Mark Frank

Sermons

Being a course of sermons beginning at Advent and so continued through the Festivals

Mark Frank

Sermons

Being a course of sermons beginning at Advent and so continued through the Festivals

ISBN/EAN: 9783337257521

Printed in Europe, USA, Canada, Australia, Japan

Cover: Foto ©Lupo / pixelio.de

More available books at **www.hansebooks.com**

SERMONS

BY

MARK FRANK, D.D.

MASTER OF PEMBROKE HALL, CAMBRIDGE,
ARCHDEACON OF ST. ALBANS,
PREBENDARY AND TREASURER OF ST. PAUL'S, ETC.

IN TWO VOLUMES.

VOL. II.

OXFORD:
JOHN HENRY PARKER.
MDCCCXLIX.

CONTENTS OF VOL. II.

A Table of the Texts of Scripture handled in the foregoing Sermons.

SERMON XXVIII.
ON THE FIFTH SUNDAY IN LENT.
1 CORINTHIANS IX. 25.

And every man that striveth for the mastery is temperate in all things. Now they do it to obtain a corruptible crown; but we an incorruptible   1

SERMON XXIX.
ON THE SIXTH SUNDAY IN LENT.
DEUTERONOMY XXXII. 29.

O that they were wise, that they understood this, that they would consider their latter end! 15

SERMON XXX.
ON THE ANNUNCIATION OF THE BLESSED VIRGIN MARY.
S. LUKE I. 28.

And the Angel came in unto her, and said, Hail, thou that art highly favoured, the Lord is with thee: blessed art thou among women . 33

SERMON XXXI.
ON PALM SUNDAY.
S. MATTHEW XXI. 8.

And a very great multitude spread their garments in the way; others cut down branches from the trees, and strawed them in the way   . 52

SERMON XXXII.

UPON GOOD FRIDAY.

1 CORINTHIANS II. 2.

For I determined not to know any thing among you, save Jesus Christ, and him crucified 67

SERMON XXXIII.

THE FIRST SERMON UPON EASTER DAY.

S. LUKE XXIV. 4—6.

And it came to pass, as they were much perplexed thereabout, behold, two men stood by them in shining garments: and as they were afraid, and bowed down their faces to the earth, they said unto them, Why seek ye the living among the dead? He is not here, but is risen 83

SERMON XXXIV.

THE SECOND SERMON UPON EASTER DAY.

S. MATTHEW XXVII. 52, 53.

And the graves were opened; and many bodies of saints which slept arose, and came out of the graves after his resurrection, and went into the holy city, and appeared unto many 97

SERMON XXXV.

THE THIRD SERMON UPON EASTER DAY.

PSALM CXVIII. 24.

This is the day which the Lord hath made; we will rejoice and be glad in it 112

SERMON XXXVI.

THE FOURTH SERMON UPON EASTER DAY.

S. MATTHEW XXVIII. 5, 6.

And the Angel answered and said unto the women, Fear not ye: for I know that ye seek Jesus, which was crucified. He is not here: for he is risen, as he said. Come, see the place where the Lord lay . . 127

SERMON XXXVII.

THE FIFTH SERMON UPON EASTER DAY.

1 CORINTHIANS XV. 19.

If in this life only we have hope in Christ, we are of all men most miserable 148

SERMON XXXVIII.

UPON ASCENSION DAY.

PSALM XXIV. 3, 4.

Who shall ascend into the hill of the Lord? or who shall stand up in his holy place? Even he that hath clean hands, and a pure heart; and hath not lifted up his soul unto vanity, nor sworn deceitfully to his neighbour 173

SERMON XXXIX.

THE FIRST SERMON UPON WHITSUNDAY.

S. JOHN III. 8.

The wind bloweth where it listeth, and thou hearest the sound thereof, but canst not tell whence it cometh, nor whither it goeth: so is every one that is born of the Spirit 185

SERMON XL.

THE SECOND SERMON UPON WHITSUNDAY.

S. JOHN XVI. 13.

Howbeit when he, the Spirit of truth, is come, he will guide you into all truth 202

SERMON XLI.

THE THIRD SERMON UPON WHITSUNDAY.

S. JOHN XVI. 13.

Howbeit when he, the Spirit of truth, is come, he will guide you into all truth 226

SERMON XLII.

THE FOURTH SERMON UPON WHITSUNDAY.

ACTS II. 1—4.

And when the day of Pentecost was fully come, they were all with one accord in one place. And suddenly there came a sound from heaven as of a rushing mighty wind, and it filled all the house where they were sitting. And there appeared unto them cloven tongues like as of fire, and it sat upon each of them. And they were all filled with the Holy Ghost, and began to speak with other tongues, as the Spirit gave them utterance 241

SERMON XLIII.

THE FIFTH SERMON UPON WHITSUNDAY.

Acts ii. 1—4.

And when the day of Pentecost was fully come, they were all with one accord in one place. And suddenly there came a sound from heaven as of a rushing mighty wind, and it filled all the house where they were sitting. And there appeared unto them cloven tongues like as of fire, and it sat upon each of them. And they were all filled with the Holy Ghost, and began to speak with other tongues, as the Spirit gave them utterance 256

SERMON XLIV.

UPON TRINITY SUNDAY.

Revelation iv. 8.

And they rest not day and night, saying, Holy, holy, holy, Lord God Almighty, which was, and is, and is to come 271

SERMON XLV.

THE FIRST SERMON UPON THE CALLING OF S. PETER.

S. Luke v. 8.

Depart from me, for I am a sinful man, O Lord . . . 283

SERMON XLVI.

THE SECOND SERMON UPON THE CALLING OF S. PETER.

S. Luke v. 5.

Master, we have toiled all the night, and have taken nothing: nevertheless at thy word I will let down the net 299

SERMON XLVII.

UPON THE TRANSFIGURATION.

S. Luke ix. 33.

And it came to pass, as they departed from him, Peter said unto Jesus, Master, it is good for us to be here: and let us make three tabernacles; one for thee, and one for Moses, and one for Elias: not knowing what he said 318

SERMON XLVIII.

THE FIRST SERMON UPON ALL SAINTS.

Psalm cxlix. 9.

Such [This] honour have all his saints . . . 336

SERMON XLIX.

THE SECOND SERMON UPON ALL SAINTS.

HEBREWS XII. 1.

Wherefore seeing we also are compassed about with so great a cloud of witnesses, let us lay aside every weight, and the sin which doth so easily beset us, and let us run with patience the race which is set before us . 351

SERMON L.

UPON S. ANDREW'S DAY.

S. MATTHEW IV. 20.

And they straightway left their nets, and followed him . . 376

SERMON LI.

PREACHED AT S. PAUL'S.

COLOSSIANS III. 15.

And let the peace of God rule in your hearts, to the which also ye are called in one body; and be ye thankful 394

SERMON LII.

PREACHED AT S. PAUL'S CROSS.

Sir Richard Gurney being then Lord Mayor.

JEREMIAH XXXV. 18, 19.

Thus saith the Lord of hosts, the God of Israel; Because you have obeyed the commandment of Jonadab your father, and kept all his precepts, and done according unto all that he hath commanded you: therefore thus saith the Lord of hosts, the God of Israel; Jonadab the son of Rechab shall not want a man to stand before me for ever . . 413

A SERMON

ON

THE FIFTH SUNDAY IN LENT.

1 COR. ix. 25.

And every man that striveth for the mastery is temperate in all things. Now they do it to obtain a corruptible crown; but we an incorruptible.

THE text is a comparison between the worldly combatant and the spiritual,—between the wrestler of this world and the wrestler with it,—between him that strives for the "mastery" over others, and him that strives for the "mastery" over himself,—between the contenders in the Olympic games and the contender in the Christian race.

And it is an apt and fit comparison. Olympus in the heathen poets is commonly used for heaven; so the Olympic exercises may well be used to resemble those for heaven, and the heavenly crown likened to the Olympic garland, without any offence, though with all advantage.

And it is as seasonable as fit. This holy time of Lent is a time of striving for the "mastery" with our corruptions, with our "corruptible" for God's "incorruptible;" a time of holy exercises upon the "corruptible" earth to obtain a crown "incorruptible" in the heavens.

And it is somewhat more accommodate and easy to our natures, as much as temperance is than fasting, as partial abstinence from inordinacy and excess than abstaining altogether.

SERMON XXVIII. Which makes me hope it will be as profitable as either fit, or seasonable, or accommodate; to teach us by comparing ourselves with the wrestlers of the world, our work with theirs, our reward with theirs, to do as much as they. Indeed, it should be more, as our work is more honourable than theirs, more honourable to master ourselves than others, our own unruly, beastly passions, than any man or beast whatever; and our "crown" more worth than theirs, "incorruptible" than "corruptible," and the obtaining it every way as easy, if we would but think it so, or set seriously to think of it: what they do, and what they do it for; how much they do, and how little they do it for; what we do, and for what we do it; how little we do, and for how much we do it; how little they get for so much, how much we may get for so little.

This is the sum of the text; and the intent is to persuade us to be as industrious and careful for a crown of glory, as they are for a crown of grass; to take as much pains for the praise of God, as they did for the applause of men; to do and suffer as much for heaven, as they for less than earth, for a few leaves that grow out of it. And both the one is the better to be understood, the other the more likely to be persuaded, if I keep the parts of the comparison together, and do not sunder them, but compare them as we go.

The two combatants. The two strivings. The two dietings or preparations. The two crowns.

The two combatants,—the temporal and spiritual: The temporal, "he that striveth for the mastery," *qui in agone contendit;* the spiritual, "we"—S. Paul, and we Christians.

The two strivings: Theirs express, ours understood; they strive for masteries, yet not they only, but "we" also.

The diet or preparing for it much alike: "they are temperate in all things;" yet not "they" alone, but "we" must too; they do it, but we do it too, or should so, by the Apostle's similitude.

The two crowns: The one "corruptible," that is theirs; the other "incorruptible," that is ours; both expressly mentioned and compared.

And by comparing them together, we shall see the great obligation that lies upon us, to be "temperate in all things;"

that is, as you shall see anon, to do all things whereby we may come at last to obtain this "incorruptible" crown of glory.

I begin with the two combatants:—The one, is any man; the other, any Christian. The first is a man and no more, the other has a relation to Christ added to him.

That man, that "every man, striveth for the mastery," to outgo his fellow some way or other, is from his very nature; there is a kind of natural contention thence in everybody to be somebody more than ordinary. If this contention were placed upon good things, or things worth the striving for, it were happy for us. But if we have no better assistance than from nature, we fix it upon games and sports, vanities and trifles; it is them we only strive about; there lies our business and our study. Πᾶς ὁ ἀγωνιζόμενος, every one of us is no better, strive and study for nothing else; and yet vain men that we are, we trouble and toil ourselves as much about such nothings, as if they were all we could desire, all we could do.

It being then so natural and necessary a condition to every one of us, to be striving for somewhat or other, to aim at some excellence or other, to be better than our neighbours in some way or other; it were to be desired that this desire and earnest pursuit were pitched right. It is so in the other of the two combatants, the Christian.

He (1) indeed is the only "man that strives for the mastery." All others strive for that only which is but slavery when all is done; "we," we Christians, alone strive for that which is mastery and excellence. The more men strive for earthlythings, the more are they brought under the dominion of them, the greater is their vassalage, and brings them no better but to cry out with Paul, in the person of the unregenerate man, "Who shall deliver me from this body of death?" It is God's service only that is perfect freedom; we are then only free when we are free to righteousness, then only masters when we can command ourselves. For *An ille mihi liber videatur cui mulier imperat?* &c. says the Heathen orator, "Can you think him to have got the mastery whom vanity commands;" whom his lusts give law to; who can neither go nor come, eat nor drink, wake nor sleep, work

Rom. vii. 24.

SERMON XXVIII. nor play, speak nor do, desire nor think, but what they would have him? *Ego vero istum non modo servum sed nequissimum servum, etiamsi in amplissima familia natus sit, appellandum puto.* "I truly," says he again, "think he is not only a servant, but a drudge, be he who he will, of never so honourable a family." I add, be his victory never so great and notable in mere vain and corruptible things; they do but press him down the more, and subject him to vanity, and leave him groaning under the bondage of corruption. The master over these is the true Christian only, who by his faith and resignation conquers all his conquests, gets the better both when he overcomes and is overcome, both when his enemy oppresses him as well as when himself subdues him; who makes all things serve his triumph, every thing enhance his glory, also things work unto his good, advance his crown. All else are but the slaves of their conquests, mere drudges to an empty name,—an airy title.

And (2) if we take ἀγωνιζόμενος, for one that strives or fights, none so truly does it as the Christian. All else do but beat the air, fight with nothing in comparison; their combats are not only merely vain, vain scufflings with air and wind, to no purpose in the world; but the very things and enemies they encounter are, at the best, but men whose Ps. lxii. 9. breath is in their nostrils, "lighter" than the very air, and "vanity itself," if we believe the Psalmist; and what great conquest over such? It is the Christian that fights indeed, [Ephes. vi. 12.] that combats enemies indeed, "principalities and powers, and spiritual wickednesses in high places," enemies strong and mighty, that go invisible, and strike and wound us when we see them not, that fight with us out of high and almost inaccessible places of defence, that have all possible advantage over us. These are enemies, if we talk of enemies, to fight with indeed. The enemies worldly men so tremble at, are but braggadocios to these; all their force and power but weakness if compared with the powers of hell and darkness. This is fighting, to fight with these, to fight with devils, and sins, and lusts; and thus the Christian is the only fighter, the πᾶς ἀγωνιζόμενος, none but he.

And if I may have leave to expound ἀγωνιζόμενος, one in an agony, as sometimes it is, none fight to agonies like Christians;

they come even to the fiery trial, even unto blood, even unto death. They did not so in the Olympic, Pythian, Nemæan, or Isthmian games; they were but games and sports to the Christian combat, that fights often to the death, must have always that intention not to give over for death itself, but continue constant to the end. So here we have in this first point, even the mastery amongst them that strive for mastery, that they strive for things not worth the striving for; that they strive indeed for slavery, not mastery; that they scarce do anything worth the name of striving or fighting; that theirs is but play and sport in comparison of the Christian combatant; and yet for all that, a great deal they do for the victory in these petty trifles; they wrestle, and cuff, and leap, and throw, and run, and try all their strength and powers. And it is worth the while to see whether we strive and contend as much in our real Christian combat, in a case worthy of the while and labour. That we are now to do, secondly, to compare our strivings, theirs and ours, the Grecian and the Christian exercises.

Five several exercises, or kinds of striving for the mastery, there was in those Corinthian games,—wrestling, cuffing, quoiting, leaping, running. All these answered in our Christian course and exercise.

1. Wrestling. "Wrestling against principalities, against powers, against the rulers of the darkness of this world, against spiritual wickedness in high places," says S. Paul. *Eph. vi. 12.* "Wrestling," secondly, with God in prayer, as Jacob did. *Gen. xxxii. 24.*

2. Cuffing and buffeting there is too. Buffeting ourselves, (i.) "keeping under our bodies, and bringing them into subjection," S. Paul's ὑπωπιάζειν, making our eyes and bodies, as it were, black and blue by watchings and fastings; cuffing or buffeting our eyes for looking after, our ears for listening to, our bodies for doing, punishing all our powers and senses for acting anything that is evil; a being "buffeted" too (ii.) "by Satan," when we forget to buffet ourselves. Cuffing and buffeting sufficient to be found in the Christian's exercise. *1 Cor. ix. 27. 2 Cor. xii. 7.*

3. Quoiting or casting. "Casting away any weight" that hinders us, any "sin that does beset us;" removing every stone of offence, "giving no offence" to any "in anything, that our ministry be not blamed;" that nothing we do, nothing *Heb. xii. 1. 2 Cor. vi. 3.*

we omit, neither our doing or our not doing, be a stone of stumbling, whereby "our brother may justly stumble, or is offended, or is made weak." Throw all such stones out of the way, and strive who shall so come nearest that "great corner-stone Christ Jesus," or the "mark of your high calling of God in Christ Jesus."

<small>Sermon XXVIII.</small>
<small>Rom. xiv. 21.</small>
<small>Phil. iii. 14.</small>

4. Leaping also is to be found among the Christian's exercises. Skipping and leaping for joy at the glad tidings of the Gospel; "leaping and praising God" with the lame man that was healed; striving who shall leap farthest in it; leaping with Abraham, (for so the word signifies,) "to see the day" of Christ; leaping with holy David before the ark; "rejoicing and leaping for joy" in the day of our sufferings for Christ; making it one of our daily exercises and businesses to praise and magnify God, and rejoice in him, in all his days, and ways, and dispensations; strive with one another who shall do it most, who shall go farthest in it.

<small>Acts iii. 8.</small>
<small>John viii. 56.</small>
<small>2 Sam. vi. 16.</small>
<small>Luke vi. 23.</small>

5. Running, we every where meet in the Christian's course. Running "the race which is set before us;" "so running as we may obtain," in the verse before the text. Christianity itself is styled a race, the Christian law the law of it, the Christian the runner, his life the course, heaven the goal; nothing more ordinary.

<small>Heb. xii. 1.</small>
<small>1 Cor. ix. 24.</small>

Besides these five single exercises in the Grecian games, there was a sixth, mixed or compounded, of wrestling and cuffing both, παγκράτιον they called it. But in Christianity all are joined, all are sometimes exercised together; the Christian must be skilled and well exercised in all; wrestle against the world, the flesh, and devil; wrestle with God, cuff and buffet himself, suffer the buffetings of Satan too sometimes, cast away all weights and stones of hinderance and offence, leap and "run" with joy and eagerness "the race which is set before us, looking unto Jesus," always, in all these, looking unto him that is both "the author and finisher of our faith."

<small>Heb. xii. 2.</small>

And being thus wholly to be kept in exercise, it will be convenient, nay, necessary, now to fit and prepare ourselves, so to diet and order ourselves, that we may so perform them as to obtain the day, to get the victory, to be temperate in all things, as well as any wrestler or runner of them all.

There are four several interpretations of the word ἐγκρατεύεται, which we here render "temperate."

1. The first is, what here we find it, to be temperate: to keep a certain set diet, whereby their bodies might be best strengthened and enabled, made nimble and active; so it signifieth to the wrestlers. To observe a spare and moderate diet, such as may most advantage the soul's business, best subdue the body and quicken the spirit, be it abstinence from some, or sometimes from all, kinds of meat and drink; so it signifies to the Christian. This the Christian's, as the other the wrestler's diet.

Very exact and punctual were they that strove for the masteries in their observances: kept their rules, and times, and kind of diet. I would the Christian now were but half so much to his rule and order. Indeed, I must confess, theirs was not sometimes a moral temperance,—it was sometimes to fulness; yet still, such as was prescribed and most conducible to their end. If we would observe as much those abstinences, which most make to the enabling us in our spiritual race or combat, I shall desire no more; there indeed fasting and all temperance will come in, will be the Christian's ἐγκρατεύεται, the Christian's being temperate in all things. A thing so necessary, that S. Jerome says no less than, *Difficile imo impossibile est, ut præsentibus quis et futuris fruatur bonis, ut hic ventrem et ibi mentem expleat, ut de deliciis transeat ad delicias, ut in utroque sæculo primus sit, ut in cœlo et in terra appareat gloriosus.*[a] "It is hard, nay impossible," no less says he, "to enjoy both present and future goods," our good things here and hereafter too; "to fill the belly here and the soul hereafter; to pass from pleasure into pleasure," from fulness into fulness; "to be first in earth and heaven too, glorious in both." He must feed spare here, that looks to be fed full there; be temperate in all earthly delights and satisfactions, that looks for heavenly either in the other world or in this either: for the full body stifles the soul; and we are not more unwieldy in body when the belly is over full, than the soul is then. Fulness oppresses even the natural spirits, makes us we cannot even breathe freely for the while; enough to show us our rational

[a] [This passage has not been found.]

spirits are not likely to be freer to breathe, or evaporate themselves to heaven or heavenwards, whilst the very natural ones themselves are so oppressed. From temperance and moderation we cannot be excused, neither in meat, nor drink, nor any thing, whatever weakness may excuse from fasting; so necessary a disposing of us it is to all Christian piety and goodness; yea, and a Christian virtue too itself.

2. The word may yet be rendered continence; so it seems to be taken, where it is distinguished from σώφρων, sober or temperate, and joined next to ὅσιος, holy, clean, or pure. A point observed by those *agonothletæ*, to abstain from wine and women for the time of their providing themselves against those games. So the poet, *Qui cupit optatam cursu contingere metam ... Abstinuit vino et venere.*[b] And our Apostle tells us of such a kind of temporary continence, very convenient for those Christians that more especially addict themselves to the Christian exercises, particularly of prayer and fasting. But no time but commands continence and chastity to all Christians whosoever, that no uncleanness be "so much as named among them;" for it becomes not saints,—it becometh not the Gospel of Christ, which is a doctrine of all holiness and purity. Nothing more weakens and indisposes the body for vigorous and noble actions,—nothing more unfits the soul for the race of Christian piety,—nothing more blinds it from understanding, nothing more keeps it from desiring, nothing more disables it from performing it,—than inordinate and sensual lusts, and indulging to them. To run, or wrestle, or combat well, we have as much need of continence, as any that ever strove for secular mastery.

3. A third notion of ἐγκρατεύεται there is to signify a constancy of mind to abstain from all things that are hurtful. Suidas and Hesychius render it, to abstain from evil; and that not only things that are truly such, but those things also sometimes that may hinder the greater good. Thus S. Paul in this chapter, a little before the text, abstains from using his Christian liberty, that he may so with the greater profit and success fulfil the course of his ministry; will not use the power he had to live upon preaching of the Gospel, but voluntarily preaches to the Corinthians upon free cost, that

[b] [Horat. De Arte Poet. 412.]

he might gain the more; becomes again "all things to all men," that by all means he might "gain some." He saw the Corinthians were close and covetous, foresaw it was like to hinder his preaching much if he put them to much charge; he therefore supersedes his power and liberty (though he convinces them, from the beginning of the chapter, that such he had, and just, and natural, and reasonable, and ordinary it was), lest he should not do so much upon them as he desired. But though we must not expect that all men should advance to this height, they must yet resolve to remove all real and faulty hinderances out of the way, abstain from all occasions and appearances of evil, which may at any time hinder or rob us of our crown, make us fall short of the goal of heaven and glory.

Sermon XXVIII.
1 Cor. ix. 22.

4. Lastly, it may signify his having all things in his power, πάντα ἐν κράτει ἔχων, the getting the mastery over himself, getting the victory over one desire after another, denying himself first one liberty, then another, till at last he has mastered all, πάντα ἐγκρατεύεται, got all into his power. Thus strove those Grecian wrestlers and racers, ordered and tempered their bodies by degrees, first to this exercise, then another; first to this height, then a higher; first to this, then to a further, till they had gotten a perfect mastery and command over all their powers and members, to use them to the greatest advantage and agility. This is the Christian's business too, to keep our soul and body in continual exercise, always doing, ever suffering somewhat, now striving against that sin, then a second; now mortifying that lust, then another; now moderating this passion, then sweetening that; one while denying himself this liberty, then another; sometimes attempting this difficulty, then some other; sometimes running after good, sometimes wrestling with evil, sometimes cuffing and crucifying an inordinate desire, sometimes throwing off such and such a habit, sometimes leaping away in fear from an occasion or opportunity of doing ill, sometimes leaping into a way or occasion of doing good, sometimes leaping for joy when it is done: whereby at length, by continual exercise and custom, we may happily come to a perfect temper in all our powers and faculties of soul and body, bring them all to an exact obedience, to "the obedience of Christ," to

"run the race," to "fight the fight," that he has set before us.

Delicatus es miles, si putes te posse sine pugna vincere, sine certamine triumphare, &c. says S. Chrysostom : [c] "Thou art too delicate a soldier for Christ, if thou thinkest thou canst overcome without striving, triumph without fighting." *Exsere vires,* &c.; put out thy strength, fight valiantly, contend fiercely, in the Christian warfare; remember thy covenant, think upon thy condition, consider thy warfare, the covenant that thou madest, the condition thou undertookest, the warfare thou gavest thy name to at thy baptism. The Christian's life is but a continual warfaring against the world, the flesh, and the devil; thy Captain calls and leads thee to it, and thy crown expects thee, not a crown of corruptible leaves or flowers, but "an incorruptible crown of glory." Be "temperate" and sober, be chaste and continent, be vigilant and constant, be diligent and active in Christ's holy work and business, that thou mayest run without falling, wrestle without being thrown, cuff without being beaten, quoit all thy labours near the mark, out-leap all evil ways, perform all thy exercises, get happily at last to the end of thy way and labour, snatch and carry away the crown prepared for thee. That is the fourth and last point of the comparison between crown and crown, the one "corruptible," the other "incorruptible."

Here indeed first, properly, comes in the "but," the comparisons before have run somewhat even; combatants, and exercises, and preparations much alike; but here nothing but the name, no comparison between mortal and immortal, vanity and reality, finite and infinite: yet let us a little compare them as we can.

The "crown" these gamesters strove for was but of leaves of pine or apple, of oak or olive, of laurel, nay, or even grass sometimes: corruptible these indeed, nay, and vain too, to do so much; *Multa tulit fecitque puer, sudavit et alsit ;*[d] to run, and sweat, and toil, and keep ado for such a toy as the best of these, how vain and foolish! The very heathen themselves, Anacharsis in Lucian,[e] sufficiently deride it.

---

[c] [This passage has not been found.]
[d] [Horat. De Arte Poet. 413.]
[e] [See the Dialogue *Anacharsis, seu de Gymnasiis.*]

Yet, as ridiculous as it seems, the greatest part even of the Christian world strive and labour for as little. What is the aim of all the great ones of the world, but leaves and grass? what get they by all their labours and pursuits, but some such business? Let them all have their desires, and it comes to no more. Let the one obtain his so much desired honour, another his beloved mistress, Pleasure, a third his darling wealth, (of one of which three kinds of leaves all their crowns are made,) and what get they but mere fading leaves? —neither fruit nor flower.

<small>SERMON XXVIII.</small>

The crown of honour, what is it but a very leaf that withers presently? The worm of envy consumes it presently, the blast of jealousy nips it in its glory, the breath of malice deads it in a trice. The crown of pleasure has a woe upon it, a woe that will consume them: "Woe to the crown of pride, to the drunkards of Ephraim, whose glorious beauty is a fading flower." All that are drunk with any pleasure, their very crowns wither upon their heads; the intemperate heat that both produces and rises from their sensual pleasures, turns the colour of their beauty, and will make their garments ere long smell rank and stink with their own corruption. The crown of riches has a worm commonly that breeds in the leaf; this oaken garland in which we place so much strength and stedfastness, has an oaken apple among the leaves that nurses a worm to consume it when we least think of it. Nay, though we had *coronam militum,* a crown, an army of men as thick as the spires of grass, to encompass and guard either our honours, wealth, or pleasures; yet they would all prove in a little time but as the grass; all men are nothing else, but particularly the rich man; so says that Apostle: "The rich man as the flower of the grass he shall pass away." He shall not stay for a storm to blast or blow him away—even the sun of prosperity shall do it: *Mole ruit sua;* his own weight and greatness shall throw him down. For the "sun is no sooner" (mark but that, "no sooner") "risen with a burning heat, but it withereth the grass, and the flower of it falleth, and the grace of the fashion of it perisheth; so also shall the rich man fade away in his ways." Mark that too, in his very "ways;" his own very "ways" shall bring him to ruin and destruction. It is so with the leaves of honour; it

<small>Isa. xxviii. 1, 3.</small>

<small>James i. 11.</small>

<small>James i. 10.</small>

SERMON XXVIII.

is so with the leaves of pleasure; the very sun no sooner rises upon them, but it withers them; the very sunshine and favour of the prince ruins them; the burning heats of their pleasures waste them away, make their pleasures troublesome and burdensome in a little while, and a while after vanish and confound them with shame and reproach; leave them nothing upon their heads, but ill-coloured and ill-seated leaves, ignominy and dishonour; nothing in their souls but dryness and discomfort; their estates too oftentimes drained dry, scarce anything but the Prodigal's husks to refresh them, or dry leaves to cover them.

Ps. cxxxii. 18.
Ps. xxi. 3.
Zech. ix. 16.
2 Tim. iv. 8.
James i. 12.
Ps. viii. 5.
Rev. xii. 1.
1 Pet. v. 4.

But the Christian's crown is nothing such; it is a "flourishing crown," a "crown of pure gold," a "crown of precious stones," a "crown of righteousness," a "crown of life," a "crown of honour," a "crown of stars," a "crown of glory," a "crown of glory that fadeth not away," in the same verse, eternal, everlasting. A "flourishing," not a withering crown; a crown of "gold," not of grass; of "precious stones," not of leaves; of "righteousness," not unjustly gotten; of "life," not unto death; of "honour," not to be ashamed of; of "stars," not stubble; of "glory," not vanity; that never so much as alters colour, but continues fresh and flourishing, and splendid

1 Pet. i. 4.

to all eternity: "An inheritance incorruptible, and undefiled, and that fadeth not away, reserved in heaven for us," says S. Peter.

And having now compared our crowns, and finding so vast, so infinite a difference between them, can we think much to do as much for this "incorruptible crown of glory," as the others do for their vain and "corruptible" one? Shall they that strive for petty masteries, for toys and trifles, for ribands and garlands, be so exact in their observances, so strict in their diet, so painful in their exercises, so vigilant in their advantages, so diligent in providing, strengthening, and enabling themselves for their several sports and undertakings; and shall we, that are to strive for no less than heaven itself, be so loose in our performances, so intemperate in meat and drink, so sluggish in our business, so careless of advantages, so negligent in all things that make towards it? Are leaves worth so much, and the fruit of eternal peace so little? Is a little air, the vain breath of a mortal man, to be so sought for;

and is the whole heaven itself, and the whole host and God of it, the praise of God, and saints, and angels, that stand looking on us, to be so slighted as not worth so doing, doing no more than they? Where is that man, *Dic mihi musa virum,* show me the man that can, that takes the pains for eternal glory, that these vain souls do for I know not how little enough to style it?

But if we compare the pains the ambitious man takes for honour, the voluptuous for his pleasure, the covetous man for wealth—mere leaves of Tantalus's tree, that do but gull, not satisfy them; the late nights, the early mornings, the broken sleeps, the unquiet slumbers, the many watches, the innumerable steps, the troublesome journeys, the short meals, the strange restraints, the often checks, the common counterbuffs, the vexatious troubles, the multitude of affronts, neglects, refusals, denials, the eager pursuits, the dangerous ways, the costly expenses, the fruitless travels, the tortured minds, the wearied bodies, the unsatisfied desires when all is done, that these men suffer and run through; the one for an honour that sometimes nobody thinks so but he that pursues it; the other for a pleasure base oftentimes, and villanous; the third for an estate not far from ruin; nay oftentimes, to ruin his house and posterity;—if, I say, we compare these men's pains and sufferings, with what we do for Christ, and God, and heaven, and happiness—true, real, immovable happiness and glory, good Lord! how infinitely short do we come of them. Shall not they rise up against us in judgment and condemn us; nay, shall not we ourselves rise up against ourselves in judgment, who have done many of these things, suffered many for a little profit, vain-glory, or vain hope, which we thought much to do for eternal glory? This we do: we strive, and labour, and take pains for vanity; we are "temperate in all things," restrain and keep in ourselves, for the obtaining sometimes a little credit, sometimes a little affection, or good opinion, from some whose love or good opinion is worth nothing; or if it be, is as easily lost, as soon removed and changed from us, is commonly both corrupt and "corruptible," without ground, and to little purpose. But for God's judgment, Christ's affection, the Holy Spirit's good love to us, for the praise of good men, of saints, and

SERMON XXVIII. angels, the whole choir of heaven rejoicing over us; nay, for heaven itself, and blessedness, and glory, all which we might obtain with the same pains, and lesser trouble, and in the same time, it is so little that we do, so far from all, that I may, without injury, style it nothing.

But for God's sake, for Christ's sake, for our own sake, let it not be so for ever; let us not always prefer glass before diamonds; barleycorns before pearls; pleasure, or profit, or honour, before heaven, and happiness, and glory. There are in heaven unspeakable pleasures, whole rivers of them there. There are in heaven infinite and eternal riches, which we can neither fathom nor number; there is glory, and honour, and immortality, and eternal life. There are all these crowns made "incorruptible" and everlasting; all running round, encircling one another like crowns, encircling our souls and bodies too like crowns, without end, without period. If we would have any crowns, honour, or riches, or pleasure, let us there seek them where they are advanced to an incorruptibility, made "incorruptible," where the leaves are turned into everlasting fruit, incorruptible honour, incorruptible pleasure, incorruptible riches, incorruptible all. Let us but do for them, thus advanced and heightened, as we do for them when they are but fading and withering, and unsatisfying, and I say no more, but you will with as much ease obtain this incorruptible and immortal, as that mortal and corruptible. God grant us grace to do so, to strive "for the mastery" over ourselves, and lusts, and sins; so to be temperate, abstemious, vigilant, and industrious in the pursuit of heaven, as we are or have been of the earth; that we may at last be crowned, not with "a corruptible" but "an incorruptible crown of glory" and everlasting life.

A SERMON

ON THE

SIXTH SUNDAY IN LENT.

DEUT. xxxii. 29.

O that they were wise, that they understood this, that they would consider their latter end!

AND if we be "they," who I am afraid we are, we are now in a good time to do it. Lent is a considering time—a time set us by holy Church to consider what we have done all the year before, what we are to do all our years that are behind, and what we shall do; what will become of us if we do not, when all our years are at an end. It begins with a day of ashes, and it goes out with a week we hear of nothing in but the preparations to a grave and the resurrection, so as it were to mind us of our latter end, make us more serious about it at this time than ordinary, from the first day of it to the last. So the text is not unseasonable, nor the wish in it unfit any way for the time. [SERMON XXIX.]

And whether this wish be Moses's or God's, this "they" his own people or their enemies, it is no matter. A good wish it is from whomsoever to friend or enemy; only it intimates, they are none of the wisest for whom it is.

For his own people (1) it might well be; them he had led out of the "waste howling wilderness;" them he had kept there as the "apple of his eye," as in the same verse; and when he brought them thence, fed them with the "fat of lambs," the "kidneys of wheat;" and upon this they grew "fat, and kicked." It is a good wish for them, "that they were wiser." [Deut. xxxii. 10. Deut. xxxii. 14. Deut. xxxii. 15.]

For their adversaries (2) it might be as well. They had as little sense, it seems; very ready to grow high at any time upon prosperities and successes, as if they, and not God, had done the business. It is a good wish for them, that they would understand a little better.

There is another people that we know, but I know not how to call them, (his or I know not whose,) they carry themselves so strangely—I pray God it be not we at last, whom the wish may suit as well as any—a people who, some of them, not long since were, as it were, in wastes and deserts like God's own people, in a condition sad enough, God knows; borne thence no great while ago upon his wings; since that set high, and fed high with corn, and wine, and many good things else, who, for all that, have not well requited God that did it. Others of them, who, because they came in no misfortune like other folk, nor were plagued like those other men, stand much, like Israel's enemies, upon their terms; their righteousness, or power, or policy, or somewhat did the work. Both are become too much unmindful of the "Rock of their salvation," as we have it, ver. 15, and have quite forgot to consider the "latter end" of things, what may be yet; that, however things stand now, "the foundations of the mountains may be set on fire" again, as the phrase is, ver. 22, if they be no wiser, either of them, than by continuance in sin to blow up the sparks; and then who can assure his house, or barns, or shop, or office, at the next turn? It is a good wish for these too, both of them, that they "would consider" a little better on it together, *in novissimo*, now at last.

For all these it may be; and, to be short and home, for all these it is. As in Moses's time for Israel and their enemies, so in ours, for us, late enemies, now friends together, that we would all be wiser once, "that we men," at least at last, "would understand the loving-kindness of the Lord, and consider the wonders that he hath done for the children of men." But, above all, that men would think of this same "latter end;" think that all things end not here, there is somewhat to be looked to after these days are done, which wise men would look to and provide for. *O si*—O that they would! God wishes it, and Moses wishes it, and you and I, all of us, I hope, may wish what they do without offence. But do it we must besides, else God will complain of us, as he does of them here in the text: for a kind of complaint it is, as well as a wish; *O si*—that they were,—a plain complaint that they were not.

But be it a wish, or be it a complaint, (and both it is,) a wish for some, "that they were wise," or a complaint of them, that they are not; for three particulars it is.

I. As a wish; it is that the men here spoken of (1) "were wise." That (2) they would understand this, somewhat or other that we shall see anon worth understanding. "That (3) they would" especially "consider their latter end."

II. As a complaint; it is for three things too: that they were none of these; that they were neither "wise," nor "understood," nor considered what they should; for *O si* is but a kind of a sigh that it is no other; a very trouble to God that men are no better.

Of both, this is the sum: that they who, in the midst of mercies, after the sharp sense of former judgments, and not yet out of the fear of new ones, forget God, and either by new sins, or retrieving old ones, slight so both his judgments and his mercies, they are neither wise, nor understanding, nor considering men, whatever they go for; but a sort that God will complain of, whoever they be, for somewhat else, and wishes to be wiser, to understand a little better, and consider now at last, lest the latter end be worse with them than the beginning.

That it may not, but that the wish may take effect, and God have no more reason to complain, let us now consider the particulars, where I must first show you for whom, before I show you for what it is. And yet I know not how you will take it.

(1.) Indeed that Israel's enemies, the heathen, should be "a nation void of counsel," that have not "any understanding in them;" that I believe may be taken well enough. [Deut. xxxii. 28.]

But (2) that Israel, God's own people, should be of the number, they a "foolish people and unwise" as it is;— [Deut. xxxii. 6.]

And that not the meanest of them neither, but they that eat the fat, and drink the sweet; the best, as we would say, of the parish, who are always wise because they are rich,— that they should not understand. [Deut. xxxii. 14.]

Sermon XXIX.
Deut. xxxii. 13.

Those (3) who "ride upon the high places of the earth," the chiefest persons, that men in honour should have no understanding. It is well Moses says it; I know not whether it be safe to say it after him.

Deut. xxxii. 27.

But (4) that wise men too, not the ignorant only, but they whose wits God seems to be afraid of, and dares do nothing for them, for fear they should misapply it; who, let God do what he can, say what he will, will say and prove any thing good against him; who are always giving reason upon reason for every thing, but why they reason him out of all, that they should come into the tale; that we, or any body, or God himself, should wish them wise,—as if they were not as wise as we could wish them,—what an affront does this simple Moses put upon them! Why, Lord, who does understand, if they do not? Or who will believe us if we say it?

Luke xvi. 8.

And yet all these are "they" the wish is for. God's enemies are fools, and God's people not so wise, says our blessed Saviour. The gallantest, the richest, the wisest of them not so wise always as they should be; not so wise, I hope, at any time, but God may have leave to wish them wiser.

Yea, every one of them, every mother's child, if they have learnt no more than they here in the chapter; learnt nothing by their afflictions but to forget them; nothing by their deliverances but to abuse them; nothing by what is past but to be discontent with the present, and yet daily pour out themselves into excesses, and never think of what may come:—if this be all the wise parts they play, as they were theirs in the text, be they who they will, they are "they" God means, God make them wiser. The wish now is like, I fear, to fit the persons as well as it does the time. And three points there are in it, I told you, to be learned:—*sapere, intelligere, et novissima providere;* to call to mind the things that are past; to understand the things that are; and to provide for things to come. To remember where we were, to understand where we are, and to consider and provide for where we may be, the three main points of wisdom; so S. Augustine[f] distinguishes the three words as the three main parts of wisdom,

---

[f] [Utinam saperent: et cætera. Ecce hic, frater mi, tria in hoc versu proponuntur: scilicet scientia, intelligentia, et providentia.—Pseudo-August. Speculum Peccatoris. Op. tom. ix. 378 C. ed. Col. Agrip. 1616.]

and so shall I. But (1) consider them as our duty; and then (2) as God's desire.

Sapere, or to be wise, that is (1) the first; and *Sapientia est per quam repetit animus quæ fuerunt:* so that learned Father:[g] "To be wise is to call to mind the things that are already past;" and the great Roman orator,[h] I may tell you, takes the words so too.

And truly Moses himself seems so to mean it; for no sooner had he called this people "foolish" and "unwise," but in the next words immediately he bids them "remember the days of old, and consider the years of many generations," as if that were the way to make them wise. Indeed, if we "be but of yesterday," or look no further back, Job will quickly tell us "we know nothing." *State super vias antiquas;* that is the rule God gives us. On the old ways there is the standing,—no foundation to build on else. New opinions and devices are but a kind of standing upon our own heads; we cannot stand so long; a building upon a tottering and boggy ground, which vents itself ordinarily into vapours, that make a noise and blustering, darken and infect the air and nothing else. Every wind, too, carries them which way it will,—this way, or that way, or any way; and, observe it when you will, once out of the old way, and they never know where to fix.

Yet (2) to be "wise," has here a notion more practical, and sends us sadly and soberly to meditate now and then upon the late condition we were in. And surely where God found us, and how he found us; how he led us about, and how he instructed us; how he kept us all the while as "the apple of his eye;" how he "fluttered over us with his wings;" how he "spread them" abroad and "bore us on them,"—I keep the expressions of the chapter, for Israel's case was much our own,—or to speak out, the desolations, and poverties, and distresses, and reproaches we were in; the prisons, the dangers, the necessities we escaped; the supplies, the reliefs, the protections we found,—we know not how,—are not things

---

[g] [Prudentia est rerum bonarum et malarum et neutrarum scientia. Partes ejus, memoria, intelligentia, providentia. *Memoria* est per quam animus repetit illa quæ fuerunt. Intelligentia, per quam ea perspicit quæ sunt. Providentia, per quam futurum aliquid videtur antequam factum est.— These words are quoted from Cicero, (De Invent. lib. ii. 160 [53,]) by S. Augustine, in the Octoginta trium Quæst. quæst. xxxi. Op. tom. iv. p. 207 F. ed. Col. Agr. 1616.]

[h] [See former note.]

would be forgotten; they are such as, one would think, would make one wise. They would be written upon our walls, and beams, and posts, and doors; written with a pen of iron, and with the point of a diamond, graven upon the tables of our hearts and upon the horns of our altars, or, as Job speaks, "upon the rock for ever." Our churches, our halls, our chambers, all our rooms hung round with the sad stories we have seen, to make them live in our memories, and in our children's after us, to make them wise by their fathers' sufferings.

And yet (3) to be wise is more still: to make these things live in our lives as well as memories, to grow good upon it. "To be wise, and to do good," the Psalmist joins. Indeed, they cannot be asunder. He is not wise who is not good. To keep my laws and do them, "this is your wisdom and your understanding;" the way to make the nations say, "This is a wise and understanding people." So God determines it.

Indeed, I come not hither to preach other wisdom; I should make my preaching foolishness then, indeed, in a truer sense than the Apostle meant it. The wisdom of God, if we can keep to it, that is our business. And "he (i.) that hearkens" to it, "he is wise," says the wisest Solomon. He (ii.) who, exalted from that low condition we were speaking of, to a high one, is lowly still, "he is wise," says he again. He (iii.) who upon the same account keeps himself under still, keeps under discipline and government, as if he felt the former lashes still, "he is wise." *Apprehendite disciplinam,* is a point of holy David's, *Nunc ergo sapite,* of the wisdom he commends.

But if you will be "wise," indeed,—and pardon me that I extend wisdom a little further than I first propounded it,— "there are four things" that are "exceeding wise," you may learn it of:—"the ants," that "prepare their meat in the summer;" "the conies" that "make their houses in the rock;" "the locusts," that "go forth all of them by bands;" and "the spider," that "takes hold with her hands, and is in kings' palaces." Were we but as wise as they: as ants, and conies, and locusts, and spiders,—and it is a shame we should not,—we would, by the experience of our former evils, prepare (i.) in good days, with the ant, for bad ones; we would (ii.) with the conies, build our dwellings in the "Rock" S. Paul says was Christ; having felt sufficiently already there is no sure building else. We would (iii.) go forth, as the locusts do, to gather all by bands, unite in the bond of peace and charity, not straggle into factions, and divide in parties, remembering what that lately came to, and may quickly come to again, if we look not to it. We would (iv.) with the spider, catch hold with our hands, keep ourselves employed in our own business, trades, or studies, and not meddle with things we either understand not, or belong not to us. We would learn of them besides to be in the palaces of the great King, the houses of God, a little more constantly than we are. This would be to be "exceeding wise."

Sermon XXIX.
[1 Cor. x. 4.]

And if to these we add the "wisdom of the serpent," as our blessed Saviour commends it to us; make it our care above all, as they say the serpent does, to save our heads— *caput Christum* and *caput regem*, Christ our head and the king our head—make it our business to keep our religion and obedience safe. Be who will else thought never so wise, I am sure there is none wiser, as God counts wisdom, than they that do so.

Matt. x. 16.

Yet, lastly, if you had rather take the rule of your wisdom from above, take it from S. James. That wisdom, says he, is "first pure, then peaceable, gentle, easy to be entreated, full of mercy and good fruits, without partiality, without hypocrisy." So to be wise is to wash our hands of what is past, to live peaceably and orderly, friendly and kindly together for the time to come, heartily promoting one another's good, without grudging or dissembling. For "in returning and quietness," it seems, is the Apostle's wisdom, as well as the Prophet's "strength;" wisdom, it seems, and strength both. I would some would understand it, that or this, nay, "that" and "this" we are to consider next. The condition we are in, that it is we are now to understand. For *Intelligentia perspicit quæ sunt*, so S. Augustine[i] defines it; and this *hoc* is most naturally the present. So, to understand this (which is the second particular in the wish) is to be truly sensible how things now go with us. Where, first, what it is we are to understand, and then what it is to understand it.

James iii. 17.
Isa. xxx. 15.

[i] [See note to page 19.]

SERMON XXIX. What " this " is we take in two particulars : God's dealing with us, and our dealing with him again. These two, the " this " the business, we are wished to understand.

Deut. xxxii. 13. (1.) And how God deals with us, " the high places of the earth " we " ride on," the places and offices we enjoy; "the increase of the fields" we "eat" of, the plenty we abound with; the "honey" we "suck out of the rock," and the "oil" that issued to us " out of the flinty rock," the same verse; those blessings which we could no more expect than those

Deut. xxxii. 14. sweet dews out of stones and flints, the "butter" and "milk," the smoothness and evenness of our conditions now ; the " fat of lambs, and rams, and goats," in the next words ; the full tables we well nigh groan at, and " the pure blood of the grape," the mirth and jollity we live in,—tell us as plain, I say, how he deals with us as they did Israel how he dealt

[Ps. xix. 2.] with them. " One day tells another," how the Almighty commands it to dart blessings on us, and " one night certifies another," how he enjoins it to shadow us with protections; both speak loud enough to have " their voices heard among us."

But how (2) we deal with him again. I would there were no voice abroad,—I would nobody heard,—I would Gath did not speak it, nor the streets of Askelon ring of it ; that the day might be clouded with darkness to cover it, and that the night were as the shadow of death, to bury it for ever; that thou, O God, however, wouldst not reckon the days of our ingratitude in the number of our months. We are surrounded with plenty, and we abuse it to excess ; we are encompassed with peace, and we disturb it with petty quarrels ; we are loaded with wealth and riches, and we lash them out in lusts and vanities; we are clothed with honours, and we dishonour them with meannesses. Our friends are given into our bosoms, and we envy some of them and slight the rest; our laws are restored us, and we live as if we had none; our religion is returned, and we laugh it out of countenance. Good discipline reviving, and we are doing what we can to break the bonds in sunder. Our churches now stand open to us, and we pass by them with neglect; our king God has set

[Ps. ii. 6, and 1.] upon " his holy hill," and the people still " imagine vain things " against him. In a word, we are " filled with all good things," and we do all the evil we can with them; we fill up our "days with iniquities," and our "nights with transgressions;" we neither consider God's dealings, nor mind our own; we understand neither "that" nor "this."

Sermon XXIX.

For to understand "this," which is the second branch of this particular, is to understand both whence and whither these mercies are, whence they come, and whither they tend.

Deut. xxxii. 27.

For the first we are too ready to say with the heathen, "Our hand is high, and God hath not done" it. God hath not done it! Why, tell me then, I pray, what were the counsels that brought things about? where were the armies that forced our passage? whence the money that smoothed the way? who confounded the devices? who fettered the forces? who divided the strengths that were against us? who turned the hearts of the fathers to the children, and the hearts of the children to the fathers? who softened our enemies? who strengthened our friends? who suppled strangers at last to pity us? who calmed the seas? who held the winds? who guided our happiness into our harbours, and even threw it into our bosoms? This cloud, that arose like Elijah's, out of the sea, out of the vast sea of God's endless mercy, and covered heaven and earth with blessings (till we are grown black, I fear, sadly black and sinful, with them); it was not, as his servant took it, "like a man's hand" at all; it was like God's all the way; it was merely God's: *Non nobis*, therefore, *Domine, non nobis*, must be our Psalm; "Not unto us, O Lord, not unto us, but to thy name only be the glory." And "this" the first way to understand his mercies: to confess from him they come, and so give him thanks.

1 Kings xviii. 44.

The second is, to learn also whither they tend. They are, in S. Paul's understanding, to "lead us to repentance:" and the time is proper for it. In the Psalmist's, to understand well is to do thereafter. So, to understand God's blessings right well, is to use them right well. And when under blessings we live accordingly, take them thankfully, use them soberly, employ them charitably,—then, and not till then, we understand them.

Rom. ii. 4.
Ps. cxi. 10.

Yet, lastly, I must add, that till we think we have no understanding, till we confess we are—what God says we are in the words just before—a nation that has none,—a nation that when time was, undid itself with its own wisdom;—whilst we would needs teach God to govern his Church and rule the world, and in a manner force him either to make the world anew again out of nothing, or make the Church into it; till we grow sensible how wisely we reformed all, till we had reformed God out of all, and all into Atheism and confusion; and that we are no wiser still than to tread in the same steps that will do it again, there will be little hope we understand God's dealings or our own. Yet this understanding our not understanding God here particularly points them to; for having immediately before said, this people, they were a nation that had not any understanding, he presently adds, "O that they were wise" and "understood" it; even "this" very thing in particular that they do not understand, as wise as they seem, or think themselves. The next point may make them wiser, if however, now at last, they will "consider their latter end;" what may be the end both of their follies and their wisdoms here, and what is like to be the end of them hereafter; what in this world, and what in the other; for *novissima* reaches both, the issues of this life and the issues of the next. *Et novissima providerent.*

(3.) Several latter ends there are, of both sorts, to be considered; but how things may, notwithstanding the fair face they carry, end yet here ere long, that consider first; and that I shall tell you without stirring out of the chapter, for God tells us it there himself:—(i.) He will "set on fire the foundations of the mountains," if we be no wiser than we have been yet. The highest mountains of our honours, the greatest mountains of our strengths; nay, the firmest foundations we can build on, shall fall all into ashes, and scatter into smoke and air.

Or (ii.) "burning heat," and "bitter destruction" shall devour us; even our zeal and bitterness against one another shall raise such flames as shall consume us all together,— "high and low, rich and poor, one with another."

Or (iii.) he will "send the teeth of beasts upon" us, "with the poison of the serpents of the dust," again; set the beasts of the people again to tear and worry us; nay, even the most contemptible persons, the vermin of the dust, they shall devour us. They shall creep like serpents into our families, poison them with errors, poison with sin, poison them with lusts, multiply too there like dust, and destroy us ere we dream on it. [Sermon XXIX]

Or, if we escape that, "the sword (iv.) without," and the "terror within, shall destroy the young man and the virgin, the suckling," and "the man of grey hairs;" nor young nor old escape the second bout. [Deut. xxxii. 25.]

Or (v.) he will "scatter us into corners;" but they shall not hide and shelter us as before; our very "remembrance" he shall make "to cease;" we shall come no more out. Not so much as an "ear," or "leg," as the Prophet speaks, "taken out of the lion's mouth," to remember us by. But a *populus non populus*,—a people that we count as nothing,—shall possess our room; anything, everything, that will but serve to root us out. [Deut. xxxii. 26. Amos iii. 12. Deut. xxxii. 21.]

Some of these, nay, all these, lastly, and more shall come upon us: "heaps of mischief," and all the "arrows" of the Almighty, till they be spent (as in the same verse), if we be no wiser than we have been hitherto; if we understand no better how to use either our bad days or our good ones. And if, after not only so many fair warnings, but so many fair enjoyments, we carelessly throw away ourselves into our former miseries, we shall also die like fools; and who can be such to pity us? [Deut. xxxii. 23.]

That all these have not befallen us before this time, that God has not torn up our foundations, nor given us over to our own wraths, nor to the people's; that he has not scattered us, nor brought some ill end or other upon us long ere this— it is not for our righteousness, I am sure: but *ne hostes dicerent*, lest some should justify their own dealings; or *ne populus diceret*, lest some others condemn God's, as if he had delivered them only to destroy them. But whatever they say, *Ego retribuam eis in tempore*, "Their foot shall slide in due time," says God; *et juxta est dies perditionis*, "the day of their calamity is at hand." [Deut. xxxii. 27. Deut. xxxii. 35.]

But if we escape all these, there are four other latter ends that must be thought on—death and judgment, hell and heaven: the *quatuor novissima*, that everybody can tell, but few consider; yet the two first of them we cannot avoid, and one of the other we must come to.

And (i.) suppose our prosperity and splendour should go

with us to the grave (and we can carry them no further), yet after we have lived like gods, to come to die like men, to be shaken with agues, or burnt with fevers, or torn with cholics, or swollen with gouts, or groan away in pain, or go out in stench—every body glad when we are gone—and at our going to be stripped of all our gallantry with a *Stulte, cujus hæc?* Thou fool, whose are all these things thou must leave behind? —to be sent away with so scornful a farewell, into rottenness and putrefaction, and so be blown into dust, and vanish into oblivion, like the meanest men, or perhaps, which is far more terrible, to be plucked away in the heat and violence of a sin, and none to deliver, is but a sad end of all our jollities and glories.

Yet hence (ii.) to be drawn to the last tribunal—that is the next stage we come to;—there to have our follies fully laid open to the eyes of all the world—not a night-folly hid; where we must give an account of every hour and minute spent, every word and thought as well as work; after all our blustering here, to be dragged thither to a reckoning for every farthing, even to the last mite, and receive accordingly, how bad soever it be. This will set us to " consider," sure, what we shall answer at that day, how to give up our accounts with joy, and come off with glory.

For we end not yet; there is still a "latter end" beyond both these; two for fail: and it is yet within your choice, which you will come to—*novissima cœli*, or *novissima inferni*, the highest heaven, or the lowest hell. This last we have; and that we will take first. It is better ending with the other.

For this, it is a place whence joy is ever banished, and where no good is; where nothing but sorrow, and sadness, and horror dwells; where the wicked lie wrapped in flames and sulphur, covered with worms, and stench, and darkness. All the racks and tortures that the wit of cruelty ever found out here are beds of down and roses to those horrid lodgings. Here, in the bitterest pains, there is some part or other well, or somewhat or other always to be found to give us ease. The light will cheer us, or the night refresh us, or sleep give us rest; company will divert the anguish, or custom lighten it, or hope lessen it, or time wear it out. But in that "place of torment"—so Dives called and felt it—nor soul, nor body, nor faculty, nor member free. The conscience of former sins, that terrifies them; the memories of former happiness, that distracts them; the understanding now what they have forfeited and might have had, that, above all, infinitely torments them. The tongue burns, and the teeth gnash, and the heart trembles, and the eyes weep, and the hands wail, and the ears are filled with continual screeches and everlasting howlings, and every member is intolerably tortured with the punishment of its own sins: and yet not so much there as a drop of water to refresh them,—not a gleam of light to comfort them,— no rest day nor night. The company of devils and damned spirits—the only company there—and amongst them, perhaps, their dearest friends, or wives, or children, infinitely increase their hell; and all is augmented by continuance: for no such thing as hope to be heard of there. It is the kingdom of despairs and terrors; "the worm dieth not, and the fire is not quenched;" all the miseries are everlasting, everlasting. This the "latter end" of all the people "that forget God," says holy David; that forget him in their prosperities: "into hell" they "shall be turned."

Nor is this the melancholy man's dream, or the contrivance of the politician, or the priest's cheat to keep men in awe. If a cheat it be, it is God has cheated you, and Christ has cheated you, and the prophets have cheated you, and the apostles have cheated you; for they all say the same thing. And would the rantingest of those brave fellows that scoff at it, sit down a little and consider,—which I am sure they never do; or should the tremblings of death begin to seize them, when their understandings are about them,—which are not always,—and open the windows into another world; then these would be the words of truth and soberness, then, "Men and brethren, what shall we do?" when, commonly, it is too late. How shall we do with these everlasting burnings? We will do anything, suffer anything, to avoid them.

Then heaven, too, the end we reserved for our last, that will begin to be thought on too, and how to get in there. There, where is joy without any sad look to shadow it; pleasure without any tang to stain it; peace without dis-

SERMON XXIX.

turbance; plenty without satiety; continual health without infirmity, nor grief, nor fear, nor hazard to impair our happiness, or sully it. Glorious, all glorious things, are spoken of thee, thou city of God. Gold, and pearls, and diamonds, and all precious stones; kingdoms, and thrones, and crowns, and sceptres; torrents of joy, rivers of pleasure, well-springs of life, dwellings of glory, seats of blessedness, and blessed company, the throne of God,—all are said of thee, thou glorious place. And yet when all is said, we must conclude with the Apostle, that "neither eye hath seen, nor ear heard, neither have entered into the heart of man the things prepared there;" or if they had, it seems it is not lawful for a man to utter them. So I must needs leave them to you to consider them.

2 Cor. xii. 4.

And truly it is time now to tell you what considering is. It is to sit down and lay your ends together, and think upon them. Consider, then, seriously, (1) whether you would have your foundations once more unsettled, your houses plundered, your estates sequestered, (they are scurvy words, pray pardon them,) your glories once again trod to dirt; whether it is good making ventures, trying God's severities the second time. For let them "smite you but once" more, and as Abishai said to David, so say I to you, "they will not smite you the second time."

[1 Sam. xxvi. 8.]

Consider, again, (2) whether, seeing however you must leave all these enjoyments, within so short a span of time as death is off us, (and we may be fetched off the stage ere we are aware, ill provided for it,) it be wisdom to lay up all our treasure and provision here; either so hoard up here as if it were for ever, or so lavish here as if it were to account for never.

And seeing to that account we must come at last, consider (3) whether such imprimises and items as the long impertinent bills of sins and pleasures will bring in, will pass current at the last audit; whether so much in purple and fine linen, so much in living sumptuously every day, so little time in the assemblies of devotion, and so much in those of vanity; whether, "Soul, take thy ease, eat, drink, and be merry,"—the living in all liberty and licentiousness,— the being hateful, and the hating one another, will pass for

[Luke xii. 19.]

a rewarding the Almighty for his mercies, when, " Come, ye blessed—go, ye cursed," come in to conclude the day.

And if they will not pass so, (as no doubt they will not,) consider (4) what will be next the end you come to, and remember but half that I have told you of those eternal fires, (and I have told you nothing in comparison,) and then tell me again, whether the strictest attendances of piety, the largest expenses of charity, the trouble now and then of doing well, the beggarliness of honesty, the restraints of temperance, the niceness of chastity, the very hardships of repentance, watching, fasting, weeping, even the greatest penances of religion, as high as the rigours and austerities of hermits and anchorets, be not far easier to be endured; and whether we can be thought wise any way, if we omit any way to prevent those flames.

Or if you had rather be led with hopes and glory, (as all ingenuous and noble natures had,) consider (5) whether all the glories ye have lived in, all the satisfaction ye have met with, all the delights ye have ever here enjoyed, or ever can, be worth one minute of those eternal fulnesses in God's presence in the heavens; when even they that counted the religious man's life but " madness," and laugh piety and honesty out of doors, were so amazed at the glory and " strangeness of the righteous man's salvation, so far beyond all that they looked for," that they even "groaned for anguish of spirit," and cried out openly, " We fools;" we fools indeed; how have we cheated ourselves of heaven, the glorious kingdom, whilst the poor Lazaruses—these poor contemptible things—crept in; and we, with all our pride, and riches, and vaunting, quite shut out.

And now I may read the text another way, as an assertion, not a wish: and I find it read so. Thus, *Si saperent et intelligerent et providerent.* If men were wise, they would both understand and consider all these things without this ado. They would presently turn *considerarent* into *providerent* too, (and so the word is rendered by the Vulgar,) and provide now for their "latter end." And the provision will not stand us in much, nor shall I stand long upon it. Three ways to do it, and you have all.

The son of Sirach's, (1) " Remember they end, and let

enmity cease," says he. Let us not spend our wits, our courage, our estates any longer in feuds and enmities, seeing God has now at length so strangely brought us all together.

The (2) way shall be his too, with a little alteration. "Remember thy latter end," and that "thou never" henceforward "do amiss." I know it is read, "Remember and thou shalt not;" but it is as true if read, Remember and thou wilt not; if you consider it as you should, you will also provide you sin no more.

To make all sure, make the provision our blessed Saviour would have you, for a third: "Provide the bags that wax not old,"—friends that will not fail you, make them to you out of the mammon you have gotten, make the poor your friends with it,—"that when ye fail, they may receive you into everlasting habitations."

And consider, lastly, for the close of this part of the text, (and I am almost at the close of all,) that all this is God's desire. He wishes it here, he wishes it all the holy text through : "O that there were such an heart in them." "O that my people would hearken to it." "O that men would therefore," (Ps. cvii.) four times in it.

And yet the second general of the text tells you, he does more; wishes it so heartily, that he complains again,— complains they answer not his wishes. And wished he has so often, that he may well complain. "How often have I!" says he; so often, nor they nor we can tell it. Only so often *noluistis*,—as often as he would, so often they would not. All the day long he had stretched out his hand unto them, sent to them by his messengers, early and late, to desire them, visited them with judgments, courted them with mercies, and yet they would not, disobedient and gainsaying people that they were. And therefore complain he does, that do what he can, he must give them up, though with a *Quomodo te tradam?*—with great regret and sorrow, —give them up for fools, men of neither understanding nor consideration—men that, like fools, throw away gold for baubles,—men that are so far from understanding or considering, that they live as if they cared not whether they went to heaven or hell.

But I love not to lengthen out complaints; in this case

I should never have done—and it is time I should. And the text only insinuating, not enlarging God's complaints, gives me an item to do so too. Only give me leave in brief to sum up all.

Every wise man, before at any time he begins a work, sits down and considers what he has to do, and to what end he does it. Oh that we would be so wise in ours; that we would retire ourselves some minutes, now and then, to consider the ill courses at any time we are in, or entering on. And when we are got into our chambers, and be still, thus commune with ourselves.

What is this business I am about? To what purpose is this life I lead, this sin, this waste, this vanity? Am I grown so soon forgetful of my late sad condition, or so insensible of my late rebellions, and of the pardon God has given me, as thus impudently to sin again? Is this the reward I make him for all his mercies, thus one after another to abuse them still? Or is it that I am weary of my happiness, and grown so wanton as to tempt destruction? Is it that I may go with more dishonour to my grave, leave a blot upon my name, and stand upon record for a fool, or worse, to all posterity for ever? Is it that I have not already sins enough, but I must thus foolishly still burden my accounts? Is it that I may go the more gloriously to hell, and damn myself the deeper? Is it that I may purposely thwart God in all his ways of mercy and judgment, cross his desires, scorn his entreaties, defy his threats, despise his complaints, anger him to the heart, that I may be rid of him, and quit my hands of all my interests in heaven for ever? Why this is the English of my sins, my profaneness, and debaucheries, the courses I am in, or now going upon; and will I still continue them?

This would be considering, indeed; and a few hours thus spent sometimes, would make us truly wise. And let us but do so, we shall quickly see the effect of them : God shall have his wishes, and we shall be wise; and we shall have ours too,—all we can wish or hope, and no complaining in our streets. All our former follies shall be forgotten, and all ill ends be far off from us; and when these days shall have an end, we shall then go to our graves in peace, to our accounts with joy, and passing by—some of us, perhaps—even the gates of hell, come happily to the end of all our hopes, the salvation of our souls, have our end, glory, and honour, and immortality, and eternal life; where we, as Daniel tells us the wise do, "shall shine as the brightness of the firmament, and as the stars for ever and ever."

Whither He bring us, who is the eternal wisdom of his Father, Jesus Christ; to whom with the Father and the Holy Spirit, three Persons, and one eternal, immortal, invisible, and only wise God, be all power, and riches, and wisdom, and strength, and honour, and glory, and blessing for ever and ever.

A SERMON

ON THE

ANNUNCIATION OF THE BLESSED VIRGIN MARY.

S. LUKE i. 28.

And the Angel came in unto her, and said, Hail, thou that art highly favoured, the Lord is with thee: blessed art thou among women.

THE day will tell you who this "blessed among women" is: we call it our Lady-day; and the text will tell you why she comes into the day, because the Angel to-day came in to her. And the Angel will tell you why he to-day came in to her; she was "highly favoured," and "the Lord was with her," was to come himself this day into her, to make her the most "blessed among women,"—sent him only before to tell her so,—to tell her, he would be with her by and by himself.

This makes it Annunciation-day, the Annunciation of the Virgin Mary, as the Church calls it, and the annunciation to her, as we may call it too. (1.) The annunciation or announcing and proclaiming of Christ unto her, that he was this day to be incarnate of her, to take that flesh to-day upon him in the womb, which he was some nine months hence, on Christmas-day, to bring with him into the world. And (2) the annunciation or announcing, that is proclaiming of her "blessed among," above "women" by it, by being thus "highly favoured" by her Lord's thus coming to her;—a day, upon these grounds, fit to be remembered and announced or proclaimed unto the world.

SERMON XXX.

Indeed, *Dominus tecum* is the chief business; the Lord Christ's being with her, that which the Church especially commemorates in the day. Her being "blessed," and all our being blessed, "highly favoured," or favoured at all, either men or women being so, all our hail, all our health, and peace, and joy, all the angels' visits to us, or kind words, all our conferences with heaven, all our titles and honours in heaven and earth, that are worth the naming, come only from it. For *Dominus tecum* cannot come without them; he cannot come to us but we must be so, must be highly favoured in it, and blessed by it. So the Incarnation of Christ, and the Annunciation of the blessed Virgin,—his being incarnate of her, and her blessedness by him, and all our blessednesses in him with her, make it as well our Lord's as our Lady's day. More his, because his being Lord made her a Lady, else a poor carpenter's wife, God knows; all her worthiness and honour, as all ours, is from him; and we to take heed to-day, or any day, of parting them; or so remembering her, as to forget him; or so blessing her, as to take away any of our blessing him; any of his worship, to give to her. Let her blessedness, the respect we give her, be *inter mulieres*, "among women" still; such as is fit and proportionate to weak creatures, not due and proper only to the Creator, that *Dominus tecum*, Christ in her be the business: that we take pattern by the Angel, to give her no more than is her due, yet to be sure to give her that though, and that particularly upon the day. And yet the day being a day of Lent, seems somewhat strange. It is surely no fasting work, no business or occasion of sadness this. What does it then, or how shall we do it then, in Lent,—a time of fast and sorrow? Fast and feast too,—how can we do it? A feast it is to-day,—a great one, Christ's Incarnation,—a day of joy, if ever any; and Lent a time of sorrow and repentance,—a great one, the greatest fast of any. How shall we reconcile them? Why thus: The news of joy never comes so seasonable as in the midst of sorrow; news of one coming to save us from our sins, can never come more welcome to us, than even then when we are sighing and groaning under them; never can angel come more acceptably than at such time, with such a message as "All hail, thou art highly favoured, blessed art thou." It is the time that angels use to come when we are fasting. So to Daniel; so to Cornelius; the time when we best hear a voice from heaven, and best understand it with S. Peter; the time when God himself vouchsafes to spread our table, as he did there, of all kinds of beasts and fowls, to S. Peter, all heavenly food and mysteries. It is the very time for *gratia plena*, to be filled when we are empty; the only time for *Dominus tecum*, for our Lord's being with us, when we have most room to entertain him. So, nor the Church, nor we in following it, are any whit out of order. *Dominus tecum*, Christ is the main business, both of our fasts and feasts; and it is the greatest order to attend his business in the day and way we meet it, be it what it will.

^{SERMON XXX.}
Dan. ix. 3, 21.
Acts x. 30.
Acts x. 13, 15, 16, 20.

Though perhaps it seem stranger too, to hear of an angel coming into a virgin's chamber at midnight, (as is conjectured,) and there saluting her. But no fear of those sons of God, if they come in unto the daughters of men. Angels are virgins,—may be with virgins in the privatest closets,—are always with them there to carry up their prayers, and to bring down blessings. No strange thing, then, to hear of an angel with any of them whom God highly favours, with whom himself is too; no wonder to hear of an angel or *Ave* to any such. The only wonder indeed to us, will be to hear of an *Ave* Mary. Indeed, I cannot myself but wonder at it, as they use it now, to see it turned into a prayer. It was never made for prayer or praise,—a mere salutation. The Angel's here to the blessed Virgin never intended it, I dare say, for other, either to praise her with, or pray unto her. And I shall not consider it as such. I am only for the Angel's *Ave*, not the popish *Ave Maria*; I can see no such in the text.

Nor should I scarce, I confess, have chosen such a theme to-day, though the Gospel reach it me, but that I see it is time to do it, when our Lord is wounded through our Lady's sides; both our Lord and the mother of our Lord, most vilely spoken of by a new generation of wicked men, who, because the Romanists make little less of her than a goddess, they make not so much of her as a good woman: because they bless her too much, these unbless her quite, at least

SERMON XXX.

will not suffer her to be blessed as she should. To avoid both these extremes, we need no other pattern but the Angel's, who here salutes and blesses her indeed; yet so only salutes and blesses her, so speaks of and to her as to a woman here, though much above the best of them; one "highly favoured," it is true, yet but favoured still; all her grace, and blessedness, and glory still no other, mere favour and no more; and *Dominus tecum*, the Lord's being with her, the ground, and source, and sum of all; virgin and day, both blessed thence. The better to give all their due, Angel, and Lord, and Lady, and you the better understanding of the text, the scope, and matter, and full meaning of it, we shall consider in the words these two particulars:—The Angel's Visitation, and the Angel's Salutation.

I. His visitation, or coming to her, in these words:—"And the Angel came in unto her."

II. His salutation to her, or saluting her, in these:—"Hail, thou that art highly favoured; the Lord is with thee: blessed," &c.

In the visitation we have,

1. The visitor. 2. The visited. 3. The visiting.—The Angel, the visitor, he. The blessed Virgin, this the visited, her. And the visiting, his coming in unto her.

In the salutation there is to be considered, both the form of it, and the titles in it.

1. The form, threefold:—(i.) "Hail." (ii.) "The Lord is with thee." (iii.) "Blessed art thou," or, Be thou blessed,— *Sis benedicta*, it may be, as well as *Es*.

2. The titles given her, they three too:—"Thou that art highly favoured," that is one. "Blessed thou," that is another. "Blessed among women," that is the third. These all so evident and so plain, that none can miss them. But to these two points, two more are to be added:—The grounds and bounds of these great titles.

1. The ground of this high blessedness and favour:— (i.) Full of grace, so our old translation and the old Latin render it; her fulness of grace and goodness, that is one. (ii.) But "the Lord is with thee," that is the main, thence all her blessedness; thereby it is that she is so highly favoured, because the Lord is with her.

2. The bounds or limitation of these titles, they come first with a χαῖρε, no other form than what is and hath been given unto men; though great they be, yet divine they be not. The greatest title, secondly, is but κεχαριτωμένη, from mere grace and favour. Thirdly, it must still, too, acknowledge *Dominus tecum.* She hath a Lord,—is a subject as well as we. And lastly, all her blessedness is but *inter mulieres,* " among women;" how much soever she excels all women, she is but *inter mulieres,* among such creatures, in the rank of creatures; no goddess, nor partner with the Godhead, either in title or worship.

By considering and laying all these points together, we shall both vindicate the blessed Virgin's honour, as well from all superstitious as profane abuses, and ourselves from all neglect of any duty to the mother of our Lord,—one so highly favoured and blessed by him, whilst we give her all that either Lord or Angel gave her; but yet dare not give her more.

And now *Dominus mecum,* and *Dominus vobiscum* too, the Lord be with me whilst I am speaking it, and with you whilst you are hearing it, and bless us both whilst we are about it, that we may learn to bless where we should bless, whom, and when, and how to do it, and rightly both accept and apply God's blessings and our own.

We are now to learn it from the Angel, his visiting and blessing the blessed Virgin here. His visit and his salutation to her. But his visit, or visitation, that stands first. Where the visitor, the visited, and his visit; the Angel, the Virgin, and his coming in unto her, are all to be considered. "And the Angel came in unto her."

And who (i.) so fit as an angel to come in to her,—to give this visit,—to give this blessing? It was a bad angel that brought the curse upon the woman—it was fit a good one should bring the blessing.

The employment (ii.) suits none so well. It was news of joy; who could bring it better than one of those who were the first sons of eternal joy,—the first enjoyers of it,—who could pronounce it better?

Who fitter (iii.) to come with a *Dominus tecum,* before the face of the Lord, with a message of his coming down to earth, than they who always behold his face in heaven? Matt. xviii. 10.

Sermon XXX. Who fitter (iv.) to come to her? She was an immaculate and unspotted virgin: and to whom do virgins' chambers lie open at midnight but to angels? God sends no other thither at that time of night; and that that time it was, may be well conjectured from Wisdom xviii. 14, 15: "When all things were in quiet silence, and that night was in the midst of her swift course, thine Almighty Word came down from heaven;" then, it seems, was the time of her conception,—of Christ's coming to her; before whom immediately the Angel came to bring the message that he was a-coming, if, as S. Bernard[k] says, he were not come already.

And (v.) with such a message to a virgin, as that she should conceive without a man, who was convenient to bring it but an angel? *Ne quo degenere depravaret affectu*, says S. Ambrose,[l] that there might not be the least ground of a false suspicion.

But (vi.) to such a virgin, one so highly favoured as to be made the mother of God, (for the mother of Christ is no less, he being God,) what messenger could come less than an angel? Prophets and patriarchs were too little for so great an embassage, and angels never came upon a greater.

Nay, (vii.) every angel neither was not fit for so high an office. The Angel Gabriel it was,—he is the ὁ ἄγγελος here. Gabriel, is by S. Jerome[m] and S. Gregory[n] interpreted *fortitudo Dei*,—the power or strength of God; and in this work it appeared indeed. God's strength and power never so much shown, as in the saving of us by Christ. It is by others interpreted *vir Deus*, or *Deus nobiscum*,—God man, or God with us. Could any be thought fitter to bring this news upon his lips, than he that carries it in his name? Especially,

Dan. ix. 21. being the same that foretold all this to Daniel,—fit that he should see to the performance who brought the promise. Petrus Damiani[o] thinks he was the holy Virgin's guardian

[k] [De Nativ. Domini, Serm. ii. falsely attributed to S. Bernard. Op., p. 1667 I. ed. Paris. 1640.]
[l] [Ne quo degenere depravaretur affatu, ab angelo salutatur.—S. Ambros. Comm. in Luc. lib. ii. p. 1633 B. ed. Paris. 1549.]
[m] [S. Hieron.Comment.in Danielem, cap. viii. Op., tom. v. p. 499 C. ed. Francofurt. ad Mœn. 1684.]

[n] [S. Greg. Hom. xxiii. in Evangelia, tom. ii. p. 478 C. ed. Froben. Basil. 1564.]
[o] [P. Damiani Cardinalis Homil. I. in Nativitate B. Virg. Mariæ (de Throno Salomonis 3 Reg. cap. x.) *Duo Leones stabent juxta brachiola*. Duo Leones sunt Gabriel Archangelus et Joannes Evangelista, quorum alter dextræ Virginis, alter sinistræ depu-

Angel,—proper therefore to bring her this good message, or any else. God had several times employed him before, to Daniel, Zacharias, and others, and found him faithful; he therefore now employs him still, that we may know, he that is faithful in the least, God will by degrees trust him with the most, the greatest matters.

{Sermon XXX.}

In a word, angels drove us out of Paradise, and now they come to let us in again. Then they placed a sword to keep us out,—now they bring the word to let us in. None now, you see, more fit for this business than an angel,—than the angel Gabriel too; whether we respect the persons, either from whom or to whom the message comes, or the message, or the time, or the way, and order of it. So we have done with him; come we now to her,—a greater than he,—if we may speak with Epiphanius,[p] and some others.

Yet I shall not give her other titles than the Scripture gives her: I am afraid to give her such as many do. A "Virgin espoused to a man whose name was Joseph, of the house of David" she was, and her "name was Mary," in the verse before the text. (1) Of royal descent and lineage; (2) espoused to a husband of the same kingly house; (3) of a name very answerable to her greatness. Of David's seed, for so her Son, the Messiah, was to be; a virgin,—for of such a one he was to come: *semen mulieris*, not *maris*; from the beginning the woman's seed, and not the man's; so necessarily a virgin then, and so plainly foretold to be by Isaiah. "A virgin shall conceive and bear" him; yea, a "virgin espoused;" (1) to conceal the mystery of his Incarnation from the devil; (2) to take away all occasion of obloquy from devilish men; (3) that the birth of our Saviour might be with all possible honour; and (4) that his genealogy might so be reckoned as all others, regularly by the man, as you see them both by S. Matthew and S. Luke.

{Luke i. 27.}

{Isa. vii. 14.}

Of a high and illustrious name besides; Maria is *maris stella*, says S. Bede:[q] "the star of the sea;" a fit name for the

---

tatus est. Gabriel enim mentem, Joannes carnem, pervigili solicitudine servaverunt.—Op., p. 248 C. ed. Lugdun. 1623.]

[p] [Epiphan. Or. de Laudibus B.V.M. Ἀγγέλων ἀνωτέρα γέγονεν ἡ Παρθένος, μειζοτέρα τῶν Χερουβεὶμ καὶ τῶν Σερα-

φείμ' ἀρέσκουσα τῷ Βασιλεῖ Χριστῷ ὡς ἀξία δούλη, κ. τ. λ.—Tom. ii. p. 298 C. ed. Petav. Paris. 1622.]

[q] [Maria autem Hebraice Stella maris, Syriace vero Domina vocatur. —V. Bede, Homil. Hyem. For. iv. quatuor temp. p. 17. ed. Col. 1541.]

SERMON XXX. mother of the bright Morning Star that rises out of the vast sea of God's infinite and endless love. Maria (2) the Syriac interprets *domina*, "a lady," a name yet retained, and given to her by all Christians; our Lady, or the Lady Mother of our Lord. Maria, (3,) rendered by Petrus Damiani,[r] *de monte et altitudine Dei*, highly exalted, as you would say, like the mountain of God, in which he would vouchsafe to dwell, after a more miraculous manner than in very Sion, his "own holy mount." (4) S. Ambrose[s] interprets it, *Deus ex genere meo*, "God of my kin;" as if by her very name she was designed to have God born of her, to be *Deipara*, as the Church, against all heretics, has ever styled her the Mother of God. You may well now fully conceive no ambassador so fit to come to such an one as her, but some great angel at the least.

And his coming to her comes next to be considered: "And the Angel came in unto her;" where we are taught both how he came, and where he found her. By his coming, or being said to come, we are given to understand that it was in a bodily and human shape. So angels often used to come in the likeness of men; and at this time it was of all ways the most convenient that the angels should come like men, seeing their Lord was now to come so; and one of them to come before him with the news. When he himself would vouchsafe to wear the livery of our flesh, it is most convenient his servants, sure, that wait upon him, (whom he sends upon his errands,) should appear at least in the same livery. Nor could his message easily be delivered in more sweetness, nor the blessed maid entertain it with less terror or diffidence any other way.

For though it could not but trouble her, as we see it did, in the following verse, to see a man at that time in her closet, ere she was aware; yet his coming in so insensibly, when the doors were shut upon her, besides perhaps the brightness of his countenance and raiment, could not but tell her it was an angel, and so abate her fear a little.

Yet observe here a difference between the Angel's coming now and heretofore: we never read of an angel's appearing but abroad, or in the temple, till now. Now they begin to

---

[r] [This has not been found.]
[s] [S. Ambros. Institut. Virg. cap. 5. Op., p. 133 D. ed. Paris. 1549.]

grow more familiar with us—come in into our closets, now Christ is coming; the kingdom of heaven, it is a sign, is come nigh unto us. And (1) it is a good item to us to keep much in our closets, seeing angels are now to be met with there. {Sermon XXX}

And (2) it is an item too for virgins to keep within: Dinah went out and met with you know whom; came home ill-favouredly. The blessed Virgin keeps in, and meets with an holy angel, and the title of "highly favoured," and "blessed," for it. The straggling, gadding housewife, meets no angel to salute her, whosoever does. If we look for angels' company and salutations, we must be much within. "A garden enclosed is my sister, my spouse; a spring shut up, a fountain sealed," says Christ. The spouse of Christ, the soul he loves and vouchsafes his company, much private, oft within,—within and at her prayers and meditation too. So was the blessed Virgin, (say the Fathers here,) blessedly employed, watching at her devotions; no way so sure to get an angel's company, or hear good news from heaven—to obtain a favour or a blessing thence, as this—as prayer and watching in our closets. {Cant. iv. 12.}

This we piously believe of the blessed Virgin; but we are sure she was within—a true daughter of Sarah in it—who it seems kept commonly within doors in her tent, "whose daughters you are," says S. Peter, "as long as you do well;" must be too in this, as well as other things, if you would do well. {Gen. xviii. 10. 1 Pet. iii. 6.}

For, lastly, to show the truth of the Angel's words, that she was full of grace, the Scripture tells us, by the Angel's coming in to her, that she was within, where, *qui habeat abundantiam gratiæ*, says Hugo[t]—they that are full of grace—keep in as much as they can, fearing the corrupt discourses and conversations of the world. None so scrupulous of appearing abroad, none more fear idle, loose, or vain discourses—which cannot be avoided by such who go often abroad—than they that are fullest of grace and goodness. Nor do they care for the salutation, favours, and compliments of men, who are "highly favoured" of the Lord. No matter at all with them to be neglected by men, who desire only to be saluted by an

---

[t] [Most probably Hugo de S. Victore. The place is not found.]

SERMON XXX. angel, as was the Virgin here, which falls next to be considered. The Angel's salutation.

Two points we told you there were to be handled in it: the form of it, and the titles in it; the form in which it runs, the titles with which it is given.

The form is in three expressions,—"Hail," "the Lord is with thee," "thou art," or be thou "blessed." Three several salutations, as it were, and that (1) for the greater reverence and honour to her; so kings and queens are commonly saluted with three adorations. (2) To show from whom he came, from Father, Son, and Holy Ghost; from all three Persons in the Trinity. That (3) she was so intent and busy at her devotions that she minded not, perhaps, his first and second salutation, he was fain to add a third; to show, lastly, the triple blessing that he came with—peace, and grace, and blessedness; that heaven was now at peace with us, grace was thence coming down apace, heaven's doors set open, and the very blessedness of heaven clearly now propounded and proffered to us. The first salutation is an *Ave*,—a salutation never heard from angel's mouth before. And it speaks (1) joy, and peace, and health, and salvation, both to her, and us by her. The Greek word is χαῖρε, "rejoice," rejoice indeed, at such a Child as now is to be born of thee, "O virgin daughter!" "Behold, I bring you tidings of great joy," of a Child, —all our joy by him,—"which is Christ the Lord."

(2.) The Hebrew word speaks, Peace be to thee. A wish for peace, the first news of heaven reconciled; the way to reconciliation being now in agitation, and to be by her. Peace from the Prince of Peace, from the Author of our peace, now coming, as joyful a salutation as we can wish, all our peace from this conception, all begun with this message, and the Angel the herald of it.

(3.) It intimates health as well as peace. We were all sick Cant. v. 8. till this day came; the best, with the spouse, "sick of love;" the worst, sick of somewhat else. None well till this news came,—till the next morning after this great conception rose with healing in his wings. Now all "hail," and whole, and well again.

(4.) It signifies a wish of salvation too. *Ave*, says one, piously, though not learnedly, *a væ*, all woe now away, temporal and eternal. Eva spelled backwards; all *Eve's* ill-spun web unravelled, undone, rolled backward by the conception of this blessed Virgin here foretold; temporal and eternal woes taken all away; nothing but joy and salvation to us, if we will hear it with the blessed Virgin, and accept it. {Sermon XXX.}

The second salutation is, "The Lord is with thee;" and it may be either an apprecation, or wishing that he would be; or an annunciation, or affirmation,—a declaring and affirming that he is; or a prediction or foretelling that he will be with her.

It was an apprecation when Boaz gave it to the reapers, that God would be with them. {Ruth ii. 4.}

It was an apprecation and an affirmation both, when the Angel gave it to Gideon: "The Lord is with thee, thou mighty man of valour." {Judg. vi. 12.}

It is affirmation, apprecation, and prediction, all three here, to our blessed Lady,—a wish that the Lord would,—an assurance that he is,—a prediction that he will be yet more signally, and more particularly, with her by and by.

It is somewhat to be saluted by an angel, and it is not common; we hear often of their coming with a message, seldom with a salutation. It is a sign of more than ordinary acquaintance and familiarity with God, and of his respect particular unto us, when he sends his angels, not only upon errands, but how-do-yous to us.

With such a salutation too as "The Lord is with thee." "The hand of the Lord was with him," it is said of S. John Baptist, and that was well; his hand, and not himself; and yet the greatest of them that was born of women was not "greater than he." But here it is he himself with the greatest among women. It is a great favour to have his hand; but it is a high one to have himself with us. {Matt. xi. 11.}

Yet the Angel says to Gideon, "The Lord be with thee," Κύριος μετὰ σοῦ; but it is here Ὁ Κύριος μετὰ σοῦ, an article, an emphasis put upon it. He is not with her, as he is with any else. *Tecum in mente, tecum in ventre,* as the Fathers gloss it; *Tecum in spiritu, tecum in carne,* with her he was, or would be presently, as well in her body as in her soul, personally, essentially, nay bodily with her, and take a body from her,— a way of being with any never heard before or since,— {Judg. vi. 12.}

a being with her beyond any expression or conception whatsoever.

And the Lord thus being with her, all good must needs be with her: all the gracious ways of his being with us are comprehended in it; so the salutation no way to be exceeded. And well may he choose to be with her—even make haste and prevent the Angel, as S. Bernard[u] speaks, to be with her. He is with " the pure in heart," with the humble spirit, and piously retired soul, and she is all. And though, by the Angel's words, we cannot conceive that the Lord was yet conceived in her, he speaking in the future; yet as sure it was, even whilst the Angel was in his salutation, as if he were already incarnate in her flesh. Upon this may well follow the third salutation, "Blessed art thou," or, Be thou blessed. Yet,

I shall not here say much of this; I reserve it to be handled amongst the titles,—only tell you it may as well pass for a salutation as the other. We still sometimes use it in our salutations; use to say, "God bless you," when we salute sometimes; so the mowers to Boaz, return his salutation of " The Lord be with you," with " The Lord bless thee." And we read that Jacob "blessed" Pharaoh when he came before him; that is, saluted him in a form of blessing.

All the famous salutations, now you see, of all former and latter times, are here rallied up in this—Daniel's " Live for ever;" for life, and health, and safety; the Angel's to Gideon, " The Lord is with thee;" Boaz' to Ruth, " Blessed be thou of the Lord, my daughter;" Tobit's to the Angel, *Gaudium tibi*, " Joy be unto thee;" Christ's to his disciples, " Peace be unto you;" the Apostles' " grace," and " peace," and " salvation," to their Churches; all in this of the Angel to the Virgin, now in treaty about Christ's Incarnation. To show us (1) all these are in Christ, all now coming to us, by his coming to us, to be found altogether no where but in him; joy, and peace, and health, and salvation, and blessedness, first rising on us by this day's business—his Incarnation. To teach us (2) good forms of salutation, blessing, and not cursing; though there are some so peevish, to say no worse, to tell us they had as lief we should say, The devil take

[u] [Pseudo-Bern. ubi supra, p. 1667 I. ed. Paris. 1640.]

them, as God bless them, or God be with them. It seems they had rather imitate the bad angel than the good: I hope we had not. Good words, if it be no more, are fittest, sure, for Christian mouths; but yet good wishes too; for he that forbids to say to some, "God speed you," intimates we should say so to others; and though the disciples are bid to "salute no man by the way,"—that is, when it will retard or hinder their holy business,—they are yet bid, when they come into a house, say, "Peace be to it." And if the Angel do it, and Christ bid it, and do it too, as he does, I hope we may and will do too; nay, and give good titles too, upon the same account: the Angel does so to the blessed Virgin; and we hasten to them. "Thou that art highly favoured," blessed, "blessed among women."

Sermon XXX.
2 John 10.
Luke x. 4.
Luke x. 5.
Luke xxiv. 36.

"Thou that art highly favoured;" but why "thou," without a name? Why not Mary here as well as after? Why? there he used her name so to dispel her fear, as it were, by a kind of friendly familiarity; here he forbears it in his reverence to her. We use not to salute great persons by their names, but by their titles; and the Mother of God is above the greatest we here meet with upon the earth. We must not be too familiar with those whom God so highly favours; that is our lesson hence. We are not to speak of the blessed Virgin, the Apostles, and Saints, as if we were speaking to our servants, Paul, Peter, Mary, or the like. It is a new fashion of religion, neither taken from saints, nor angels, nor any of heaven or heavenly spirits, to unsaint the saints, to deny them their proper titles, to level them with the meanest of our servants. We might learn better manners from the angel here—manners, I say, if it were nothing else; for we dare not speak so to any here that are above us, and we think much to be *thoued*, without our titles, by that new generation of possessed men, who yet with more reason may call the best man thou, than we the Apostles, John or Thomas.

Luke i. 30.

But to descend to a particular survey of these titles here: "thou that art highly favoured," so our new translation renders it; "full of grace," so our old one hath it, from the Latin, *gratiæ plena;* and both right; for κεχαριτωμένη will carry both. Grace is favour; God's grace is divine favour;

SERMON XXX. high in grace, high in his favour; full of his grace, full of his favour,—all comes to one.

Now there is *gratia creata* and *increata,* " created grace" and " uncreated grace." Created grace is either sanctifying or edifying; the gifts of the Holy Spirit that sanctify and make us holy; or the gifts that make us serviceable to make others so. The first to serve God in ourselves: as faith, hope, charity, and other graces; the second, to serve him in the Church : such as the gift of tongues, of prophecy, of healing, and the like. Of each kind she had her fulness according to her measure, and the designation that God appointed her.

For sanctifying graces, none fuller, *solo Deo excepto,* " God only excepted," saith Epiphanius.[x] And it is fit enough to believe that she who was so highly honoured to have her womb filled with the body of the Lord, had her soul as fully filled by the Holy Ghost.

For edifying graces, as they came not all into her measure, she was not to preach, to administer, to govern, to play the apostle, and therefore no necessity she should be full of all those gifts, being those are not distributed all to any, but *unicuique secundum mensuram,* to every one according to his measure, and employment, and not at all times neither; so neither is she said to be less full for wanting them. There is one fulness of the fountain, another of the brook, another of a vessel; one fulness of the sea, another of the river, another of the pond; and yet all may be full. Christ himself is said to be full of the Holy Ghost, and S. Stephen is said to be full, and others said to be full; yet Christ, as the sea or fountain,—they as the rivulets or rivers; and yet all as they can hold. It is so in earth, it is so in heaven : and with such a fulness as the brooks or rivers is our Virgin full, and with no other. Where any edifying grace was necessary for her, she had it as well as others; more perhaps than others. Where it was not necessary, it was no way to the impairing of her fulness, though she had it not. As the banks of the rivers rose, or the channel was enlarged, so were those

---

[x] [Epiphan. Or. de B. V. M. Χαῖρε κεχαριτωμένη στυλοειδὴς νεφέλη ἡ τὸν Θεὸν ἔχουσα τὸν ἐν τῇ ἐρήμῳ τὸν λαὸν καθοδηγήσαντα, τί εἴπω ; καὶ τί λαλήσω ; ὅτι χωρὶς Θεοῦ μόνου πάντων ἀνωτέρα ὑπάρχει.—Tom. ii. p. 293. ed. Petav. Paris. 1622.]

graces; but *inter mulieres,* "among women," at the end, makes me inclined to think the fulness of apostolic endowments do not any way belong to her, women not being suffered in the times of the Apostles but to teach their children or servants at home : never thought so full of the Spirit as to be sent to blow it all abroad.

And indeed it is not said here, "full of the Spirit," but "full of grace," and that is commonly understood of sanctifying grace, of which it is very convenient that we believe none fuller than she ; and the original κεχαριτωμένη will not enforce it much higher in the business of created grace.

But in respect of the increated grace, that is, of Christ, with whom she was now so highly favoured as to be with child, none ever so filled with grace indeed. This was a grace of the highest nature, of which created nature was never capable ; κεχαριτωμένη well rendered, highly, "highly favoured ;" for it is most highly can be imagined ; and this is her first title, "O thou that art highly favoured ;" high in God's grace and favour—so high, as to be made his mother, then, sure, made a fit receptacle for so great, so holy a guest, by the fulness of all grace and goodness.

From this follows the second title, "blessed," blessed of God, blessed of men ; blessed in the city, and blessed in the field. Cities and countries call her blessed ; blessed in the fruit of her body, in her blessed child Jesus. Blessed in the fruit of her ground, her cattle, her kine, and her sheep, in the inferior faculties of her soul and body ; all fructify to Christ. Blessed her basket and her store, her womb and her breasts ; the womb that bare him and the paps that gave him suck. Blessed in her going out and in her coming in, the Lord still being with her ; the good treasure of heaven still open to her, showering down upon her, and the earth filled with the blessings which she brought into the world when she brought forth the Son of God. Blessed she indeed that was the conduit of so great blessings, though blessed most in the bearing him in her soul, much more than bearing him in her body. So Christ intimates to the woman that began to "bless the womb," that is, the mother "that bare him ;" Luke xi. 27, 28. "Yea, rather," says he, " they that hear the word of God and keep it ;" as if he had said, She is more blessed in bearing the word in her soul than in her body. But blessed she is; Elisabeth, by the Holy Spirit, fell a-blessing her when she came to see her; and she herself by the same Spirit tells us, "all generations shall call her blessed." So we have sufficient example and authority to do it. And I hope we will not suffer the Scripture to speak false, but do it.

And do it to her above all women, *Benedicta tu in mulieribus*—that is her third title. Most blessed, none so blessed; none ever had child so blessed; none ever bore or brought forth child as she.

Benedicta in mulieribus, "blessed among women;" she (1) indeed only blessed; all others subject to the curse of *in dolore paries,* of conceiving and bringing forth in sorrow— she wholly free from that—she a perpetual Virgin before, and in, and after child-birth. Christ came into her womb insensibly; came forth, as it were, insensibly too, without groan or sorrow to her. "Blessed (2) among women;" they all henceforth saved by her child-bearing; "Notwithstanding she," that is, woman, "shall be saved in childbearing," *i.e.* διὰ τεκνογονίας, "by her child-bearing," says a learned commentator, not their own, but hers, by the child she bore; and they therefore shall call her blessed.

"Blessed" (3) "among women;" that is, none more blessed than the best, the highest of them; none above the mother of God; none, sure, so good as she,—which now brings me to consider the grounds of all this honour, all these titles.

The first is grace, *gratia plena,* χάρις in κεχαριτωμένη, that always the ground of God's favour and all our blessedness; so she tells us in her hymn, *Respexit humilitatem.* It was the humility of his handmaid that God, in this high favour of the Incarnation of his Son, respected in her. Humility the ground of all grace within us,—all grace without us,—of God's grace to us,—of his graces in us,—the very grace that graces them all too. Humility makes them the most lovely, pride disgraces them all, be they never so many, though indeed they can be truly none that are not founded in and adorned with humility.

The second ground of blessedness is in the text too, *Dominus tecum,* the Lord's being with her. From Christ's being with her and with us it is that we are blessed. From his Incarnation begins the date of all our happiness. If God be not with us all the world cannot make us happy, much less blessed. From this grace of his Incarnation first riseth all our glory; so that, "Not unto us, O Lord, not unto us, but unto thy name give the praise," must she sing as well as we; and they do her wrong as well as God, that give his glory unto her, who will not give his glory to another, though to his mother, because she is but his earthly mother,—a thing infinitely distant from the heavenly Father. Nor would that humble handmaid, if she should understand the vain and fond, and almost idolatrous styles and honours that are given her somewhere upon earth, be pleased with them; she is highly favoured enough that her Lord and Son is with her and she with him: she would be no higher sharer. You may see it in the last particular, the bounds and limitations of her titles and blessedness.

1. For, first, how full soever she be of grace, it is yet but grace and favour; it is no more. God's mere favour so exalted her, *respexit* only, his respect to her, his free looking on her, no merit or desert, κεχαριτωμένη, he hath highly favoured her indeed, but he has done, done it in the *præter*, before she could conceive or imagine it.

2. The salutation here, except the titles given her by the angels, is not much more than what he gave to Gideon, or what Boaz to his harvesters. Enough to make the Papists afraid, one would think, of those extravagant, at least, if not blasphemous, titles they give her, of their closing their books and studies with *Laus Deo et Virgini Mariæ*, joining her in partnership with God, as if they were as much beholding to her as him. I am sure they learned not this from the Angel; he brings no divine but human titles and salutations to her. And he knew how to give titles, though not flattering ones, as Elihu speaks in Job.

3. All her honour and blessedness is from *Dominus tecum*, the Lord's being with her. He is her Lord as well as ours. More, indeed, he is with her than with us or with angels either, *plus tecum quam mecum*, as some gloss it; but he is her Lord still for all that, and she is content so to acknowledge it and leave us a penned hymn in witness of it, to give him the sole honour of her magnifying and being magnified.

SERMON XXX.

Lastly, though it be *benedicta*, it is but *inter mulieres*, "among women," all this is; and they are but creatures: a creature-blessedness, a blessedness compatible to the creature; all to show us that when we exceed this way of honour to her, or this way of blessing her, we are all out in our *Aves*,—we know not what we say. And it is well for some that their ignorance excuses them, that they understand not what they speak.

Give we her in God's name the honour due to her. God hath styled her "blessed" by the Angel, by Elizabeth; commanded all generations to call her so, and they hitherto have done it, and let us do it too. Indeed, some of late have overdone it; yet let us not therefore underdo it, but do it as we hear the Angel and the first Christians did it; account of her and speak of her as the most blessed among women, one "highly favoured," most "highly" too. But all the while give *Dominus tecum*, all the glory, the whole glory of all to him; give her the honour and blessedness of the chief of saints,—him only the glory that she is so, and that by her conceiving and bringing our Saviour into the world we are made heirs, and shall one day be partakers of the blessedness she enjoys, when the Lord shall be with us too, and we need no angel at all to tell us so.

Especially if we now here dispose ourselves by chastity, humility, and devotion, as she did, to receive him, and let him be new-born in us. The pure and virgin soul, the humble spirit, the devout affection, will be also highly favoured; the Lord be with them and bless them above others. Blessed is the virgin soul, more blessed than others, in S. Paul's opinion; blessed the humble spirit above all. For God hath exalted the humble and meek, the humble handmaid better than the proudest lady. Blessed the devout affection that is always watching for her Lord in prayer and meditations; none so happy, so blessed, as she; the Lord comes to none so soon as such.

1 Cor. vii. 40.

Yet not to such at any time more fully than in the blessed Sacrament to which we are now a-going. There he is strangely with us, highly favours us, exceedingly blesses us; there we are all made blessed Marys, and become mothers, sisters, and brothers of our Lord, whilst we hear his word, and conceive it in us; whilst we believe him who is the Word, and receive him too into us. There angels come to us on heavenly errands, and there our Lord indeed is with us; and we are blessed, and the angels hovering all about to peep into those holy mysteries, think us so, call us so. There graces pour down in abundance on us,—there grace is in its fullest plenty,—there his highest favours are bestowed upon us,—there we are filled with grace, unless we hinder it, and shall hereafter in the strength of it be exalted into glory—there to sit down with this blessed Virgin and all the saints and angels, and sing praise, and honour, and glory, to the Father, Son, and Holy Ghost, for ever and ever.

Thus, by being full of grace, and full of those graces, we also become Marys, and the mothers of our Lord; so he tells us himself, " He that so does the will of my Father, he is my mother." Let us then strive to be so, that the angels may come with heavenly errands to us, our Lord himself come to us, and vouchsafe to be again born in us, and so bless us, fill us with grace, receive, and set us highly in his favour, and fill and exalt us hereafter with his glory, and with this blessed Virgin, and all the saints and angels, we may sing praise, and honour, and glory, to him, Father, Son, and Holy Ghost, for ever and ever.

A SERMON

ON

PALM SUNDAY.

S. MATT. xxi. 8.

And a very great multitude spread their garments in the way; others cut down branches from the trees, and strawed them in the way.

SERMON XXXI.
John xii. 13.

THE "branches" in the text point you out what day it is. S. John calls some of them at least "palm branches," and the Church calls the day "Palm Sunday," *Dominica Palmarum*, the day wherein our blessed Lord, riding as "Lord and Bishop of our souls,"—his visitation to Jerusalem upon an ass,—was met with a kind of solemn procession by the people, "a very great multitude of them," says our Evangelist, and had his way strewed with boughs, and bespread with clothes the best they had, as is usual in princely entertainments, and triumphs, and processions.

And it is both a day and business worth remembering, wherein we see the triumph of humility, whereby we are taught both humility and its reward, Christ's mercy and man's rejoicing in it, Christ's way of coming to us and our way of going out to him to meet and entertain him: things worthy consideration. All that was this day done were so, but they are many; and though they all concern us much, yet our own duty concerns us most,—to know with what dispositions, which way, and how to meet and receive our Lord, come he never so meanly, never so slowly to us; upon horse or ass, by mountain or valley, gloriously or humbly to us; though come he how he will it will be humbly,—the greatest imaginable condescension even to come unto us.

I shall stir out neither of the text nor time to mind us of our duty in the way of receiving Christ, nor desire more matter to spend the hour than the words will give me. Only I must take both the letter and spirit of them. If we look to the history and letter, many remarkables we shall meet with; if to the mystery and spirit, more and more punctually to our purposes. By both we shall be abundantly fitted against Christ's coming to us, and for our due receiving him, the sacramental, within few days now at hand, not excepted; nay, the spirit of the words may be as fitly applied to that, to the sacramental receiving him, as any other; to teach us how to receive and meet him there as well as any where else.

Consider we the words, then, under both notions,—what they did as to the letter,—what we are taught to do by the mystery and spirit. In each these three particulars:

I. The persons that go out to meet Christ and entertain him; the multitude, "a very great multitude."

II. The ceremony and respect they meet him and entertain him with; some "spread their garments in the way; others cut down branches from the trees, and strawed them in the way."

III. The way and place they meet and entertain him in, both the one and the other "in the way."

There they met him,—so they there entertained him, so many hundred years ago, in the literal sense; in the same way and manner in the spiritual sense are we to entertain him every year and all our years and days to come. And by thus canvassing the text, and taking both senses of it, we shall plainly see we have good reason to remember a Palm Sunday,—the Church so to entitle it, so to prepare us both to the Passion and the Resurrection, by spreading still before us these branches of palms and olives, by insinuating this way unto us as the properest to entertain our Saviour in, to usher in the thoughts of both the Passion and Resurrection, both his and ours, and fit us for them both.

I begin with the persons of the day, and them I find the

SERMON XXXI.

"multitude." A "multitude" for their quality; a "very great multitude" for their number.

(1.) The "multitude" for their quality are the common people. And, *Interdum vulgus rectum videt*, says the poet,[y] "Sometimes," it seems, "the common people see what is right." No people of so low or mean understanding but may come to the knowledge of Christ, and understand the ways of salvation. The rabbins had a proverb, that *Non requiescit Spiritus Domini super pauperem*, "The Spirit of the Lord rests not upon the poor;" and the Pharisees had taken up somewhat like it, when they give the people no better style than ἐπικατάρατοι, than of "cursed," and such as "know not the law." Their blessing, then, comes by Christ, it seems; so they may well honour him upon that score. Πτωχοὶ εὐαγ-γελίζονται, "To the poor the Gospel is preached," is one of the tokens he sends S. John Baptist, to evidence himself the true Messiah; quite contrary to the Pharisees' *Hic populus qui non novit*, "This people that knoweth not the law." The "Gospel," the law of Christ, the far better law, "is preached," it seems, "to the poor" by him, and *spiritus* is now joined with *pauperes*. The spirit and poor together we find in his first sermon and first beatitude, "the poor in spirit;" and a while after, *Quam difficile*, &c. "How hardly shall they that have riches enter into the kingdom of God!"—the condition altered, the poor advanced, the rich depressed, a good reason why the "multitude" should follow and respect him, and a great testimony of our Saviour's mercy and humility so to honour mean things.

John vii. 49.

[Matt. xi. 5.]

Matt. v. 3.
Mark x. 23.

Yet (2) that the "multitude" may not forget themselves, as they are too prone to do, to ride, you know whither, when they are set a-horseback; they may remember, Christ would "not commit himself unto them." He needed not their honour; he knew what they would do in a few days hence, cry as many "Crucifys" as they did to-day "Hosannas;" as fast to crucify him as now to bless him. Indeed, they are easy to be seduced and led away by any "wind of doctrine," new teachers and seducers. We have found it so of late; Christ and his Church, and his religion more dishonoured by the madness of the multitude than he

John ii. 24.

[y] [Hor. Epist. II. i. 63.]

was honoured here. They have stripped himself and his Church of all the garments and ornaments to clothe themselves, instead of stripping themselves or spreading their own garments to honour him. Yet, for all that, of such giddy pieces as these Christ does not always refuse to be honoured, that we may know he does not deal with us after our sins, nor reject us for our weaknesses, much less condemn or damn us for them before we have committed them.

Nay, perhaps, (3,) he accepts this honour from this "multitude," that he might show us what all worldly honour is; how fickle, how inconstant, how vain it is, to puff up ourselves with the breath of men, to feed ourselves with their empty air. They that are now ready to lick the dust of some great man's feet, and spread not their garments only, but their bodies for him to go over—not only to cut down boughs to strew his way, but to cut down every one that stands any way in his way if he would have it—will, within a few days, upon a little change, be as ready to trample upon that great one they so much honour, and even cut his throat if he command any thing that pleases not their humour, or crosses their private interests and designs. This very "multitude," so eager to-day to exalt Christ to the highest in their loud hosannas, are as fair on Friday to exalt him to the cross by their louder cryings. He yet would suffer them to give him honour, that you might know all earthly honour what it is.

But (4) he thus receives this honour from the "multitude," that he might provoke great ones by their example. S. Paul tells us that "salvation was come unto the Gentiles to provoke the Jews to jealousy," that they might, in a holy strife and indignation, endeavour to outgo them. It is the like intended here, that we might think much that simple men and women should outstrip us, the ignorant know more of piety and religion, do more at least; the poor and meanest bestow more, much more, on Christ than we with all our wit, and wealth, and greatness, and honour. Rom xi.11.

And in this (5) appears as well his power as providence and wisdom, that he should out of such stones as these "raise up children unto Abraham," that he should thus "out of the mouths of babes and sucklings perfect his own

SERMON XXXI.

praise," make the child as eloquent as the orator, the women as valiant in his service as the stoutest men, the people understand that which the learned doctors would not see.

Luke x. 21. "Even so, O Father, for so it pleased thee to reveal those things to babes and sucklings, and hide them from the wise." His only doing it was neither their doing nor deserving, and it is "marvellous in our eyes," an evidence of the freeness of his power, that he can do what he pleases, that he does what he lists; no man can hinder him; none able to contradict him.

This (6) shows his omniscience and his truth, that nothing that he foretels, not a tittle of it, shall fall any time to the ground. He had foretold it by his prophet, that the "daughter of Zion should rejoice, and the daughter of Jerusalem shout for joy:" and here we have it to a tittle; even their sons and daughters doing it; "a very great multitude"

Zech. ix. 9.

Matt. xxi. 15.
Matt. xxi. 10.

it is, and children and women in it; "children in the Temple," and "the whole city moved;" all sexes then, that the prophecy might be fulfilled to the last letter. So punctual is he of his word.

Yet to fulfil it fuller, it is "a very great multitude" in the text, that we (1) might know that he that was here met by so great a company was the Saviour of all, as many as would come, that would spread their garments to receive him, make him any kind of entertainment, though but strew boughs and rushes for him. That (2) the world might know that he was going to his Passion, he went freely too; he could as well have used these multitudes to preserve himself as thus strangely to do him honour; made them have bespread him with arms and weapons as well as arms and boughs of trees; strewed the way with their bodies in his defence, as well as their garments in his honour; but he would suffer death, and therefore would not suffer that. To tell us (3) that he should be served hereafter by great multitudes, and not by little handfuls of men and women; this was but a forerunner of the great multitudes of those that should hereafter believe on him.

Upon such grounds as these it is that the Eternal Wisdom so uses this "great multitude" here to set forth his glory, makes them do that which themselves yet do not understand;

to tell us (1) he is a Saviour of the poor and needy as well as of the rich and wealthy; that he does not (2) utterly refuse man's service though he knows it is not to last long; to teach us (3) all the glory and honour we receive from men is but transitory and quickly vanishing; to provoke us, (4,) by their doings, to a godly jealousy and contention to outdo them; to ascertain us (5) of the exact performance of every ἰῶτα of his promises; to intimate, lastly, to us, that he is the Saviour of us, willingly comes to suffer that he may be so, that he may purchase a Church, "great multitude," by it to himself. Thus you have some kind of glimmering light why this "great multitude" are employed in this way of honouring him by the way. And yet there is a mystery beyond it.

This "multitude" throngs together, to inform us (1) how Christ would be served and honoured—with full assemblies and congregations. The places where he comes he loves to see crowded with devout worshippers, to hear them encouraging and heightening one another with, "O come, let us worship and fall down, and kneel before God our Maker," and by outward reverence, gestures, and expressions, provoking one another to his service.

It instructs us, (2,) that there is neither man nor woman, master nor servant, old man or child, poor or rich, to be out in giving glory to him; all sexes, ages, and conditions to flow together to do him service; the very children to lisp it out; they that have not a rag to cover shame may have a leaf to honour him; they that cannot, are not able to cut down a bough, may strew it yet; that cannot lift a branch, may hold a twig, do somewhat or other to his entertainment.

It preaches (3) to us, that there is nothing readier to serve him than the poor in spirit; that the spirit which most does him honour, which is ever most ready to do it to him, is the poor and humble spirit, such as ranks itself lowest, thinks meanest of itself, none so mean in the meanest multitude. Here is the spirit of this "very great multitude," the spiritual sense it speaks, a serving Christ with a poor and humble spirit, and bringing ourselves, and all ours, our very children, to speak or point out his praise, to do it too "in the great congregation," as the Psalmist speaks, to "praise him among much people." [Ps. xxxv. 18.]

58 A SERMON ON PALM SUNDAY.

SERMON XXXI.

And not only so, but with much ceremony too; so we read in the next particular, some "spread their garments in the way; others cut down branches from the trees, and strawed them in the way."

II. These ceremonies, neither of them, were strange among the Jews, in the days of joy or triumph, or the inauguration of kings and princes. When Jehu was anointed king, we find every man hasting to take his own garment and put it under him; spreading them as carpets for him to walk on. And in the Feast of Tabernacles, it was commanded them to "take boughs of goodly trees, branches of palm trees, and the boughs of thick trees and willows of the brook, and so rejoice before the Lord;" whence afterward it became usual in all feasts of solemn joy to do as much. So we read, Simon entering the tower of Jerusalem, "with thanksgivings, and branches of palm trees;" and when Judas Maccabæus had recovered and cleansed the temple, "they bare branches, and fair boughs, and palms also," rejoicing for it. So that the reason is ready, why the multitude met Jesus in this fashion. They would long before have made him king; they believed he was the Messiah, the King of Israel; and therefore thus go out to meet him and receive him. They had heard his word, they had seen his miracles; "Never man," say the very Pharisees' officers, "spake like" him; with more authority and power he, than all their Jewish doctors and rabbis all together,—never man did such things as he,—and therefore no wonder if the people do some strange things too, to express their opinions of him.

2 Kings ix. 13.

Lev. xxiii. 40.

1 Macc. xiii. 51.

2 Macc.x.7.

But the matter is not so much what they do, as what we learn by Christ's suffering them to do so. And by it we (1) first gather, that Christ is no enemy to outward ceremonies and respects, to outward civilities and expressions.

That (2) he dislikes not neither even the ceremonies of solemn joys and triumphs, of respects done to kings, and princes, and great persons, or public congratulations with them in the days of their joy, or of any public joy, or particular gladness, as occasion shall present it.

That (3) he rejects not even the old and ancient ceremonies —is as much content with such as any other; these were no other, and yet he sticks not to receive them, stumbles not at them.

Nay, (4,) even in his service and for his own honour he accepts them; is not only content, but pleased also that they should do them to himself. It is the Pharisees only, and pharisaical spirits; men of mere pretended piety and religion, whose devotion is only to be seen of men, whose whole business is to appear holier than others, not to be so, that find fault with the doing it, that would have them rebuked for it. To whom Christ answers, that if they did not, "the stones" would do more; they, even they, would both "cry out" against them for their silence, and not doing it, and do what they could to express that joy of his coming to Jerusalem, of which they seemed so insensible. The very trees would bow themselves, and every branch shake off its leaves, and spread the ways, if men should not spread their garments; break off themselves, if they would not cut them down to strew them; the very stones of the wall fall themselves into an even pavement, to kiss the feet of their Lord and Maker. Insensible and senseless stones, are men the while, that deny Christ external reverence, outward worship, reverent and ceremonious approaches to him, that make I know not what senseless arguments and excuses, idle scruples and pretences against old good significant ceremonies in his service to his honour. The very stones confute them, and Christ's telling us, they would cry if men should not, signifies as well, they would bow, and worship, and fall down, beautify the ways and places where he comes, if men should not,—rear themselves into temples and altars, if men should be so irreligious not to raise and employ them to it. I now spare any other confutation.

We learn, (5,) by Christ's thus suffering them, and God's secret moving them, thus to spread the ways with boughs and garments, that he would be acknowledged to be that great He, to whom all creatures owe themselves, to whom all are to be devoted, who is to be served with all, even to a thread; the trees to pay their boughs, and men their garments—to strip themselves to the very skin, and consecrate even their garments to his honour, to lay them at his feet, to resign all to him, to be content that he, nay, the very ass

Sermon XXXI.

Luke xix. 39.

SERMON XXXI.

he rides on, should trample on us, if it be to his praise and glory, that that may be augmented by it.

Lastly, This spreading the way with garments and palm branches, was the way of entertaining conquerors in their triumphs; and by his disposing it at this time to himself, he gave them to understand, that he was the conqueror over death and hell. In this only differing from other conquerors, that he triumphs before his conquest—none so but he, because none certain of the victory till it be perfected but he. This might go for a mystery among the rest, but it concerns those persons peculiarly, and those times. The mystery of this point as it concerns us, we are next to see; how these garments and branches, this spreading and strewing, belong to us,—how we are still so to spread our garments and strew branches before Christ.

Zech. xiv. 14.

Now, garments (1) pass in the account for riches; and he that either bestows plentifully upon the poor, that clothes the naked, and feeds the hungry, and supplies the needy with any thing to cover, comfort, or refresh him, and spreads God's holy house and table with offerings, gives or does any thing to beautify his service, to add honour and solemnity to his worship, spreads his garments before Christ.

(2.) Garments are reckoned among necessaries; and he that not only out of his superfluity, but, as the Apostle testifies of the Corinthians, out of his poverty also, abounds unto the riches of liberality, that spares somewhat from his necessities, spreads even his inner garment at the feet of Christ.

2 Cor. viii. 2.

But (3) the garments the multitude here spread were honorary; the outward vestments and more honourable, that we might know our honours also are to be laid aside; nay, laid down to be trod upon by any ass for Christ's sake, we to count nothing of our honour in comparison of his, tread all under foot, and reckon nothing so honourable as the reproach of Christ.

(4.) Garments are a shelter from the injury of wind and weather, of heat and cold. Yet if Christ's business require it of us, we must not think much to lie open to storm and tempest, to be deprived of house and shelter, of robes and rags—nothing too much—nothing enough for Christ.

(5.) To spread our garments under one's feet, was construed for a profession of subjection and obedience to him for whom we spread, or to whom we send them; so to spread our garments in the way of Jesus, is to profess, and promise, and begin obedience to him, the chief spreading the way that he desires, the best way of entertaining him.

Sermon XXXI.
2 Kings ix. 13; 1 Kings x. 25.

(6.) Our righteousness is called our garment. This also we are to spread before him, that he may consecrate and hallow it; till he has set his mark upon it, and sealed it, it will not pass for current; all our righteousness and obedience must have his stamp to confirm it, his robes to lengthen it, his righteousness to make it right.

Rev. iii. 4; xvi. 15.

Lastly, to spread our garments to receive him, may have a kind of reflection upon the preparation we are making for the blessed sacrament. We must open our bosoms, disrobe ourselves, spread our garments, stretch out our hands, open our bosoms by confession, disrobe and dismantle ourselves by renouncing all former vanities, spread all the good thoughts, and affections, and desires we can, stretch out our souls in all holy vows and resolutions, to receive and entertain him. Nay, all the former garments and spreadings may again be repeated and remembered here. We must spread our garments upon the backs of the poor, spread ourselves before the altar upon the pavement with all humility and devotion, neglect and trample upon all private respects and interests, lay aside all vain desires of honour and greatness, despoil ourselves of all trust and confidence in ourselves, or in the arm of flesh, faithfully protest and renew the vow of obedience and subjection, acknowledge our own no righteousness till he accepts it; thus spread our garments all we can, to receive him with joy and honour.

But if it so fall out, that we either have not some of these kind of garments, those we have be not worth the spreading, we may yet " cut down branches from the trees, and straw in the way," at least where our garments will not reach. Now several sorts of branches there were, which we may conceive the "multitude" made use of. Two more particularly, palms and olives; yet from Nehemiah we may gather more; " olive branches, and pine branches, and myrtle branches, and palm branches, and branches of thick

Neh. viii. 15.

trees," he reckons up, and bids them fetch to make them tents and tabernacles, the like likely also here; and in Leviticus, willows are added to; in brief, any such as were at hand, that grew by the way from Mount Olivet to Jerusalem. These to the letter; shall we see what spirit we can draw from them?

1. "Branches of palm trees" by name, S. John tells us, they came out of Jerusalem to meet him with. And palms (i.) are the emblems of patience and perseverance; they cannot be depressed with any weight; but the more you press them the more they rise; and so may teach us the patience of the Cross, not to look sad for any hardship that shall befal us in the way to Christ; but the more we suffer for him, the more to bear up and lift up our heads, that our redemption draweth nigh. Palms thence (ii.) are signs of victory, so being here given as it were to Christ, they intimate to us both to whom to give the glory of all the victory we get over our sins and passions, and so to labour ourselves against them, that we may be thought worthy to overcome them.

2. "Branches of olives" could not probably but be here too; the meeting was upon Mount Olivet, a place full of olives; and olives are the emblems of peace and meekness, of mercy and softness: nothing so smooth, so softening, so suppling as oil, to teach us what spirit we are of if we be Christ's; this the offering he is most pleased with, the disposition he most delights in; his way is spread with "olive branches," is a way of sweetness,—his yoke an easy yoke, full of rest and peace to the wearied soul; the Christian's way must be so too,—a sweet and quiet temper in us through all our ways.

3. We may have leave to conjecture from that cited place of Leviticus and Nehemiah, there were other sorts besides. Pine branches, or as some render the word, branches of balsam and cedar trees.

Now the pine and cedar are tall, straight, and upright trees, and may mind us of high heavenly thoughts, pure and upright intentions, straight and regular affections, to run forth to meet him with.

In particular, (1,) the pine is a tree, says Pliny, that is never but bearing fruit; it has perpetually three years' fruit upon it, and ripens month by month. What a glorious tree is this to present to Christ! a soul always bearing fruit, fruit after fruit, fruit upon fruit, "adding to faith, virtue; to virtue, knowledge; to knowledge, temperance; to temperance, patience; to patience, godliness; to godliness, brotherly kindness; to brotherly kindness, charity," as S. Peter advises us; bearing still one fruit upon earth, for the great years, the three great ages of our life—youth, manhood, and old age, till we bring our years to an end.

<small>Sermon XXXI.

2 Pet. i. 5, 6, 7.</small>

The cedar next, (2,) is a sweet lasting wood—will not take worm, corrupt, or lose its scent; and the branches of it shadow out thus much to us, that in the actions we present to Christ, there be no worms, no bye intentions, no corrupt affections,—all sweet, and incorrupt, and a continued constancy, and continuance in them.

The balsam, or balm tree, (3,) is a tree medicinal to heal and cure wounds. And "is there no balm in Gilead, no physician there?" says the prophet Jeremiah. If there be not, here there is; upon Mount Olivet there is here, upon Mount Calvary there is, in Christ's death and passion, to which he here is going; let us then bring balm branches thence, and strew the way; acknowledge our Physician, in whom our health; He that heals the lame, the blind, the sick, and all.

<small>[Jer. viii. 22.]</small>

(4.) Nehemiah mentions myrtle branches, as usual in such solemnities as these. It was a tree, says Pliny, dedicated to love; and the boughs of it may teach us upon whom all our love is to be bestowed,—all upon Christ, all upon Christ.

At the Feast of Tabernacles, from whence this spreading the ways were borrowed, we read of willows, "the willows of the brook;" and they may denote unto us, that we are to sit down with the willows a little by the waters, look upon ourselves in the streams of repentant tears, and then bring our branches so watered to strew the way of Christ.

There is yet *lignum nemorosum*, the branches of thick trees behind, to tell us that we are to strew the ways not here and there with our piety and good works, but thick every where, as thick as may be, that so we may even cover the way, hide the earth, all appearance of earth, or earthly, sensual, worldly desires and thoughts, when we are coming to receive our Lord.

Thus I have brought you to the trees, showed you what to spread Christ's way with; you must now cut down the branches, and strew the way; take others in your hand and present him with. And with joy, and gladness, and thankful hearts, both accept the infinite favour he does you to come to you, and rejoice in it. It is time now I say somewhat of the "way" he comes, the "way" you are to meet him in.

III. Between Mount Olivet and Jerusalem it was, from the mount into the temple. Upon the mount he preached, and in the temple he taught, and there in his word you are to meet him; and that the word pass not away as the wind and empty air, you are to come to it with prepared hearts, to open your ears, to spread your hearts to entertain it, to bring the boughs of olives,—peaceable and pliant dispositions; boughs of palms,—conquered passions; boughs of cedar,—constant resolutions; boughs of myrtle,—loving affections, to it; and from Mount Olivet to Jerusalem, remember it is from the mount of peace to the city of peace, that you may not forget to come in the unity of the Church's peace, without schism, or faction, or schismatical and factious intentions, if you look to meet Christ there.

In both Olivet and Jerusalem you see there is a mystery: the "branches" and "garments" cover mysteries all the "way," are kind of sacraments; and in the blessed sacraments it is we receive Christ Jesus. Throw we then our "garments" in the way, cast all our own from us, that we may have none but Christ; bring palms, and pines, and olives, cedars, and myrtles, and willows; all thick and all green, verdant, pleasing graces, virtues, and affections to them; spread them all at the foot of the altar—that is the ass that Christ rides on; the holy elements they that carry him, they that convey him to us. There is our Conqueror, let us bring palms; there is our Peace-maker, let us bring olive-branches; there is "the Lord our righteousness," let us bring the upright pine; there is our "sweet-smelling savour" in the eyes of God our eternal redemption, let us bring cedar-boughs; there is the great Physician of our souls, let us bring him balm; there is our love, let us bring him myrtle;

there is the well-spring of our life, let us bring willows; there is the fulness of our good and happiness, let us bring him the branches of thick trees.

Sermon XXXI.

That we may do it better, remember this "way" is the way to the Cross; this procession to his Passion. This the way, his Cross and Passion the meditation we are to receive him in. Let us readily strip ourselves of all our "garments" for him who is stripped presently of all his for us. Let us cover him with palms, and crown him with olives; let us make it our business and delight to be always strewing his way before him, to be doing all our endeavours we can to entertain him. Let us leave no branch of virtue out—spread them as thick as possibly upon this earth of ours—cover ourselves with them, that we may be the "way," our souls and bodies the "way" for him.

And now you see, I hope, how fit Palm Sunday is to usher in the Passion, to precede the receiving Christ; the very trees of the wood have told you it: I shall do no more—spread the boughs no further. It is you now must strew them, or I have but hitherto strewed in vain.

The work is not to be done singly by the preacher,—it is the "multitude" that is to do it too; it is to be done in public, it is to be done in private, it is to be done by the Apostles, it is to be done by the people, it is to be done by men, women, and children, old and young, poor and rich— all to bear a part by the way, if they hope to come to the happy end; every one either to spread his garment, or strew a branch, or bring a sprig; some one thing, some another— but all something to the honour of Christ; to do it with much solemnity and respect, outward and inward, all of it, as to one that deserves all that we can do to strew our souls, to strew our bodies, to fill our hands, to spread all our powers and affections, to entertain him; to strew our souls with palms and olives, pines and cedars, myrtles and willows, patience and meekness, uprightness and constancy, love and repentance, and all holy virtues—as thick, as full, as fair as may be; think nothing too much, nothing enough to do or suffer in his service.

Then shall our "garments" truly cover us, and keep us warm; then shall our "trees" bring forth fruit, when boughs and garments are thus employed; then shall our " ways " be strewed with peace, every one " sit under his own vine," and drink the wine of it; then shall our " branches " cover the hills, and " stretch out unto the river." He that is the " Branch " in the Prophet's style, shall so spread them for it, give us the " tree of life " for these lifeless boughs, and for the spreading our " garments " over him, spread his garment over us,—the " robe of his righteousness," the garment of glory, where, strewing our " garments" and " branches" with this " great multitude " in the text, we shall, with that " great multitude " in the Revelation, " of all nations, which no man can number, stand before the throne, and before the Lamb, clothed with white garments, and palms in our hands," singing and saying, " Salvation unto our God, which sitteth upon the throne; and to the Lamb, Blessing, and glory, and wisdom, and thanksgiving, and honour, and power, and might, be unto our God for ever and ever." Amen.

A SERMON

UPON

GOOD FRIDAY.

---

1 Cor. ii. 2.

For I determined not to know any thing among you, save Jesus Christ, and him crucified.

AND this being Passion day, I am "determined not to" preach "any thing among you" to-day but "Jesus Christ, and him crucified." I cannot preach any thing more seasonable, nor you hear anything more comfortable, nor any of us "know any thing" more profitable. S. Paul himself thought nor he nor his Corinthians could—" determined" so here, *ex cathedra*. And the holy Church has thought and "determined" so too: to send no other Epistles, to preach no other Gospels to us this week through, than of "Jesus Christ, and him crucified;" as if the sum of the Gospel, the Gospel itself, were nothing else; no other knowledge worth the knowing, at least at this time, these days, to be thought of or intended.

Not but that we may lawfully have other knowledges besides, intend other knowledges too, at other times, in their proper times; not but that we may know more of Jesus Christ himself than his being crucified; but that all the knowledges of him tend hither, "Jesus" and "Christ," his salvation and office, clearest seen here, best "determined" hence; that all other knowledges are to be directed hither, to Jesus Christ, are but petty and inconsiderable in respect, and only worth the knowing when Christ is in them, and we

SERMON XXXII.

2 Cor. xii. 15.

with Christ crucified in them, our affections mortified and humbled by them; that especially at this time nothing is so fit to take up our thoughts, to employ our meditations,—nothing not of Christ himself, no act or story of him,—as his crucifixion.

And yet the text affords us a plainer reason and account of this so "determined" knowledge, from the two pronouns, "I" and "you." None so fit for this "I," for an Apostle, a preacher, a divine, to be "determined" to, to determine from, to be "determined" by, as "Christ, and him crucified;" nothing so fit to fasten his resolutions against the crosses and thwartings he is like to meet with in the world, even among them he bestows and spends most upon, and would be bestowed and "spent" himself for,—as this Apostle for these Corinthians,—as the consideration of the cross of Christ. And no knowledge fitter for this "you," for the Corinthians,—people now divided into schisms and factions,—than to think of Christ crucified, rent and torn in pieces by them; thus crucified again by them through their divisions, who was crucified to unite them, to bring all into one body, under one head, by his body on the cross, into himself the head, Christ Jesus.

For there were at the time of this Epistle, among the Corinthians,—as there are now among us,—some that much boasted of their knowledge, as if they alone knew all that was to be known,—more than S. Paul, than a hundred S. Pauls; made themselves heads of factions and schisms upon it, and drew parties after them. In this, indeed, differing from the heads of ours, that they vaunted of their human learning; ours have nothing but ignorance to boast of. They would have faith reduced to reason—these ruled by fancy; yet in this agreeing both, in their ignorance of the cross of Christ, or sure quite forgetting it, and making schisms, and sowing heresies in the Church of Christ, though perhaps we could find them some Socinianized wits too, that would fain bring all to natural reason, and really deny the very effects of the cross of Christ, his satisfaction and redemption; the very denying, in effect, "Christ crucified," or any knowledge of it.

To beat down these great boasters, and all vain braggers, S. Paul resolves upon two points in the text, a seeming ignorance and a real knowledge; a seeming ignorance, to confound their seeming knowledge; a real knowledge, to confound their real ignorance: "not to know," and "but to know;" "not to know," that is, not to seem to know anything; yet "to know," to know every thing that is worth the knowing, "Jesus Christ, and him crucified;" the whole way of salvation. So to teach us besides, and all that should come after him, what to determine, and how to determine, both of our ignorances and knowledges; what "not to know," things that have no profit, but only breed strife and debate, schisms and divisions, "not to know" such things among them, to do others hurt by our knowledge. What "to know—Jesus Christ, and him crucified;" that to be sure to know, and nothing but him and it, and in order unto it or him; thus to determine and be "determined," the only way to profit and benefit both ourselves and others, at any time, with our knowing and not knowing: to know what, and how far to know, and not to know: what to determine of, and where to be determined.

Thus we have brought the text to its own natural division, to hinder our unnatural ones; S. Paul's double determination: one for ignorance, the other for knowledge; one, "not to know," the other, "to know." A determination too, in a double sense as well as a double object; a double determination about not knowing, and a double one about knowing; a determination to both, and a determination of each.

I. A determination not to know, to seem ignorant,— "I am determined not to know."

A determination of this not knowing, or seeming ignorant, it is but seeming, only so "determined," or put on; it is but "among you,"—it is but in comparison of the following knowledge, which is the only saving knowledge.

II. A determination to know, not to be really ignorant, though not "any thing" but is something, though not *that* those false teachers vaunted of.

A determination or determining of this knowledge, (1,) to "Christ;" (2,) "Christ Jesus;" (3,) "Christ Jesus crucified;" that, and nothing further, now further, among them; nothing else to determine himself, or them, or his, or their knowledges by at any time; nothing, save that,—nothing saving, but that.

Thus the text determines both our knowledge and

ignorance, and limits both, shall determine and limit our discourse. God grant we may all so be determined by it, that both our ignorance and knowledge may hence learn their bounds and limits, and all end at last in "Jesus Christ, and him crucified."

I begin with S. Paul's determination, "not to know any thing among" the Corinthians; where we have, (1,) the things he is determined not to know; (2,) the not knowing them; (3,) the determination so to do; (4,) the determining how far, and among whom, how, and where to be ignorant, and not know them.

And, first, many things there are not to be known, of which it is good to be ignorant. Some things that are not worth the knowing,—light and trivial things, which only rob us of those precious minutes which a Christian should spend upon nobler thoughts.

Some things we are the worse for knowing, which only infect the soul, and instead of knowledge bring blindness and ignorance upon it: Adam and Eve's unhappy knowledge, when we will needs be knowing more than God will have us, curious and vain arts and sciences, of which it is far better, with those in the Acts, to burn the books than read them.

Some things we can scarce do worse than know them, whose very knowledge is a guilt whereby we are perfected in wickedness, grow cunning in contriving, subtle in conveying, experienced in managing sin or mischief.

Some things, again, there are which it is best "not to know," sins from which the safest fence is ignorance, whose knowledge would but teach us to do them, or leave in us a desire and itching after them, *Nitimur in vetitum;* sins which else, perhaps, we had never thought of or attempted, the not knowing of which had kept us safe, because we cannot desire things we know not.

Some things there are, again, which though good and commendable, yet of which we may say, and say truly, it is very pleasant and useful too "not to know" in time and place; and such is this "any thing" of the Apostle's; human learning and sciences, natural reason and artificial eloquence, tongues and languages, disputes and questions, whereof sometimes a real ignorance, sometimes a seeming one, will do more good than all of them together.

SERMON XXXII.

For diversity there is in the not knowing, as well as in the things not to be known; many ways of not knowing. For "not to know" is (1) really to be ignorant; which in good matters, if it be not voluntary or affected, but either by reason of a natural dulness or incapacity, or for want of education which we could not have, or because we had not the means or time to come to the knowledge of it, or if we were not bound "to know" it, is no sin,—may not only excuse from punishment but from fault. Thus the poor simple man that knows not a letter, nor understands half what others do, not the tenth part that others do, may know enough of "Christ crucified" to bring him into heaven, when many that are more learned shall stand without. But this ignorance, for the most part of it, must not be determined by us; we must not, the meanest of us, resolve and determine with ourselves to be ignorant, or remain so in any spiritual or heavenly business, but "to know" as far as our condition requires, or will give us leave. Yet in mere human knowledges even a resolved ignorance may do well, when your knowing would take up more time than it is worth, when it would rob us of better, or hinder us in the more necessary improvements of our souls, when there is just fear it will but make us insolent or impertinent; better far "not to know" a letter, not to speak a tongue, but what the nurse and mother taught us, than be the nimblest orator or skilfullest linguist or rarest philosopher, if nothing be like to come of it but the disturbance of the Church, the seducing others, and vain glory in ourselves. In this case we may, with S. Paul, even determine to be ignorant, more ignorant still, especially in unprofitable, curious, or impious knowledge or ways of knowing.

However, even in the best and most necessary of these it may be requisite "not to know" (2) in a second sense; that is, not to seem to know them; to bear ourselves sometimes as if we did not. There are some we may have to deal with that are suspicious of being deceived by too much reason and philosophy, with whom it is only the way to work, to renounce,

SERMON XXXII.

as it were, all art and logic, and discourse, as if we were wholly ignorant in them, that we may so by S. Paul's own way, of "becoming all things to all men," to the ignorant as ignorant of every thing but salvation, by plainness and condescension to their humour win them to the truth. And indeed, wherever eloquence, language, philosophy, or natural reason are like more to lose than gain a soul, more to vaunt themselves than preach Christ; "not to know," that is, to seem not to know them, or deal by them, or build upon them, or make show of them, but conceal them, is the best.

"Not to know" them (3), in a third sense, is not to teach them, not to teach them when we should be teaching Christ, or teach them instead of Christ,—natural reason for divine faith, moral philosophy for the only divinity.

"Not to know" them (4), fourthly, to profess and make our whole business of them, to make knowledge our whole profession, as if religion consisted in knowing only, and they the best Christians that knew most. Alas! *Nos doctrinis nostris trudimur in infernum*, is too true: "Many a learned man is thrust at last into hell with all his knowledge." We may "speak with the tongues of angels," and "have all knowledge, all faith" too, even to a miracle, and to do miracles, and yet for all that be "but sounding brass and tinkling cymbals;" mere noise and vapour, not so good as the prophet's reprobate silver, but mere brass and copper, that will not pass with heaven for current money, nor be received into the treasuries of God; better it is "not to know" at all than to know only and no more, to know and not do; we shall only get the more stripes by the bargain; and however we seem to know God, not to be known of him, or acknowledged by him, but sent away by Christ with an—"I know you not."

The things then not to be known, and the not knowing, being things of so difficult or doubtful nature, best it is now that we determine somewhat of them, that we may know both the things and knowledge, or rather not knowledge that is fittest for us.

The "any thing" the Apostle means expressly is set down in the former verse under the terms of "excellency of speech" or "wisdom;" and that "wisdom" to be "the wisdom of the world;" of the wise and prudent, moral philosophy; of the scribe, law and history and philology; of "the disputer of this world," natural philosophy, mathematics, astronomy, astrology: all which S. Paul seems determined not to know.

Sermon XXXII.

1 Cor. i. 20.

It is ἔκρινα, he has so judged it, so judged and passed sentence upon all those knowledges as to give a μή τι, to give a negative to them all. In things of moment it is good to be determined and resolved. It is for want of this judgment and determination that we lose ourselves so oft ere we are aware, and not only consume our days in knowledges that do not profit, in searching out endless genealogies and disputations to no benefit of the hearers, without the least edification. Settle we and fix ourselves upon this point in all our knowings, and not knowings, to do all to edification, that whether we know any thing or not, whether we know every thing or nothing, it be all to the glory of God; and then even our ignorance will save us as well as our knowledge: only with this item, that it be a determining by ἔκρινα with the Apostle here, a determination with judgment to discern and judge what things are fit not to be known, what to be known; what knowledge and time and pains to bestow upon them; what we are to be wholly ignorant in, what in part, what really not to know, what to seem only not knowing in, what to conceal, and what to teach, what to make our profession of, and what to know only by-the-bye; how far, and where, and when to know them.

And this is the very determining our determination I spake of for a fourth consideration. I shall set no other bounds either to our knowledge or object, or our determining ourselves to it, or in it, than what we have within the bounds of the text, because my determination is to hasten to the knowledge of "Jesus Christ, and him crucified."

To determine, then, this determination of S. Paul's, " not to know any thing," take we the words as they lie, and consider who it is that has thus "determined." "I," it is, that S. Paul himself it is, an Apostle, and a great knowing one too. Yet "I have determined not to know." Sciences

SERMON XXXII.

Acts xix. 8.
Acts xvii. 28.

there are that are below an Apostle, that become not him whatever they do others. The Apostles were to act all by the power of the Spirit; were not to study words and human arguments, though we sometimes find them "disputing" too, and quoting poets and human authors; were not to pretend to such worldly wisdom, that the glory might be wholly God's, and the whole world convinced, that as the Christian faith was not established by mortal strength, nor settled by worldly power, so it was not persuaded by human wit or interests, and was therefore truly divine and heavenly.

But, (2,) even the successors of the Apostles, the ministers of the Gospel,—though they have now only this ordinary way of enabling them to their office,—are yet so to use their knowledge as if they used them not, their chief work being Christ's, and these only as ways to it, remembering their great business to be "to know Christ crucified," and to teach him, and not to know anything but in order to it; at least, not to profess anything above or equal with it, that may swallow up the time which ought to be spent in divine employments. Thus this not knowing is first determined by the person: persons wholly interested in the business of heaven not to turn their studies into a business of the world, persons designed to an extraordinary office, not to deal in it by extraordinary means, but guide all according to that rule and way and work that God has set them.

But the not knowing the secular sciences is not only limited to spiritual persons; there are limits within which all must keep as well their ignorance as knowledge. When at any time they will determine not to know it must be (1) by ἔκρινα, by judgment and discretion, not promiscuously: such things as sound judgment propounds unnecessary, dangerous, or unfruitful.

It must be (2) by a *non judicavi quicquam*, whatsoever knowledge we have of human sciences we must judge and reckon it as nothing, determine it to be no other than dross and dung, than building with hay and stubble, in respect of the knowledge of Jesus Christ, not anything to that.

It must be, (3,) too, without putting any estimate upon

ourselves for any such knowledge; we must still think we know nothing whilst we know no more. "Moses," a man, as S. Stephen styles him, "mighty in words and deeds, and learned in all the wisdom of the Egyptians;" yet when God would send him of his errand, considering that, tells God he was not eloquent, neither heretofore nor since he had spoken to his servant, but slow of speech and slow of tongue. And Isaiah, that seraphic prophet, cries out, he is a "man of unclean lips;" so little valued they all their knowledge, when they had but a glimpse of that great knowledge God was now imparting to them. How much soever we think we know before, when we once come to the knowledge of Christ, or but our thoughts to come to know a taste of the riches of the fulness of the knowledge of Christ, we then know we know nothing, count ourselves dolts and idiots, mere fools and blocks, for squandering away so much time and cost and pains upon those empty notions whereby we are not an inch the nearer heaven, and it may be, the further from God, after all our labour. Then only we begin truly to know, when we can pass this sentence upon ourselves, that we know not anything; when we are so humble that we think so, at least think not anything of ourselves for all we know.

(4.) We must "determine not to know any thing" at all of human sciences or natural reasonings, rather than to determine ourselves by it, renounce it rather, all knowing, and turn all to believing; not fix our faith upon natural principles, or believe no further than we can know; rather than so, we had far better know nothing, set it up for a resolution, however, in the matters of faith not to know, that is, not to go about to determine them by reason: for the "natural man" he understands them not; they are foolishness unto him; a foolish thing to him to talk of a God incarnate, of a crucified Saviour, of a religion whose glory is the cross, and reward he knows not where nor when.

Or, (5,) he is only "not determined to know any thing;" so the negative is truly joined, not to his knowledge, but to his determination, "not determined;" if he know it he counts it but by-the-bye; his main business is something else; human knowledge is but by-the-way and *obiter*; he intends

SERMON XXXII.

them not for his doctrine, nor yet to prove or stablish his doctrine upon them, as upon foundations, nor preach moral and natural philosophy for divinity; but to advance both the one and the other: all philology, language, and history, to the service of Christ and the glory of his cross; to use our rhetoric, to set forth his sufferings, the merit, and benefit, and glory of them: our natural philosophy, to find us out the God of nature in all his works: moral philosophy and history, to dissuade vice and encourage virtue, even by the light of nature: the knowledge of the heavens and heavenly spirits, to declare his excellent and wondrous works: our criticisms, to sift out truth, and our languages to express it: in a word, not so much to know any of them, as God through them; not them properly, but Christ Jesus by them. There is no fear of human sciences thus determined.

Yet there is one way more to determine our not knowing by,—by the persons with whom we have to do. Our doctrines,—for so we told you, and for the chief meaning here we tell you now again, to know here signifies to teach,—our doctrines are to be proportioned and fitted for the auditory. It was no meaner a man's practice than S. Paul's, to the weak to become as weak, to gain the weak; to the weak and simple, not to speak mysteries and speculations; to them that were without law, as without law, plain, honest dealing, not quirks and quillets, to gain such; not to know any such thing among such as they. Yet sometimes, upon the same ground, to do quite contrary, to confound the wisdom of the world, by that which that counts foolishness; the strength of the world, by that it reckons weakness; the honourable things of the world, by things which that esteems base and ignominious. The Corinthians gloried in their learning and eloquence; S. Paul, to confute their vanity, undertakes to do more by plainness, and rudeness of speech, and ignorance, than they, all of them, can by all their wisdom and rhetoric; among them, he will make no use of anything but the contemptible knowledge of the cross of Christ, and yet do more than all their philosophers and orators. Where learning will serve but to ostentation, and the ear only tickled by it, or human applause not edification, schism not peace, the issue of it; among them, "not to know any" such thing, is best of all; for "let all things be done," says the Apostle, "to edification;" and if that will be done best by plainness, to use plainness; if by learning, to use that; as the "you" are that are to be edified, so the "I," the minister to deal with them; if they be puffed up with human knowledge, to humble them to the A B C of the cross, to exalt and preach up that above all knowledge whatsoever; if divided into schisms by the several sects of philosophy, or the masters of them, to unite all again into one, as so many pieces into one cross, among them to cry up no knowledge, but thence or thither.

So then, now to sanctify all our secular knowledges and ignorances, thus we are to determine them: to know our times, and place, and persons for them; to keep measure and order in them; to profess none that are wicked, or only vain and curious, and to no profit; to submit our knowledge to faith, and our determination to the Church's; not to overvalue them, or ourselves by them, but only make them handmaids to guide us to the cross of Christ, and there with Mary Magdalen and the good women, stand weeping at it; "not to know any" of them otherwise; to resolve and determine nothing of Christ by them, and "not to know" them where they will know no submission and order. I come now to our knowledge, and it is indeed the only saving one, "Jesus Christ, and him crucified;" nothing save that,—nothing to that.

For you may now take notice, that it is not an absolute determination "not to know," a decree for ignorance, but a determination with a *but*, "not any thing save;" then save something, something to be known still. Some have been blamed for making ignorance the mother of devotion, yet themselves that blamed them have advanced it to be the mother of religion, now, whilst they set up mere ignorants, —I might say more,—to be the apostles of it; fit teachers, I confess, of their religion, which so much abhors the cross of Christ as to cast it off their own shoulders upon other men's, and the name of Jesus, as to reckon it superstition to respect it.

But this great preacher of the cross, as much as he seems "determined not to know," had yet languages more than

SERMON XXXII.

1 Cor. xiv. 26.

1 Cor. xiv. 18.

SERMON XXXII.

Acts xix. 8.
Acts xix. 9.
Acts xvii. 28.
Titus i. 12.

Mal. ii. 7.

Matt. xv. 14.

Luke xxi. 15.

all these Corinthians he writes to,—tells them of it too; though he will not boast of it, "disputes" even in Corinth, in the "Synagogue" of the Jews, and in the "schools" of the Gentiles; quotes Heathen poets too to the men of Athens, and to Titus,—that we may know that the preachers of the Gospel may read other books besides the Bible,—shall never read that to understand it if they do not. It is only in some cases and with some persons, we are not to make profession of them, and merely too upon private determination, as our own wisdom and prudence shall direct us; not that God or Christ has determined the least against it. God would have his people to seek his law at the mouth of the priest; and adds the reason,—because "his lips should keep knowledge." And Christ Jesus, though he made poor simple fishermen his Apostles to divulge his Gospel, yet he would not have the "blind lead the blind," for fear of "falling both into the ditch;" and therefore promises to give them wisdom,—such "wisdom as all their adversaries should not be able to gainsay,"—and sends down the Holy Ghost, with the gifts of tongues to sit upon them all; so little is there to be said for the ignorant and unlearned man's teaching from them, who before they went about that work were so highly furnished and endued. And though the Apostle here resolve the Corinthians to make no profession of those great knowledges; yet it is to shame them only from the great estimate and confidence they set upon them, and reduce them to humility, and into order, and to edify them, that he chooses and prefers to speak among them but five words in a known tongue, before all languages to no purpose.

And indeed, all tongues are too little to speak of that the Apostle is here about, "Jesus Christ, and him crucified;" all knowledges not sufficient to make us know him, and teach him as we should. We had need have all tongues and knowledges,—all words and eloquence, to set it forth.

Well then, at least let us about it, to see what it is "to know Jesus Christ, and him crucified." It is the determination of this determined knowledge. "to Christ," "to Christ Jesus," "to Christ Jesus crucified;" to this only, and no other object among them.

A knowledge this, the most profitable, the most happy,

the most glorious,—even eternal life it is, "to know Jesus Christ." Nor does his crucifying abate anything of the glory of it. S. Paul makes it his only glory; with a "God forbid that he should glory in anything," as here, "not know any thing" else, "but in the cross of the Lord Jesus Christ." Indeed, hence flows all our happiness: the wound in his side, is the hole of the rock in which only the soul can lie secure; the water that issued out thence, is the only laver to cleanse it in; the blood, the only drink it lives by; the wood of the cross, the only tree of life; the title of it, better to us than all the titles of the earth; the reproach of it, better than all the honours of the world; the pains of it, sweeter than all the pleasures under heaven; the wounds, better cordials and restoratives to a sick soul than all the physic nature or skill affords. There is not a grain of that holy wood, but of more worth than all the grains of gold that the Indies can afford. There is not a vein in that crucified body of Jesus, but it runs full with heavenly comfort to us. There is nothing in "Christ crucified," but man glorified. Who, indeed, would not be determined to fix all his knowledge here—to dwell here for ever? But so immense and vast is this happy subject, that I must limit it; yet I shall give you notions that you may improve, whilst I tell you "to know Christ crucified" is to know him as we do other things by the four causes of it: the efficient, the material, the formal, and the final. So to know him, is to know who crucified him, for what he was crucified, how it was he was crucified, and to what end he was crucified?

It was (1) his own love that moved him to it,—it was God that sent him and delivered him up to it,—it was Judas that betrayed him to it,—it was both the Jews and Gentiles that had the hand in doing it. And what know we hence but this: his infinite goodness, God's unspeakable mercies, man's base ingratitude; this mystery in all: how vastly God's purposes and man's differ in the same business, how infinitely good and gracious God is, even where men are most wicked and unthankful.

Know we then, (2,) the material cause of his sufferings for a second, and the matter for which he suffered was our

Sermon XXXII.
John xvii. 3.
Gal. vi. 14.

SERMON XXXII.
Isa. liii. 8.

iniquities; "for the transgressions of my people," says the Prophet, "was he smitten." And to know this is to deplore it, to abhor and detest ourselves, who were the causes of so vile using the Son of God.

Know we, (3,) and consider the formal cause, the manner of his crucifying, a death most cruel, most lingering, most ignominious; to have his back all furrowed with whips and rods, to hang naked upon the cross by the hands and feet, and them nailed to it through the most tender parts, where all the organs of sense are quickest; to be given vinegar and gall to drink, when he most needed comfort and refreshment; to be mocked and scoffed at in his sorrow too, derided by his enemies, forsaken by his friends as he hung; to have the weight of all the sins of all mankind upon him; to have God as it were leave him to struggle under them without the least glimmering of his presence; to see in his soul all the horrors of all the sins of men; to feel in his body all the torments that a body so delicate beyond the bodies of the sons of Adam, by reason of its perfection, must needs feel beyond all others, and groan and die under the fury of an angry God, now visiting for all the iniquity that was before or after, should be committed by the world. To know all this, and by this, no sorrows like his sorrows, is at least to sit down and weep at it; however, not to pass by regardless of it.

And know we (4) the end why all this was?—even to redeem us from all our sins; or, as it is in the chapter before this, "That he might be made unto us, wisdom, and righteousness, and sanctification, and redemption;" that "by his blood we might have entrance into the holy of holies,—into heaven itself."

1 Cor. i. 30.
Heb. x. 19.

This you all know as well as I,—every one will say he knows it all. Yet I must tell you, you do not know it as you should, if you sit not down, and sometimes determine your thoughts upon it; unless you sadly meditate, and thankfully think upon it; unless you value the meditations and discourses of it above all other thoughts, all other talk; unless you set by other business ever and anon, to contemplate this. To know in Christianity, is to do more than fill the brain with Scripture notions,—it is to fill the heart too with devout affections; therefore we read in Scripture of an understanding heart, and wisdom is said, in the holy phrase, to be seated there. And when the heart evaporates itself into holy affections, and desires Christ, then we are only said to know him.

But, "to know Christ Jesus crucified," is more than so; it is in S. Paul's meaning, "to be crucified with him," to "take up our cross and follow him;" to make profession of him, though we be sure to come to execution by it; to go with him as S. Thomas exhorts, though we die with him; to be willing to suffer anything for him; to deny our own wisdom and repute, and ourselves, for his service; to be content to be counted fools for his sake; our very wisdom and preaching, foolishness; if we may save any by it, to count all as nothing, so we may know him, and be known of him.

marginal: Gal. vi. 14. [John xi. 16.]

We cannot think much, sure, to be crucified with him, who was crucified only for us; to suffer something for him, who suffered all for us; if we but know and consider who it was was crucified, and for whom he was so,—the Son of God for the sons of men,—the most innocent for the greatest sinners,—the most holy for the most wicked,—for such who even deny him after all he has done for them.

This speak we, this preach we, this profess we, this determine we upon with S. Paul to know, to think, to speak, to teach, to preach, to profess this, and nothing else; ever crying out to him with that good old Father, *Deus meus et omnia, Deus meus et omnia*: "This crucified Jesus is my God and all, this Christ crucified is my God and all;" all my thoughts, all my heart, all my knowledge, all my profession; he is all in all, I know nothing else, I value nothing else; I know him though never so disfigured by his wounds; I will acknowledge him, though in the midst of the thieves; I am not ashamed of him, though full of spittle and reproach; I will profess him, though all run from him. Alas! I know not any thing worth knowing, if they take him away.

And yet to know him has one degree more: When our understanding knows anything, it does (says the philosopher) become the same with it. So to know Christ, then, is to become like him; to know Christ to be anointed, is to

SERMON XXXII.

be anointed like him also with holy graces; to know him Jesus a Saviour, is to be a saviour to the poor and needy, to deliver the widow and fatherless from the hand of the oppressor; to know him to be crucified, is to crucify our affections and lusts. Thus we know him as he is here, and by so knowing him here, we shall at last come to know him hereafter; where we shall know him perfectly, know him glorified for here knowing him crucified, and all things then with him; for now not knowing anything but him, know God, and happiness, and eternal glory, and ourselves partakers in them all.

THE FIRST SERMON

UPON

EASTER DAY.

S. LUKE xxiv. 4—6.

And it came to pass, as they were much perplexed thereabout, behold, two men stood by them in shining garments: and as they were afraid, and bowed down their faces to the earth, they said unto them, Why seek ye the living among the dead? He is not here, but is risen.

"AND" to-day, the day "it came to pass." This the day wherein this great perplexity both rose and was resolved. It rose from the not seeing "the body of Jesus" in the grave. It was resolved by the hearing here, he was risen thence.

^{SERMON XXXIII.}

^{Luke xxiv. 3.}

Thus rise the greatest perplexities still, and thus they are resolved. From the miss of Christ, which way soever, truly or falsely conceived by us, they come, and at the very hearing of him again they vanish. To be sure, they stay not at all after he "is risen," and we hear it; and God will not let it be long before we hear it; he will not suffer those to be long perplexed that seek Christ heartily, affectionately, and devoutly, though with some error in their heads—as here, poor souls, they had—if they have no wickedness in their hearts, and spices and ointments, good works and charity, in their hands. Some angel or other shall be sent to them ere long, to pacify their troubled thoughts, to disperse their fears, and raise up their drooping heads.

SERMON XXXIII.
Luke xxiv. 10.

"Mary Magdalene, Joanna, Mary the mother of James," with "other women," found it so to-day. And to-day also, and from this day now forward, shall we so find it too, if we seek our Lord but with that affection, that holy fear, that humility, as they; so humbly bowing down our faces, so "afraid" to miss of him, so "perplexed" when he is from us.

This is a day when perplexities cannot stay, fears cannot tarry with us, our heads cannot long hang down; the news of it is so full of gladness, of comfort, and of joy. At the rising of this day's Sun of righteousness, our perplexities pass away as the clouds before the sun; our tears melt as the dew before it; and we turn up our heads like flowers to the sunbeams. It is a day the fullest of all good tidings,—as the seal and assurance of all the good news we heard before it. The Angels fly every where about to-day, even into the grave, with comfortable messages. "Why weepest thou?" says one; "Fear not," says another; "Why seek" you "among the dead?" says a third. What do you at the grave?—"he is risen," says the whole choir; he whose rising is all your risings, who is your Saviour now complete, and the lifter up of all your heads; and go but into Galilee and you shall see him.

Matt. xxviii. 5.

But this only hearing of him must for this time content us; we shall one day see him as he is; till then, if we hear of him with our ears, and feel him in our hearts, and see him in our conceits; if so hear as to believe him risen, and our hearts listen to it (for the heart has two ears as well as the head,—nature has given to it such a form as has been observed in the dissections,—to teach us that our hearts within us, as well as our ears without us, are to give ear to him that made, to him that saves them), if they do, we need not be the least perplexed for not visibly seeing him. All believers that then were did not see him so; five hundred, indeed, we read of all at once; but they were not all that were then believers:

Acts x. 41.

"Not to all," says S. Peter, expressly, "but unto witnesses chosen before of God." There is a blessedness, and it seems, by the manner of speaking, somewhat greater, for them

John xx. 29.

"that have not seen, and yet have believed."

Be we then content to-day to hear that he "is risen," with the first news and tidings of it. From a good mouth it comes, to good souls it comes, in good time it comes; from the mouths of angels to good women, and very seasonably, when they were "much perplexed," much "afraid," and much cast down for want of such a message. And though we cannot here see Christ as we desire, yet be we pleased to see ourselves, our own sad condition upon the loss of him, in these women's perplexities, fears, and downcast looks,—our way to seek him, humbly, with our faces down as not worthy to look up—reverently, with fear and trembling, as afraid to miss him—solicitously, much perplexed, to want him, as they were, in the text. And that we may not give up our hope, be afraid, or cast down for ever, look we upon the bright "shining garments" of the two Angels here (for these "men" are no less),—it is a joyful sight,—and rejoice at the good success that always follows them that so seek him—Angels and good news. The women found it here—heard the good news from the Angels' lips. You must be content to hear it from mine; yet you know who says it, *Angelus Domini exercituum est;* "The priest is the angel" or messenger—that is enough—"of the Lord of hosts;" too much for me, poor sinful wretch. But look not upon me, but upon them that here first told the news, and see in the text these three particulars :—

I. The sad condition, for a while, of those that either are without or cannot find their Saviour, Christ, in three particulars: they are "perplexed," they are "afraid," they "bow down their faces to the earth," they go all the while with downcast looks.

II. The only ready way to find him, after a while, by being here "perplexed" for his loss and absence, by being "afraid" to miss him, by looking everywhere, up and down, to find him, or news of him; going poring up and down, looking where we looked before, and casting down, not our "faces," but ourselves also "to the earth," in all humility, to search after him.

III. The good success, at last, of them that thus diligently, reverently, and humbly seek him, in three points more: to see Angels, to be directed right, and be made partakers of the joyful news of a resurrection, of Christ's resurrection by them, who is both the ground of ours, and the first-fruits of them that rise.

SERMON XXXIII.

The sum of all is this,—That though it sometimes fall out to us that we lose Christ, or cannot find him for a while, and so fall into perplexities and fears, and go up and down dejected, with downcast looks; yet if we so seek him with a solicitous love, a reverent fear, and humble diligence, we shall meet Angels after a while, to comfort us and bring us news of our beloved Lord, and find him risen or rising in us ere we are aware. And the close of all will be our duty, and the duty of the day, (1,) to make ourselves sensible of the perplexed and sad estate of those that are without Christ, who have lost him in the grave, or know not where he is, or how to find him; and thereupon, (2,) so set ourselves to seek him that we may be sure at last to hear of him, and be made partakers of his resurrection.

It is a glad day, I confess; yet I begin with the gloomy morn that seemed to usher it in to these poor women,—their sadness upon the imagined loss of their dear Lord, truly representing to us the sad condition of those who are deprived of Christ, or think they are so. The glory of the day will appear brighter by this morning cloud; the news of the resurrection will be the welcomer when we first see what poor, troubled, frighted, dejected pieces we are without it; we will have the higher thoughts of him, now risen, when we feel how disconsolate a thing it is to be without him, even without his body here, though dead and buried.

"And it came to pass," says the text, "that they were perplexed thereabout;" and it will quickly come to pass that the best of us all will be perplexed to lose anything of our Lord's, much more his body, if we love him. They were good souls, such whose devotion and affection death itself could neither quench nor alter, that were so here, that we might know even devout and pious souls may both err concerning Christ, and sometimes want him too; seek him sometimes, with these here, where he is not, where we falsely imagine him to be, and not find him presently neither, when we look for him where we left him.

Luke xxiv. 12.

No wonder they here, poor women, were so perplexed. Men, the great S. Peter, knew not what to say to it; "departed, wondering." Indeed, it seems a wonder at the first, that such who love Christ so dearly, seek him so early, should yet miss of him; that such, too, should be in so great an error about him, as to think the Lord of life could be held in death; but so poor a thing is man, that, as such, he is perpetually subject to error and mistake, and may thereupon easily lose the sight and presence of his Lord. The Spouse, in the Canticles, complains, her " beloved had withdrawn himself, and was gone;" she "sought him, but could not find him;" she "called to him, but he gave" her "no answer;" and thereupon tells the " daughters of Jerusalem" that she is " sick of love;" that is, so perplexed and troubled at his absence that she is not able to hold up her head any longer, no more than these are here.

Sermon XXXIII.

Cant. v. 6.

Cant. v. 8.

Nothing certainly but doubts and perplexities can involve us when we have either lost our love or fear it; to be sure, nothing but doubts when we have lost him who is the only truth that can resolve us; nothing but perplexed ways when we have lost him who is "the way." Which way can we resolve on, when our way is gone? What can we think can hold him whom the grave cannot? If in a sealed sepulchre, under a mighty stone, the dead body be not safe, where can we think to sit down in security?

To lose a token or remembrance of a friend's, how are we troubled! but to have his body stolen out of the sepulchre, his grave rifled, and his ashes violated, how impatiently would we take it! You cannot blame them for being much perplexed for so great a loss.

I shall show it greater in the mystery. The body is the Church; and to have that taken from us, the Church, that glorious candlestick removed, and borne away we know not whither, what good soul is there that must not necessarily be perplexed at it? What way shall we take when they have taken away that which is the pillar of the truth, and should lead us in it? Whither shall we go when we know not whither that is gone, where they have laid it, or where to find it? Poor ignorant women, nay, and men too, may well now wander in uncertainties—as they do—full of doubts and perplexities, full of cares and troubled thoughts which way to take, what religion to run to, what to leave, and what to follow, seeing the body—to which the eagles used to flock, the most eagle-eyed, the most subtle and learned used to be

SERMON XXXIII. gathered—is removed away, and we have nothing to gather to, scarce a place to be gathered together in. Well may we now fear what will become of us, and what God means to do to us, how he intends to deal with us, having thus suffered our Lord to be taken from us.

"Afraid" they were that they had lost him quite. I pray God we may have no cause to fear the same fear. When Christ was but asleep, the Apostles were afraid at a blast of wind that rose, and "cry out they perish," whilst he but sleeps. Anything scares us, if Christ watch not over us; not the visions only of the night, but the very noises of the day; any light air or report affrights us, and blows us which way it please,—to any side, any faction, out of fear. What hold, then, is there of us—what little thing will not scare us when he is absent quite? When his body, the Church, is removed from us, where can we stay our wavering souls, or fix our trembling feet? Christ was no sooner dead and gone, but away run all his disciples into a room together, and shut up themselves, "for fear of the Jews;" so coward-like and faint-hearted are we all when the Captain of our salvation is slain before us; nor can it be other, all "our life" being "hid in him," and all our spirit only from his presence.

Matt. viii. 25.

John xx. 19.

[Col. iii. 3.]

Part of these women's fear, was at the sight and congress of the Angels. Even Angels themselves do but scare us if the Lord of the Angels be not by us. Nay, even God himself is but a terror to us, and "a consuming fire," without Christ; it is with him only, under the shadow and shelter of his wings, that we dare approach that inaccessible light, that consuming fire. Lose we Christ, and we lose all our confidence in heaven, all the ways of access to heavenly things, all the pleasure and comfort of them; we are nothing but agues, and fears, and frights,—not courage enough even to look up; we, with these perplexed souls, go bowing down our faces to the earth.

[Heb. xii. 29.]

"Thou didst hide thy face from me," says holy David, "and I was troubled;" the very hiding of God's face sore troubled him. What think you to hide his whole body would do then? Why, then he goes "mourning all the day long." So did the two disciples that went to Emmaus: they walked sadly, and talked sadly, and looked sadly, like men

[Ps. xxx. 7.]

Ps. xxxviii. 6.
Luke xxiv. 17.

disconsolate and forlorn, such as were ashamed to show their faces in the city, after this was come to pass; durst not look anybody in the face upon it. Alas! how could it be otherwise with them? All their hope was gone: he that they looked should have redeemed Israel could not redeem himself; nay, his body stolen out of the grave, and conveyed they knew not whither. Well may they bow down their faces to the earth, having now little hope above in heaven, he being gone and lost by whom they only hoped and expected it.

Indeed, if he be either so gone from us that we have no hope to find him, or he be found in that condition in which there is no hope,—as there is none in a dead Saviour, wherever he be,—no wonder if our faces then bend wholly to the earth, if we look no further. Let us take our portion in this life, for we are like to have no other: without Christ, and Christ "risen" too, hither it is we fall, no looking higher, not an eye to heaven, so much as in a prayer, if we have not *per Dominum Jesum*, Christ Jesus at the end of it; in and through whom only we can with confidence look for a blessing thence, and without whom at the end the prayer is to no end or purpose.

II. Yet in as sad a condition as this we speak of, we are not utterly without hope if we again look upon the words at a second view. For now, they as well decipher to us the condition of those that seek as of those that have lost their Lord and Master. We may be as much "perplexed" in our search as at our loss, as well "afraid" to miss as startled at our loss, as well "bow down" our "faces to the earth" in seeking as in sorrowing. And thus in the second view of the text it is.

(1.) They had lost their Master's body, and were now not only troubled at the loss, but how to find it, where to look it. Surely, take but away his body—the Church, and the wisest of us will scarce know to find him; one will run this way, another that way, after him; one will stand weeping at the sepulchre, and think that a sad melancholy posture and business is religion only; another will run thence from the sepulchre as fast as he can, and think the finding Christ so easy a business that it does not require either a groan or a sigh; others will be walking to Emmaus, up and down, now

SERMON XXXIII. to one sect, now to another, and from Jerusalem most commonly, from the city of peace, out of the bonds of unity, every one by himself, which way pleases him, if Christ's body,—the Church, be once removed out of our sight. Our best way is, with the disciples, into our chambers altogether till we can get a better place, with all the company we can make, to our devotions and our prayers; or if we will step out a while to the sepulchre, let it be but to pay a tear upon it, to vent our troubled souls, to express how we are troubled at our sins that have made us lose our Lord, or at our negligence that he is slipped from us whilst we were asleep, lulled in soft pleasures; or at our slowness, that we come so late to seek him that he is gone before we come. This is so to seek as to be "perplexed thereabout," and there is no true seeking him without it.

Heb. xii. 28. But (2) with fear too we are to seek him; "with reverence and godly fear," that the only acceptable service and seeking Phil. ii. 12. of him "with fear and trembling," no hope either of Saviour or salvation without it. "Afraid" of the "two men in shining garments" they were here; and if Angels, habited like men too and in so cheerful attire, be so terrible, what think you is that excellent Majesty: if we cannot see those Rev. xxii. 9. our "fellow-servants," as they style themselves, without fear (for we seldom read of the appearing of an Angel but either coming or going he strikes some terror) how say some among us, that in the approaches to God we need not be afraid? Alas, deluded souls! they conceive not God, or Christ, as either of them should be conceived; they neither seriously consider the majesty of God or Christ, nor their own unworthiness, nor how hard a thing it is to find Christ, that are not afraid either to miss him in the search by their unskilfulness, or lose him by their sins. He that looks to be comforted by an Angel must not think much to be afraid, how great a claim soever he conceives he hath in Christ. [1 John iv. 18.] "Perfect love," indeed, says the Apostle, "casts out fear," but it is servile fear and no other. Mary Magdalen, to [Luke vii. 47.] whom Christ bears witness that "she loved much," yet she also is "afraid." The more for that she loved so much,—for the more we love, the more we fear to lose the thing we love; the more we love, the more we fear to offend the person whom we love, nay, the more we fear to miss; and the more earnest we are to seek, the more likely are we to find what or whoever we set to seek for. Seek him with filial fear, or love and fear; that is the second.

(3.) Yet if we seek Christ, we must also, thirdly, seek him with our "faces bowed down to the ground;" and that is (i.) the fashion of those that seek earnestly: and so he must be sought with all the earnestness we can.

And it is (ii.) a token of diligence in the search, much like that of the poor woman that sought her groat, that lighted a candle, swept her house, raked in the dust, looked into every corner, peered into every chink to find it. Do we so in seeking Christ light up the candle of faith kindled from the flame of love; sweep we the houses of our souls with the besom of repentance; look we into our dust, consider what we are made of, what poor dusty things we are; ransack every corner of our hearts, every cranny of our thoughts, that so we may, if not find him there, yet make all clean for him against he comes; and we shall commonly find he will come gliding in when we think not of it, we shall hear of something rising in our dust after we have so raised it, by the breaking and contritions of repentance.

And it is (iii.) the posture of humility, and of the humble he will be found; they shall not miss of him whoever do; to them his grace, to them his ways, to them his dwelling. The lower we bow down before him the higher will he lift us up. James iv. 6. Ps. xxv.

And, lastly, the "face bowed down to the earth" is the look of them that mourn: we must seek him as his father and mother did; seek him sorrowing, sorry that we have been so long without him, that we so carelessly lost him; then, after a day or two, we shall be sure to find him: nay, if our sorrow begins, as here in the morning of the day, if we begin betimes to be exceeding sorrowful, the morning shall not pass ere we hear at least some tidings of him: nay, we shall not stir from the grave, but we shall hear it ere we go; some good Angel or other shall bring us some glad message or other from him, and tell us where he is. So it follows, "as they were perplexed, behold, two men stood by them in shining garments: and as they were afraid, and

SERMON XXXIII.
Ps. ix. 10.

bowed down their faces to the earth," this news they tell them, that " he is risen."

" God never faileth them that seek him," says the Psalmist, never them that seek him as these did, with careful and troubled souls, such he never does refuse;—" with reverence and godly fear," such he never does reject;—with earnestness, with diligence, with humility, with godly sorrow, those he visits presently either by himself or by his Angel.

And, which is very observable, and as comfortable, " as they were perplexed, and as they were afraid, and bowed down," says the text, that is even when they began to be so, before their perplexities had misled them, or their fears undone them, or their faces licked the earth; as they began only to hang their heads, and their spirits began to faint, and their souls to be troubled, " two men" on a sudden, whence they cannot tell, and which way they came there they knew not; but there they stand to disperse both their sorrows and their fears by what they have to tell them. Three grand points we observe in this apparition of the Angels, to make that great success that those who faithfully and devoutly seek Christ may promise themselves upon it.

1. They see a vision of Angels. It is their good hap ever to meet blessed spirits who seek the Lord of spirits, to meet them here, to be with them ever hereafter, to meet one or two of them here at times, to meet ten thousand times ten thousands of them hereafter.

To meet them here (i.) even at the sepulchre in the midst of sorrow, even then to receive comfort from them, even in the grave, in our greatest afflictions.

To meet them (ii.) like " young men," so says S. Mark, sprightly, and able to defend us.

To meet them (iii.) in " shining garments," tokens of some exceeding joy and gladness, which we may expect, and shall find from them.

To meet them (iv.) " standing " by us, that is, ever ready to comfort and assist us.

To meet (v.) " two " of them together, not one single comforter alone, but comfort upon comfort, deliverance upon deliverance, spiritual and temporal, one at the right hand and another at our left.

But, (vi.) lastly, hereafter to be sure we shall meet them in full choirs, when we rise out of our sepulchres, then like "young men" indeed, both they and we, then to be always so, never die again, never grow old, nor our garments neither, but have them always shining.

[margin: Sermon XXXIII.]

2. The next point of the good success is to receive direction from them. Two parts of it there are: first, to recall us from the wrong, and then, secondly, to set us right.

"Why seek you the living among the dead? he is not here;" that is the correction of our judgments and affections. "He is risen;" that is the setting them to the right.

For a traveller, when he is out of the way, to be told he is so, is a thing any of us would take well; and when we are straggling out of the way to heaven, going out of that safe, and fair, and happy way into the bogs of the world, and mires of lusts and ditches of hell, to have an Angel, "one of a thousand," as Job speaks, but a messenger of the Lord of hosts to call out to us that we are wrong, is certainly a happiness if we understood it; and such God sends always to them that seek him truly, if they will but turn their heads at the call and look after him. Well, but what says he that so calls out to us, why, "why seek you the living among the dead?" What is that?

[margin: [Job xxxiii. 23.]]

(i.) They "seek the living among the dead," that seek salvation by the law of Moses, long since dead and buried.

(ii.) They "seek the living among the dead," that seek it by the works of nature, by the power of them: nature without grace is dead: *Verebar omnia opera mea,* says holy Job; there is not in us one poor work to trust to.

[margin: [Job ix. 28.]]

(iii.) They "seek the living among the dead," that seek salvation, that think to be saved by a mere outward holiness, by the outward body of religion without the inward life, by forms of godliness, whether they be merely ceremonial performances of religion, or great shows and pretences of godliness without the power of it in their lives and conversations.

(iv.) They, lastly, "seek the living among the dead," that seek Christ upon worldly interests, that take up their religion upon by-respects, that do it for carnal or worldly affections. But, say the Angels, "he is not here." Christ is not here; Christ the Saviour is not, that is, our salvation is not to be found in the law of Moses or by the law of works, or in mere external performances or great pretences, or in worldly and carnal hearts,—they are but graves and sepulchres all, which we too much and too often bury our souls in, and stand weeping by, and are much perplexed at if we cannot find it there, but must be forced from thence to a new search, as here the women are to leave these kinds of seeking, all of them, and betake us now to think of him as risen thence. For so the Angel says he is: "he is risen." And in this he both tells us what to conceive of him, and at the same time to put off all our perplexities, and tears, and sorrows to rejoice with him. " He is risen."

"Risen," (i.) and not raised; others, indeed, have been raised from death, the Sareptan's child, the widow's son; one of these, Mary's brother, Lazarus; but none " risen " but he: he raised himself, they did not so; he raised them all, must raise us all too, will raise us by his resurrection. For,

" Risen," that is, (ii.) his body risen, that is, we members of it to have part also in his resurrection; for if our head be risen the members also will follow after.

Must (iii.) in the interim follow him, so raise our thoughts above the earth as to seek him now above; to seek those things which are above; that is it the Angel directs us to, by telling us "he is risen," so pointing us where now to fix our thoughts, to leave the sepulchre to bemoan itself, to cast off all the ways and paths of death, to throw off all worldly perplexities, fears, and sorrows; or, in the midst of them, to take a ray at least from their " shining garments," and put on the looks of joy and gladness. This both the direction they give us and the joy they make us partakers of.

To tell us "he is risen" whom we seek, he is alive whom we bemoan for dead; he that is our head, our hope, our love, our life, our joy, our comfort, our crown of rejoicing, he in whom we trusted, we may trust still, hope still, joy in him still, for "he is risen" and alive.

That is the close we are now to make to-day, that the answer we are to give to the Angels' speech, that the application of the text; to make it full, run we once more over it.

Grow we, then, first, as sensible as we can of our sad condition without Christ, how the grave,—the last place of rest from all troubles,—has nothing in it without him; how our souls cannot be at quiet without him; how our hearts cannot but tremble when he is gone, our spirits faint, our faces look sad and heavy, dull and earthy, when he is from us. Let us upon this sit down and weep and be troubled, and tremble at it, that we may not at any time give him occasion henceforward to desert us, or leave us comfortless at the grave, but send his Angels thither to direct and to conduct us to his joyful presence.

When we are thus made sensible what we are without him, we then, secondly, certainly will make after him with all care and reverence, all earnestness and diligence, all humility and devout repentance, troubled at his absence, fearful of our own unworthiness, and truly humbled for our sins that drove him from us; perplexed to lose him, fearful to offend him, vigilant to seek him, that so at last we may recover him; for you see he is recovered from the grave, and may again be by us recovered to our souls.

This the duty both our own necessities and the opportunity of this great day require of us.

The business we are next to go about exacts as much. We are with these women come here to seek the Lord's body, and I shall anon give you news of greater joy than here the Angels did the women. They say, "he is not here, but he is risen." I say, but "he is risen, and is here," will be here by and by in his very body. Your eye cannot see him, but your souls may there see and taste him too.

"Lift up then your heads, O ye immortal gates, and be [Ps. xxiv. 7.] ye lift up, ye everlasting doors, that the King of Glory may come in." Look up and "lift up your heads, for your salva- [Luke xxi. 28.] tion draweth nigh." "Bow down your faces" no longer "to the earth," neither look here as to an earthly business. Look not sad but cheerful now to-day, (I hope you have looked sadly enough already in your chambers upon your sins,) you may here put on another face. Yet if you be somewhat "perplexed" and troubled at your sins, or "afraid" of your own unworthiness, or your souls and bodies bowed down as low as can be in humility,—I shall say you are the fitter to receive your joys, and to be made partakers of the Angels' company, which, as the Apostle tells us, are present in holy places; and if ever there, there more especially, at so great a mystery as this, which they themselves bow down themselves to look into, and wing about us, say the Fathers, to assist the celebration all the while, you will be the fitter too to receive the joyful news that this day brings us, of Christ's rising; being only so cast down and prepared in all humility to receive it.

Yet learn we something from the Angels too, as well as from the women: for "behold," says the text, as if it meant we should look upon them too, and learn by their standing, constancy, and resolution, by their clothing in "shining garments," purity, and innocence, and all good works, whereby we are so to shine as to glorify "our Father which is in heaven;" by their correcting the good women's error, to correct our own, and not let our brother either perish or go astray for want of good and timely admonition,—a prime work of charity which this business so requires; by their advice, no longer to "seek the living among the dead;" no more to seek Christ for earthly profits or respects; and by their so readily publishing the news of Christ's rising, to be this day ever telling it, every day thinking of it, and so living as if we believed a resurrection.

So shall it come to pass, that however we come, we shall not depart perplexed, but in peace; not in fear, but in hope; not in sorrow, but in joy; and shall one day behold him risen, whom we now only hear is, and meet him with all his Angels "in shining garments," in the robes of eternal glory.

He who this day rose, raise now our thoughts with these apprehensions, raise our thoughts to the height of these heavenly mysteries, make us this day partakers through them of his resurrection by grace, and in his due time also, of his resurrection to glory.

THE SECOND SERMON

UPON

EASTER DAY.

S. MATT. xxvii. 52, 53.

And the graves were opened; and many bodies of saints which slept arose, and came out of the graves after his resurrection, and went into the holy city, and appeared unto many.

AND this is the third day since the first of these was done, since "the graves were opened;" and the first day that all the rest, that the "bodies of saints arose," came forth, "went into the holy city, and appeared,"—the blessed day of our "Saviour's resurrection." So we have both passion and resurrection in the text, and not amiss; the one to usher in the other,—the passion, the resurrection,—both comfortable when together: to see the passion end so glorious, the darkness of so sad an evening open itself at last, after a little respite, into so lustrous a morning,—the most lustrous that sun ever shone in, the most joyous thus to meet the grave and the holy city, Christ and his saints together.

SERMON XXXIV.

This day the very stones cry out, and send forth the deceased saints, as so many tongues, to speak the glory of their Redeemer. And if the "graves" open their mouths, can we hold our peace? If the dead bodies of the "saints" appear to-day in "the holy city" to celebrate the day, shall not we appear with our living bodies in the holy mount, to do as much? The "grave cannot praise thee, death cannot celebrate thee," says Hezekiah; and "the dead praise not

Isa. xxxviii 18.
Ps. cxv. 17.

SERMON XXXIV. thee, O Lord," says David; yet here they do. They thought then they could not,—we see now they do; and shall not the living do so too? "The living, the living, he shall praise thee," says Hezekiah; and, "but we will praise the Lord," says David. That is agreed on both hands that the living shall: the father to the children, make known the truth of this day's great wonder, declare it one to another from generation to generation,—keep the day in remembrance throughout all generations.

Indeed, if we be not more senseless than the day, more silent than the grave, the house of silence, we cannot hold to-day; up and arise we will, and into the holy places to set [Ps. cxv. 17.] forth the wonders of the day. "They that go down," as the Psalmist speaks, "into the silence," and into the land [Ephes. ii. 1.] where all things are forgotten, who are either "dead in trespasses and sins," or are resolved to forget all that their fathers have seen or done, or has been done for them, who are in the dark, the darkness of ignorance or error, departed from the Church, out of the marvellous light into the land of darkness; they show not of these wonders among the dead in their own congregations, nor tell of the loving-kindness, faithfulness, and righteousness of this day, in that great destruction they have made. But we will, I hope, we that are among the living stones, in the communion of holy Church, will praise the Lord,—do as much as the graves and now risen bodies, wherever we appear.

For upon this day hang all our hopes. We were hopeless till it came; hopeless when it was come till we knew it, and no great hope of us if we forget it now it is. This day Christ rose out of the grave. If he had not risen, had had no resurrection, there had been no hope of ours. If nor hope nor resurrection, we had been of all men most miserable; and if we do not thankfully remember both, we are but miserable unthankful wretches; no sooner the day forgotten, and such days put down, but all our happiness put down with them, we of all the nations under heaven presently most miserable, miserable times quickly after this happy day, with the rest of its attendants, was unhappily voted to be forgotten. So much does it concern our happiness with the "saints" in the text, to solemnize it in the "city," if the city intend either to be holy or happy, so much to make much, both of all texts and times, that may bring it to our remembrance, all days and words, texts and testimonies, either of "Christ's resurrection" or our own.

This text then among the rest,—wherein we have both a testimony and evidence of "Christ's resurrection," and a pledge and symbol of our own. Two general points, which we shall consider in the words. Or more particularly thus: A testimony of the truth of "Christ's resurrection," and an evidence of the power of it. A pledge of the certainty of our "resurrection," and a symbol of the manner of it, both of our "resurrection" to grace, and our "resurrection" to glory.

The testimony of the truth of "Christ's resurrection:"— (1.) In the "bodies of the saints," arising, and "coming out of their graves." (2.) In their coming "into the holy city," and there appearing "unto many," telling and declaring it.

The evidence of the power of "his resurrection" to be seen:—(1.) In opening the "graves." (2.) In raising the "saints' bodies that slept" there. (3.) In sending them "into the holy city." (4.) Sending them thither to "appear to many."

The pledge of our "resurrection" it is:—(1.) That they that rise are of those that slept, saints and members of the same body with us. That, (2,) it is no phantasm, no fantastic or mere imagined business, for they "appeared to many."

The whole business of their "resurrection" is a symbol and signification of ours, both of that to grace and that to glory. (1.) Of that to grace: the grave, and sleep, the symbols of sin and sleeping in it, the bodies rising thence, of the souls rising out of sin; their going "into the holy city," of the souls passing from sin to righteousness and holiness; their appearing to many, of this righteousness manifested and appearing unto all. A symbol (2) it is of the "resurrection" unto glory, where the grave first opens, then the body rises, then "into the holy city," into new Jerusalem it goes, and there appears and shines for ever.

Thus you have the text opened as well as the graves; we must now go on to raise such bodies of doctrine and comfort out of it as may bring us all "into the holy city," serve to

SERMON XXXIV. make us holy here, and happy hereafter, partakers here of the first resurrection, and hereafter in the second. He that here opened the graves, and raised the dead bodies out of their sleep, open your ears and hearts, and raise your understandings and affections, that we may all of us have our share in both—rise first to righteousness, then to glory. "Christ's resurrection" is the pattern and ground of both; we therefore begin with that, with those words first that bear witness to the truth of it, that Christ is risen.

A double testimony we gather of it in the words, from the rising of the dead saints, and from their appearing.

It was a sign indeed that the resurrection was well towards, when the graves began to open; we could not but see somewhat of it even in those dark caverns, when they once began to let in the light; some hope of rising, even when a body begins to yawn; some hope the body might come ere long to recover its long-lost liberty, when the prison doors were wide set open, and the shackles of death knocked off the legs; some sign and hope, I say, it would be so, that there would be a resurrection of some, of some one or other, by and by.

But the graves being opened at Christ's passion, they could be but hopeful prognostics at most of "his resurrection;" a testimony it could not be; but when out of these opened graves the saints arose out of their sleep, they could tell us more certain news of it than so. And being but members of that body of which Christ Jesus was the head, we must needs know the head is risen when the body is got up; the head first ere any member could, be it never so holy, never so much "saint." He is "the head of the Church," says the Apostle, and the Church the body; and if any part of the body be raised to life, the head you may be sure is—first too. For if Christ be "the first-fruits of them that sleep," and "the first-begotten from the dead," as he is styled; if we see others risen, other dead bodies walking and alive, there is no witness more true than that He is. The first-fruits ever before the crop: "Christ the first-fruits, afterwards they that are Christ's," says S. Paul — out of order else; and the "first-begotten" ever before all the rest; second, and third, and fourth, and all witness the "first-begotten" was before them,

Eph. v. 23.

1 Cor. xv. 20.
Rev. i. 5.

1 Cor. xv. 23.

"the first-begotten from the dead," risen before the other dead. [Sermon XXXIV.]

And it seems it is not a single witness; they were many dead bodies here that rose; and "in the mouth of two or three witnesses" "shall every word be established," much more in the mouths of many witnesses. [Deut. xvii. 6. Matt. xviii. 16.]

And if these be from the dead, surely then the most incredulous will believe. "Nay, Father Abraham," says Dives, "but if one come from the dead, they will" believe, yea, and "repent" too. Here is more than one,—here is "many," that not so much as any of Dives's brethren,—the most voluptuous, secure, customary, and obstinate sinner,—can be incredulous after this, or have reason to doubt the truth, or have the power to contradict it. To satisfy either particular curiosity or infidelity, God does not use to send us messengers from the dead; he sends us to "Moses and the prophets" there, for our instruction; does not press men from hell or heaven, or raise them out of their beds of rest, to send them on an errand to us, (though perhaps little can be universally, though ordinarily it perhaps may be, defined in this particular, for the ignorance we are under of the condition of the bounds and limits of the dead.) "If they will not believe Moses and the prophets," says Father Abraham, "neither will they believe if one rise from the dead." If they will not believe the living word, the word of the living God, no likelihood that they should believe the word of a dead man, especially when they cannot be certain but it may be the devil, the father of lies and falsehood. But not of one only rising from the dead,—that to be sure; no man so simple to venture his faith upon a single testimony, and such a one as that. Or if he would, God does not use to do extraordinary miracles, where the ordinary means of probation or information are sufficient. [Luke xvi. 30. Luke xvi. 29.]

But in this great business that concerns all mankind, he is pleased to step out of his ordinary course to give us, for once, some extraordinary satisfaction, that all ages afterward might be sufficiently convinced of the truth of Christ's resurrection from heaven and earth by the testimony of the dead and living, that there might be no occasion hereafter to doubt for ever. He raises, therefore, a great company to attend the triumph of his Son's resurrection, and to bear witness to it.

And as it is not a single witness, so it is not, secondly, a single testimony; it is not from their rising only, but from their going into the city, and there appearing unto many. For sure neither their journey nor appearance was to tell stories of the dead, what is done either in the grave, or heaven, or hell, to satisfy the curious soul with a discovery of those chambers of silence, or the "land where all things are forgotten;" and therefore all forgotten, that we may know they remember when they come thence to tell us nothing that is there; their business was to wait upon their Lord, that had now set them at liberty from the grave, and divulge the greatness and glory of his resurrection. When Moses and Elias appeared upon the holy mount, at Christ's transfiguration, talking with him, S. Luke tells us, they "spake of his decease, which he should accomplish at Jerusalem." And it is highly credible the discourse of these saints with those to whom they appeared, was of his resurrection. Their going into the city was not merely to show themselves, nor their appearance merely to appear, but to appear witnesses and companions of their Saviour's resurrection.

Nor is it probable that the saints, whose business is to sing praise and glory to their Lord, should be silent at this point of time, of any thing that might make to the advancement of his glory.

Yet you may do well to take notice, that it is not to all, but "to many" only, that they "appeared:" to such, as S. Peter tells us of Christ's own appearance after his resurrection, as were "chosen before of God," "witnesses" chosen for that purpose, that we may learn indeed to prize God's favours, yet not all to look for particular revelations and appearances. It is sufficient for us to know so many saints that slept arose to tell it,—that so many saints that are now asleep, S. Peter, and the twelve, S. Paul, and five hundred brethren at once, all saw him after he was risen—so many millions have fallen asleep in this holy faith,—so many slept and died for it, that it is thus abundantly testified both by the dead and living, both by life and death, even standing up and dying for it; and a Church raised upon this faith through all the corners of the earth, and to the very ends of the world. SERMON XXXIV.

But to know the truth of it is not enough, unless we know the benefits of Christ's resurrection: they come next to be considered; and there is in the words evidence sufficient of four sorts of them:—(1.) The victory over sin and death both—" the graves were opened." (2.) The resurrection of the soul and body; the one in this life, the other at the end of it—" many dead bodies that slept arose." (3.) The sanctification and glorification of our souls and bodies; the dead bodies that arose out of the graves "went into the holy city." (4.) The establishing us both in grace and glory: they " appeared unto many." All these, says the text, after " his resurrection," by the force and virtue of it.

(1.) Indeed, it seems "the graves were opened," death almost vanquished, and the grave near overcome, whilst he yet hung upon the cross, before he was taken thence; death's sting taken out by the death of Christ, and all the victories of the grave now at an end, that it could no longer be a perpetual prison; yet for all that the victory was not complete, all the regions of the grave not fully ransacked, nor the forces of it utterly vanquished and disarmed, nor its prisoners set at liberty, and itself taken and led captive, till the resurrection. It is upon this point S. Paul pitches the " victory," and calls in the Prophet's testimony; upon this it is he proclaims the triumph,—" O death, where is thy sting? O grave, where is thy victory?"—even upon the resurrection of Jesus Christ, which he has been proving and proclaiming, the whole chapter through, with all its benefits, and concludes it with his " thanks " for this great " victory." 1 Cor. xv. 54. 1 Cor. xv. 55. 1 Cor. xv. 57.

So it is likewise for the death and grave of sin: the chains of sin were loosed, the dominion of it shaken off, the grave somewhat opened, that we might see some light of grace through the crannies of it, by Christ's passion; but we are not wholly set at liberty, not quite let out of it, the gravestone not perfectly removed from the mouth of it, till the Angel at the resurrection, or rather the " Angel of the Covenant," by his resurrection, remove it thence—remove our sins and iniquities clean from us.

(2.) Then indeed the dead soul arises; then appears the

SERMON XXXIV.
1 Pet. ii. 24.
Rom. vi. 4.

second benefit of his resurrection; then we rise to "righteousness" and "live;" then we "awake to righteousness," and "sin no more." So S. Paul infers it,—"That like as Christ was raised from the dead by the glory of the Father, even so should we also walk in newness of life." This resurrection, one of the ends of his; our righteousness attributed to that, as our redemption to his death.

From it it comes that our dead bodies arise too. Upon that Job grounds it,—his resurrection upon his Redeemer's. Job xix. 25. "I know that my Redeemer liveth." Well, what then? Why, I know too, therefore, that "though after my skin worms destroy this body, yet in my flesh I shall see God." The Apostle interweaves our resurrection with Christ's, and Christ's with ours; his as the cause of ours, ours as the effect 1 Cor. xv. of his, (a good part of 1 Cor. xv.) If Christ be risen, then we; if we, then he; if not he, not we; if not we, not he. And in the text it is evident, no rising from the dead, how open soever the graves be, till after his resurrection, that we may know to what article of our faith we owe both our deliverance from death, and our deliverance into life here in soul, and hereafter in our bodies, by what with holy Job to uphold our drooping spirits, our mangled, martyred, crazy bodies, by the faith of the resurrection; that day, the day of the Gospel of good tidings, to be remembered for ever.

(3.) So much the rather in that it is a day yet of greater joy, a messenger of all fulness of grace and glory to us, of the means of our sanctification, of our rising saints, living the lives of saints, holy lives, and of our glorification, our rising unto glory; both doors open to us now, and not till now; liberty and power given us to go "into the holy city," both this below and that above, now after "his resurRom. iv. 25. rection," and through it. "He rose again," says S. Paul, "for our justification;" to regenerate us to "a lively hope;" 1 Pet. i. 3. "blessed be God" for it, says S. Peter; that we might be Rom. vi. 5. "planted together in the likeness of his resurrection," says S. Paul; grow up like him in righteousness and true holiness; and when the day of the general resurrection comes, rise then also after his likeness—be conformed to his image— bear his image who is the heavenly, as we have borne the image Phil. iii. 21. of the earthly—"our vile body" changed and "fashioned like his glorious body, according to the working whereby he is able to subdue all things to himself;" whereby, in the day of his resurrection, he subdued death, and grave, and sin, and all things to him. [Sermon XXXIV. 1 Cor. xv. 27.]

(4.) And to show the power of his resurrection to the full, there is an appearing purchased to us by it—an appearing here in the fulness and lustre of grace, such as may appear unto all men to be such—not a few, but many, many graces, all graces obtained by it; nay, "it does not yet appear what we shall be" by it, but "when he shall appear, we shall be like him," says S. John; our righteousness and glory last for ever. "He died once," says the Apostle, "but being raised, he dieth no more;" no more did these in the text; no more shall we, but live for ever. Not only grace and glory, but perseverance in the one and eternity in the other, apparently no less accruing to us by the virtue and efficacy of his resurrection; good news from the grave the while, and from the late-raised prisoners of it, who are now, thirdly, as well the pledges of the certainty of our resurrection, as the evidences of the power of Christ's. [1 John iii. 2. Rom. vi. 9.]

A double pledge we have here of our resurrection,—one from the "many dead bodies of the saints that slept, arising out of their graves;" the other from their going "into the holy city," and their appearing "unto many."

In the first, then, are four particulars to assure us of it:—

(i.) We find dead bodies here arising, to assure us such a thing there may be, such a thing there is, as a resurrection of the body; that bodies, be they never so dead, may be quickened,—never so corrupted, may rise incorruptible; you may see them rising here. And,

(ii.) "Many" of them there are, that we may see it belongs not only to a few, to some particular persons; this many is but the usher to S. Paul's "all"—"we shall all" arise and "stand before the judgment-seat of Christ." [Rom. xiv. 10.]

(iii.) Saints' bodies they are said to be, and they are our fellows, members of the same body; and if "one member be honoured, all the members are honoured with it," says S. Paul. Indeed, the "bodies of the saints" only shall rise with Christ, rise to enter "into the holy city;" but all shall rise; for "all" shall appear, "every one to receive the things done in his [1 Cor. xii. 26. 2 Cor. v. 10.]

SERMON XXXIV.
John v. 29.
John v. 28.

body, according to that he hath done, whether it be good or bad;" "they that have done good, to the resurrection of life; and they that have done evil, unto the resurrection of damnation," says He that rose himself to-day. "For all that are in the graves shall hear his voice, and shall come forth;" none be left behind, though the best come first. The saints have only the prerogative, not the only privilege of the resurrection.

For, (iv.) it is said the "bodies" of them that "slept," that we may know that all that sleep, that all that die, shall awake again and rise at last. He that lies down only to sleep, lies down to rise; and good and bad, how sad soever the one's dreams be, how full of terror soever be the wicked man's sleep in death, are both said to sleep. Jeroboam and Rehoboam, Baasha and Omri, and Ahab, and Joram, are said all of them to sleep with the fathers, as well as David and Solomon, and Joash, and Hezekiah, *obdormierunt simul*, they all sleep together the sleep of death, and so shall likewise rise together; though as there is difference in sleep, some sweet, some horrible, so in rising too, some sad, some joyful when they awake; but sleep necessarily intimates and supposes some awaking and rising after it; it is else somewhat more than sleep. Thus, by the rising of the dead bodies of these saints, so many rising, rising as men out of their sleep, not as saints out of a privilege, we have one strong pledge of our resurrection, of which they only lead the van after our great Captain, the Lord Jesus Christ.

A second we have given us, from both their going "into the holy city," and their appearing "unto many."

[Acts xxvi. 26.]

It was not *in obscuro*; "this thing was not," as S. Paul speaks, "done in a corner," not in a house or churchyard, (where are all the apparitions we now hear of,) not in a country village; no, not an ordinary city neither, but in the great metropolis, Jerusalem itself; called holy for what it had been, not what it was,—for it was now the most sinful city,—or called holy yet for the Temple's sake, that yet stood firm: an item, by the way, to tell us how long a city may be styled holy, so long as the Church stands sacred and inviolate in it, and no whit longer. But be the city holy or not, that which is done there by many, is not likely a private business, has witnesses enow to give credit to it.

But to put all out of question, the there appearing "unto many," will certify it was no phantasm, no particular fancy, or imagination of some silly, simple, or timorous persons, but a business of the greatest certainty; whether you take "many" for the "many," or many people and folk together, or for "such who were before chosen," as the Apostle speaks, "to be witnesses," to whom the "resurrection" should be revealed, as to men of credit, repute, and understanding.

Nor does the word "appearing" any way prejudice but confirm it,—the word ἐνεφανίσθησαν, is from ἐμφανίζω, to make plain and certify; to give us a full knowledge and manifestation of a thing, so used, when either persons or things really and truly appear before us. So the publicness of the place, the number and fitness of the persons, and the way and manner of appearance, is evidence enough of their real resurrection, and a second pledge to us that it concerns more than themselves, (though themselves were "many," even the "many" they "appeared to," too;) whole cities, all cities, holy and unholy, all the world, of which that city was but an emblem and signification; a place from whence God did as it were, out of his own house and palace, dispense his providence through all the earth; and the saints besides thus going after the resurrection "into the holy city," an intimation whither the saints go when they are risen; the whole action, a symbol of what is done in both the first and second resurrection; what we are to do in the one, and expect in the other, or what is done both in the one and the other; and so, lastly, we now consider it.

For the similitude the first resurrection, or the resurrection of the soul from sin to righteousness, bears to this of the dead bodies in the text, we have it very like both for thing and order.

The graves in which the souls lie buried, are either our corruptible bodies, or corrupt passions, or stony hearts, or continued ill customs, which so entomb the spirit, that it lies dead without any spiritual life and operation. The opening of the graves, is the loosing the chains of those earthly affections, bodily depressions, wicked habits, and hardened hearts. The souls that are dead in trespasses and sins, are those dead bodies fuller of stench, and worms, and

Sermon XXXIV. rottenness, than any dead body whatsoever, full of infamous and stinking sins, worms of conscience, and worms of concupiscence, rotten resolutions and performances; continuance in sin is the sleep of death. Holy purposes and resolutions are the rising out of it. Walking thenceforward in the ways of righteousness, is going into the holy city, and the letting our righteousness so shine before men, that God may be glorified, is the appearing unto many.

And the order is as like,—our justification or spiritual resurrection well resembled by it. God first, for the merits of Christ's death and passion, breaks open the stony heart, looses the fetters of our sins and lusts, all worldly corruptible affections in us; opens the mouth of it to confess its sins; then the soul rises as it were out of its sleep, by the favour of God's exciting grace, and comes out of sin by holy purposes and resolutions; resolves presently to amend its courses; then next it goes into the holy city, by holy action, endeavour, and performance; so goes and manifests its reconcilement to the Church of God,—and at last makes its resurrection, repentance, and amendment, evident and apparent to the world, to as many as it any where converses with, that 'all may bear witness to it, that it is truly risen with Christ, now lives with him. This the order, this the manner of our first resurrection, from the death of sin to the life of grace.

Our second resurrection to the life of glory, is but this very resurrection in the text acted over again. As soon as the *consummatum est* is pronounced upon the world,—as soon as Christ shall say, as he did upon the cross, "All is finished," the end is come, the Archangel shall blow his trumpet, the graves open, the earth and sea give forth their dead, and the dead in Christ shall rise first; then they that 1 Thess. iv. 14. be alive at his coming; "for if we believe that Jesus died and rose again, even so them also that sleep in Jesus shall God bring with him;" and they shall "come out of their graves, and go into the holy city," the new Jerusalem that is above, and there appear and shine like stars for ever. Indeed the ungodly and the wicked shall arise too, and appear before the great tribunal; but not like these "saints," for "into the holy city" they shall not come. Rise and come forth they shall, but go away into some place of horror, some gloomy valley of eternal sorrow, some dark dungeon of everlasting night, some den of dragons and devils, never to appear before God, but be for ever hid in the arms of confusion and damnation.

As for the godly, the "holy city" is prepared for them,—for us, if we be like them. Saints and angels are the inhabitants of this "holy city,"—no room there for any other; if our bodies then be the "bodies of" holy "saints," then "into the holy city" with them, and not else; no part in the new Jerusalem, if no part in the old; no portion above, if none below; no place there with angels, if no communion here with "saints;" no happiness in heaven, if no holiness on earth. They are the "bodies of the saints," you hear, that go "into the holy city,"—they that rise from the sleep of sin, and awake to righteousness,—that rise from the dust of death, to the rays of glory.

And this now may hint us of our duty, to close with them for the close of all. It has been shown before what is the first resurrection, without which there is no second, namely, a life of holiness : a dying to sin, and a living unto God. And this is a resurrection we are not merely passive in, as in the other. We must do somewhat here towards our own resurrection, at least to finish it. We must open our mouths, which are too often, what David styles, the wicked man's throat; even open sepulchres, and by confession send out our dead, our dead works, confessing our iniquities; we must awake out of our sins, and arise and stand up by holy vows and resolutions; rear up our heads, and eyes, and hearts, and hands to heaven; "seek those things that are above, if we be risen with Christ;" get up upon our feet, and be walking the way of God's commandments, walking to him; get us "into the holy city," to the holy place, make our humble appearance there; express the power of "Christ's resurrection" in our life, attend him through all the parts of it all our life long.

This the great business we are now going to, requires of us more particularly to come to it like new-raised bodies that had now shaken off all their dust, all dusty earthly thoughts, laid aside their grave-clothes, all corrupt affections

Sermon XXXIV. that any way involved them, and stood up all new, all fitly composed for the "holy city," dressed up in holiness and newness of life,—thus come forth to meet our new-risen Saviour and appear before him. This the way to meet the benefits of his passion and resurrection: for coming so with these saints out of their graves, Christ's grave also shall open and give him to us; the cup and paten wherein his body lies, as in a kind of grave, shall display themselves and give him to us; the spirit of Christ shall raise and advance the holy elements into lively symbols, which shall effectually present him to us,—and he will come forth from under those sacred shadows, into our cities, our souls, and bodies, if they be holy; and his grace and sweetness shall appear to many of us, to all of us that come in the habit of the resurrection, in white robes, with pure and holy hearts.

Here, indeed, of all places, and this way above all ways, we are likeliest to meet our Lord now he is risen, and gone before us; this the chief way to be made partakers of his resurrection, and the fittest to declare both his death and resurrection, the power of them, till his coming again.

And to declare and speak of them, is the very duty of the day; the very grave this day, with open mouth, professes Christ is risen, and gives praise for it, that it is no longer a land of darkness, but has let in light; no longer a bier of death, but a bed of sleep. But "shall thy loving-kindness, O Lord, be known in the dark," or "shall the dead rise up" again, "and praise thee?" Yes, holy Prophet, they shall, —they did to-day; and if his loving-kindness shall not be known in the dark, the dark places shall become light, now the "Sun of righteousness has risen" upon them.

[Psalm lxxxviii. 10.]

But shall the dead rise up again and praise him, and shall not we? Shall the graves open, and shall not our hearts be opened to receive him, nor our mouths to praise him for it? Was it the business of the dead saints to-day, to rise to wait upon their Lord, and shall not the living rise to bear them company? Shall the whole city ring of it, out of dead men's mouths, and shall not our cities and temples resound of it? Shall they tell the wonders of the day, and we neither mind the day nor wonders of it? Surely, "some evil will befal us," as said the lepers at the gates of Samaria, "if we

[2 Kings vii. 9.]

hold our peace." It is a day of good, of glorious tidings, and we must not, lest the grave in indignation shut her mouth upon us, and the holy city bar us out. Open we then our mouths to-day, and sing praises to Him who made the day, made it a joyful day indeed, the very seal of happiness unto us. Open we our mouths, and "take the cup of salvation," as the Prophet calls it; "the cup of thanksgiving," the Apostle styles it, "and call upon the name of the Lord." Open our mouths now as the grave, and he will fill them. Open our mouths as the grave, and be not satisfied,—give not over our prayers until he do. Raise we all our thoughts, and desires, and endeavours to entertain him; go which way he shall send us, appear what he would have us, attend him whithersoever he shall lead us; and when he himself shall appear, he will lead our souls out of the death of sin to the life of righteousness; our bodies out of the dust of death into the land of life; both souls and bodies into the holy city, the new Jerusalem, where there shall be no more death, neither sorrow, nor crying, nor any more pain, but "all tears shall be wiped away," all joys come into our hearts and eyes, and we sing merrily and joyfully. All honour and glory be unto Him that hath redeemed us from death, and raised us to life, by the power and virtue of his resurrection. All blessing, and glory, and praise, and honour, and power be unto him, with the Father and Holy Spirit, for ever and ever.

[Ps. cxvi. 13.]
[1 Cor. x. 16.]
[Rev. xxi. 4.]

THE THIRD SERMON

UPON

EASTER DAY.

Psalm cxviii. 24.

This is the day which the Lord hath made; we will rejoice and be glad in it.

Sermon XXXV.

"This is the day which the Lord hath made." And if ever day made "to rejoice and be glad in," this is the day. And the Lord "made" it, made it to rejoice in. Τὴν ὕπατον πασῶν τῶν ἡμερῶν, as holy Ignatius,[z] a day of days, not only "a high day," as the Jewish Easter, but the highest of high days, highest of them all. A "day," in which the sun itself rejoiced to shine; "came forth like a bridegroom," in the robes and face of joy, and "rejoiced like a giant," with the strength and violence of joy, *exultavit,* leaped and skipped for joy "to run his course," as if he never had seen day before; only a little "day-spring from on high," as old Zachary saw and sung, never full and perfect day; the kingdom and power of darkness never fully and wholly vanquished till this morning light, till this day-star, or this day's sun arose, till Christ rose from the grave, as the sun from his Eastern bed, to give us light, the light of grace and the light of glory, light everlasting.

John xix. 31.

Ps. xix. 5.

[Luke i. 78.]

And this sun's rising, this resurrection of our Lord and Master, entitles it peculiarly the Lord's making. This "day" of the week, from this "day" of our Lord's resurrection,

[z] [S. Ignat. Epist. (interpol.) ad Magnes. c. ix.]

styled Lord's day ever since. And of this day of the resurrection, the Fathers, the Church, the Scriptures understand it. Not one of the Fathers, says that devout and learned Bishop Andrews,[a] that he had read, (and he had read many,) but interpret it of Easter day. The Church picks out this Psalm to-day, as a piece of service proper to it. This very verse in particular, was anciently used every day in Easter week; evidence enough how she understood it. And for the Scriptures, the two verses just before: "The stone which the builders refused, the same is become the head of the corner: this is the Lord's doing, and it is marvellous in our eyes,"—to which this day comes in presently and refers, applied both of them by Christ himself unto himself in three several places,—rejected by the builders in his passion, —made the head of the corner in his resurrection; the first of the verses applied again twice, by S. Peter, to the resurrection. For these doings, these marvellous doings, a day was made,—made to remember it, and rejoice in it, as in the chiefest of his marvellous works. And being such, let us do it. Let not the Jews outdo us: let not them here rejoice more in the figure, than we in the substance; they in the shadow, than we in the sun. It is now properly Sunday, this "day," ever since, a day lighted up on purpose for us, by the Sun himself, to see wonderful things in, and as wonderfully to rejoice in. "Abraham saw this day" of Christ's as well as Christmas: saw it in Isaac's rising from under his hand, from death "as in a figure," says the Apostle; "saw it and was glad" to see it, exceeding glad,—as much at least to see Christ and Isaac delivered from death, as delivered into life. Abraham's children, all the faithful, will be so too, to see the day whenever it comes. It now is come by the circle of the year, let us "rejoice and be glad in it."

SERMON XXXV.

Matt. xxi. 42; Mark xii. 10; Luke xx. 17. Acts iv. 11; 1 Pet. ii. 7.

John viii. 56.

Heb. xi. 19.

I require no more of you than is plainly in the text, to confess the day, and express the joy. Both are here as clear as day. *Dies gaudii, et gaudium diei;* "a day of joy, and the joy of the day." Easter day, and Easter joy; a day made, and joy made on it; a day ordained, and joy appointed;

[a] [Andrewes. Of the Resurrection, Serm. VI. Anglo-Cath. Library, vol. ii. p. 270.]

SERMON XXXV. God making the day, we making the joy upon it. Or if you please, *ordo diei, et officium diei;* "an order for the day, and an office for the day."

The order for the day: "This is the day which the Lord hath made," ordered and ordained.

The office for it: "We will," or, let us "rejoice and be glad in it:" *Exultemus et lætemur;* an office of thanksgiving and joy ordained and taken up upon it. The first is God's doings, the second ours. And ours ordered to follow his,— our duty his day; the Lord's day requires, sure, the servant's duty. Both together, God's day and man's duty, make up the text, and must the sermon. But I take my rise from the day's rising. The Lord's order for the day: "This is the day which the Lord hath made."

Wherein we have,

(1.) The day designed. (2.) The institution made. (3.) The preeminence given it. (4.) The institutor expressed. (5.) The ground intimated. (6.) The end annexed. "This is," designs the day; God's making, that institutes it; the ἡ ἡμέρα, the "the" gives it the preeminence; the Lord is the institutor; the ground is understood in the "this," this "day" when that was done that went before (ver. 22); and the end, by the annexing joy and gladness to it. Of these particularly and in order; then of the office, *exultemus, lætemur,* and *in ea,* outward and inward joy, and our directing and spending both upon it. But *hæc est dies,* the day designed is our first design. "This is the day."

"This"—first, is a sign of a particular. God made all days, all in general, but this in particular. Particular days are of God's making as well as others. God made such from the beginning, all days in the week, but the Sabbath in particular; all days in the month, but the new moons in particular; all days in the year, but the feasts and fasts, the Easter, the Pentecost, the Feast of Tabernacles, the great Kipparim in particular, to his service in particular among the Jews. And among the Christians particular days may

Rom. xiv. 6. be observed too. "He that observes a day, may observe it unto the Lord." And upon particular order we have such,

1 Cor. v. 7, 8. *Pascha nostrum immolatum;* our Passover is slain, and we
Rev. i. 10. must keep a feast, we have an Easter. We have the Lord's

day thence, and we may be "in the spirit upon" it; a "first day of the week," and we may "break bread," and make collections upon it. *Panem frangere,* and *collectas facere,* make meetings, and celebrate sacraments upon it. We have the Apostles at their pentecost; S. Paul, after that, making a journey to be at it; the Spirit descending on it, to sanctify it particularly to God's service, to take it, as it were, away from the Jewish into the Christian calendar. We have a *hodie natus est,* a day for Christ's being born, taken up from the examples of an host of angels, by all Christian people (for I can scarce call them Christians any of them that deny it) ever since; a day of his incarnation too, whence the Christian era, all Christian accounts of the year have since ever begun and run; a proof sufficient to show, Christians have their observations of days as well as Jews, particular days and feasts, nay, and fasts too, upon Christ's *in diebus illis jejunabunt,* his particular injunction of them,— days all particularly made for his own service.

The fault that the Apostle finds with the Galatians, for "observing days, and months, and times, and years," was for the observing the Jewish ones, not the Christian,—for falling back to the beggarly rudiments of the law, as he there expresses it in the verse before, as if the Gospel rites were not sufficient, or that they being afraid to suffer for the cross of Christ, studied such poor compliances to avoid it. Else some particular days have been always set apart, to the more especial and particular remembrances of God's benefits and Christ's; many of these days in the devoutest and purest times, in the ancientest calendars. This of Easter in particular among the rest. So particular, that generally all the Fathers and interpreters pitch upon it, as the day designed and deciphered here.

Other secondary interpretations, I confess, they make, some of them, but this the prime, though to some other upon occasion, or by-the-by, they apply it too.

1. To the day of the incarnation first. Then this stone, upon whose exaltation this day is founded, was "cut out of the mountain without hands,"—Christ's body framed without man's help.

2. To the day of his nativity. Then *factus est in angulum,*

this stone was made, made more plainly in little Bethlehem, a corner of Judæa.

3. To the day of his passion. Then he was rejected by the builders, the Scribes and Pharisees, and people of the Jews; *Nolumus hunc,* take him who will, "We will not have him;" "disallowed indeed" then "of men," says S. Peter.

4. To the day of the Gospel, the whole time wherein that glorious light displays itself to all the corners of the world.

5. To the weekly Lord's day, the Christian's day of rest and joy, the weekly resurrection day, that rose, as S. Jerome speaks,[b] *post tristia Sabbata,* out of the sad Jewish Sabbath, after the sad Saturday of Christ's passion, to the primacy over the other days.

6. To the day of the general resurrection, when this stone, "elect and precious," as S. Peter styles it, shall appear in its full brightness and glory to all the corners of the earth; at which day we are bid by our Saviour to "look up, and lift up our heads:" that is, to rejoice and be glad when we see it coming.

7. To Christ himself it is applied,—the day in this verse as well as the stone in ver. 22. He is both Daniel's and David's stone; Zachariah's and David's day-spring or day. *Ego sum dies,* S. Ambrose reads it[c] for *Ego lux,* "I am the day," and "he that walketh in the day," in me, he "stumbleth not."

Nay, lastly, we find it sometimes applied to any day of famous and notable mercies and deliverances, wherein any great blessing has been given. Thus to the letter, it is here applied to David's coming to the crown, after his long being rejected by Saul's party. Thus, in the Council of Constantinople, under Agapetus, for the blessing or election of Cyriacus, a most learned and pious bishop there.

1. But all these, though they may be applications, they are not so properly explications of this "day." To this of Easter it most fully points. Then the stone so lately rejected by the builders, became the head stone of the corner, the head of the Church, to unite both corners of the building, Jews and Gentiles, into one holy temple; then were the hearts of the disciples filled with joy and gladness; the prophecy

---

[b] [S. Hieron. Comm. in Marc. xvi. 1. Op., tom. ix. 91 C. ed. Francof. 1684.]   [c] [S. Ambros. de Mysterio Paschæ, cap. 5. Op., p. 440 C. ed. Paris. 1549.]

here fulfilled,—the joys completed in the exaltation of the Son of David, which the Jewish people here began for the exaltation of David, but prophesied of Christ's, though perhaps they knew no more than Caiaphas what they said.

<small>SERMON XXXV.</small>

The incarnation, the nativity, the passion, the time of the Gospel, the Sunday or Lord's day, the day of the universal resurrection, the particular days of God's mercy to us, are all days of God's making, and to be kept and celebrated with joy, even the passion itself with spiritual joy and gladness; and Christ is the day that gives light to all these days, —enlightens all; yet both day and joy, and the Lord's making of them to us, can fit not one, nor all of them, so properly as this "day" that now shines on us, Easter day.

2. Thus we have found which this day is, what day it is that is here so particularly designed and pointed out, which in the text is said to be made, and now to be considered how or what it is made. Of common days, it is said only that they be or are; so "the evening and the morning were the first day;" and "the evening and the morning were the second day;" and so of all the rest. The evening came and the morning came, light and darkness succeeded one another, so the day came, no making else. But of this, it is punctually said that it was made,—something in it or in the making, more than ordinary. <small>Gen. i. 5.</small> <small>Gen. i. 8.</small>

"Made," (1,) that is, made famous by something done upon it; death, and hell, and all the terrors of darkness, this "day" put to flight for ever by Christ's only resurrection.

"Made," (2,) that is, appointed and ordained for something. So *Deus fecit Dominum et Christum,* God is said to have made our Saviour "Lord and Christ;" and of Christ, that *fecit nos reges et sacerdotes,* that he "made us," that is, ordained us, "kings and priests," as God had him both Lord and Christ, and upon this day both; so that it is no wonder if the day too be said to be made,—made or ordained and appointed to be remembered. <small>Acts ii. 36.</small> <small>[Rev. v.10.]</small>

"Made" (3) to be celebrated too,—to be kept anniversary as a solemn day of joy and gladness, of praises and thanksgivings. Thus, *facere diem Sabbati,* and *pascha facere,* is to keep the Sabbath and the passover. What is there in Latin to make the Sabbath and the passover, in our English is to <small>Deut. v. 15.</small> <small>Matt. xxvi. 18.</small>

SERMON XXXV. keep them, to make up, or make out the day in God's worship and service. When God is said to make a day, it is for himself, and we can make none but to him; mar days we do, when we spend them upon any thing, or any else,—they are never made but when on him. The greater sin theirs then that unmake the days that are thus made, that both unsaint the saints, and unhallow the days, and profane both; that make them for all but him, all business but his, as if the holiness of the holiday were the only offence of it, that which made the day, or for which the day was made, the only reason to them to unmake it.

3. But however it pleases some to mar what God has made, yet made days there have been many, are, and shall be. Themselves are not yet so impudent to deny us all, not the Lord's days yet, which yet are but so many little models of this great day. But of "made" days all are not alike; some high days, some not so high, though the one and the other made and constituted for God's service. Of "made" days this is the highest; ἡ ἡμέρα, "the day," so we told you out of Ignatius;[d] so we now tell you out of S. Augustine,[e] *Principatum tenet*, "It is the prime." "As the blessed Virgin among women, so this blessed day among the days," says he. "The most holy feast of Easter," the good Emperor Constantine calls it four times, in one Epistle[f] to all the Churches; *solenne nostræ religionis festum*, a little after, the "solemn feast of our religion," by which we hold our hopes of immortality—the very day of all our religion and our hope. *Illa videtur dies clarior illuxisse*, sings Lactantius,[g] "The fairest day that ever shone." The sun, which so many hours withdrew its light, and hid its face in sable darkness, went down sooner into night at our Saviour's passion, and to-day rose so much sooner, restored those hours to lengthen, or increased its beams to enlighten this glorious day in the opinion or else rhetoric of Chrysologus,[h]

[d] [S. Ignat. *ubi supra*.]
[e] [Pseudo-August. Appendix de Diversis, Serm. li. Op., tom. x. 612 E. ed. Col. Agr. 1616.]
[f] [Euseb. De Vita Constant. lib. iii. c. 17. seq.]
[g] [Pseudo-Augustinus (?) *ubi sup.* p. 612 D.]
[h] [S. Petri Chrysologi Serm. lxxxii.

Sol qui præter horam, ut Domino pateretur, abscesserat, claritate cum resurgeret Dominus ante tempus occurrit: et qui, ut suo commoreretur Auctori, ipsam meridianam suam mortificaverat claritatem, ut consurgeret Auctori suo, evictis tenebris antelucanus erupit. —P. 126. ed. Aug. Vind. 1758. Cf. Pseudo-Augustin. *ubi supra*.]

Eusebius, and S. Augustine. If so, it was "the day" indeed, none like it ever since; but if not, there were two suns rose to-day to enlighten it—the sun of heaven, and the Son of God, who is also styled "the Sun" in the strictest spelling, "the Sun of righteousness,"—needs must it be a glorious day indeed which is gilded with so much light, so many glorious rays.

All days were night before; nothing but dark clouds and shadows under the law of Moses; nothing but a long unevitable night under the law of nature; nothing but a disconsolate night of sorrow under the power of sin and darkness: this was the first bright "day" that dispelled all darkness quite. A kind of spring of day, or glimmering twilight there was abroad from the first preaching of the Gospel, but men could scarce see any thing; not the disciples themselves; their eyes were ever and anon held, not fully opened, till the grave itself was this day opened, and gave forth Christ to open the Scriptures to them by the evidence of the resurrection. Ἡ ἡμέρα, "this is the day," when all this was done, when this marvellous light shone forth, to enlighten all the world. The day of all the days before or since.

4. And now, it may well be so when the "Lord made" it. All his works are wonderful, all perfect and complete, deserve articles and notes to be set upon them. But when he sets the note himself, and gives the article, then to be sure it is somewhat more than ordinary—somewhat he would have us to observe above the rest. And when he entitles himself to it, or challenges it unto himself, day itself is not more clear than that such a "day" must be observed.

Things that are exceeding eminent and full of greatness, wonder, or perfection, are commonly attributed unto God. This "day" is such at least, because it is said "God made" it; a peculiar work and ordinance of his, more than the common ordinance of day and night; and if God made it, what is man that he should mar it, or the son of man that he should unmake it? or how dares man or son of man make little of that which God made so great?

So great as to call it his; so great as to make it the mother of one-and-fifty daughters, of all the Lord's days in the

SERMON XXXV.

year besides. This is the Lord's doing indeed. None could alter the Sabbath into the "Lord's day" but he. None put down that, and set up another; abolish the seventh and set up the first, but the Lord of all, and may do all, what he pleases in heaven and earth, lord it everywhere how he will. Herein he shows he is the Lord, and this "day" the lady of the year, from whence so many little weekly Easter days take both their rise and name. All the former days God made, the Lord made this, the Lord Christ the ground and author of this day; Christ's rising raising this to that height it is.

Now, God or Christ is not only said to do or make that which they do immediately by themselves, but that also which they do by those to whom they have committed such Luke x. 16. authority. So Christ tells us, "He that heareth you heareth me;" he that heareth his Apostles, his Church, his Ministers, heareth him himself; their commands are his, their orders his, so long as they are not contrary to his word. And thus we may evidently without much labour deduce the day to be his making.

From the Apostles' times it came. Polycarpus,—that Rev. ii. 8. "angel," as is conceived, "of the Church of Smyrna,"—kept Easter, saith Irenæus, with S. John, and with the rest of the Apostles.[i] The great difference about the time of keeping Easter between the Eastern and the Western Churches, was grounded upon the different keeping of it by the two great Apostles, S. Peter and S. John : S. John keeping it after one reckoning, S. Peter after another; S. John keeping it after the Jewish reckoning, upon the fourteenth of the month Abib : S. Peter much after the account as now it stands, upon the Sunday following; but all the controversy was about the time, not about the keeping it; none denied or questioned that but Aërius, none left it at liberty but the *Cathari*, both registered for heretics about it. So confident were they it was from the Lord.

And that from him, at least by the Apostles, Constantine in Eusebius [k] is direct. Ἠν ἐκ πρώτης τοῦ πάθους ἡμέρας ἄχρι τοῦ παρόντος ἐφυλάξαμεν· "Which day," says he, "ever since the first day of his passion, we have kept until this present."

[i] Euseb. [Hist. Eccles.] lib. v. c. 24.
[k] [Euseb. De Vita Constantini, lib. iii. cap. 18.]

"We have received it of our Saviour," says he a little after. And again, "which our Saviour delivered to us." Thus *Dominus fecit* then indeed. And that so it was either from his own command or from his Apostles, the whole practice of the Church is ground enough, in all ages still observing it, even in the hottest times of persecution, some in caves and some in woods, and some on shipboard, and some in barns and stables, and some in gaols, keeping it as they could, says Eusebius; so scrupulous were they of omitting that "day" upon any hand, that the Lord "had made" them: and the great contentions about the time of keeping it shows as plain they thought it more than a human institution; they might else have easily ended all the controversy and laid down the day.

But they had not then so learned Christ, had not learned the trick of lightly esteeming days, and places, and things, and persons, and offices dedicated to God's service, which God had made, or were made to him.

5. Especially made upon such an occasion as this "day" was. This "day;"—what day is this? The "day" wherein the "stone" that was disallowed by men was approved of God, and exalted to the "head of the corner;" wherein the chief "corner-stone" of Sion was laid, and Sion begun to be built upon it, when we had ground given to build upon, and stones to build with, by Christ's resurrection; that is the ground and occasion of the day. And a good one too: for had he not risen we had had no ground to build upon; we had perished in our sins; been swept all away like so many houses built upon the sand. We had had neither place for faith, nor ground for hope, nor room for preaching; our "preaching vain, your faith also vain,"—all vain, all come to nothing. His being "delivered for our offences" had been nothing, if he had not been "raised again for our justification," as it is Rom. iv. 25. It is to this day we owe our justification; it is from this day we are made just and holy; from this "stone's" being made the "head stone of the corner" we made "lively stones, built up into a spiritual house," or building, as S. Peter speaks. From his becoming this day "the chief corner stone," it is in that we now have confidence, as S. John speaks, and creep not into corners to hide our faces—that we dare boldly look up

1 Pet ii. 5.

SERMON XXXV. to heaven, and come unto him, and that we call not to the hills to hide us, or to the mountains to cover us from the presence of God, or the face of man or devil. Our faith and hope, our souls and spirits, are all raised by this day's raising; we are all made by this day's being made; we had else better never have been made, for we had been marred and undone for ever.

6. But by this "day" it seems we are not: for this rejoicing and gladness that now follows close upon it shows what a kind of day it is, for what it is made, even to be glad and to rejoice in, a feast or festival. God is no enemy to the Church's feasts, whoever be; calls to us to blow up the trumpet for feasts, as well as bid us to proclaim a fast. Indeed he more properly makes the feast and we the fast, for he only gives the occasion of the one and we of the other; he benefits, and we sins; *Deus nobis hæc otia fecit.* So no wonder that the "day" that he has made be a good day,—a day of good things, such as we may well rejoice in— a festival.

Yea, and a set one too. His making, you heard, was an appointing or instituting it. Though God would sometimes have free-will offerings he will not always trust to them. If he leave all to the wills of men, the fires will oft go out upon his altars, his house stand thin enough of people, and his priests grow lean for all the fall of his sacrifices, if he come once to the mercy or courtesy of men. They would quickly starve him and his religion out of doors. But set feasts he always had; set services and offerings; would not leave himself or his worship to man's devotion, for "he knew what was in man." He made this "day," made it a feast, —a day of joy and gladness. Let us now, therefore, to our office, to "rejoice and be glad in it;" that is the second general, thither now are we come.

Three points we told you we would consider in it, *exultemus, lætemur,* and *in ea.* Three parts in our office—rejoicing, gladness, and the right ordering both. Outward expression, inward gladness, and right placing them. Both words, I confess, ἀγαλλιασώμεθα and εὐφρανθῶμεν, in the Septuagint, and *exultemus* and *lætemur* in the Latin, have something outward in them; yet *exultemus* is more for the outward, *lætemur* somewhat more within; a joy of the heart with some dilatation only of it, *lætitia quasi latitia*, a stretching out the heart and sending forth the spirits; *exultatio* of *saltatio*, a kind of skipping or leaping for joy, the spirits got into all the parts and powers, ready to leap out of them for joy.

[—]*Sermon XXXV.*

Being thus both involved one in the other, I shall not trouble myself to distinguish them, but only tell you hence, that, first, the joy that God requires in the things that he has made, or any time makes for us, is not only inward, it must out into outward acts; out into the mouth to sing forth his praise, "in psalms and hymns, and spiritual songs;" *Eph. v. 19.* out into the hands to "send portions to the poor for whom nothing is prepared;" out into the feet to go up to the house *Neh. viii. 10.* of God with the posture as well as the voice of joy and gladness, to go up with haste, to worship with reverence, to stand up cheerfully at the hymns and songs of praise; our very bones, as David speaks, to rejoice too; the very clattered bones to clatter together and rejoice; all the parts and powers of the body to make some expression in their way and order.

But not the powers of the body alone, but all the powers of the soul too: "Praise the Lord, O my soul, and all that *Ps. ciii. 1.* is within me praise his holy name." Our souls magnify the Lord, our spirits rejoice in God our Saviour; our memories recollect and call to mind his benefits and what he has done for us; our hearts evaporate into holy flames and ardent affections and desires after him; our wills henceforward to give up themselves wholly to him as to their only hope and joy. It is no perfect joy where any of them is wanting. It is but dissembled joy where all is outward. It is but imperfect gladness where all is within. It must be both. God this day raised the body, the body therefore must raise itself, and rise up to praise him. He this day gave us hope he would not leave our souls in hell; fit, therefore, it is the soul should leave all to praise him that sits in heaven. He is not worthy of the day or the benefit of the day, worthy to be raised again, who will not this day rise to praise; not worthy to rise at the resurrection of the just who will not rise to-day in the congregation of the righteous to testify his

SERMON XXXV.

joy and gladness in the resurrection of his Saviour, and his own. He is worthy to lie down in darkness in the land of darkness, who loves not this day, who stands not up this day to sing praises to him that made it.

And now I shall give you reason for it out of the last words, *in ea*, "in it." In it, and for it. As short as they are they contain arguments and occasions, as well as time and opportunity to rejoice in.

Rejoice, first, (1,) "in it," because this day it is, a particular day of gladness and rejoicing. Let us do what the day requires. It is a day of joy, designed for it, let us therefore "rejoice in it."

Rejoice, (2,) because the "Lord made" it. All the works of the Lord are matters of joy to the spiritual man, even sad days too, much more glad days such as this.

Rejoice, (3,) because the Lord's people have ever made it such. God has always made them to rejoice in it, to contend and strive who should do it best or nearest to the point.

Be glad, (4,) for the occasion of it, the resurrection of our Lord and Master, and the hopes thereby given us of our own; all benefits of Christ were this day sealed unto us, all his promises made good, all so hang upon this day that without it, "we, of all men," says the Apostle, had been "most miserable;" none so fooled, so wretched, so undone, so miserable as we.

[1 Cor. xv. 19.]

Rejoice, (5,) because God bids us; it is an easy and pleasant precept. If we will not be glad when he commands us, certainly we will do nothing that he commands us, especially when he gives us so great occasion of joy when he commands it.

Rejoice, (6,) because the very Jewish people do it here. They had but little cause of joy compared to ours; they saw but a glimmering of this joy at most, saw the resurrection but afar off, and yet you hear they cry out, "We will rejoice and be glad in it." And is it not a shame that we Christians, who see it clearly, and pretend to believe it fully, should not as much exceed them in our joy as in our sight, in our gladness as in our faith? Clearly so it is.

Rejoice, (7,) because "it is a good thing to rejoice;" to rejoice in God's mercies and favours to us, in Christ's crown and glory, in his day and way. The very angels themselves put on this day the white garments of joy and gladness, we find them in them.

SERMON XXXV.

Luke xxiv. 4.

Rejoice, lastly, to-day, because this day is the first of all our Lord's days ever since. We count them feasts and days of joy, and we meet together upon them to rejoice in, to give God praise, and thanks, and glory. It is a piece of worse than nonsense to say we are to do it upon these days, and not on this, from which only and no other they had their rise and being. All that we commemorate or rejoice in on every Sunday is more eminently and first in this,—this the great yearly anniversary of that weekly festival, the time, as near as the Paschal circle can bring it to the time, that the resurrection fell upon.

For these, and for this day, so made to mind us of all these, let us now take up the resolution of these pious souls,—"We will rejoice and be glad in it,"—in the day, and on the day, and for the day; that is the very work and business of the day, *opus diei in die suo,* " the proper work of the day in the day itself."

And here is now a way particularly before us to rejoice in. *Lætari* is taken sometimes for *latè epulari.* To rejoice is to eat and drink before the Lord in his house or temple. "And thou shalt eat there before the Lord thy God, and thou shalt rejoice, thou, and thy household." Here now we are before him,—the table spread, and our banquet ready: let us eat, drink, and be merry, and rejoice before him; only rejoice in fear, and be glad with reverence. "This is the day which the Lord made," and all Christians observed for the celebration of this holy banquet and communion; never let the day pass without it; excommunicated them that did not, one day or other of or about Easter, receive the blessed Sacrament; the greatest expression of our communion with God, and Christ, and all his saints, and our rejoicing in it. You may see this people, in the Psalm, within one verse, blessing him that "cometh in the name of the Lord," blessing the minister that comes with it, wishing him and all the rest that be of the house of the Lord, good luck with their business, God's assistance in his office and administration. And in the next verse calling out aloud, "God is the Lord which hath showed

Deut. xiv. 26.

[Ps. cxviii. 26.]

SERMON XXXV.

us light; bind the sacrifice with cords, even to the horns of the altar:" God has showed us light, and made us a day; let us now bind the sacrifice, the living sacrifice of our souls and bodies, with all the cords of holy vows and resolutions, "even to the horns of the altar," and there sacrifice and offer up ourselves, even unto our bloods, if God call to it; all our fat and entrails, the inwards of our souls, our hearts and all our inward spirits; the fat of our estates; our good works and best actions, the best we have, the best we can do, all we have, or are, even at the altar of our God with joy and gladness; glad that we have anything to serve him with, anything that he will accept; that we have yet day and time to serve him, that he has not cut us off in the midst of our days, but let us all live to see this day again, and have the liberty as well as occasion, yet to rejoice in it. Upon this comes in David now presently with—" Thou art my God, and I will thank thee; thou art my God, and I will praise thee." O let us do so too: cry out one to another, as the Psalm concludes, " O give thanks unto the Lord, for he is gracious, and his mercy endureth for ever." Turn all our rejoicings into thanks and praise, make it a day of praise, that so rejoicing worthily this day, we may be thought worthy to rejoice in that day; opening and dilating our hearts and mouths with joy to-day, in this day of Christ's particular resurrection, we may have them filled with joy and gladness at the day of the general resurrection; this day of the Lord convey us over happily to that, these our imperfect joys be advanced or translated into everlasting ones, into a day where there is no night, no sorrow, but eternal gladness and rejoicing for evermore.

THE FOURTH SERMON

UPON

EASTER DAY.

S. MATT. xxviii. 5, 6.

And the angel answered and said unto the women, Fear not ye: for I know that ye seek Jesus, which was crucified. He is not here: for he is risen, as he said. Come, see the place where the Lord lay.

BUT is he not here?—what do we, then, here to-day? "Come, see the place where the Lord lay." Why, it is not worth the seeing now; it is but a sad place now he is gone; no place worth the seeing or the being in, if he who is our being be not there. Old Jacob's *Descendam lugens in internum*, is all that we can look for; we must go down with sorrow to the grave.

But "fear not," though. Our Lord, indeed, is gone, but risen and gone away himself; they have not stolen him away. He is past stealing; "he is risen," and alive. Nor is he gone so, neither, but we may find him anon again in some better place. Had we found him here in the grave to-day, it had been sad indeed. He had been lost, and we had been lost, and both lost for ever. "He is risen, he is not here," are the words that disperse the clouds and clear up the day,—make it so clear, that *Videtur mihi hic dies cæteris diebus esse lucidior*, says S. Augustine;[1] *sol mundo clarior illuxisse, astra quoque omnia et elementa lætari:* "Never any day so bright; the sun, the stars, and all the elements

SERMON XXXVI.

---

[1] [Pseudo-August. Appendix de Diversis, Serm. li. Op., tom. x. 612 D. ed. Col. Agr. 1616.]

SERMON XXXVI.
Matt. xxviii. 3.

more sprightful and glorious to-day than ever;" they even dance for joy. The Angels themselves to-day put on their glorious apparel, bright shining robes to celebrate this glorious festival at the grave; a place where they this day strive to sit; sent thither to dispel our fears, and disperse our sorrows, and raise our hopes, and advance our joys.

And indeed it was no more than needed when this day first arose; no more than what needs still to those who "seek Jesus which was crucified," who go out with these tender hearts to the grave to weep. They need comfort and encouragement, direction, and other assistance too. They lie open to fears and troubles, to errors and mistakes often in their seekings. They had need of an Angel to guide them, and the news and certainty of a resurrection to support them; and by this we find here, shall so find it, if they truly seek him.

This is the business both of the text and of the day. The whole business of the Angel here, and of his speech to the women that sought Jesus that was crucified. In which, when I have shown you,

I. The persons—the Angel speaking it, and the women to whom it was spoken,—I shall show you then,

II. In the speech:—
Somewhat (1) to disperse the fears.
Somewhat (2) to approve and encourage the endeavours.
Somewhat (3) to correct the search.
Somewhat (4) to inform the judgments.
Somewhat (5) to confirm the faith of those who here seek, or shall at any time hereafter set themselves to seek "Jesus which was crucified."

For, (1,) "fear not ye," says the Angel; there our fears are dispersed. (2.) "I know you seek Jesus which was crucified;" there our endeavours are approved of or encouraged. (3.) "He is not here;" there is our search corrected. (4.) "He is risen, as he said;" there is our judgment informed. (5.) "Come, see the place where the Lord lay;" there is our faith confirmed. All you see plain and orderly in the text, both the particulars and the sum of it.

I shall go on orderly with the particulars; and so show you, first, the persons—both the speaker—and to whom it is spoken. The Angel is the speaker, and stands here first. I shall begin with him. {Sermon XXXVI.}

And an excellent speaker he is. The tongues of angels above all the tongues in the world besides. You will say so anon, when you have heard his speech examined. In the meantime a word of him.

S. Matthew mentions here but one; S. Mark no more; S. Luke two. S. Matthew's Angel sat upon the stone which was rolled away from the mouth of the sepulchre; S. Mark's sat on the right side of the sepulchre, within; S. Luke's Angels stood by the women, as they stood perplexed in the sepulchre. And S. John speaks of two Angels more—"the one sitting at the head, the other at the feet, where the body of Jesus had lain." And yet in all these diversities no contradiction. The story runs smoothly thus:— {Matt. xxviii. 2. Mark xvi. 5. Luke xxiv. 4. John xx. 12.}

These pious women mentioned here come early to the sepulchre to embalm their Master's body; whilst they yet stood without, for fear, this Angel in the text that sat before the door, upon the stone he had rolled away, invites them to come in, where they were no sooner entered but they saw a second Angel, sitting, who entertained them almost with the same words, and is he remembered by S. Mark; when they had awhile perused the bowels of the grave, and found nothing there but the desolate linen in which their Lord's body had been wrapped, being somewhat perplexed at the business, they were comforted by two other Angels, which immediately appeared, to resolve their doubts, and sent them to the disciples to tell the news, and are those spoken of by S. Luke; whereupon away they haste; only Mary Magdalene returns again with S. Peter and S. John, who having looked and entered into the grave, away they go; but she stands still without, and weeps, till two other Angels, as S. John relates, show forth themselves to stop her tears and divert her moans, and show her her Lord, standing at her back.

Thus we need no synecdoches, no ὕστερον-πρότερους, no strained figures to make things agree. But thus, you see, "Angels are all ministering spirits, sent forth to minister for them who shall be heirs of salvation," as the Apostle tells us. They stand by us when we think not of them. They speak to us often when we do not mind them. In the {Heb. i. 14.}

very grave, in our deepest melancholies, in our saddest conditions; at the head and at the feet of them they take their places and sit to comfort us; but especially, when we descend into the grave to seek our Lord; when we cannot be satisfied unless we may even die with him; when we are crucified and dead to the whole world but him; when our only business is both in life and death to be with him, then to be sure we shall not want Angels to attend us; at every turn they stand ready for us; upon all occasions they are still at hand. A strong consolation this (1) in all afflictions; a brave encouragement (2) in all good undertakings; a good item, (3,) too, for our good behaviour, to carry ourselves well, soberly, modestly, piously, in all conditions, "because of the Angels," as the Apostle speaks, that thus stand about us, that are everywhere so near us.

1 Cor. xi. 10.

So near us, that they often answer our desires ere we can speak them. We read not of a word the women said to the Angel, yet, says the text, he "answered." Thus, many times God answers us by himself or by his Angels ere we utter our necessities or breathe out our thoughts. He does not always delay his mercy till we beg it; he prevents us with his lovingkindness.

Ps. ciii.

He did so, to be sure, to-day by sending it by such messengers. Angels have wings,—so they were graved and painted in the Tabernacle and the Temple,—his comforts had so too, to-day. The message of the resurrection,—the greatest of our comforts,—could not upon this account come by a better hand. By an Angel, then, (1,) that it might be with the greater speed.

By an Angel, (2,) that it might be with the greater honour. Angels are glorious things, honourable ambassadors; and such are not sent on petty errands, nor can that embassy be slight on which such persons come.

By an Angel, (3,) that the benefit might look with more convenience. It was an Angel (i.) that shut the gates of paradise against us and drove us thence into the territories of the grave; the more convenient, sure, that the Angel again should roll away the stone, and open the gates of heaven out of those confines of death into which he drove us. He had (ii.) been employed in the news of our Lord's incarnation and first birth out of the womb; the fitter to be sent with the tidings of his resurrection and second birth out of the grave.

By an Angel, (4,) that it might be told with all the advantage it could possibly. Such news is fittest for Angels' tongues; men know not how worthily enough to speak it. Thus (i.) for the greater speed, and so our greater comfort; for the greater honour, (ii.) and so our greater and humbler thanks; for the greater convenience, (iii.) and so the greater confirmation of the analogy of our faith; for the greater advantage, (iv.) and so our greater and readier acceptance of it, was this first news of the resurrection given us by an Angel, though nor men nor angels sufficiently fit for it.

Angels, certainly, the fittest of the two—they the fittest for the news; and yet methinks meaner ambassadors might be fitter for the persons to whom it is told. Angels and women, the "sons of God and the daughters of men," are no good matches; though I must tell you, too, such women as these,—such who outrun the Apostles themselves in affection and duty to their Lord, whose love triumphs over the power of death, whose early piety prevents the morning watch and shames the sun,—are company for Angels to make up their choirs.

But it is not without reason that the Angel first appears to women—that they are honoured here with the first news of a resurrection. There is a mystery in it. The woman (i.) was first deceived by an angel of darkness; it was therefore most convenient she should first be undeceived by an Angel of light. The woman (ii.) was the first that fell; somewhat the more requisite that she should hear first of the hopes to rise again. Thus does the Almighty Wisdom proportion all things to us; thus does the Eternal Goodness contrive all things for us with order and convenience, *et respondent ultima primis*, and all things answer one another, first and last.

Yet all must not look for Angels to comfort or instruct them. S. Peter and S. John came to the sepulchre, but found no such favour—they came too late; the Angels were gone before they came: the women had been before them, and had gotten the blessing. It is they that watch and rise up early to find their Lord that meet Angels at their prayers.

SERMON XXXVI.
Gen. xxxii. 26.

When the day breaks the Angel must be gone, to say his matins, says the Chaldee; he will stay no longer. When we come lagging in with our devotions, God's answers come lagging too; extraordinary favours are the rewards only of extraordinary attendance.

But, what! those two great Apostles not so highly favoured as poor silly women? What! is Mary Magdalene the sinner, too, among the rest, preferred above them? It is so; women and sinners, and any above us, above the greatest Apostles, the greatest clerks, in God's favour, if above them in their devotion and piety to their Lord; it is so, and we must be content; nay, if God please to prefer the weak and meaner things of the world, upon any account, either such as are so, or such as we conceive so, at any time before us, we have no more to say, but, Even so it pleased thee, O Father; and learn upon it to be humble, and not think too highly of ourselves; as those weaker things are hereupon also not to be afraid or terrified at their weaknesses, but called to here by the Angel not to fear: "Fear not ye," which is the proem or first part of his speech, to which we are now come.

Four things here there were that possibly they might fear: (1,) the glorious presence of the Angel; (2,) the ghastly countenances of the soldiers; (3,) the unsettled face of the yet almost quaking earth; (4,) and the sad sight and horror of the grave. Yet, "Fear not," says the Angel, not any of these.

Rev. xix. 10.

(1.) Not me,—not an Angel, first. Angels are our "fellow-servants," and of our "brethren that bear the testimony of Jesus," as well as we. We need not fear them—they will do us no hurt; nay, they are always ready to do us good. Somewhat I confess there is in it that makes them commonly

Luke i. 13.
Luke i. 30.
Luke ii. 10.

thus preface all their speeches, as, "Fear not, Zacharias;" "Fear not, Mary," and "Fear not," to the shepherds. All is not so well between heaven and us as should be; all not so wholly well but that we may be afraid sometimes of a messenger from thence. Yet fear not for all that; they come not to us thence but with "good tidings," especially when they come in raiment, "white garments," as the

Mark xvi. 5.

Angel does; or a "long white garment," as S. Mark's Angel. That is neither a fashion nor a colour to be afraid of, for any that "seek Jesus which was crucified," or hope to see the face and enjoy the company of holy angels, though some now-a-days are much scared with such a garment, when the angels or messengers of the Churches appear in it. But μὴ φοβεῖσθε, "fear it not;" it is but an innocent robe; no more hurt in it than in the Angel that wore it. It is the robe of innocence and the resurrection; no reason to fear it: "Fear not ye," not this bright appearance.

No, nor (2,) that black one neither, of the ghastly countenances of the amazed soldiers. They, alas, are run and gone! There was no looking for them upon him they had crucified. They indeed had reason to be afraid that the earth that trembled under them should gape and swallow them; that the grave they kept, being now miraculously opened, might presently devour them; that he whom they had crucified, now coming forth with power and splendour, might send them down immediately into eternal darkness for their villany. Nay, the very innocent brightness and whites in which the Angel then appeared, might easily strike into them a sad reflection and terror of their own guilt, and confound them with it,—and I am afraid when the Angel's "long white garment" does so still, it is to such guilty souls and consciences as these soldiers that it does so; such who either betrayed their Lord to death, or were set to keep him there. Such, I confess, may fear even the garments of innocence that others wear. But they that seek Christ crucified may be as bold as lions. *Non timent Mauri jacula nec arcus, Nec venenatis gravidas sagittis, Christe, pharetras.* Thy disciples, O blessed Jesu, now thou art risen, will fear nothing, nor darts, nor spears, nor bows, nor arrows, nor any force or terror, any face or power of man whatever. And ye good innocent souls, ye good women, "fear not ye," your own innocence will guard you; these soldiers shall do you no hurt; their shaking hands cannot wield their weapons, nor dare they stand by it,—they are running away with all speed to save themselves. So, (2,) fear not them.

Nor fear (3,) the quaking earth that seems ready either to sink them or sinks under them; it is now even settling upon its foundation. The Lord of the whole earth has now once again set his foot upon it, and it is quiet, and the meek,

SERMON XXXVI.

Ps. xlvi. 1, 2.

such as seek Christ, they shall now inherit it. But "though the earth were moved," and though "the hills were carried into the midst of the sea," yet "God is our hope," the "Lord is our strength," and we "will not, therefore, fear," says David. No, "though the waters thereof rage and swell, and though the mountains shake at the tempest of the same," do earth what it can to fright us, "God is a present help in trouble;" why, then, should ye be afraid? " Fear not."

(4.) No, not, lastly, the very grave itself, that King of Terrors, that is now no longer so to you. Though tyrants should now tear your bodies into a thousand pieces, grind your bones to powder, scatter your ashes in the air, and disperse your dissolved atoms through all the winds, no matter; this Angel and his company are set to wait upon your dust, and will one day come again and gather it together into heaven.

Rom. viii. 38.

Nothing can keep us thence, nothing separate us, "nor life, nor death," says the Apostle. Fear nothing, then, at all: not ye, however; for "ye seek Jesus which was crucified." That is an irrefragable argument why you should not fear. And such give me leave to make it, before I handle it, as an encouragement of our endeavours; an encouragement against our fears, before I consider it as an encouragement to our work.

And, indeed, ye who dare "seek Jesus that was crucified," amidst swords and spears, and graves, of what can you be afraid? He that dreads not death needs fear nothing. He that slights the torments of the cross, and despises the shame of it; he that loves his Lord better than his life, that dares own a crucified Saviour, and a profession that is like to produce him nothing but scorn and danger and ruin, he cannot fear. *Illum si fractus illabatur orbis, impavidum ferient ruinæ:* "The world itself, though it should fall upon him, cannot astonish him." Nothing so undaunted as a good Christian, as he that truly "seeks Jesus that was crucified."

And there is good reason for it. He that does so is about a work that will justify itself; he needs not fear that. He whom he seeks is Jesus,—one who came to save him from his sins; he needs not fear them. This Jesus being crucified, has by his dying conquered death: "O death, where is thy sting?" He needs not fear that. And though die we must, yet the grave will not always hold us, no more than it did him. "He is not here," nor shall we be always here—not always lie in dust and darkness; no need to fear that. Nay, "he is risen" again, and we by that so far from fear that we know we shall one day rise also. For the chambers of death, ever since the time that Christ lay in them, lie open for a return, are but places of retreat from noise and trouble, places for the pilgrims of the earth to visit, only to see "where the Lord lay." Thus is every comma in the text an argument against all fears that shall at any time stop our course in seeking Jesus that was crucified. And having thus out of the words vanquished your fears, I am now next to encourage your endeavours: for "I know ye seek Jesus," &c.

"I know it," says the Angel: that is, I would not only not have you be afraid of what you are about, as if you were doing ill, but I commend you for it, for it is well that you "seek Jesus which was crucified;" you need not be afraid, you do well to do it.

Yea, but how dost thou know it, thou fair son of light, that they seek him? Alas! it is easy to be known by men and women's outward deportment, whom they seek. Let us but examine how these women sought, and we shall see.

(1.) They come here to his sepulchre; they not only followed him to his grave a day or two ago,—the common office we pay to a departed friend,—but to-day they come again to renew their duties and repeat their tears. Nor do they do it slightly or of course.

They (2) do it early, "very early," as if they were not, could not be, well till they had done it; so early, that it was scarce light; nay, "while it was yet dark," says S. John; they thought they could not be too soon with him they loved. Mark xvi. 2.

They (3) came on with courage as well as haste. They knew there was a guard upon the sepulchre; yet for all that, venture they would,—they feared them not. The day they knew, too, would come on apace, and there would be eyes upon them, so may be presumed not to be ashamed of their Matt. xxvii. 66.

Sermon XXXVI.

Mark xvi. 1.

[Ps. cxxxii. 4.]

Master or their work. No, nor were they neither afraid (4) of cost or charges, for "They had bought rich spices," and sweet ointments, and had brought them with them "to anoint him." They were resolved to be at charges with him.

That (5) would not be done without solemnity and ceremony neither; that they were resolved on too—resolved to pay their last duty to their Lord with all funeral solemnities and honours.

And by this time we have more than a guess, when men "seek Jesus that was crucified." (1.) If they follow him day after day. (2.) If their devotions be so eager on him, that they give him their attendance at the earliest hours, "suffer not their eyes to sleep, nor their eyelids to slumber, nor the temples of their head to take any rest," till they have found him. (3.) If neither the fear or shame of men can keep them from him. (4.) If the grave itself be more their desire than their fear, willing to be dissolved to be with him. (5.) If shame for his name be (as it was to the Apostles) the matter for their rejoicing. (6.) If, for his sake, they spare no cost upon his altars, which represent his tomb and present his body; nor upon the poor, who are the members of his body. (7.) If they think much of no cost, pains, or time; no duty or reverence too much for him. When we find any thus disposed and doing, we may confidently say of them, They "seek Jesus that was crucified," and we thus know it of a certain.

And indeed we had need of good certain signs to know it by. For many there are that cry, Lord, Lord, and yet Christ himself does not know them he professes. Many that talk of the Lord Jesus, and pretend to cast out devils too, sometimes, and do miracles in his name; have his name the Lord Jesus commonly in their mouths, and talk of it at every turn; yet if you mark it, it is one King Jesus; if any Jesus, it is in his kingdom, not on his cross; not Jesus crucified. No; the doctrine of the cross was to the Jew a scandal, and to these men foolishness. The very sign of the cross disturbs them. Fools they were thought, you know, a while ago, that would take up the cross and follow him, when they might with more case follow him in his kingdom, (as was then much talked of when the kingdom was in their own hands,) and reign with him. But whatever was the business of those times, the business of this is, Jesus crucified. And if we had no other proof that they still seek not "Jesus which was crucified," but that they are yet ashamed to give any reverence to his name, so to acknowledge him; ashamed too, of the very badge of Jesus crucified, the sign of the cross upon which he was; not only ashamed of it neither, but not ashamed to oppose it, and write and preach against it, and disturb the peace of the Church and simple souls about it; if, I say, we had no other argument against them, that they seek not "Jesus which was crucified," I know not how they would invalidate, and less, answer it. He certainly that cannot endure the sign, would less endure the thing itself, nor seek him certainly that hung upon it, if he must succeed him there.

Nay, we ourselves, who profess right enough, live not, I am afraid, sometimes, as if we sought or served a crucified Jesus, or indeed a Jesus. Our devotions to him are dull and heavy, slow and careless; we come to Church, as if we cared not whether we came or no; we are niggardly and sparing in the embalming of Christ's body,—to the Church, and to the poor; we are afraid of pains and charges in his service; we are ashamed too often to be found doing well, lest the wits and gallants of the age should laugh at us; afraid to be too ceremonious, lest we give offence to I know not whom; ashamed of patience or humility, lest we should be thought poor-spirited Christians; that is, the servants of so poor-spirited a Lord, that would rather suffer himself to be so horribly abused and crucified, than to head his Father's legions to fight for him.

He that sees how we have kept our Lent, how we always keep it; how little we mortify our lusts, how little we restrain our passions, how much we indulge our appetites, how far we are from crucifying our sins, or subduing our flesh, or dying to the world; how profuse men and women are in their apparel, how studious of vanities, how poured out in riots and excesses, how given up to their sports and pleasures, how continually taken up in some or other of these, when they are even walking to their tombs, and should

SERMON XXXVI. be thinking upon their graves; how every day they still post off all serious and religious thoughts, and never think of Christ or of his cross,—either what he did, or what he suffered for them, or what he would have us to do upon it; he cannot but say, "I know ye seek" not "Jesus that was crucified." I see no balms in your hand, no spices in your laps, no tears in your eyes, no sorrow in your faces, no funerals by your garments, no solemness or seriousness at all in any of your demeanour, that carries any semblance of relation to Jesus crucified. All so loose, so fine, so quite of another fashion, that certainly it were a tyranny over my faith, to impose upon me to believe that you "seek" any such as a "Jesus that was crucified;" that any such as you do so at all.

I did not think to have made so severe an observation, but that I find men think commonly that strict devotion is but women's work,—they themselves may live with greater freedom,—but so it is not; it is only this seeking Jesus we have spoken of, can really arm us against the grave, or fit us for the resurrection. And great persons do so too; too often think it is for those only of lesser rank, the simpler and the mean ones; they, forsooth, have enough to do to dress, and visit, and talk idly, and take a liberty from morn to night, answerable to their greatness, their fortune, or their youth. This story of Jesus crucified spoils all the sport, and lays all their honour too soon in the dust. Well, notwithstanding, we had better all of us have the Angel here than they commend us; his testimony rather that we "seek Jesus that was crucified," than their wits that make light of it.

And yet, methinks, they here are but slenderly rewarded for it, for all their pains. Now they have done all, "he is not here." That we called the correction of their search.

And however we think of it, it is a good reward to have an Angel set to keep us right, to tell us when we do amiss. Ps. cxli. 6. Let me never want one, O Lord, to do so; "let him smite me friendly, and reprove me." There are even "balms," says the Psalmist, that will "break one's head," and smooth ways we often stumble in. Smoothing and anointing does not always cure us; too often betray us. To tell us always, "O Sir, you are right; you do well, excellently well," is but a way to ruin us. "Thou art the man," is better far; "you are out,"—"he is not here;" "you seek wrong," when we do so, as necessary, as to tell us we seek right, when so we do. Indeed, the women were right, both for him they sought and the way they sought him; but for the place, that they were amiss in. Even "in many things we offend all," says S. James. For "there is no man that sinneth not." And it is our happiness when we are timely told it, that we go not wrong too long.

<small>SERMON XXXVI.

James iii. 2.
2 Chron. vi. 36.</small>

And it was timely here, indeed; the Angel would not have them enter in an error. It was a good work they came about, but he would not let them do it upon false principles. Men do so often—do that which is good upon a wrong ground; seek Christ too often so.

Sometimes, (1,) they seek him in the grave; that is, in fading, dying things, in earthly comforts, or for such things; but he is not there.

Sometimes, (2,) they seek him in the graves of sins and lusts, whilst they yet continue in them; whilst they are yet in their rebellions, schisms, pride, covetousness, malice, envies, and disorder, they pretend to seek him, even none but him; but his body fell not, as those Israelites, in the graves of lust. He is not there.

Sometimes, (3,) they seek him in a melancholy fit, in a humour sad as the grave, in a mood of discontent, all godly on a sudden. They have buried a friend, or son, or wife, or brother—are disappointed of a preferment—have missed of an estate—lost an expectation; and are now, forsooth, for a fit of heaven, a seeking Christ; but "he is not here;" you will see it quickly, if the day clear up again; the monk will quit his cell, the dog will to his vomit, he is presently where he was.

Sometimes, (4,) they seek him in outward elements, in mere ceremonies and formalities, and mind no further; think if we hear a sermon, or come to prayers, make a formal show of piety and religion, all is well. But if we bring not somewhat also within, some hearty inward devotion with us too, "he is not here" neither. A few linen clothes you may find, perhaps, that look fair and handsome, and the external lineaments of a sad, sober piety, like the dimensions of the grave; but dead men's clothes they are, and a grave, an empty grave, it is still; if our hearts be taken up with them, stopped and buried there, " he is not here."

Sometimes, (5,) we seek him perfectly in a wrong place, where the malice of his enemies only thrust him for a time amidst dust and rubbish; he is not there : he will be sought in " the beauty of holiness;" now " he is risen," there shall you find him; for he does not love to dwell in dust, though amongst us that are so. We must find him a fitter place to be in. Now " he is risen," and we are risen, our low condition changed into a higher, our poverties into plenties, our rags into robes, our houses almost into courts, it is fit his house and courts should also rise into lustre and glory, and he not in badgers' skins whilst we dwell in cedars, nor lie upon the cold stones or earth whilst we lie upon silks and velvets.

And now you see why it is when we seek Christ we so often miss him. We seek him where he is not to be found— amidst graves and sepulchres—whilst we are dead in trespasses and sins; or buried over head and ears in earth and earthly interests; or only in some sad distemper, when we are so weary of ourselves that we wish for death; or only in dead elements and rites, without the life or spirit of devotion; or with that slightness and neglect as if we thought anything good enough for him, or that he would be content with any clod of earth to lay his head on.

But these are the mysteries of the grave. He was not to be found, lastly, even in the grave, without a mystery; he could not be held in the grave they laid him. " It was not possible," says S. Peter; God had promised he would not leave him there—that his flesh should "see no corruption." Here was the mistake these good women made; they either understood not, or had forgot this promise; and believed not his own, that he would rise again. This is that S. Luke's Angels even chide them for, for forgetting: " Why seek you," say they, " the living among the dead ? Remember what he spake to you while he was yet in Galilee, saying, The Son of man must be delivered into the hands of sinful men, and be crucified, and the third day rise again." It was a piece of infidelity, it seems, now to seek him in the grave; so that well may the Angels ask them why they do it.

SERMON XXXVI.

Indeed, our Angel here is not so rough; but you must know this was the first time of their error. When they had been told it once or twice before,—first, by S. Matthew's Angel, and then S. Mark's, that he was not there, it would make even an Angel chide, to see them still continue in the same mistake. At the first it is Angels' method to be smooth in the business of reproof.

Nay, and sometimes to pave our way to it, with a " fear not ;" I do not mean to hurt you,—what I am to tell you is only for your good. This is but with Balaam's Angel, to stand only in our way with a sword drawn to hinder us from a fruitless journey; or, at the worst, but to smite us friendly with it, that we may go no further on upon wrong surmises.

And yet " fear not,"—" he is not here!" Is not the inference ill? Are they well joined? Why, " he is not here;" and therefore fear seems a better consequence. If he be not here, we have lost all our labour, all our cost. If he be not here, somebody has stolen him hence, and taken away even that little comfort that was left us of seeing him once again, and doing our last office to him. Thus Mary Magdalene complains indeed. Well, but for all that, depose your fears; if you should find him here you might fear indeed, and despair for ever. He had deluded you, he had broken his promise with you, that he would come again; he was no Saviour, but his body a mere dead trunk, like other men's; your hopes were all taken away, and all of you undone for ever. But now he is not here, you may hope better, and dread no longer; and I shall quickly put you out of all fear indeed, for I shall tell you now, " he is risen," as he said.

John xx. 13.

And now indeed, O blessed Angel, thou sayest something: away all my fears, " he is risen."

Why then, (1,) he is above the malice of his enemies, and of all that hate him. They, and the soldiers that crucified him, may be dismayed, and look all like dead men for fear, but I shall never be dismayed hereafter, seeing death has no more dominion over him.

For, (2,) if he be risen, we shall rise one day too. If our head be risen, the body, ere long, will rise also. He is

SERMON XXXVI.

1 Cor. xv. 22.
1 Cor. xv. 12.

Acts iv. 10.
John x. 30.

Col. iii.1, 2.

"the first-fruits;" the whole lump, of course, will follow after. So certain, that the Apostle tells us, that in him we are all already "made alive;" and with indignation asks, how some among them durst be so bold to say there was "no resurrection of the dead," seeing "Christ is risen."

But is he not rather raised than risen, (3,) that they durst say so? Was it by his own power, or another's? By his own, sure; for all the Evangelists say unanimously "he is risen." Indeed, it is said, that "God raised him from the dead." It was so; for he was God himself, "he and his Father one:" so God raised him, and yet he raised himself; was not raised as the widow's son, or Jairus's daughter, or his friend Lazarus; but so as none other ever were, or shall be raised and risen, and yet so risen as not raised by any but himself: that is a third note upon "he is risen."

And (4) risen so as to die no more. All they did, but he not. He conversed awhile with his disciples upon earth, so by degrees to raise them too; but after forty days he ascended into heaven. Risen, surely, to purpose—risen above all heavens—risen into glory.

And if thus risen, we have good cause, (1,) to raise our thoughts up after him, entertain higher thoughts of him than before; though then we knew him after the flesh, yet now with the Apostle henceforth to know him so no more.

Good cause, (2,) if he be risen, to raise up our affections after him; "set our affections," as the Apostle infers it, "upon things above," and no longer upon things beneath; set them wholly upon him.

Nay, and (3) raise ourselves upon him; build all our thoughts and hopes upon him; build no longer upon sand and earth, but upon that Rock that is now risen higher than we, in whom we need fear no storms or tempests; we cannot miscarry.

And, in the meantime, lastly, now "he is risen," let us rise and meet him; rise in haste with Mary, yet not to go to the grave to weep, as they thought of her, but to cast ourselves at his feet, and cry, "Lord, if thou hadst been here,"—if I had found thee in the grave, my brother and I, and all my brethren, had died indeed, been irrecoverably ruined and undone. And yet, for all that, "come," now, and "see where the Lord lay;"—be your own eyes your witnesses that "he is risen." [SERMON XXXVI.]

And it is but just that in so doubtful a condition of affairs, and a change so unheard of, you should seek an evidence not to be contradicted. "Come," then, and "see" it; the place will show it, and your eyes shall behold it.

Indeed, that "he is risen," as he said, to a tittle, to a day, as soon as ever it could be imagined day, is an argument that not being here, he is truly risen. Yet it is fit that we should be certain he is not there.

For it is fit that we should be able "to give a reason of the faith that is in us," says S. Peter. We can neither believe unreasonable things ourselves, nor imagine others should believe them. We are not to take our religion upon trust from an Angel: *si angelus de cœlo,* says S. Paul; not from an Angel coming from heaven itself. Some Angel, it seems, thence, may, speaking to an absolute possibility, preach some other doctrine than what we have received; "but believe him not," says the Apostle, if he do. But suppose an Angel thence can speak no other, yet there is an Angel that is from below, from the pit of darkness, that can transform himself into an Angel of light. We had therefore need take heed to our own eyes, too, as well as to our ears. The best way to fix them is to look first into the grave of "Jesus that was crucified;" see what we can find there to make good what the Angel tells us, be he who he will. "Try the spirits," says S. John, "whether they be of God," before we trust them. See whether things are as they are presented. It is but dark day yet; we may be deceived if we look not narrowly into the business, even to the very inmost corners and crannies of the grave. "Come see," then, what is there. [1 Pet. iii. 15.] [Gal. i. 8.] [1 John iv. 1.]

Nothing but the "linen clothes" that wrapped him in, says S. John, and "two Angels," says S. Luke. Well, this was enough, indeed, to prove he was not there. But how proves it that he was risen? Had not somebody stolen him thence? The grave was closed, the stone was sealed, the guard was set, and who durst come to do it? His disciples? Why, they were stolen away themselves for very fear. And it is not probable they would venture for him through a [John xx. 6, 7. Luke xxiv. 4.]

SERMON XXXVI. guard of soldiers when he was dead, that ran from him when he was alive. The Jews? Why, they set a watch to keep him there. The soldiers? Why, who should hire them? or, why should they take money to deny it, if they were hired to it? Besides, it was against the Jews' interests to give so fair a ground to the report of his resurrection, and his disciples had so little subtilty to maintain so forlorn an interest as theirs, that it looks not like a piece of their contrivance; and so poor a purse, God knows, they had that they could not fee so largely as to reach it. Nay, and the linen clothes left all behind, are a kind of witnesses against it. It is not probable they would have stolen the dead body and left them when they came to steal, and the laying them so in order by themselves requires more leisure than a thief's haste. So being clearly gone, and clearly none to own the theft, and none to prove it, and nothing to evince it, it is plain he must be risen, as he said. We have now, then, no more to do than "see the place where," &c.

And where he lay we call the grave: a good place sometimes to go into; "the house of mourning better to go into than the house of mirth," says Solomon, who had tried both; best to recal our wandering thoughts to prepare both for a comfortable death and joyful resurrection.

But Christ's grave, or sepulchre, has more in it than any else. There sit angels to instruct and comfort us; there lie cloths to bind up our wounds; there lies a napkin to wrap up our aching heads; there is the fine linen of the saints to make us bright white garments for the resurrection.

You may now descend into the grave with confidence; it will not hurt you; Christ's body lying in it has taken away the stench and filth and horror of it. It is but an easy quiet bed to sleep on now; and "they that die in Christ do but sleep in him," says S. Paul, and "rest" there "from their labours," says S. John.

1 Thess. iv. 13.
Rev. xiv. 13.

" Come," then, and "see the place," and take the dimensions of your own graves thence. Learn there how to lie down in death, and learn there also how to rise again; to die with Christ and to rise with him. It is the principal moral of the text and the whole business of the day. In other words, to die to sin and live to righteousness, that when we must lie down ourselves, we may lie down in peace and rise in glory.

SERMON XXXVI.

I have thus run through all the parts of the text. And now I hope I may say with the Angel, "I know ye" also "seek Jesus that was crucified," and are come hither to that purpose. But I must not say with the Angel, "He is not here." He is here in his word, here in his sacraments, here in his poor members. Ye see him go before you when ye see those poor ghosts walk; you hear him when you hear his word or read, or preached. You even feel him in the blessed sacraments when you receive them worthily. The eyes and ears and hands of your bodies do not, cannot; but your souls may find and see him in them all.

Some of you, I know, are come hither even to seek his body too, to pour out your souls upon it, and at yon holy sepulchre revive the remembrance of the crucified Jesus; yet take heed you there seek him as you ought. Not "the living among the dead," I hope. Not the dead elements only, or them, so as if they were corporally himself. No; "he is risen" and gone quite off the earth, as to his corporal presence: all now is spirit, though Spirit and Truth too; truly there, though not corporally. "He is risen," and our thoughts must rise up after him, and think higher of him now than so, and yet believe truly he is there. So that I may speak the last words of the text with greater advantage than they are here; "Come, see the place where the Lord lies."

And "come, see the place," too, "where he lay;" go into the grave, though not seek him there. Go into the grave and weep there, that our sins they were that brought him thither. Go into the grave and die there; die with him that died for us; breathe out your souls in love for him, who out of love died so for us. Go into his grave, and bury all our sins and vanities in that holy dust. Go we into the grave, and dwell there for ever, rather than come out and sin again; and be content (if he see fit) to lie down there for him, who there lay down for us. Fill your daily meditations (but now especially) with his death and passion, his agony and bloody sweat, his stripes and wounds, and griefs and pains.

SERMON XXXVI
[Col. iii. 1.]

But dwell not always among the tombs. You come to seek him; seek him then, (1,) where you may find him; and that is, says the Apostle, "at the right hand of God." "He is risen," and gone thither. And seek him, (2,) so as you may be sure find him. Not to run out of the story,—seek him as these pious women did; (1) get early up about it henceforward, "watch and pray" a little better; he that seeks him early shall be sure to find him. Seek him (2) courageously; be not afraid of a guard of soldiers; be not frighted at a grave, nor fear though the earth itself shake and totter under you. Go on with courage, do your work, be not afraid of a crucified Lord, nor of any office, not to be crucified for his service. Seek him (3) with your holy balms and spices, the sweet odours of holy purposes, and the perfume of strong resolutions, the bitter aloes of repentance, the myrrh of a patient and constant faith, the oil of charity, the spicy perfumes of prayers and praises; bring not so much as the scent of earth, or of an unrepented sin about you; seek him so as men may know you seek him,—know by your eyes, and know by your hands, and know by your knees and feet, and all your postures and demeanours, that you "seek Jesus that was crucified;" let there be nothing vain, or light, or loose, about you; nothing but what becomes his faith and religion whom you seek, nothing but what will adorn the Gospel of Christ. You that thus "seek Jesus which was crucified," shall not want an Angel at every turn to meet you, to stand by, support and comfort you in all your fears and sorrows, nor to encourage your endeavours, nor to assist you in your good works, nor to preserve you from errors, nor to inform you in truths, nor to advance your hopes, nor to confirm your faiths, nor to do anything you would desire. You shall be sure to find him too, whom your souls seek; and he who this day rose from his own sepulchre, shall also raise up you from the death of sin first to the life of righteousness, and from the life of righteousness, one day, to the life of glory; when the Angel shall no longer guide us into the grave, but out of it,—out of our graves and sepulchres into heaven, where we shall meet whole choirs of angels to welcome and conduct us into the place where the Lord is; where we shall behold, even with the eyes of our bodies, "Jesus that was crucified," "sitting at the right hand of God," and sit down there with him together in the glory of the Father.

To which he bring us, who this day rose again to raise us thither, "Jesus which was crucified." To whom, though crucified—to whom for that he was crucified, and this day rose again to lift us up out of the graves of sins, and miseries, and griefs,—be all honour and power, praise and glory, both by Angels and men, this day, henceforward, and for ever. Amen.

THE FIFTH SERMON

UPON

EASTER DAY.

1 Cor. xv. 19.

If in this life only we have hope in Christ, we are of all men most miserable.

Sermon XXXVII.
AND if this day had not been, we had been so miserable indeed, and without hope of being other. If Christ had not risen there had been no resurrection, and if no resurrection no hope but here; then "most miserable" we Christians, to be sure, who were sure to find nothing but hard usage here, tribulation in this world, and could expect no other, or no better there.

Happy then this day to us; happy we that this day came, which opens to us a door of hope—have reason, therefore, to remember it, and with joy to keep it, as the first dawning of a better hope, the day-spring of all our happiness. This day our Head is risen, and with him our hope has enlarged its borders, and made a prospect into the other world, sees some comfort there for our sorrows here. This day's bright-shining beams have lightened our eyes, that now we shall not sleep in death; a Sunday indeed, the first true Sunday that ever shone, wherein the Sun of righteousness arose out of the chambers of the grave, to guide our feet out of misty darkness into marvellous light—out of the paths of the dead into the land of the living—out of this miserable into a blessed life by Christ's resurrection.

I know the Apostle gathers his argument somewhat otherwise. If there be no resurrection, says he, then is Christ not risen; if Christ had not, be not risen, say we, there is not, will not be a resurrection. To the same purpose both he and we, both of us making Christ's rising the cause, the ground of ours. If he, then we; if not he, not we neither. Our grounds the same.

And the inferences the same too. For whether we say, If there be no resurrection Christ is not risen; or, If Christ be not risen there is no resurrection, we affirm both—Christ's rising and our own. And if either be false, we are found false witnesses,—both, nay all. Not S. Paul only, who saw him last, but those also that saw him first—but "Cephas also and the twelve"—but "five hundred brethren" at a clap, who saw him all at once. S. James too, and all the Apostles, who both eat and drank with him after his resurrection, who bare witness of it, and preached it to the world, preached our resurrection from it. False witnesses,—liars all,—all the Fathers, all the preachers ever since, who preached nothing so much as both the one and the other. So if either be false, "our preaching is vain," (but that, perhaps, is little in the world's account, who could peradventure willingly spare both preachers and preaching too,) nay, but "your faith is also vain," your hope is vain, "you are yet in your sins;" and when you die you perish, and "miserable" you are, both alive and dead. Miserable deceivers we, to preach,—miserably deceived, you, to trust a Saviour who could not save himself, but is dead and perished; miserable both you and we, to continue in a religion so groundless, so unprofitable, so troublesome, so uncomfortable, so hopeless, whence little good is to be expected here and less hereafter, as it must needs be, if there be no other hope in Christ, but only here.

But the comfort is, the text is but a supposition,—what would become of us, if our hope were only here? Now, a mere supposition, as it infers a necessary consequence upon the supposal: so, being but a mere supposition, it as evidently proves a real truth contrary to the supposal. "If in this life only we have hope" supposes that so it is not truly, though, truly, so it might be. And we were "most miserable"

Sermon XXXVII.

[1 Cor. xv. 5.]

[1 Cor. xv. 15.]

says, in effect, that so we are not, though upon the supposal so it would be.

So that by this we have two general parts to handle in the text: (1,) What our "hope" might be, and what then might be the issue. It might be only "in this life" (such hopes there are); and then the issue would be misery. Then, (2,) what our "hope" is, and what, therefore, the success. It is not "in this life," therefore in the other; or not "in this life only," then in both,—a double hope, a lasting and everlasting hope. And then the effect sure will be good; if the other end in misery, happiness must be the close of this. The first of these is true only upon supposal, the second true without it. The first the Apostle only supposes, to prove the absurdity of denying a resurrection, or our hope in Christ concerning it; the second he truly means,—that the Christian's hope in Christ is not only here, and he is therefore the most happy of the world, because it is not, though if it were, he of all were the most desperately "miserable."

The sum must be to teach us, (1,) where not to place our hope; and, (2,) where to place it; (3,) what is the effect of an ill-placed hope; and, (4,) what of that which is rightly set. By both, showing us even the necessity of a resurrection, and of a faithful expectation of it.

And two kinds of "hope," now, with their several effects, shall divide the text—a false one, and a true one.

I. A false hope. In Christ, "in this life only."

And its effect: Misery—misery, both in this life and in the other. "Most miserable;" "of all men most miserable," then, in both lives, to be sure.

II. A true hope. Not "in this life only."

With its effect: Happiness—double happiness, here and hereafter both; that also, not "in this life only;" for if the other makes its owners the most miserable, this then, by the law of contraries, makes most happy in this world, as well as in the other; though there most, because there is most,—yet here too, because here is some.

The first, "hope," and its effect, more plainly expressed; the second, and its effect, as necessarily implied; both of them together, the full contents of the text.

I shall, for once, begin with the false hope, because the

Apostle's purpose here seems more especially to be, to beat down that; which once done, a few words and a little time will serve for the other. And as the Apostle here does but only intimate it, so it shall serve us anon but to touch it, lest we too much transgress the bounds both of text and time.

To search then thoroughly into the vanity and misery of a hope that reaches short of heaven, we shall consider these four particulars:—(1,) That such a "hope" there is—a false hope in Christ. That (2) that which is in him "in this life only" is such a one. That, (3,) the effect of it is misery—all those that have it "miserable;" they that "have hope in Christ," "in this life only," miserable they. Yet, (4,) of those, some more miserable than others, some "most miserable;" we, of all,—we apostles, we the ministers, we the preachers of it,— "most miserable" of all, of all the rest. "If in this life only we have hope; we, of all," &c.

That a false hope there is, even in him who is "the hope of all the ends of the earth," I would we could not say. But a false belief there is in him, nay, many false ones; therefore a false hope too, yea, many such. For all hope presupposes a belief; and such as our belief, such is our hope also.

We could easily, peradventure, bear it, were that hope only false which is in things below, in things transitory. Why? They deceive themselves, are inconstant to themselves, no wonder then if so to us. Health loses itself when it fails its master; riches decrease not more to their owner than to themselves; pleasure fades at the same time wherein it leaves the pursuer; honour becomes but air, when it is departed from him it honoured; all earthly hopes only therefore fail us, because their own natures fail them; the things we hope for perish, and we therefore lose them. All this might be endured to be failed by failing hopes.

But that a hope in him who cannot fail should fail us—a hope in him that cannot deceive should delude us, who could think it? Yet, too true it is. Such a hope, many such a one there is. When, though the object be right, or at least materially so, even Christ our Saviour; yet either (1) the formality, or way of apprehending him is wrong, or (2) the ground false, or (3) the reason none, or (4) the order ill, or (5) the managing of it naught, or (6) the nature of it not

Sermon XXXVII.

I. General.
1. That a false hope in Christ there is.

right, or (7) the strength of it not competent, or the continuance too short. We shall best understand what this false hope in Christ is, by considering what is required to make up that which is the true one. And to it are required, (1,) a right apprehension, (2,) sure grounds, (3,) good reason, (4,) order, (5,) discretion, (6,) purity, (7,) steadfastness and constancy.

(1.) True hope should have a right apprehension of its object, as well as an object that is right. It is not enough to justify our hope that we say it is in Christ, unless it be in Christ truly apprehended. To conceive Christ so to be the Saviour of sinners, as remaining sinners; to imagine he will give us heaven because we imagine it; to expect he should violently draw us thither whether we will or no; to hope that he will save us without doing anything ourselves, is presumption, at the easiest I can speak it; but some part of it is blasphemy, viz. to make Christ so to receive sinners as even to approve the sins, by taking the persons into favour, and justifying them, or declaring them to be just and righteous whilst they wilfully continue in them; and so far from truth it is, as that himself professes he came not to save them otherwise than by "calling" them "to repentance." Yet, as bad a hope as it is, it is too common now, commonly professed and preached too, as well as practised, though most injuriously to Christ, and as dangerously to themselves.

(2.) "Hope," that is, true hope, should be well grounded. Now there is a groundless one,—that must needs be naught. The ground of hope is the word of God. "In thy word do I hope," says David; and, that in the Scripture ye "might have hope," says S. Paul. That which hath other foundation is without foundation. God's word, not man's comment; Christ's promise, not man's fancy, must ground our hope. To hope we shall be saved only because we hope so; to hope God will save us only because he is merciful, infinitely merciful; or that we shall to heaven because we persuade ourselves we are elected and predestinated, or conceive ourselves the only saints and darlings of the Most High; to make either our own groundless and sudden hopes, or God's general mercies only, or temporal successes and prosperities (which are common also to the most wicked), or rash and obscure fancies of predestination and election, or our own merely imagined holiness and saintship; or, yet, some new revelation or inspiration, or some extraordinary strange light and motion within us, (which may as well proceed from him who too often changes himself into an angel of light, as from the Father of lights, for aught we know; nay, for we know it does so, if it be contrary to any parcel of God's revealed will in Scripture, that from God it is not, if it be so;) upon any of these, I say; nay, upon all of them together, (yea, though the prophets we have chosen to ourselves, add their word to it to assert it,) to found our hope is to build it upon the sand, that when any storm shall come from heaven, any wind or tempest of God's displeasure beat upon it,—when temptations, afflictions, or persecutions, sickness, or death, shall smite the corners of this specious building of our hope, down it falls, and in the dust, there lies our hope; yea, the fall is great; so much the greater by how much the higher, the larger built. He that will ground his hope aright must not be too sudden. *Qui crediderit ne festinet,* says the Prophet: Let him not be too hasty to believe. "He that believeth shall not make haste." To God's general goodness and promises he must add some inward feelings; for his opinion of being predestinated or elected, he must find some ground from his effectual calling, inward sanctification and renovation, constancy of faith and resolution, as well as from God's goodness and mercy. His holiness and saintship too he must not measure by his own conceit, but by the square of God's commandments. Does he do that which is holy and just? Then a saint—not otherwise, in the Scripture phrase. New revelations beyond the word of God he must renounce, if he mean not to reject the word of God as insufficient; and his new lights and inspirations he must bring to the light of God's written word,—his teacher's doctrines must be tried also by the same evidence and rule, and answer to it too, or his hope will be as groundless as his who never heard of Christ or God,—only serve to make him miserable. For so he is, and so will be, who thus fixes not his ground, who has nothing else but those foresaid imaginations to go upon.

Nay, (3,) reason, too, is required to our "hope." "Be ready," says S. Peter, "always to give an answer to every man that asketh a reason of the hope that is in you." Hope without reason is an unreasonable hope, fit for beasts, not men; unreasonable to be required of reasonable men. He that requires me to hope contrary to reason, requires of me either an impossibility or a folly. I cannot truly hope that which is impossible to my reason, that which I really conceive impossible; or I am a fool to go about, desire, or pursue it, whilst I think so. Hope above hope I must; nay, "hope against hope" I may too, sometimes, as Abraham is said to have done; that is, against the ordinary course of nature or affairs; but then only though, when greater reason persuades me to hope against it than to fear with it; when God expressly sends me word, or some other way assures me he will transcend the ordinary way with me, and not bind himself to laws of inferior nature and course, and then indeed it is greater reason that I should believe God than rely upon natural reason and ability or ordinary providence and common course. But then I must have either an Angel from heaven to tell me so, or an evidence from God which I can neither resist nor deny; a full evidence, besides, that it is God that so assures me, that he it truly is who requires my belief; otherwise I am to trust no further than reason will assure me, nor hope more, nor otherwise from Christ or God than true reason grounded upon God's holy word and possibilities, and probabilities, too, will move me to. To hope other is but to be our own deceivers.

(4.) True "hope in Christ" should be rightly ordered. First faith, then hope, then rejoicing in hope, then assurance,—not assurance at the first dash, nor rejoicing neither. Hope hath a kind of torment with it at the first, when the thing we hope for is either delayed or a great way off. The nearer we draw to it the lesser is our torment, the nearer are we to our rejoicing. Whatsoever joy rises before we come somewhat nigh the thing we hope for, is either none or very little: and if faith enter us not into our hope, if hope be grounded upon opinion only, not on faith, it will scarce hold a shaking fit; see the Apostle's order, first, "tribulation," then "patience," then "experience," then "hope," then, and not before, that "hope" which "maketh not ashamed." Till you have been tried and tried again, patiently endured affliction and temptation, till your patience be grown into experience, till you are become an experienced Christian, have had experience both of God's favours and his frowns, and are become an experienced soldier in the Christian warfare, one well versed in that holy trade, you cannot have "the hope which maketh not ashamed." All hope that rises not in this method will but shame you. In a word, first, the "hope" of righteousness, in the order I have told you; then the blessed "hope" of glory. All other is preposterous and no better in the upshot than that which is in this life only; for it will not hold, or not hold beyond it, though it talk never so much of another. No, without the hope of righteousness here,—a hope that expresses itself by righteousness in this life,—no hope, no true hope, I am sure, of glory in the other.

SERMON XXXVII.

(5.) There is a fifth "hope" that is as vain, which neither knows how to go about nor pursue its ends, nor entertain them neither when they come. A kind of people there are who lay claim to much "hope in Christ;" yet, when good motions arise within them to beget this hope, they either carelessly neglect or wilfully quench them; when God shows them ways to confirm it they mind it not; nay, when salvation itself seems to knock at their very doors they sit still, and stir not so much as to open and let it in; or if it fall out that they entertain it, it is with so much vanity and self-conceit, so much empty prattle and boasting of itself, so much show and specious profession, that Christ, in whom it is pretended to be all, is least of all seen in it. True hope is never without humility and discretion; it takes all opportunities to confirm and raise itself; manages its motions with all carefulness, sobriety, humility and godly fear; expects nothing but what in prudence it may; slips no time but what of necessity it must; uses whatsoever means it possibly can, yet without the least vain ostentation, to attain what it wishes and desires.

(6.) To this end, sixthly, it endeavours after holiness. The "hope" that does not so is no true "hope in Christ" at all. "Every one that hath this hope purifies himself," says S. John;—"hath his soul purified in obeying the truth unto unfeigned love of the brethren," adds S. Peter. S. Paul

1 John iii. 3.
1 Pet. i. 22.

calls it a "hope of righteousness;" and the Psalmist joins to it doing good. "Hope, and be doing good," as if there could be no good "hope" without doing good, unless it did purify us to all obedience and love. This is the only "hope in Christ" we read of for approved and sound; a pure, holy, obedient, operative, charitable hope. Whatever hope else is said to be in Christ does but usurp the name, and is no such, and brings us no whither but to the end of the verse, to be "most miserable."

Sermon XXXVII.
Gal. v. 5.
Ps. xxxvii. 3.

Yet, (7,) steadfastness and constancy must be added to make "hope" complete. Upon faith it must be grounded, as we told you, and faith can admit no wavering. "Sure and steadfast," the Apostle calls it;—"hope without wavering,"—anchor-hope, and helmet-hope, strong and sure. Sure! nay, "sure and firm unto the end," too. So sure as that it carries rejoicing with it, as if it had already obtained. No doubtful, sad, melancholic, wavering or unconstant piece of business, as the hopes of the world are, now up, now down, now merry, now sad; nor as those false hopes in Christ without ground taken up, without discretion pursued, and with impurities and impieties daily defiled, will one day prove. No, nor yet any impatient expectation, but a "hope with patience," as the blessed Apostle; a quiet and "patient waiting for Christ," to be content to endure anything, though never so hard, any time, though never so long, and think nothing too much for his sake. There are so many men's hopes of the contrary nature, so impatient of any service or hardship, or endurance for Christ, that with most it is come to more than an "if;" if they have only a false hope in Christ, so it is without an "if" too evident, too common, the more the pity.

Heb. vi. 19.
Heb. x. 23.
Heb. iii. 6.
Heb. vi. 11.

1 Thess. i. 3.
2 Thess. iii. 5.

I have been somewhat long in discovering the false hopes we have in Christ, which little differ either from impudence or presumption, to say the least, because the religious world, as they would be accounted, is too full of them; because so many deceive themselves with their false glitterings, and will needs be, forsooth, the saints, the only saints who "have hope in Christ," who neither know the nature nor feel the power of it. More false hopes even in Christ there are, but such as may well be reduced to these heads; as many false hopes as false beliefs, and they are more than I can tell you, more than any can; more, however, than the day would give us leave to tell you, if we would or could.

A "hope in Christ," (1,) that misconceives him; (2,) a groundless, (3,) unreasonable, (4,) preposterous, (5,) indiscreet, (6,) unholy, (7,) a wavering, inconstant, and impatient hope, are the only false hopes I have informed you of; you may reduce all others to them but this one behind, which the Apostle seems to imply by the rule of contraries, when he tells us of a "hope" he had, which made "him use great plainness of speech," whereby he insinuates, that the hope "through Christ to Godward" "by the ministration of the Spirit, not the letter," as he styles it, delights not in a kind of canting language, which nobody understands but those of the same craft and occupation, none but themselves; no, nor themselves neither,—though by an uncouth kind of holy language, through spiritual pride, they would fain seem to speak mysteries. No, "the Father of lights" uses no dark-lantern language. If they mean good why may we not understand them? If they fear not the detection of their falsehoods, why do they cloud themselves and meanings in unscripture-like phrases? If they hoped like Christians they would speak like such, not like barbarians, and then should we plainly understand them. For S. Paul's hope in the place forementioned, and the hope of the Fathers ever since, was in plainness of speech,—we know what it means,—from which these men so professedly swerving, we may justly suspect they are swerved also from the hope of the Apostles and all Christian Fathers,—have set up also a new hope different from theirs, and are become a kind of Christians different from them. This is a note you shall scarce meet with; but the observation of the hopes of our times compared with those of the Apostles' times, and S. Paul's words, brought it to my hands; and it almost seems the symptom, by thoroughly examining it, of all false, heretical and groundless hopes through all ages in sects and heresies, as they rose; the changing the Catholic and received phrase into other terms: a new uncouth language for new and uncouth faiths and hopes.

By what has been said you may now easily find out

Sermon XXXVII.

2 Cor. iii. 12.
2 Cor. iii. 4, 6.

SERMON XXXVII. whether your "hope in Christ" be as it should be, whether it will make happy or miserable. And by the same you may as easily perceive how false hopes generally delude the world. Yet, to give you only a short prospect of them all together now at last, that you may see them fully and yet briefly too, take it thus:

For men to play the devils and yet pretend to hope in God; to study schism, faction, and contention, and yet pretend hope in the "Prince of Peace;" to run all the ways of destruction and yet hope salvation; to strive for nothing but this world, this only in all their carriages, and yet hope for another; to look for their portion and happiness hereafter, and yet will needs have all that is here; to hope for another life and lead this no better; to be so solicitous to place Christ's kingdom here, and yet mind none other but their own; to keep ado to set up "King Jesus" here, as they love to speak, and yet not suffer him to reign or rule in any of themselves; to hope for the reward of peace-makers, to be called the saints and children of God, and yet be the only peace-breakers, peace-disturbers in Church and State, nay, and the great war-makers too; to hope for the reward of being persecuted for Christ, and yet daily persecute him in his members, and that even for his sake too, for his religion and a good conscience; to hope for the reward of the meek, the poor in spirit, the pure in heart, which amounts to as much as heaven and earth, and yet be the most impure and proud and haughty, exalting themselves "above all that is called God," proud of virtues and graces, and proud of sins, enormous sins too,—are such riddles and contradictions, are such groundless, senseless, impudent hopes, that, whatever they pretend of Christ, they are not only such as are in this life only, fading, vanishing and vain, but so only in Christ, as in the mere sound and noise and echo of the name, and even the greatest injury that can be done it, the vilest abuse that ever the name of Christian hope yet suffered.

Yet are we to proceed to another still. A hope in Christ, only for this life, the second particular we propounded, a hope that pretends no further than this present life. In this so much the more modest than the other, in that it pretends no further than it acts; in this only different from the other.

This denies the resurrection, the other the power of it; this more expressly, the other implicitly; this sometimes both in words and deeds, (so much the honester,) the other in deed only, in words never, so much the proner to deceive us. But who are they, now, whose hope in Christ is only in this life? Or, what is it to hope in Christ in this life only? Let us see a little.

(1.) They plainly "have hope in Christ in this life only," who deny his resurrection. For if he be not risen, if he be yet in the grave, and his body among the atoms of the dust, alas! there must needs our hope end too,—thither must it go, and sleep there for ever. He was no more than a poor man as we, if he be not risen; and if our hope be in man "whose breath is in his nostrils," then when God takes away his breath he dies, and our hopes die with him. The point of Christ's resurrection, then, is the hinge of all our hope. Best to keep close to that article, or we lose all our religion quite, and must go seek some other. If he that should save us be not able to save himself; if our hope be hid in him, and he hid for ever in his ashes; if he that should deliver us, delivered not himself from death, we have no reason to expect beyond it, and then little comfort to look beside it, upon any good we can here get by it.

(2.) They who deny our resurrection, can hope no further in Christ than in this life only. If we rise no more, here is all we look for. And if Christ, in whom we hope, can do us any good, it must be here, for he has nowhere else to do it, if when we die we perish. So to deny a resurrection, is plainly to confine our hope within this present world, to the narrow limits of an uncertain life. Yet such there were in the Apostles' times, as appears, some among the Corinthians, who "said there was no resurrection of the dead." Of which sort also were Hymenæus and Philetus, who affirmed "the resurrection was past already,"—nothing more to be expected; and thereby, says S. Paul, "overthrew the faith of some." I cannot punctually point out to you, amidst the confused rout of errors and heresies, which now swarm and reign amongst us, any such who dare yet expressly say so much. Yet if they who are so hot for Christ's temporal reign upon earth, (of which there are good store,) be not such, they look

Sermon XXXVII.

That hope in Christ in this life only, is a false hope also, and what it is.

1 Cor. xv. 12.

2 Tim. ii.

SERMON XXXVII.

very like them; like men, I am sure, who "have hope in Christ in this life only," or at least too much in it, more than they should; and if we may guess at them by their actions, they and many other of that pious rabble seem to mean it, and would express it, if it were time to do it; or it may be, do it already in their congregations and private meetings, if we could come to hear them. I am sure it concerns them much, that there be no resurrection, and to think so too, if they desire to go on confidently and quietly, without the throbs of an accusing and condemning conscience in the courses they are in.

(3.) Such are they also truly in effect, who deny Christ's satisfaction, who will acknowledge no other benefit from his life, or death, or resurrection, than good example. If he be risen only for himself, or not risen at all, it is all one to us; all one, I say, to us, if we have no benefit by his resurrection. I think they will not say themselves, we can rise out of the grave, only by a pattern. If there be no power in his resurrection that extends to us, well may he be risen, but we shall not rise if he raise not us. We know then quickly where is all our hope.

(4.) Such are they again, who only follow Christ for loaves, who only therefore embrace or follow the Christian faith, and take up Christ's religion only to maintain themselves, and such or such a sect thereof, because it is the only way they see to live and thrive by. Here at this prospect, now, you see there are more hopes in Christ in this life only, than perhaps before you did imagine; whilst you behold so many change their religion, new form their faith, new model their profession, alter and assume opinion after opinion, for this poor thing we call a life, for the poorest things of it, to save the skin or gain a penny. An act so unworthy of a Christian, that it blasphemes the name, and makes us yet put another "if" to the Apostle's. If this be faith in Christ, any is. If this be true, there is none vain. If these be *Christi fideles*, who are *infideles?* If these be Christ's faithful ones, who are infidels? Who, but those who look for another world, who believe that Christ is risen, and they shall one day rise after him, and therefore in the interim, rise above this foolish world and the things of it in all their thoughts?

THE FIFTH SERMON ON EASTER DAY.

(5.) Many other hopes there be, which have too much tincture of this life in them, too much infected with the interests of this present life; which seem so much to be possessed with it, that upon loss of friends, or liberty, or estate, or honour, or the fear of such probable or threatened losses, the men that have these hopes only, they grieve, and moan, and fear, and are perplexed, and troubled, and amazed, as men "without hope," as the Apostle styles them, without hope of a recompence of a reward,—as if Christ either could not, or else would not, make them a recompence for all their sufferings, all their losses; and therefore go like men forsaken and forlorn, not weighing how infinite ways Christ can at any time both return them here, and beyond desire or imagination reward them all hereafter,—but grieve as if there were no other world but this,—nothing to make amends for ever. I say not, that these kind of hopeless hopes are any thing near so bad as the other, yet bad they are, and have too much both of distrust and worldly interest in them. Though they deny not a resurrection, they seem to fear it; though they reject not quite the thoughts of another world, yet they seem to doubt it; though they now and then think well of Christ, they dare not trust him, unless they can feel him and his reward in present with him. The other indeed bid defiance to him, or else march impudently against him in his own colours; these only shrink from him, yet do enough to make us see too much of their hope in Christ is fixed here, enough to embitter all their lives, and make them miserable, if they settle not their souls a little better, and rouse up their spirits to eternal hopes.

(6.) Nay, more than so. Those very spiritual joys and inward comforts which we feel within us, and which sustain us in all our miseries, are but delusions, dreams, and fancies, if there be no resurrection, if we or they must end here; poor slender hopes to uphold us, if they rest only in present complacencies. The Turk,—for aught we can say,—has as much in the service of his Mahomet. The idolater feels the same, if perhaps not more, when he has done his sacrifice to his idol; he is pleased, no doubt, and much rejoices in it when he has done his worship. Every false sect, no doubt, has some like complacencies within, whereby it is confirmed

Sermon XXXVII.

[Ephes. ii. 12.]

SERMON XXXVII. in its superstitions; and, it may be, the more to fasten them, Satan, that metamorphosed angel of light, does, by adding somewhat of sensible pleasure to them, make those inward illusions and delights far sweeter in the apprehension than the true Christian's, many times. Nay, and the resolute sinner shall find a kind of subtle delight and appearing contentment in the custom of his sins, (especially of spiritual sins, false zeal, heresy, schism, singularity, or the like); does so commonly for a while, till conscience begin a little to remember him; would do so for ever but for the tang and touch of conscience, which ever and anon strikes in on a sudden and thwarts or allays them, which yet it could not do if there were no resurrection to call them to account. So that those great pledges and forerunners of our eternal happiness would be either none, or not what they are, or but the fading glances of a perishing hope, if they had not a relish from those infinite and everlasting joys we look for. And whoever he is, that shall endure what a Christian must, only for those slender (and peradventure uncertain) contentations here, (which yet truly are not so much, or it may be, none at all to fully reasonable souls, if they bring not with them the promises of a fuller stream of a yet-to-be-expected satisfaction,) whoever he be, he does but vainly place his labour. It is the glances of the other world, that make any thing look beautiful in this. It is only those eternal sweetnesses above, which give the taste to all these below, of what kind soever, if they relish truly well. And be our hopes, though in Christ himself, fed with any thing but them, or with things that have relation to them, we may put them all into this number, that the Apostle reckons only to make "most miserable."

Be they hopes in Christ without an eye (i.) to his rising out the grave; or, (ii.) without our rising thence: (iii.) do they deny the power of Christ's resurrection; or, (iv.) mind him only for worldly things, not regarding other; or, (v.) through infirmity, fix too much upon things of this life; or, (vi.) please themselves only in some inward complacencies and delights, without reference to eternal blessings,—they are no other. If any of these ways only we have hope in Christ, we have hope in him in this life only, and are of all men most miserable; which close puts me in mind now of the third particular. The effect of all these if-hopes, these but supposed, vain hopes, misery, and the worst the most misery. "We are then of all men most miserable."

Sermon XXXVII.

"Miserable!" But what should make us so? What, but that which makes up misery? Pain and loss. Lost joys, deluded hopes, and real pains, troubles, and infelicities. We shall not need to go out of this very chapter, which has given us the text, to find enough to make up a bulk of misery.

3. The effect of false hopes, misery.

i. For loss.

i. Loss.

(1.) We have lost our head. Christ is not risen, if our hope be only here. He is dead still, if there be no resurrection, and we are at the best but walking ghosts, horrors to others and to ourselves. We may well go with the disciples to Emmaus, a word that signifies forlorn people; go among forlorn people indeed, if he be dead still. We have lost our spirits, our senses, our life and all, if our head be gone; we are a generation of senseless, lifeless, silly people to be Christians still.

Loss of all good.

(2.) We have lost our labours and our sufferings too. What availeth it that "we stand in jeopardy every hour" if the dead rise not at all? "If after the manner of men I have fought with beasts at Ephesus, what advantageth it me if the dead rise not?" What are all S. Paul's labours and travels, watchings and fastings, whippings and imprisonments; his suffering cold and nakedness, hunger and thirst, contumelies and reproaches; his journeys and his shipwrecks, his so many perils both by sea and land; his chastening his body and keeping it under; his so often perils of death by treachery, by hostility, many other ways; his so many persecutions, and after them even death itself? To what purpose all these if there be no place or opportunity hereafter to reward them? What mean these foolish Christians so to subject themselves to cruel mockings and scourgings, to bonds and imprisonments, to stoning, burning, sawing in sunder, to swords, and racks, and gibbets? What mean they to wander up and down in sheepskins and goatskins, when they may have better clothing far cheaper? To wander up and down from house to house, when they may at an easier rate have houses of

1 Cor. xv. 30, 32.

SERMON XXXVII.

their own? To wander up and down in deserts and mountains, in dens and caves of the earth, when they may with greater ease have stately buildings and glorious palaces to dwell in? Why are they so foolish to be thus "tortured" and tormented, and "accept of no deliverance," if it were not that they might "obtain a better resurrection?" as the Apostle speaks, Heb. xi. 35, and so on. Else if there be no such business," Let us eat and drink," says S. Paul, " for to-morrow we die." Let us crown our heads with rose-buds in the spring and take our fill of loves; let us stretch ourselves upon our beds, and drench ourselves in pleasures, deny nothing to our desires, abridge ourselves of no delights, care not by what means we rush into riches, pleasures, lusts, and honours: if there be no other world let us take our portion here, and let us not be such fools and madmen to lose all here and hereafter too. This is better doctrine than the cold precepts of Christianity, if there be no other hope than what is here. But "be not deceived" for all this, says our Apostle; it is but "evil communication" this; though so it were not, but good wise counsel rather, if there were nothing beyond this life. But awake, awake to righteousness, for there is a resurrection, where both our labours and our sufferings shall be remembered all.

Heb. xi. 35.
[1 Cor. xv. 32.]

1 Cor. xv. 33.

1 Cor. xv. 14.

(3.) We have lost our faith if our hope in Christ be only here; "your faith is vain;" our religion is gone, there is no such thing as that in Christianity, then. Religion is our business towards God, but if Christ be not risen,—as he is not, if we can hope in him no further than this life only,—then he is no God, so our religion is but foolery, and we miserable fools to busy our heads so much about it; about the name, and nature, and worship, and service, and trusting of a dead Redeemer, that can neither help himself nor us; no, nor hear a prayer, nor grant a request, nor reward a duty, nor punish an injury done to him.

Nay, (4,) we have lost our very hope too. If we have no hope but here, we have none at all, we can hope for nothing that flees not from us. Do we hope for honours or riches by following Christ? We see daily we are deluded. Do we hope for happiness by it upon earth? We see nothing but misery about us, and death before us. Nay, do we hope indeed for any good by Christ yet lying in the grave? What is it that a dead Saviour can give us more than the dead idols of the heathen? We see and feel our hopes in this life already vain, and for hereafter we can see nothing at all without a resurrection.

^{Sermon XXXVII.}

Yes, say some now-a-days. If the soul live we may be happy without a resurrection, though the body rise not, if the soul be but immortal. Fond men! who consider not how "if the body rise not, then Christ is not risen," (the Apostle's own way of arguing, ver. 15,) and then our faith which was in Christ being perished, as being no other than in a helpless, hopeless man, the soul can neither enjoy, nor expect a happiness from or by him, and has lost all other by following him already. Not considering, again, how the greatest misery that can betide the soul is to wander desolate and disconsolate for ever without both her body and her Christ, deprived eternally of all kinds of hopes. Not considering, lastly, that the soul's immortality necessarily infers a resurrection, it being but a forerunner and a harbinger for the body, to which it hath so natural a reference and inclination, that happiness it could have none when separated from the body, if it did not perceive the certainty of its body's rising awhile after to accompany it. It could not without that certificate but be incessantly tormented with its own unsatisfied and ever-to-be-unsatisfied longings, which it could throw off no more than it could its own nature and essence, it being essentially created and deputed to the body.

1 Cor. xv. 15.

But loss makes not all our misery. Not only loss of good but sense of evil concurs also to make us miserable. And here is enough of this, too, for us, if in this life only be our hope. "You are yet in your sins"—that first. And what greater evil, I pray, than sin? What greater misery than to be under the dominion of it? To be torn in pieces with the distraction of our sins, to be tormented with inordinate desires, to be hurried up and down with exorbitant lusts, to be enslaved to the drudgeries of so base commands, to be racked with the terrors of a wounded conscience, to be distracted quite with the horrors of inevitable damnation, to be at war continually within ourselves, to be commanded by every petty lust, to be a drudge to every

ii. Pain, or sense of evil.

filthy sin, to have a soul and body full of nothing but pollution, nothing clean, nothing pure, nothing quiet, nothing peaceable within it; thus to persist and continue, thus to live and die, neither our own masters nor our own men,—no misery more miserable. You talk of slavery and tyranny; there is none like this of sin and lusts. "Ye shall die in your sins," says Christ to the Jews, as the greatest misery he could leave them under. Sinned we have all, and die in them too we must all of us as well as they, for all Christ, if we have no hope in him but here. He is not such a Saviour as can deliver us, if he have not delivered himself; or if he have, and we yet will not hope in him beyond this life, and the things of this life, we shall also die in our sins and be miserable as well as they.

This is ill enough, yet there is a worse misery behind: we shall perish, too. "Then all they also who are fallen asleep in Christ are perished,"—perished for ever; whether you take it for annihilation, or for damnation; whether for being dissolved into nothing, or being damned for ever, either of them is misery enough.

Let the best befall you that can, it is to perish into nothing, and yet there are that say it is the worst; that to be annihilated is worse than to be damned; perversely, I fear, more to maintain a cruel opinion against God's goodness,—which in some men's favour merely they have undertaken obstinately to defend,—by setting up an absolute reprobation, than that either sense or reason can persuade any unprejudiced judgment that it is so. Well, be that kind of perishing what it will, let that be it, to have our breath vanish into the soft air, as the wise man phrases it, and have our bodies disperse into insensible atoms, or rather to become truly nothing, you cannot think it but a misery; if for nothing else, yet for this, that men of honour and understanding should become no better than the beasts that perish, to have so fair and glorious a building as man's moulder into nothing. And if death alone be terrible, to die into nothing is to nature much more, insomuch as it is further from the principles of it than any the most horrid corruption or putrefaction. "If a man die, shall he live again?" in Job's worst agony was but a question: but if a man once fall into nothing, he, the same he, cannot live again, is no question at all. He shall not—cannot. Something may be made of nothing, but the same thing cannot be re-made out of it. There is not anything, hell only excepted,—for we, however, for our parts will except that,—can be so bad, so far from all the properties of all kind of good, metaphysical, physical, and moral too, as this *non ens*, this "nothing" we must resolve into at the best that can befall us if there be no resurrection.

But I may go a strain higher, and tell you but the truth. If there be no resurrection, yet they that "sleep in Christ," sleep (if I may use so soft a word) in damnation too. The soul is immortal,—however some in this worst of ages are so impudent to give out it is not, because they truly wish it were not, and it much concerns them that it should not, yet—the soul, I say, is immortal, and cannot die, must therefore upon necessity be miserable, if it depart its lodging without hope either of seeing its expected Saviour, or her beloved body ever again; must needs wander, and pine, and fret, and desire, and despair, and be never satisfied, find no content in anything, no ease in any turn of thought, or motion of desire; restless and unsatisfied every way, every where for ever.

Nay, again, whether there be any resurrection or no, "if Christ be not risen" too, we may yet perish everlastingly, amidst the everlasting fires. For our Saviour will prove none, our religion none, our recompence no other than those burnings.

Nay, lastly, if there be a resurrection, and if Christ be risen too, yet if our hope be not risen also,—if we believe, and hope, and desire, no further than this life only,—if our endeavours and labours be only for this life we live,—if our hopes be none other than one or other of those false ones which I have told you of, the place of eternal torment and despair is only what we can expect, even so to perish, there to be miserable for ever.

Sum up now the issue of our hopes, without relation to another life, and tell me what they are all else but misery. To lose our head, our life, our Saviour, our pains and labour, all our sufferings too; to lose our faith, our religion, our

SERMON XXXVII.

hope and all, to live and die without it; to live perpetually under the tyranny of sins, and lusts, and devils, and in death to depart uncomfortably into torments, or, at the best, to be no more, to become mere nothing; to live a miserable, wretched, tedious life, full of rigours and austerities, denying ourselves the freedom and pleasures that all others take; a life full of afflictions and miseries too, for no better a recompence than mere nothing at the last, nothing at the best, yea, worse rather, than what we can imagine nothing at the most, and that without any hope for ever, has all the ingredients of the utmost misery.

And yet in miseries there are degrees, and of miserable persons degrees too: some more miserable than others,— some "most miserable." It is the last of the four particulars of the first general. " We, of all men, are most miserable."

4. The persons which are most miserable of all.

We Christians, that you have heard,—we, of all religions, the " most miserable." But of all Christians, we, the Apostles,—we, the ministers of Christ,—we, the " most miserable " of those who are the most miserable company,—we more miserable than all the world beside. This is still behind.

1 Cor. xv. 15.

Two things the holy Apostle, in this very chapter, adds to make it so. We are then " found false witnesses of God." What could be said more to our dishonour? To be nothing else but a company of base, impudent liars, to make a trade and profession of it to gull people into misery, to be the devil's own ambassadors and agents to bring in souls daily into hell; to add this dishonour to our misery, not only to be miserable Christians, but both the causers of their miseries by so dishonourable a baseness as a perpetual course of lying, and the wilful authors of our own, is that which adds much height to our already too great misery.

1 Cor. xv. 14.

To this there is an addition yet, " our preaching " is also " vain " and needless. We are persons of whom there is no use; our function so far from holy, that it is but folly; our labour and studies (from the first of those tedious days and broken nights of studies, of our exhausted spirits, and neglected fortunes and preferments, to attend our work) to no purpose at all. Thus, besides those common miseries of a hopeless life, with other Christians, we have most vile dishonour, and a whole lost life, and a whole vain course of labour added to increase our misery. *Sermon XXXVII.*

A third addition we have by the same pen in this Epistle, and so forward to augment our misery beyond a parallel. *1 Cor. iv. 9, 10, &c.* We are men " appointed unto death," " made a spectacle unto the world," unto " angels," unto " men ;" " fools for Christ's sake," " weak" and " despised," hungry and thirsty, and " naked," and " buffeted," and without any " certain dwelling-place," outed at any body's pleasure ; labouring day and night ; reviled, persecuted, defamed by every tongue ; made " the filth" and " off-scouring " of the world, and " of all things, even to this day ;" hated and envied of all kind *1 Cor. iv. 13.* of men ; " the world hateth you," says our Master, for whose *John xv.* sake it does so. Hated of all men, said I ? yea, hated of *19.* God too, if our preaching be vain, and there be no hope in Christ but here. Miserable fools, sure ; no such fools in the world again as we, to endure all this in vain, to place, or keep ourselves in so slavish, so dishonourable, so troublesome, so afflictive, so contemptible a condition, when with the same, or easier pains, less cost, fewer broken sleeps, more worldly content, larger liberties, fuller friendships, freer entertainments, greater hopes, we might take many several ways and courses of life more profitable, more pleasurable, more honourable. Nor can we be so ignorant of ourselves and parts, many of us, nor find we else any other reason to distrust, but that we might in any other way promise to ourselves as much power to manage other means of thriving than books and papers, as any others, if we would apply ourselves to the same ways and undertakings with them. And had we no other hope but here, you should quickly find we could do so, were we not confident we serve a Master, the Lord Christ, " whose service," as it " is perfect freedom," so it is perfect honour, whatever the world imagine it, or please to call it ; were it not for the hope of a resurrection, when we shall find a sufficient recompence for all the affronts, contempts, and ill-usages we suffer here, where these ragged blacks shall be gilded over with the bright beams of glory,—where we, whose office it is to " turn many unto righteousness " (whatever be the success), if we do our duty, shall shine like " stars for *Dan. xii. 3.* ever and ever." So now you see the scene of the text is

SERMON XXXVII. altered quite; there is evidence enough by our willingly and knowingly subjecting ourselves to all these fore-mentioned sufferings, that our " hope in Christ " is not only here, and we no longer, never, " miserable." All before but a supposition; this the truth, (which I told you should be the second general, though only summarily and exceeding briefly,) that our hope, the true Christian's hope, is not in Christ for this life only; and therefore whoever is, he, to be sure, is not " miserable."

II. General. The Christian's hope is not in Christ for this life only. That our hope is not only here, is evident by so many signs, that I shall only need but show and name them as I pass. We willingly suffer hardships, bear restraints, deny our freedoms, debar ourselves many lawful liberties, lay by our hopes of worldly honour, think not of the most profitable and probable preferments; we contend to rigours and austerities; we watch our paths, we mark our steps, we make scruples where the world makes none; we accept restrictions in our lives, that the worldling and gallant laugh at. The whole business of our life is to be accepted of Christ our Saviour; we remember his benefits, we observe his days, we believe his resurrection, and keep this feast upon it; we solemnize the memory of all his other glorious actions, sufferings, and mercies, with all holy reverence and godly fear, with thankfulness and love ; we hear his word, and study it; we strive to do his will, and fulfil his commandments, at every point passing by the satisfactions of our own inclinations and desires; we receive his sacraments and believe their power; we by this day's solemnity confess his rising, and profess our own; we leave all worldly interests for his, bid adieu to all contentations which stand not with that which is in him; we suffer anything gladly for his sake—to be counted fools and madmen, despised and trampled on, reviled and persecuted, exiled and tortured, and slain for his sake, for our hope in him, for that we fear to displease him, to lose his reward. These are full manifestoes of the true Christian's hope, what it is he looks for, what he means. For who now can think by the very naming of these doings and sufferings, truly acted and willingly undergone, that our hope is either not in Christ, or not in him beyond this life, who so easily contemn this, all the glories and pleasures of it, and choose with deliberation and full consent that only in it which the world counts misery or affliction? Especially if he but consider that we are not crazed men that do so, but have our senses perfect, our understanding clear—clearer, many of us, than the greatest part even of understanding men—the same passions with other men, as sensible of any evils or afflictions, naturally, as any others, and yet notwithstanding choose all this for our hope's sake in Christ only.

Sermon XXXVII.

And when all these shall be new heaped, and more embittered to the ministers of the Gospel, above others, through the spite of the world and the malice of the devil, on purpose to drive them from their hope, and they daily see and know it, are they such miserable fools and madmen, think you, not only to persuade others to these courses, but themselves also so readily to undergo them, when they might enjoy all liberties and pleasures at an easier rate, as well as others, did they not verily believe and hope, and even see and feel already, by evident testimonies both within and without, an abundant recompence hovering over them, laid up for them, superabundant, in a resurrection?

World, now do thy worst against us, thou canst not make us miserable, do all thou canst, not miserable at all. We scorn thy spite, we contemn thy malice: we shall have another world when thou art none; we shall outlive thy malice, thyself. Whilst thou art in thy greatest pride and glory, lo! we trample on thee; and when thou thinkest thou hast laid both us and all our honour in the dust, we are above thee; thou art made our footstool; and thou thyself, as scornfully as now thou lookest upon us, shalt be one day forced to vomit up those morsels of us which thou hast swallowed, and wilt thou, nilt thou, bring all our scattered ashes and least atoms of our meanest parts together, and humbly offer them at the feet of the meanest Christian soul whom thou at any time despoiledst of them, and either shrink away confounded with our glory, or else be glad of a resurrection as well as we; whilst those miserable wretches that thou so much courtedst and delightedst in, and that thy prince, who ruled and abused thee to all his lusts, shall down together into eternal misery, when those poor, despised Christians, whom thou so much malignedst, shall reign in glory.

That the Christian, of all men, is not miserable.

SERMON XXXVII.

Miserable they were not here, maugre all the world could do against them; they had that peace, that joy, that contentment still within, which the world could neither give nor take away. They found an unspeakable, as well pleasure as glory, in their very afflictions and bitterest sufferings, being exceeding glad, and counting all joy to be made so like their Master, whose ministers or whose servants they were; with him, "despising the shame" and trouble of a contemptible and afflictive life or death, for "the joy set before them," for the hope they saw at the right hand of the throne of God. Thus feeling nothing that could be truly or properly called misery, whilst they "took pleasure in infirmities, in reproaches, in necessities, in persecutions, in distresses for Christ's sake," as S. Paul professes he did; whilst it all served only to their contentment here, and augment their happiness and glory hereafter, they sure lost nothing then, they are not miserable now, who are so fallen asleep. And lift up your heads, ye drooping Christians; still, they shall not be miserable, that so at any time fall asleep, but rise and live again, and be yet more happy, every one in their order, every star their glory, every star a different ray, according to their hope and sufferings here; as no men so little miserable here, if all things be truly pondered, so no men so happy hereafter as the Christians; they, "of all men," above all men, souls and bodies, both pastor and people, all that live and die under the glorious hope of a resurrection by Christ, who place not their hopes or affections in this life, but in him and in the other,—of all men, they, most blessed, most eternally blessed.

[Heb. xii. 2.]

2 Cor. xii. 10.

To which blessed estate, after this life ended, he who is our "hope," and who, we hope, will keep us in it,—he in whom we trust, and I trust shall do so still, not for this life only, but the other too—but for ever,—he, of his mercy, convey and bring us all, every one in his due time and order, even our Lord Jesus Christ. To whom with the Father and the Holy Spirit be all praise and glory, not in this life only, but for ever and ever. *Amen.*

A SERMON

UPON

ASCENSION DAY.

PSALM xxiv. 3, 4.

Who shall ascend into the hill of the Lord? or who shall stand up in his holy place? Even he that hath clean hands, and a pure heart; and hath not lifted up his soul unto vanity, nor sworn deceitfully to his neighbour.

"WHO shall ascend," indeed, if none must ascend but he that is clean and pure, and without vanity and deceit? The question is quickly answered, None shall, for there is none so: dust is our matter, so not clean; defiled is our nature, so not pure; "lighter," the heaviest of us, "than vanity," and "deceitful upon the balance," the best of us; so no ascending so high for any of us.

Yet there is one we hear of, or might have heard of to-day, that rose and ascended up on high, was thus qualified as the Psalmist speaks of, all clean and pure, no chaff at all, "no guile found in his mouth." Yea, but it was but one that was so: what is that to all the rest? Yes, somewhat it is. He was our head; and if the head be once risen and ascended, the members will all follow after in their time.

Indeed, it is not for every one to hope, any but such as are of his, that follow him, that belong to him. It is a high privilege that the Psalmist stands admiring at, and therefore not for all; yet for all that will; for who *shall* here is a who *will*, set up for all that will accept of the condition. *Quis ascendet* is who *will*, as well as who *shall*. They that will

SERMON XXXVIII.

Ps. lxii. 9.

1 Pet. ii 22.

take the pains, will do what they can to be clean and pure, they shall. His innocence and purity shall help out for the rest, when they have done their best. But if any man will ascend he must do his best, must be clean and pure with Christ, and through him, or he shall not ascend and rise up after him. It is the lesson we are to learn, from Ascension-day to Whitsunday, how to ascend after Christ "into the hill of the Lord," how " to rise up in his holy place," even to have " clean hands" and " pure hearts," " not to lift up our minds to vanity, or swear to deceive our neighbour," to have our hands ascend, and our hearts ascend, and our minds ascend, and our words ascend, as into his presence—all ascend after him.

The Psalm is one of them which the Church appoints for Ascension-day, and I see not but it may very well pass for a kind of prophecy by way of an ecstatical admiration at the sight of Christ's ascension. So it passed with the Fathers, and with our fathers too,—may so with us; for never was it so fulfilled to a tittle as by Christ and his ascension. He, the only "he" of clean hands, and pure heart, and holy mouth, and holy " all;" he the first that entered heaven, that got up the hill, that entered into the "holy place not made with hands." Not any doors so properly "everlasting" as those of heaven, nor they ever opened for " any king of glory to come in," as it is ver. 7, but him. I cannot tell how we should expound it otherwise, without much more metaphor and figure.

Yet I will allow it too for the prophet's admiration at the foresight of the happiness of God's peculiar people, and their condition: that God, whose the "whole earth is and all its fulness," should out of all its places choose Sion for his place; he " whose the world is, and all that dwell therein," as it follows there, should choose out the Jews, amongst all the dwellers, to dwell among, them only to serve him upon that hill; that, further, this God, whose all is, should still of this " all" so particularly honour some as to give them the privilege of his hill and holy place, his solemn worship and service, to go up first into his holy places upon earth, and then afterwards ascend into the " holy places"—the heavens,—for the word means one as well as the other.

Who are they? What a sort of people are they that are so happy, so much exalted upon the earth, and over it! It is worth the admiring, worth the inquiring, and we find it presently who they be, even such as have "clean hands," and "pure hearts," that "lift not up their minds to vanity, nor their mouths to wickedness or deceit."

Sermon XXXVIII.

In sum, these are the only men that shall ascend those everlasting hills, those eternal holy places, that are only worthy to enter into God's houses and holy places of the earth too, obtain those admirable privileges that are innocent and pure, and just and true, the only men worth the admiring, as the Church and heaven, the hill of the Lord and his holy place, are the only things are worth it; heaven is for none but such, and when we enter into the holy places we should all be such, as none have right to enter them indeed but such.

Well, now the business of the text is in brief the way to Sion and to heaven, to the hill of the Lord and his holy place, both that here and that hereafter; where we have,

First, the condition of being admitted thither.

Then, the condition of them that are. The first in the former of the two verses, the second in the latter.

I. The condition of being admitted or ascending "into the hill of the Lord," or standing up in his holy place, what it is; that is, what, or how great a business it is to be God's peculiar people, to be allowed to enter into his courts here and into heaven at last; what it is; why,

It is (1) a privilege; some one, not every one; some few, not all. Who shall? is, all shall not.

It is (2) a high one. It is an ascent, a rise; it is to a hill, and "the hill of the Lord:" who shall ascend,—who shall rise up; "Who shall ascend into the hill of the Lord? who shall rise up?"

It is (3) a holy one; it is to the hill of the Lord, to a holy place.

It is (4) an admirable one; the Prophet starts aside, as it were, from his discourse, and wonders at it, who it is should be so honoured.

It is (5) a glorious one. For the hill of the Lord is not only an earthly hill, his holy place; not that only made

Sermon XXXVIII. with hands; the words are as appliable to that of heaven, and glory, and so understood.

It is yet (6) hard to be come by. It is an ascent hard and steep; a high hill, no easy plain; raise and rouse ourselves up we must to get it; stand up to get and keep it.

And lastly,—that we may take in all the possible senses of the text,—it is Christ's proper privilege, his *præ aliis*, his first and above all others, therefore delivered in the singular, *quis* not *qui*, who is *he*, not who are *they* that shall? Though they, others also shall, yet they but by him; he first, they after; he properly rises and ascends, they more properly are raised and drawn after him.

II. The condition now of them that are so thus admitted to all these privileges, is,

(1.) That they "have clean hands."

That (2) they "have pure hearts" too.

That (3) they "lift not up their mind to vanity."

That (4) they "swear not deceitfully, or to deceive."

The privilege we are to speak of is a real one, a high one, a holy one, an admirable one, a glorious one; and though hard to be come by, yet to be come by, though through him. The condition upon which we are to come by it: (1,) innocency; (2,) purity; (3,) righteousness; (4,) truth; yet all too little without him. He ascended to this purpose, that we also might ascend after him; that is the lesson we are now to teach you. Two parts it has—the condition of the privilege of the hill of the Lord, and the conditions of our performance for it; the one, the condition to be obtained; and the other, the conditions to be performed: the admission "into the hill of the Lord" and his "holy place," that the condition to be obtained; innocence and purity, freeness from vanity and deceit, they the conditions to obtain it. I now enter upon the first, to show what is the condition we may ascend to; what a great and glorious one it is to ascend "into the hill of the Lord," and to rise up in his "holy place."

1. Several senses I intimated to you of the words: (1,) some understanding by "the hill of the Lord" and "his holy place," the material hill and house of Sion, and thence our Christian churches; (2,) others, the spiritual house and

building, the faithful and true members of the Church; (3,) others, the eternal house of heaven, the hill of Sion which is above. Each of them is called God's "hill," or "holy place." Sion, God's "hill;" the Temple, his "holy place;" the Church, the "house of God," not to be used like our own houses, and therefore a "holy place;" the faithful, the "temples," the "dwellings," the "buildings," the "house of God." Heaven, lastly, is called "Mount Sion;" the "holy place;" the "true tabernacle and sanctuary." Be it which of these it will, or be it all, to ascend into any of them is a condition worth the considering, to be admitted into God's house and temple, to be admitted into the family of true believers, especially to be exalted so high, as into heaven. To be in any of these conditions, is to be in good condition, a condition which is,

<small>SERMON XXXVIII.
Ps. ii. 6; lxviii. 15.
Exod. xxvi. 33.
1 Cor. xi. 22.
1 Cor. iii. 17.
2 Tim. i 14.
1 Cor. iii. 9.
Heb. iii. 6.
Heb. xii. 22.
Rev. xiv. 1.
Heb. ix. 12.
Heb. viii. 2.</small>

(1.) A privilege, a peculiar favour, not for every body to arrive at; it is a question who shall get it; "not every one," says Christ. The faithful, they are a "little flock;" "a chosen generation;" "few" there are of such; only a parcel that Christ has "given him by his Father." "To you it is given," says he himself. To some it is given, to some it is not. So a privilege it is to stand thus upon Mount Sion with the Lamb; to be in the number of those that "follow him whithersoever he goes."

<small>Luke xii. 32.
1 Pet. ii. 9.
Matt. xx. 16.
John vi. 39.
Matt. xiii. 11.
Rev. xiv. 4.</small>

And it will prove a privilege (2) to be of those that go up to the "house of the Lord," among them that "keep holyday," that is, that go up to serve him there. Now, he has "not dealt so with any nation," any but his own. "If I shall find favour in the eyes of the Lord, then he will bring me again, and show me his ark and his habitation," says David. And if a favour it be, not to be debarred the house of God in Shiloh or Jerusalem, is it less, think we, to be allowed the liberty of Christian Churches, to praise God in the great congregations? S. Paul counts it a mercy, this "gathering together unto him;" much comfort in it, as in the coming of our Lord Jesus Christ, which is there joined with it. *Non omnes* I am sure we find it; all have not the privilege: we are out of God's favour the while, and he seems to have no delight in us, when he denies us at least to suspend the showing it, as he did there to David when he fled from

<small>Ps. cxlvii. 20.
2 Sam. xv. 25.
2 Thess. ii. 1.</small>

178 A SERMON ON ASCENSION DAY.

SERMON XXXVIII.
Absalom; a privilege, sure, all count it to have a place to serve God in together; there would not else be such contention for it, who should, and who should not.

But for that hill of hills, (3,) far exalted above all hills, to ascend thither, to be lift so high, that is a privilege without contradiction. It is given to none but "for whom it is prepared;" "few there are that find it;" it is merely "at our Father's good pleasure to give it;" "neither of him that wills, nor him that runs, but of God that shows mercy;" we have no other claim but mercy to it. Only, fear not (i.) for all that, says Christ; he ushers in the privilege so; and, (ii.) strive to enter too, says he, for all that; though the gate be strait, it is not impassable for them that strive and labour for it; and then, (iii.) too, admire his goodness, say we, who yet leaves ope the gate to enter to any penitent sinner that will strive and labour for it; who sets up a *si quis* in the market-place, sets it upon the doors and screens of our churches and chapels; sets his prophets, too, to proclaim and cry it, Who will "ascend," who will come and "stand up in his holy place," come serve him here a while, and reign with him for ever? This privilege, though all attain not to, is not such as any are absolutely excluded from; that no more enjoy it, is because they voluntarily exclude themselves: they shall not, because they will not take the pains; it is no decree against any, though a privilege for some.

Matt. xx. 23.
Matt. vii. 14.
Luke xii. 32.
[Rom. ix. 16.]
Luke xii. 32.

Such a one indeed it is, and a high one too; a high privilege (1,) to be sons and heirs to the Most High, can be no less; to be raised so to the tops of the hills, above all the nations of the world: "You only have I known of all the families of the earth." To be the only men that God knows, that he takes notice of in the world, to be a "kingly priesthood," "made kings and priests;"—this is high. And,

Amos iii. 2.

1 Pet. ii. 9.
Rev. i. 6.

High it is, too, (2,) to be admitted into his house and holy temple. Every one came not there, not all the Levites, not all the priests. A high favour it was, allowed to some only to enter there. Why, "the Lord loveth the gates of Sion more than all the dwellings of Jacob," says the Psalmist. All the high places and palaces of the earth are not in so high esteem with God as the very gates and ports of Sion; to be suffered but to peep in there is a higher honour, to be a door-keeper in the house of God a greater happiness, than to dwell in the most magnific buildings of the world. David, a king himself, had rather be there than anywhere. And he that shall consider the primitive zeal of Christians to these hills, how they never thought enough bestowed upon them; how often they frequented them; how they would not pass without going in and worshipping; how the pious and devout souls thought it a happiness to look that way, and a great comfort in the midst of their desolations and captivity,—cannot but confess they all thought high enough of the favour that God allowed them in receiving them into those hills and holy places.

{Sermon XXXVIII.}

A higher privilege yet it is to get up the other hill, to be admitted into heaven when all is done; so high, that Christ says "it is not his to give;" the Father hath reserved it to himself, and there is nothing higher situated than it. The very name of "hill," the phrase of the text, sufficiently shows, if it be a privilege, it is a high one; hills are the highest places of the earth; the Church is a "beacon upon a hill," every true disciple a light there at least. The houses of God used to be thought "high places" too, and so had in honour. And for heaven, it is styled "the everlasting hills." So to be admitted to the privilege of any of them must needs be a high one. {Matt. xx. 23.}

(3.) "High" and "holy" too, that is a third addition to the privilege. Many high privileges that are not so. Holy is the highest, most like to the Most High. To be saints, to be called to holiness, as S. Paul says we are; to be a holy nation, as S. Peter says; to be "priests," as you heard before; to have holiness engraved upon our foreheads, is to be holy persons; "every pot in Jerusalem" to be "holiness to the Lord," is a privilege, and a holy one too. {1 Pet. ii. 9.} {Zech. xiv. 21.}

To go up like saints to the hill of Sion, to keep holy-day there; to worship before the holy altars of the Lord of hosts; to drink and eat in holy vessels; to be part of his holy portion; to be made partakers of his holy word, and there praise the God of holiness in his holy congregation, is a holy honour that is done us. The highest privilege that wants this, the highest palace that is without this, is but the tents of ungodliness, and "they," says David, "will but make us

SERMON XXXVIII.

afraid." Let my privilege, O God, be holy, or I care for none; that is that must bring me to his holy hill, and to his dwelling; that hill in which he dwells amidst cherubims and seraphims, and all his host. Whither, thirdly, to ascend is the height of the holy privilege.

(3.) His holy heaven, that is the style; the "holy of holies," S. Paul calls it; the very seat of the most holy God, and holy angels, and holy saints. It cannot there sure be suspected to be the holy privilege, and the privilege of the holy only to come thither.

(4.) This holiness must needs make it to be admired too. An admirable privilege we told you it was; it is our fourth point now. And David, as if he had been all this while in a kind of swoon at the contemplation of it, breaks out now upon a sudden, with a "Who is he?" and what a thing is this to "ascend into the hill of the Lord," and to rise up in "his holy place!"

Indeed, we cannot sufficiently admire it, that God should raise up dust and ashes to such a height as to make it a co-heir with Christ, as to make a hill and holy place of it for himself to dwell in; *Ὦ Βάθος*, says the Apostle, "Oh the depth!" Who can find it out? who, who can reach it?

[Rom. xi. 33.]

That he should pitch his place and dwell among us, give us free access, liberty to come and go unto him, to approach him when we will, speak to him what we will, eat and drink with him when we will too,—what can be stranger? who can wonder at it enough? How terrible is this place! it put poor Jacob into a cold sweat to think of it before it was built. Will the Lord dwell on earth? Is it true? says Solomon; can it be so? Lord, what am I, says holy David, and my people, that we should but offer to it? Lord, what is it that we should be allowed to touch so holy ground with our unhallowed feet, look upon so holy a sight with our unholy eyes, that such a glow-worm as man should be set upon a hill?

Gen. xxviii. 17.

But above all, Lord, what is man, Lord, what is man, that thou shouldest so regard him as to advance him also into the holy hill of heaven too? Lord, what can we say, what can we say? Shall corruption inherit incorruption? dust, heaven? a worm creep so high? What! he that lost it for an apple, come thither after all? he in whom dwelleth no good thing be let stay there where none but good, and all good things are? He that is not worth the earth, worth naught but hell, be admitted heaven? Lord, what is man; or rather, what art thou, O Lord? How wonderful in mercies that thus privilegest the sons of men! Admirable it is; worth the whole course of your days to admire it in, and you can never enough. It will appear yet the more by the glory that accompanies it. It is a glorious privilege indeed, even admirable for its glory.

Even in all the senses we take the words it is (5) a glorious privilege: glorious to be saints, they are heirs of glory: glorious to be saints in churches; for the angels that are there to wait upon us, and carry up our prayers; for the beauty of holiness that is seated there; for the God of glory, whose presence is more glorious there. But it is without comparison to be saints in glory. Grace is the portion of saints; that is one ray of glory. The Church, "the house of God," is "the gate of heaven;" that is the entrance into glory. What, then, is heaven itself? what is it to enter there, into the very throne of "the King of glory?" "Lift up your heads, O ye gates; lift up your heads," and let us poor things in to see "the King of glory." "The hill of the Lord" can be no other than a hill of glory; "his holy place" is no less than the very place and seat of glory.

And being such, you cannot imagine it, (6,) but hard to come by; the very petty glories of the world are so. This is a hill of glory, hard to climb, difficult to ascend, craggy to pass up, steep to clamber, no plain campagnia to it; the broad, easy way, leads somewhither else. The way to this is "narrow;" it is rough and troublesome.

To be of the number of Christ's true, faithful servants, is no slight work: it is a fight, it is a race, it is a continual warfare; fastings, and watchings, and cold, and nakedness, and hunger, and thirst; bands, imprisonments, dangers, and distresses; ignominy, and reproach; afflictions, and persecutions, the world's hatred and our friends' neglect; all that we call hard or difficult is to be found in the way we are to go. A man cannot leave a lust, shake off bad company, quit a course of sin, enter upon a way of virtue, profess his religion, or stand to it, cannot ascend the spiritual hill, but he will meet some or other of these to contest and strive with. But, not only to ascend, but to stand there, as the word signifies; to continue at so high a pitch, to be constant in truth and piety, that will be hard indeed, and bring more difficulties to contrast with. And yet to rise up (to keep to that translation), that is, to rise up in the defence of holy ways, of our religion, is harder still; to blood it may come at last, but to sweat it comes presently—cold and hot sweats too—fears and travails, that is the least to be expected.

Nor is it easy, as it often proves, to gain places to serve God in. Temples are long in building; that of Jerusalem sixty-four years together. Great preparation there was by David and Solomon to that before, and no little to the rearing of the tabernacle. It was three hundred years and upward that Christianity was in the world before the Christians could get the privileges of sanctuaries and churches. The more ought we sure to value them, that we come so hardly by them. We would make more of the privilege, if we considered what pains and cost, and time they cost; how unhandsome religion looks without them; how hard it is to perform many of the holy offices where we want them; how hard it would be to keep religion in the minds of men, if all our churches should be made nests of owls and dragons, and beds of nettles and thistles. Yet I confess, it is hard, too, to enter into those holy places with the reverence that becomes them, to rise up holy there. Every one that comes into the church does not ascend; he leaves his soul too oft below, comes but in part; his body that gets up the hill, the mind lies grovelling in the valley, amongst his grounds and cattle. Nor may every one be said to rise up or "stand in his holy place," that stands or sits there in it, unless his thoughts rise there, unless his attention stands erect and steadfast up to heaven when he is there; he is indeed in the place, but he unhallows it; it is no longer holy in respect of him. He must ascend in heart and soul, raise up eyes and hands, voice and attention too, that can be properly said to " ascend into the hill of the Lord," or rise up " in his holy place." Which how hard it is, the very straggling of our own thoughts there will tell us; we need not go to the prophet to find a people that sit there as if they were God's people, and yet are not; that hear his word and stand not to it; that raise up their voices, and yet their hearts are still beneath: we can furnish ourselves with a number too great of such, enow to tell us how hard it is to "ascend into the hill of the Lord," and rise up " in his holy place," so few do it.

Sermon XXXVIII.

And if these two ascensions be so hard, what is the third! "the very righteous are scarcely saved." If by "any means I may," says S. Paul. Suppose he may not; he is afraid, at least, after all his preaching, he should "become a cast-away," fall short of the goal, miss the crown, come short of the top of the hill, of the holy place. So hard a thing is heaven; so clogged are the wings of our soul, so heavy and drossy are our spirits, and our earth so earthy, that it is hard to ascend so high. We feel we find it; and they but deceive themselves that think it is but running a leap into heaven, a business to be done wholly or easily upon our death-beds, when we can nor stir nor raise up ourselves or our heads. Who shall ascend? Whatever question it is, it is most certainly an assertion of difficulty. Who shall ascend? no man can read it, but he will read hardness in the ascending.

1 Pet. iv. 18.
1 Cor. ix. 27.

And yet it would be harder but for the last consideration of the words, that it is a kind of admiration of the prophet's at the foresight of Christ's ascension; he, in his spirit, foresaw his Saviour climb this hill, and wondered at it. From his ascending, some of the difficulty is abated: he has led the way, traced a path, opened a door into heaven unto all believers; so we used to sing in the *Te Deum*. I need not tell you he has ascended in all the senses of the words : no height of holiness but he has, none frequenter in the temple than he was, none in heaven till he came thither; he the first that made our dull earth ascend so high. He rose and ascended up on high, without the least help of metaphor or figure; rose from the grave, ascended into the hill, ascended thence " into the hill of the Lord," " stands there at his right hand;" S. Stephen saw him so. Never said prophet any thing that more punctually fell out than this; he may well admire it, and so may we.

Acts vii. 55.

Yea, and praise him too. To him we owe all our ascensions, all the height and ascensions of our spirits in grace and goodness, all our privileges to worship him in holy places, all our assurances and hopes of heaven, and the possession of it. His rising raises us; his ascending makes us ascend. He the only prime singular one, we only as parts and members of him.

What is then left us to do? What for all this privilege? Why, if Christ's grace, and God's worship, and heaven itself be such privileges, I hope we will not be so silly to forego them, or betray them. Seeing they be so high ones, we cannot be so unworthy now to do any thing beneath them, any base or unworthy thing. Being holy ones too, we will not be so profane to pollute ourselves or them with lusts and sacrileges. Being so admirable privileges all, we cannot certainly but adore God's mercy in them. Being glorious ones too, we must glorify him for them, count all things dross and dung in comparison of them. Being yet hard to come by, the more need we have to labour for them, set all our powers, make it all our work to get them; to get grace and worship, and glory, to "ascend the hill" and "holy place" with all holiness, as the way to glory. In a word, seeing all this privilege comes by Christ, it is him we are to thank and serve, and worship upon his own hill, and in his own holy place, till the time come, till we ascend in glory. And yet there is something more behind; the way to this hill, the conditions required to obtain this privilege, what we are to perform that we may obtain it. To have "clean hands," and "pure hearts," "minds not lift up to vanity," and "mouths that will not swear to deceive our neighbour." For he only "shall ascend into the hill of the Lord," he only shall rise up "in his holy place;" he only is a true believer, he only truly worships God when he comes to church to worship, he only shall go to heaven that hath clean hands, &c.

THE FIRST SERMON

UPON

WHITSUNDAY.

S. JOHN iii. 8.

The wind bloweth where it listeth, and thou hearest the sound thereof, but canst not tell whence it cometh, nor whither it goeth: so is every one that is born of the Spirit.

"THE wind bloweth;" and this day it blew to purpose. "A mighty rushing wind" there was that this day "filled the house" where the disciples were assembled. And it blew truly "where it listed," when it blew only in that chamber where they were. And the sound of it was heard sufficiently when "Parthians, and Medes, and Elamites, the dwellers in Mesopotamia, and in Judea, in Cappadocia, Pontus, and Asia, Phrygia, and Pamphylia, in Egypt, and in the parts of Libya about Cyrene, and strangers of Rome, Jews and proselytes, Cretes and Arabians," all of them this day heard it framed into articulate voices, into tongues as many and divers as the countries they came from. Yet could not any of them tell whence this wind blew, whence these sounds came, for "they were all amazed, and in doubt, saying one to another, What meaneth this?" Nor could the disciples themselves, but in general, that from heaven it came, nor whither it went when it retired from them.

_{SERMON XXXIX.}

_{Acts ii. 2.}

_{Acts ii. 12.}

This day then was this text fulfilled in your ears, oh happy disciples! Nicodemus might to-day, by experiment, understand what in this chapter he could not apprehend, the "wind" and "Spirit" both together, and feel the workings

SERMON XXXIX. of them both; there both in one descent together, though here he did not when they were put in one word together; where whether *Spiritus ventus*, or *Spiritus Spiritus*, both πνεύματα, were understood, expositors have disputed, and it stands yet upon the question. The ancients restrained the words to the Holy Spirit, and translate it *Spiritus*; the modern expositors to the wind, and translate it *ventus*.

To do both right we shall join both senses, understand the words as a similitude made by our blessed Saviour to instruct both Nicodemus and us in the ways of the Spirit, and in the knowledge of the spiritual regeneration, by the likeness of the wind.

So two similes there will be in the text. *Sicut ventus sic Spiritus*, and *Sicut Spiritus sic spiritualis*.

The first similitude is between the wind and the Spirit.

The second between the Spirit and the spiritual man, or "him that is born of the Spirit."

In the similitude betwixt the wind and the Spirit, we shall observe,—

I. The nature of them both in πνεῦμα, breath, or wind, or spirit; it signifies them all.

II. The power and operation both of the one and of the other; they blow, both of them, where they list.

III. The plainness of their sounds: "thou hearest the sound thereof;" both of them easy enough to be heard.

IV. The obscurity, yet, of both their motions: ye know of neither of them, whence they come, or whither they go.

According to these four points will the second similitude be extended too. "He that is born of the Spirit" will be like the Spirit in all four. In his nature, in his operations, in his plainness in some particulars, and his obscurity in others. "So is every one that is born of the Spirit."

But to tell you fully the true condition of him "that is born of the Spirit," I must tell you first the nature, the operations, and the properties of the Spirit. And to tell you the nature, the operations, and the properties of the Spirit, I must show you also those of the wind; that so by the more perfect discovery of them we may the more perfectly admire them, and adore and magnify him to-day, who this day gave us both the occasion and means to hear and understand them.

I. I begin now to compare the nature of the wind and Spirit. Πνεῦμα the word is, and may be translated both. It is so in the text. Some are for *ventus*, some for *Spiritus:* breath they are both. The one the breath of heaven, the other of the air; the one, God's; the other, the world's.

SERMON XXXIX.

Indeed, the wind is a kind of breath or spirit, but a spirit, in the nicest and subtilest sense, it is not. A body it is, and not a spirit; yet the nighest thing it is we have to liken the Spirit to, as near a simile as we can find for it; but the Spirit of the day is so a spirit as in no sort a body. Τὸ Πνεῦμα, with an article and an emphasis, a Spirit above all spirits, the prime Spirit; a Spirit by essence, an essential Spirit, or essentially a Spirit; a Spirit by procession, the Spirit proceeding: personally that Spirit which "proceedeth from the Father," and "from the Son," which was this day breathed first of all solemnly into the world to quicken it to a heavenly life. *Spiritus Dei,* and *Spiritus Deus,* the Spirit of God, and the Spirit which is God, and the only Spirit that can bring us all to God.

John xv. 26.
John xvi. 7.

But this great nature is too great to comprehend, too infinite to pursue. Nor can the simile reach it; it falls short; and so must I and you when we have done our utmost. It is an easier project for us both to fall upon the power and operations of it, though I foresee we shall often there be at a stand too. Yet, to help ourselves as well as we can, we will consider the operations; first by themselves, then by their effects, and then, thirdly, by their course and compass. By themselves first.

II. (i.) The wind, you hear, blows, and so the Spirit blows. Yet the Spirit is not, blows not neither, like every wind. There are whirlwinds that make a horrid noise, that whirl every way about, and turn the world up topsy-turvy, upside down; the wind that is but *spiritus*, a direct and orderly breathing, does not so. *Spiritus vertiginis* is but *vertigo spiritus,* the spirit of giddiness that the Prophet speaks of, is but the *vertigo,* or turning of the brain,—an abuse of the name, not a spirit, but a mere humour that makes us giddy,— has made this nation so too long.

Isa. xix.14.

(ii.) Blustering and stormy winds there are, ἄνεμοι rather than πνεύματα, *graves violento flamine venti;* but this no such.

SERMON XXXIX.

Spiritus rather than *ventus*, ours is here; a calm and peaceable one, a breath rather than a wind; a Spirit proceeding from the God of peace, bequeathed and sent us by the Prince of peace; so still and even that it did not so much as disorder a wreath of that holy flame which this day encircled the heads of the disciples, but let that heavenly fire sit quietly upon them.

Acts ii. 3.

(iii.) Nor is it of this wind to which this Spirit is compared said *flat* here, but *spirat*, not said to blow by a word that signifies commonly only the ordinary and natural blowing. All is supernatural here. It is neither whirling, we told you first; nor blustering, we said secondly; nor puffing wind, we tell you now: it is a meek, an humble Spirit; from the beginning it "moved upon the waters," but did not swell them into waves or billows, as natural winds commonly do; nor does it now; but only guides all our waters, passions, and motions, into their proper place with sweetness and order, which is merely a supernatural work.

Gen. i. 2.

(iv.) And yet, as soft and smooth as it blows, it is the "Spirit of power," a "mighty wind;" and rush in it does, oft-times, at first with a little sudden and eager violence; yet two syllables, one single *fiat*, and all is done. Strange things, we know, are done by a very little wind; and that one word of this one Spirit made the world out of nothing, and can as easily make nothing of the world. He can remove the greatest rocks and mountains, not only with the breath of his displeasure, but of his pleasure too, his easiest breath. He blew the gods of the heathen out of their thrones, and spake all their oracles dumb; blew all their spirits in a moment thence, and yet the voice of his breathing was scarce heard. He does so still, throws down all the holds and fortresses of the devil in us *sine strepitu*, without noise. Some rushing mighty wind sometimes may go before it to rouse our dulness and awake us, but the Spirit is not there. Some earthquake of servile fear may shake us first, and affright us from some ill action; but the Spirit is not there. Some fire or fiery trial may first burn or scorch us, and thereby make us look about us, or some kinder fire warm us into a better temper than formerly we were in; but the Spirit is not there neither. But when these outward dispensations have suf-

Acts ii. 2.

ficiently disposed us to attention, then comes the "still small voice," and there is the Spirit that silently glides into our souls as the small dew into a fleece of wool. Such a still, smooth, sweet breath of wind is the true resemblance of the Spirit, and when this comes it works wonders; that minds me of the next particular—the effects of both the "wind" and "Spirit."

SERMON XXXIX.
1 Kings xix. 12.

Two especial effects the "wind" has—to purify and to refresh. These are the prime effects of the Spirit too.

(1.) When the Holy Spirit enters into the heart it purifies and cleanses it from all pollution. This made David pray, "Create in me, O Lord, a clean heart." Yea, but how, O blessed prophet? Why, as it follows, "by renewing a right spirit within me." That is the way to make him clean. No way but that—but that will. For the Spirit is compared to "fire," and that purifies; to "water," and that cleanses; and here to "wind," and that blows away all the chaff and dust that is either in us or about us.

Ps. li. 10.

Acts ii. 3.
John iv. 10.

(2.) The Spirit refreshes, too. It "renews the face of the earth;" it giveth "rest" and quiet; it "upholds" and establishes the faint and decaying spirit; it refreshes us in our bonds, and sets us free; it comforts us in all distresses, for he is ὁ Παράκλητος, "the Comforter," that should come into the world.

Ps. civ. 30.
Isa. lxiii. 14.
Ps. li. 12.
Rom. viii. 15.
John xiv. 26.

(3.) Nay, I may add one thing more. It not only refreshes us when we are faint and weary, and almost dying, but it revives us even when we are dead, is a "quickening Spirit." Like that wind the naturalist tells us of, which in the spring time quickens the dull dead earth into herbs and flowers. Such a wind is this Spirit, that gives life to every one that comes into the world; for he is the "Spirit of Life."

John vi. 63.

Rom. viii. 2.

But that which adds somewhat still to the fuller glory of these effects, and must not be passed without a note, is, that it is Spirit still—this wind blows still. For, however the winds are not always in a noise and bustle, yet some spirit of air there is that moves in the deepest stillness. *Spiritus* there is always, though not *ventus;* some tender breeze, though no gale of wind, there is always stirring. And if there were not continually some such sweet breathings of the Holy Spirit upon us, when those strong and louder blasts seem to be lulled asleep, we were but dead men, and might sleep for ever; but such there are, and we live by them.

I might, but I will not, add any more to the effects either of the wind or of the Spirit. I pass on to their course and compass, to show you how far their effects and powers reach. "The wind bloweth where it listeth," and the "Spirit where he willeth."

And here I must tell you, ὅπου θέλει, *ubi vult*, is a large circuit. *Ubi* is "where," and *ubi* is "when," and *vult* is what you will, especially when it is his who "worketh all things according to the counsel of his will." So that it will be no stretching to say either of the wind, or of the Spirit, that it bloweth (1) where it lists, and (2) how it lists, and (3) as much as it lists, and (4) on whom it lists, and (5) when it lists.

(1.) The wind blows where it lists, on this side or on that side, or on any side, anywhere, and everywhere. The Spirit does so too, only with more propriety to *ubi vult*, doing out of the liberty of its own will, what the wind only does out of the subtilty of its nature. No place lies exempted from the power of his will. It finds S. Paul and Silas in the prison, and blows up the organs of their voices into songs and hymns. It finds Manasseh in the dungeon, blows there with his wind, and the waters flow out of his eyes. It finds S. Matthew at the receipt of custom, and blows him out of a publican into an Apostle. It blows S. Peter and S. Andrew out of their boat to the stern of the Church of Christ. He blows upon some in their journey, as upon S. Paul; upon others at home, as upon Cornelius; upon one in the bed, upon another at the mill, upon Jonas in the whale's belly. No place beyond his compass, not the isles of the Gentiles, not the land of Uz, not the deserts of Arabia. Here and there, even amongst them, he blows some into his kingdom. In a word, no chamber so secret, but it can get into; no place so remote, but it can reach; none so private, but it can find; none so strong, but it can break through; none so deep, but it can fathom; none so high, but it can scale; no place at all, but it can come into; and none so bad, but some way or other it will vouchsafe to visit. It makes holy David cry out as in an ecstasy, "Whither shall I go then from thy Spirit? or whither shall I go then from thy presence? If I climb up into heaven, thou art there; if I go down to hell, thou art there also. If I take the wings of the morning, and remain in the uttermost parts of the earth, even there also shall thy hand lead me, and thy right hand shall hold me." No place, it seems, in heaven, or earth, or sea, or hell itself, can hold him out.

Nor can any hold him to this or that way of working neither; for he bloweth (2) how he lists; sometimes louder, sometimes softer, sometimes after this manner, sometimes after that. He raises new inclinations, or he cherishes the old; he changes the tempers of men or disposes them; he removes opportunities of doing ill, or he propounds opportunities of doing good; he scares us with threats or allures us with promises; he drives us with judgments, or he draws us with mercies; he inflames us within, or he moves us from without, which way soever it pleases him. No wind so various in its blowing. Different ways he has to deal with divers men: and "diversities of gifts" he has for them too, 1Cor.xii.5. "differences of administrations, diversities of operations." To one he gives the "word of wisdom," to another the "word of knowledge," to another "faith," to another the "gift of healing," to another the "working of miracles," to another "prophecy," to another "discerning of spirits," to another "divers kinds of tongues," to another the "interpretation of tongues," all from the Spirit, says the Apostle, in the fore-cited chapter. Nor was this only for those times. He still breathes diversities of gifts and graces, as he pleases. On some, sanctifying graces; on others, edifying; on others both. To some he gives a cheerful, to others a sad spirit; to some a kind of holy lightness; to others a religious gravity; to one a power wholly to quit the world; to another, power to stand holy in it; to one, an ability to rule, to another a readiness to obey; to one courage, to another patience, to a third temperance, and so to others other graces, as he thinks fittest.

(3.) Yet of these gifts, to some more, to some less, not to all alike; nay, not to the same person always alike neither, but (3) as much only as this Spirit will. All have not faith alike, nor hope alike, nor charity alike, nor courage alike, nor patience alike; neither all virtues, nor any virtues all alike.

SERMON XXXIX.

2 Kings ii. 9.

2 Kings ii. 21.
2 Kings iii. 15.

2 Cor. xii. 2.
2 Cor. xii. 7.

2 Cor. xii. 9.

Rom. xi. 35.
Rom. ix. 18.

Upon some the "abundance" of the Spirit dwells, upon others he breathes only; some have had ecstasies, others but only moderate breathings. Elijah had abundance of the Spirit, yet Elisha has it "doubled." And yet this very same Elisha, that presently upon it divides Jordan with the wind of a mantle, and restores waters to their sweetness, and earth to its fruitfulness by a cruse of salt, in but the very next chapter cannot so much as prophesy without a minstrel, is not so much as in a disposition to receive this divine Spirit, without the help of an instrument of music to rally his spirits into harmony and order. S. Paul, who was but even now "caught up into the third heavens," feels by-and-by such a "thorn in the flesh," that of all that great extraordinary proportion, he has no more left him than a poor pittance—a mere sufficiency.

(4.) And the person is as much in his own power as the measure is. He blows not only what, but upon whom, he will. He is no man's debtor; "he will have mercy upon whom he will have mercy." What! if he to show his justice will no longer breathe upon some persons who have so long despised his mercy, and yet to make known the riches of his glory, will yet breathe somewhat longer upon others that, for aught we know, may have deserved as little, who can complain, seeing he blows sufficiently upon all, and is not obliged either in justice or mercy to do more, but justly may do all, where or upon whom he will.

One *ubi* there is behind. He is free also for his own time; for he (5) bloweth when he listeth. Upon some in the womb, as upon S. John Baptist; upon others in the cradle; upon some in their childhood, upon others in their youth, upon others not till grey hairs cover them. In the morning, at the third, the sixth, the ninth hour, in the evening, in the still of night, in our sleep, and when we are awake, are all his times as he pleases to make them or dispose them. In prosperity, in adversity, in the midst of tears, or in the midst of smiles, in health, in sickness, whensoever it pleases him. He called Samuel in his childhood, David in his youth, S. Paul in his manhood, Manasseh in his age, and that which without contradiction shows the unlimitedness of his power —the thief upon the cross.

I shall dismiss this point, if you please, to take home with you these corollaries or lessons hence.

(1.) If "the Spirit bloweth where it listeth," we are not certainly to exclude any place or nation from these blessed gales, or with the Donatists to confine him to any corner of the world, or to the Church or congregation we are of, as if he could blow no where else. Learn charity.

(2.) If "the Spirit bloweth how he listeth," we do but show our folly to prescribe him his way. He knows what best he has to do, how best to manage us to salvation. Learn discretion.

(3.) If it be as much, too, only as he lists, it is not sure our merit or desert if we have more of him than others, nor perhaps their demerit always who have less. Whatever it is, it is more than we deserve, both they and we. Let that suffice to humble us and make us thankful. Learn humility.

(4.) If it be only upon whom he pleases, it is certainly sometimes upon some we know not. So we have no reason to pass a censure upon any man's soul. Learn to think well of all.

And so much the rather in that (5) he bloweth when he will. If he has not already, he may hereafter breathe upon him or her thou doubtest most. If thou perhaps thyself feelest him not within thee now, thou mayest ere long. Learn hence to despair neither of thyself nor any one else.

In a word, seeing all his actions are so free, all his blessings and all the ways of them so wholly in his own breast, let us all resign up all our wills to his, and submit them wholly to his pleasure for time and place and manner and measure, and bid him do with us what he pleases.

Yet for all this, would we not now willingly know somewhat of these mysterious and stupendous operations? There is somewhat, I confess, towards it in the next point, and I shall show you it, that though you cannot perfectly discern the motions of the Spirit, you may yet hear the sound thereof; that is the third general of the text, the plainness of the sound, both of the wind and of the Spirit, easy enough both of them to be heard. "And thou hearest the sound thereof."

SERMON XXXIX. III. For the "wind," I need not tell you it, it speaks loud enough sometimes to wake the drowsiest sleeper; though we cannot see it we can hear it. And so we may the Spirit too, as invisible as he is. Now, two sounds there are of the Spirit—an outward and an inward.

They that heard the Patriarchs, the Prophets, and Apostles preach, they heard the outward; so in S. Stephen's case the Acts vi. 10. Jews are said "to resist the Spirit by which he spake." They that now hear them read or preached, they still hear Matt. x. 20. the sound of the Spirit. For so Christ tells us, "it is not they," the Prophets and the Apostles, that speak, "but the Spirit that speaketh in them."

The inward sound of the Spirit is to be heard too. When thou perceivest pious and godly motions rise within thee; when at any time good desires come upon thee; when holy resolutions spring up within thy bosom; when thou feelest thy soul overspread with heavenly light, and the Divine truth preaching to thine understanding, then thou hearest the inward sound, then this Holy Spirit begins to discourse and converse with thee. And truly, though none of these be properly sounds, but only metaphorical, yet they are plain expressions of the Spirit, and may well go for the sounds of it to discern it by. Yet, that you may not mistake false sounds for true ones, if you recollect what has been spoken scatteredly already in the discourse, of the nature, operations and effects of the Spirit, you will easily find the true ones to be these.

If the motion that at any time within us be pure and heavenly, calm and gentle, if it purify our hearts, if it cleanse our affections, if it penetrate the bones and marrow, if it cool the fevers of our lusts, if it blow out the coals of our wrath; if it blow down the fortresses of sin, if it blow up good resolutions, if it blow away the dust that hangs too often upon our good actions, the interests and by-respects, if it refresh the wounded spirit, if it warm us with holy flames; if it quicken us to all obedience to God and man; Gal. v. 22, 23. if it cause the "fruits of the Spirit" the Apostle speaks of, to bud up in us, then it is doubtless from this Spirit, and they are all as so many several kinds of sounds that loudly speak his being and breathing in us. Whatever motion, sound, or language is not consonant to one or other of these, SERMON XXXIX. let men talk of the Spirit what they will, they are not of the Spirit in the text, nor does it make them spiritual men that have it.

Thus far our knowledge of the Spirit extends; these are the sounds it makes within and without us. But our ignorance of it extends further. More of it there is that we know not, than that we know; for notwithstanding all this deciphering of the nature, effects, and sound of the "wind" or "Spirit," the obscurity of the course it takes and the motion it moves in is far greater; "for thou canst not tell whence it cometh, nor whither it goeth." Nor wind nor Spirit.

IV. For the "wind" first. They are but general notions we entertain of it. "God brings the winds out of his treasure," says the Psalmist. Out of those hidden chambers they come, but where those chambers are we cannot tell. On a sudden they arise, ere we are aware, and away they go; and who can follow them? Who can trace their steps, or track their way, or overtake them in their lodging at night or tell us where it is? Ps. cxxxv. 7.

Ask philosophy, and let that answer you, Whence is it that the winds arise? It answers you, From a thin and airy vapour drawn up out of the earth towards the middle region of the air, but repercust, or beaten back, by the grossness of some intervening cloud, which drives it down obliquely with that violence we hear and feel. This, or something as obscure, is all the knowledge we can get of it. For, ask now, Where that vapour rose? it cannot tell. Which way it went? it knows it not. In what part of heaven it first became a wind? it cannot point it out. What is become of it, now it is gone? it resolves you not. Into what part of the world it is retired when all is still? it cannot answer you.

We use to say, from the east, or from the west, from the north, or from the south; yet so uncertain must we needs confess the first point of their motion, and so many points do they vary ere they come at us, and so quickly are they gone by us, that the wisest of us all cannot tell exactly either whence they were, or whither they will.

But yet again, if it be no more than such a kind of wind

SERMON XXXIX. as is in the text, not *ventus* but *spiritus*,—a mere breath of wind or air,—that undoubtedly we know not whence it comes or whither it goes.

And yet the ways of the Spirit are more unsearchable: we know not anything at all of his eternal procession—it was before any time we can imagine. We know nothing of his course or motion all that infinite while before the world began. We understand nothing distinctly of it ever since. His motions are so intricate, so various, and so infinite, we cannot comprehend them. The dispositions, the gifts, the graces he works daily in us, we know not how they rise, or how they spread, or how they vanish. Descend we a little to particulars.

We are sometimes moved, we feel, by the words of the preacher, by the reading of a chapter, by a devout book or a godly story, and yet we know not why more now than at another time; why at this time by a little touch and not before by long persuasions; why sometimes by weak and slender, at other times not by any means; why to virtue, ofttimes contrary to our former natures and dispositions, without any occasion given, all sensible interests and motives clear against it, whilst to another, more easy and kindly to us, we cannot be wrought. Nor know we what becomes of any of those holy motions when they depart, or we thrust them from us.

But if we should go about to dive into those hidden secrets of his counsel, why he should blow upon us, and not upon others as good as we; why upon the Jews so fully, upon all the world besides so sparingly; why he should take this woman from the mill, and not the other that works by her; why of two in the same bed he should refuse the one and choose the other; why he should by the same words and motions to two several men of the same tempers and education, and at that time, as near as can be conjectured, in the same way and disposition, breathe effectually upon the one and not the other, save this man presently and leave the other to himself:—we are here wholly at a loss; they are mysteries of which we can say neither whence it is, nor whither it tends, but only to the glory of his grace, and because it so pleases thee, O blessed Spirit.

And seeing now we have told you all we can of *sic Spiritus*, of the first similitude,—the similitude betwixt the wind and the Spirit,—let us now see what we can make of *sic Spiritu natus*, of the second similitude betwixt the Spirit and every one that is "born" of it: "So is every," &c.

SERMON XXXIX.

Second General. That "he that is born of the Spirit" should be some way like it is no wonder, because he that is begotten may well be like him that begets, he that is born like her that bore him. But how he comes either to be so begotten or born, or be so like, that may easily put us to a stand, yet that too will come in as one part of the similitude. For four points of likeness we shall observe between the Spirit and him that is born of it, as we did before between the wind and the Spirit itself. Like they are in their natures, in their operations, in their sounds, and in their motions, in the evidence of those and the obscurity of these.

1. They are like in nature first. The Spirit spiritual and heavenly, and so is he that is born of it. He breathes nothing but heaven, speaks nothing else, lives there, his "conversation" wholly there, "his affections all upon things above," his fashion not according to this world at all; his face, his eyes, his hands, his feet, his ways look thither all. He is so like him that he is now perfectly another thing than what he was before; new soul, new understanding, new will, new affections, new all, body and all; that framed into new obedience, quickened to a new life, a mere new creature every way; nothing of earth or flesh, but all spirit now. You shall see the likeness of his nature plainer in the second resemblance—the likeness of his actions and operations to those of the Spirit.

Phil. iii. 20.
[Col. iii. 2.]

2. The operations of the Spirit we told you, (1,) were calm and peaceable, and so are his who is born of the Spirit. "Love, joy, peace, long-suffering, gentleness, goodness, faith, meekness, temperance,—these are the fruits of the Spirit," and he that has the Spirit has all these; he that has not, is none of his.

Gal. v. 22.

The effects (2,) of the Spirit are purifying, refreshing, and quickening. And he that has this Spirit, as well as "he that has this hope" the Apostle speaks of, (i.) "purifies himself" from all uncleanness both of flesh and spirit;

[1 John iii. 3.]

SERMON XXXIX. then (ii.) refreshes and comforts others, all that need it; and (iii.) brings forth also all good fruits, is fruitful in good works; they mistake sadly that think themselves or others spiritual men without them.

3. And yet the strangest operation is behind. "The Spirit bloweth where it listeth." And can we make the Spirit and spiritual man agree here too? Let us try a little. Two things there are in it: a power and a liberty of blowing. It is evident there must be power to do anything everywhere, and as evident there must be liberty to do everything anywhere. And both in power and liberty we shall find them like; and first in power.

The "Spirit" is a Spirit of power; he that is born of it is a man of power. An "host of men cannot so much as make him afraid." Sin itself cannot overcome him; "he that is born of the Spirit he sinneth not." He is able, with Samson, to break all the cords of it, to smite all such Philistines before him, when this Spirit comes upon him. "Nor death, nor life, nor angels, nor principalities, nor powers, nor things present, nor things to come, nor height, nor depth, nor any other creature" can overcome him. Over all these he is more than conqueror. Those things which before we were regenerate seemed impossible, when we are once born again are light and easy; we can do anything then through his Spirit that dwelleth in us. Stablish us once with this free Spirit, and it is not cold or nakedness, hunger or thirst, wearisome journeys, or dangerous shipwrecks, stripes or imprisonments, racks or gibbets, fire or fagot, that can force us from our hold, or overpower us. This very Spirit upholds us in all our pains, and at length blows away everything that troubles or offends us.

Ps. xxvii.2.
1 John v. 18.

Rom. viii. 38.

Nor is this "Spirit" only a Spirit of power, but of liberty also, and "where the Spirit is, there there is liberty," says S. Paul; that is, he that has it is free too. Free he is (1) from the bondage of Moses' law, "redeemed" from under that. Free (2) though not from the obligations yet from the rigours of the moral law. Free (3) from sin, made free from that, from the dominion of it. Free (4) from the captivity of the devil, recovered out of his snares. Free, lastly, from the dominion of death; the sting of it is lost, the victory

2 Cor. iii. 17.
Gal. iv. 5,6.
Gal. iii. 13.
Rom. vii. 6.
Rom. vi.18.
2 Tim. ii. 26.
1 Cor. xv. 55.

of it gone. So is every one free that is born of the Spirit. Well may now his fame go out into all the world and his name into all the corners of the earth. And indeed, it does so in the next words, in the next point of the similitude, "Thou hearest the sound thereof." Evident it is, and evident it is to any; heard it may be, and any one may hear it; thou, and thou, and thou, every thou that will.

Evident it is, first. The Spirit is not a fancy, nor are the operations of it so neither. The Spirit, though it cannot be seen itself, yet something there is of it that may be heard; heard, somewhat of it, by the hearing of the ear; the effects not always in the understanding only; these very ears we carry are oft refreshed with the sound of it; our very senses sensible of the strength and power of it. And he that tells us of grace or religion all within, of so serving God in the Spirit, that neither our own nor other bodies are the better for it, or show any signs of it, has turned his religion and devotion into air and imagination, and not to Spirit. By his fruits you shall know as well the spiritual man as the prophet.

Nor has he, secondly, one peculiar ear-mark, one tone and canting dialect to discern him by. He that is born of the Spirit is a free and noble and generous spirit, uses a language that every body may understand. It is not the mystery of the Spirit, but the mystery of iniquity that thus envelopes itself in a private and affected phrase, which sounds, it is to be feared, the spirit of schism, singularity, and rebellion, and not of love and peace. And yet as plain a sound as the Spirit's is, it is not, lastly, without some obscurity, but that is not of the sound; that is plain and open; but of the motion and course, of which we may have leave to be ignorant, and in many things can be no other. That is the last point wherein the Spirit and spiritual man are alike. Thou canst no more tell whence or whither those great things the regenerate man acts are, than whence the wind or Spirit comes, or whither it goes.

4. But that so it is the amazements and doubts that this day possessed those who were the witnesses of the wonders of this day's work, and their several judgments and conjectures concerning the Apostles this day filled with this Holy Spirit, will make it without question. Some said, "What

Sermon XXXIX.
Acts ii. 12, 13.
Acts xxvi. 24.
1 Cor. iv. 13.
2 Cor. vi. 9, 10.
1 Cor. ii. 14.

meaneth this? Others said mocking, These men are full of new wine;" all were "amazed and in doubt." The Apostles seemed such strange things to them now, since the Holy Ghost had fallen upon them, that they knew not now what to make of them, or of anything they did. In the progress afterward of their lives and courses they were as little understood as much misconstrued by the world. They were thought fools and madmen, when most wise and sober; condemned for wicked when they were most innocent, "reckoned the scum and offscouring of the world," when they were the treasures and jewels of it; judged as dying, when they only truly lived; accounted sorrowful, yet were always rejoicing; esteemed poor, yet so far from being so that they made many rich; thought to have nothing, and yet possessed all things. So it was then, so it always was, so it ever will be. The world will never, never can conceive the nature and way of him that is "born of the Spirit." We know not what to make even of his γεγεννημένος in the text, whether to read it "born" or "begotten," for it is both; and how he should be both by the same Spirit, or how the same Spirit should be both father and mother to him, we cannot tell. How he is begotten by the Spirit; how he is new born; the ways of his birth, the ways of his life, the way of his death; how he is wrought, and formed, and moulded out of his old, stiff, stubborn temper into mildness and softness; how the old man is mortified in all his members; how the new man rises and grows in all his parts; how he resists so many strong temptations; how he can so cheerfully renounce the world; how he can so wholly deny himself; how he can so merrily pursue a troublesome and despised virtue; why he should do all this, when there appears nothing but trouble, sorrow, and disadvantage by it, are all mysteries so obscure and dark that night itself is midday to them. Nor is it less to see with what calmness and contentedness he passes hence through pains and tortures, nor can we conceive the glory and happiness that attends him. Thus is the spiritual hero's life and death a mystery, so far above the apprehension of dull-eyed earth, that it knows no more of its course or motion than it does of the winds, neither what it is, nor whence it comes, nor whither it goes.

But, after all these mysteries, I end in plainness. It is a [Sermon XXXIX.] day, indeed, as well as a text of mysteries and wonders; but both day, and text, and wind, and Spirit will be all satisfied if they can leave these plain lessons upon our spirits.

That (1) we now get us up with Elijah, "to the mount of God," get us often up to his holy places to expect this holy wind and spirit. [1 Kings xix. 11, 13.] (2.) That there we wrap our faces in our mantles as he did his in his, cover them with all reverence and humility to receive him. That (3) we go out with him too, and stand in the entry of our caves, every one in his place ready to worship and adore him when he comes. That (4) we there listen carefully to the sound he makes as he passes by, attentively to hear his voice, and know his will, and do his pleasure. That (5) we take the "wings of the morning," as holy David speaks, our earliest devotions and prayers, to convey us to his presence, that he may blow and breathe upon us, and we daily find and feel him purifying, quickening, and refreshing us, and every day more and more drawing nearer to us, or us nearer to himself. [Psalm cxxxix. 9.] And then no matter whether we know whence he comes or whither he goes, so he thus take us with him when he comes, and carry us thither with him when he goes where he eternally with the Father and the Son resides in glory.

Even so, O blessed and eternal Spirit, blow upon us, and this day keep thy festival among us for Jesus Christ his sake, to whom with the Father and thyself be all our wonder and admiration, all worship and adoration, all our praise and glory, from this day for ever. *Amen.*

THE SECOND SERMON

UPON

WHITSUNDAY.

S. JOHN xvi. 13.

Howbeit when he, the Spirit of truth, is come, he will guide you into all truth.

SERMON XL.

AND of such a Spirit never had the world more need than now; never more need of one to guide us into all truth than at this time, wherein we are pestered and surrounded all with error, with all sorts of error; never more need that "the Spirit of truth" should come to guide us than now, when there are so many spirits up and abroad that men know not which to follow. "Come, Holy Ghost, eternal God," never fitter to be sung than now.

For, by the face of our hemisphere, we may seem either to have lost him quite, or with those in S. Peter, we may [2 Pet. iii. 4.] ask, Where is the promise of his coming? When he is come indeed, he will guide us into all truth, yea, but when is that? When comes he?

Why, this day he came; this day was this Scripture fulfilled; this day this promise made good. The Spirit of truth came down from heaven upon the Apostles this day, so that from this day forward they spake all tongues and truths, who before were both ignorant of the one and could not bear many of the other.

Well, but the Apostles are dead, and all the disciples that could pretend to those gifts and prerogatives are dead, and we neither speak with tongues by the Spirit, nor understand all truths any of us, nor can yet hear of any that do. Is his promise then utterly come to an end for evermore? Certainly either come he is not, or lead us he does not, or into truth he does not, or into but a little, and that but very few of us; or we at this end of the world have no part or portion in his coming: something or other there is, some reason or other to be given why this wind, this Spirit, does not blow upon us.

That he is come, this day of Pentecost plainly tells us; that he is come not to go again, Christ's own promise that he should "abide with us for ever" does assure us; that to us too it is he comes, though not visibly, as this day, yet invisibly every day,—which is as much for truth, though not for tongues,—S. Peter tells us in his sermon this day out of the prophet Joel, that the "Spirit is to be poured upon all flesh," so upon ours too; and the Spirit for his part is always ready, ever and anon calling us to "come." So that the fault will lie upon ourselves, not the Spirit, that he guides us not into all truth.

SERMON XI.

John xiv. 16.

Acts ii. 17.

Rev. xxii. 17.

The truth is, men are not disposed as they should be. He that looks into their ways and pursuits after truth may see it without spectacles. Other spirits are set up, new lights advanced, private spirits preferred, all the people are become leaders, every man thinks himself of age to answer for himself, and to guide himself, so that there is either nobody to be guided—all the Lord's people being kings and priests and prophets—or else nobody will be, but according to their own fancies, prejudices, interests, and humours. This is the true posture, the very face of religion now-a-days, and the true reason that this Spirit of truth ceases to guide them into truth: for, he leads none but those that will be led, and they will not. He is only sent to guide, not to hale them on or drive them forward. To you, disciples, such as are willing to be taught; not to them that will be all masters. To those that could not bear all truths then; not to those that would not then, nor to those that will not now, who make Christ's promise of none effect to themselves by their own perverseness.

Time was—and this day it was—when he found men better disposed for his coming, found them together at their prayers, not, as now, together by the ears; of one accord,

SERMON XL.

1 Sam. xiii. 11.

not in sects and factions, waiting all for the promise of his coming, not preventing it as Saul did Samuel, with a foolish sacrifice, only, as himself confesses, "lest the people should forsake him," and, as is usual now, not to stay the coming of "the Spirit of truth," but to set up one of their own, no matter of what, to keep the people from scattering and forsaking them, any spirit, so it can keep them to them.

Acts i. 4. They were to wait for the "promise of the Father," which was the Spirit of truth. They did, and had it. Do we so, and so we shall too. Our case still is the same with theirs. They could not bear all truths together, no more can we. They stood in need of daily teaching—we do more. They wanted a guide—we cannot go without him. Truth is still as necessary to be known as then it was. To this purpose was the Holy Spirit promised, to this purpose sent, to this purpose served, and serve he does still, the necessity being the same, like to be the same for ever; only fit we ourselves to receive him when he comes; and howbeit things look strangely, and this promise seems almost impossible now, the Spirit of truth will come, and "when the Spirit of truth is come, he will guide them," &c.

The words are Christ's promise of sending the Holy Spirit, now the fifth time repeated, to raise up the spirits of the drooping disciples, now ready to faint and die away, upon the discourse of their Lord's departure. He was now shortly to bid adieu to the world and them; yet so much he loved them that he would not leave them comfortless; though himself, who was their only joy and comfort, was to go away, yet he would not leave them without another Comforter. Though he that was "the way," must ascend, yet a guide should presently descend to guide them after him; though he who was "the truth" must back to heaven, yet the "Spirit of truth" should forthwith come down to guide them into all truth, to bring them thither. So that here, even without a guide, you may easily find two considerables.

1. The advent, or coming of the Holy Spirit: "When he, the Spirit of truth, is come."

2. The intent or purpose of it, the end and benefit of his advent or coming: " He will guide you into all truth;" that is the business.

THE SECOND SERMON ON WHITSUNDAY.

SERMON XL.

In the first we shall consider,
(1.) His title, "he, the Spirit of truth."
(2.) His motion, "is come."
(3.) His time, "when," indefinite it is here, but a due time it has, and we will strive to learn when it is.
(4.) His manner of coming: (i.) invisibly, as a Spirit; (ii.) effectually, as a Spirit of truth; (iii.) gently; and (iv.) softly: both implied in the word or term of "coming;" (v.) suddenly too sometimes, "when" he is come; as if so suddenly, that we should not feel or know it till he is.

In the second—the intent or benefit of his coming—we shall observe,
(1.) The benefit, what it is; to lead (2) whither? "Into truth." Into truth, (3) how far? "Into all truth." Yea, but (4) to whom all these? To you, even to lead you; you, and you, and you, all of us, in our way, in our order, one after another. Yea, but, lastly, lead us, and into truth, and into all truth; but how? Ὁδηγήσει, says the text, show and make and draw us out a way, and conduct and move and actuate us in it.

When we have thus considered them single and apart, we will join them again together and so leave them;—tell you how the leading is always proportionate to his coming; as he comes, so he leads. If he comes miraculously and extraordinarily, so he leads; if invisibly and ordinarily, so he leads; as much as he comes into us, so much he leads us; as is his coming so is his leading and no other; the one answerable to the other.

And, lastly, all this we shall make good from Christ's promise here: (1,) that his promise we have for it, who will not, cannot fail us; (2,) promise upon promise; (3,) a promise with a *non obstante*, with a "howbeit;" that howbeit all else should fail, this should not; howbeit to the world this Spirit may prove something else than a guide, a reprover, or a judge, yet to us he shall be a guide into the way of truth. This will be the sum, these the heads of my discourse, which that I may happily pursue, Come, thou, O Spirit of truth, and guide my thoughts and words this day, that I may teach thy ways unto the people, and declare thy truth.

SERMON XL.

We are to begin with the Spirit's advent, or his coming; for come to us he must before he guide us; and that his entertainment may be according, inquire we, first, Who it is? His titles here will best inform you: "He the Spirit of," &c.

1. "He!" what is "he?" "He" is a relative, relates to an antecedent, refers to some person mentioned before. Who is that? (1,) "The Comforter." Who is "he?" "The Comforter, (2,) which is the Holy Ghost"—(3,) one that the "world cannot receive;" so great, that the world, as wide as it is, cannot contain him; so good, that the world, which, as S. John speaks, lies in wickedness, cannot receive him; (4,) a Comforter that shall "abide for ever;" an eternal Comforter, (5,) "whom I will send unto you from my Father;" a heavenly Comforter, "which proceedeth from the Father," (the same verse,) a Comforter who is the very "Spirit of God," or God the Spirit proceeding. This is "he" we speak of; this is he that is said here to come, that is said still to come.

John xvi. 7.
John xiv. 26.
John xiv. 17.
John xiv. 16.
John xv. 26.

2. Well may the Evangelist stand and stop at his ἐκεῖνος here; stand and take breath here at this "he;" as if he knew not how to go further, how to call him, how to express him: he, the Comforter; he, that abides for ever; he, whom the world cannot receive; he, the Holy Ghost; he, that proceeds from the Father and the Son: all this he had said already, and more he thought he could not say, and therefore now here makes a halt as I may say, "he," and no more, to give us time to consider of the greatness of the person that is to come, and to prepare for his coming.

Yet to confirm all that before he has said of him, as he began the promise of him under the name of "the Spirit of truth," so he concludes it with the same title, that we might know all that he has said is truth, all that Christ has promised of him is no more than truth; for he is the Spirit of truth: "the Spirit of truth."

John xiv. 16, 17.

1. To make good and true all that Christ had promised, the very seal and signature of our redemption, to seal the conveyance of our inheritance to us; to make that good, "to bear witness with our spirit that we are the children of God;" to make all good to us both in heaven and in earth.

Ephes. iv. 30.
Ephes. i. 14.
Rom. viii. 16.

2. He is "the Spirit of truth," because the Spirit of God and Christ. God is truth, and Christ is the truth; and "the Spirit of God" he is, and "the Spirit of Christ" he is; so, to be sure, "the Spirit of truth," if of God and Christ.

3. The Spirit of truth is "the Spirit of prophecy;" those "holy men spake as they were moved by the Holy Ghost"—"who spake by the prophets," says the Nicene Creed; and prophets they are not, but liars, who speak not the truth, nor is it prophecy, if it be not truth.

4. "The Spirit of truth," for that as he inspires grace, so he doth truth too, all supernatural truth to be sure: for truths there are many and spirits there are many, but no truth but from him, nor no "Spirit of truth" but he himself; he is the fountain of truth," as in him and from him it is we live and breathe; he breathes into us this breath of life, the spirit of life from this Spirit; so from this "Spirit of truth" all the truth that at any time breathes from us, even natural truths and the truths of reason; but that is not it. Inspired truths, spiritual truths, they are the proper effects of this Spirit: other truths may be from him, nay, are originally all from him, as all good from God that eternal source of goodness; but they may sometimes arise and breathe from our own spirits within, or be put into us by other spirits, by the ministry of angels from without; but inspired truths from this Spirit alone.

Angels, indeed, are sometimes the "messengers" of it, but never called the "spirits" of it; they bring it, they do not breathe it: when they have brought it and done their message, be it never so true, never so comfortable, it will not comfort, but amaze us; it will not sink into us, but lie only at our doors till this Spirit breathe and work it in. He alone *Spiritus veritatis*, the Inspirer of truth.

Hence it is that this Spirit of all spirits is only called "the Comforter," for that he only lets in the comfort to the heart, whatever spirit is the messenger. Be it the angels, those spirits and messengers of heaven, or be it the ministers, those messengers upon earth, with all the life and spirit they can give their words,—no comfort from either, unless this "Spirit of truth" blow open the doors, inspire and breathe in with them. Truth itself cannot work upon our spirits but

SERMON XL.

John xiv. 17.
1 Cor. ii. 11.
Phil. i. 19.
Rev. xix. 10.
2 Pet. i. 21.

by the spiration of this Spirit of truth. It is but a dead letter, a vanishing voice, a mere piece of articulate air; the best, the greatest, the soundest truth no other; it has no spirit, it has no life, but from this Spirit of truth.

To conclude this point. It is not, when "the Spirit of truth is come," or, when "he, that is, the Comforter," is come, though both be but one, "he shall guide you"—neither title single; but "he," "the Spirit of truth," both together: to teach us, first, (1,) that the truth which this Spirit brings is full of comfort, always comfortable. Startle us it may a little at the first, but then presently, "Fear not," comes presently to comfort us: trouble us it may a little at the first, nay, and bring some tribulation with it, as times may be: but ere the verse be out, ere the words be out almost, "Be of good cheer," says Christ, it is but "in the world," and I "have overcome the world," and in me "ye shall have peace," that came before; so that tribulation is encompassed with comfort. "Ye shall be sorrowful" indeed, "but your sorrow shall be turned into joy;" the first is no sooner mentioned but the other follows, as fast as the comma will let it. Christ's truth, and this Spirit's truth, is the Comforter's truth, as well as the Spirit's, and have not only spirit to act and do, but comfort also in the doing, and after it, to be sure. Nay,

Joined so, (2,) "he, the Spirit of truth," to teach us again, that nothing can comfort us but the truth, no spirit hold up our spirits but the Spirit of truth. Lies and falsehoods may uphold us for a time, and keep up our spirits, but long they will not hold; a few days will discover them, and then we are sadder than at first. To be deluded adds shame to our grief; it is this Spirit only that is the spirit of our life, that keeps us breathing and alive; it is only truth that truly comforts us; which, even then when it appears most troublesome and at the worst, has this comfort with it,—that we see it, that we see the worst, need fear no more; whilst the joys that rise from false apprehensions or lying vanities, indeed from anything below this Spirit of truth and heaven, bring so much fear of a change, or close, or too sudden an end, that I may well say they have no comfort with them. They flow not from this Comforter, they come not from this Spirit; that is the reason they have no comfort, no spirit in them. It may well occasion us as soon as we can to look after this "he, the Spirit of truth," and for our own sakes inquire where he is, watch his motion, what, and whence, and whither it is.

II. To understand the motion and coming of the Spirit, what it means, we can take no better way than to peruse the phrases of the holy book, under what terms it elsewhere does deliver it. The first time we hear of it we read it "moving;" the next time "striving with man;" then "filling" him; then "resting upon" him. Sometimes he is said to "come;" sometimes to "enter into" us; sometimes to "fall upon" us; sometimes to be "put upon" us; sometimes to be "put into" us; sometimes to breathe, sometimes to "blow upon" us. All these ways is he said to come; whether he move us to good, or strive with us against evil, or fill us with sundry gifts and graces, or rest upon us in their continuance; whether he comes upon us in the power of his administrations; or whether he enter, as it were, and possess us wholly as his own; whether he appear in us, or without us; whether he come upon us so suddenly, and unusually, that he seems even to fall upon us, or be put upon us by ordinary ways and means; whether by imposition on, or breathing in; whether by a softer breath, or a stronger blast; whether he come in the feathers of a dove, or on the wings of the wind; whether in fire or in tongues; whether in a visible shape, or in an invisible power and grace: they are his comings all—sometimes one way, sometimes another—his comings they are all. Yet but some, not all of his comings, for all "his ways are past finding out," and teach us a lesson against curiosity in searching his out-goings.

And yet this word "come" sounds somewhat hard for all this still. Did we not say he was God? And can God be said to "come" any whither, who is everywhere? Nay, of this very Spirit expressly says the Psalmist, "Whither shall I go then from thy Spirit?" And if I cannot go from him, what needs his coming? "Coming," here, is a word of grace and favour; and certainly, be we never so much under his eye, we need that, need his grace, need his favour: nay, so much the more because he is so near us, that so we may do nothing unworthy of his presence. But he speaks to us after the manner of men, who, if they be persons of quality, and come to visit us, we count it both a favour and honour. So, by

SERMON XL.

inversion, when God bestows either favours or honours on us, when this holy Spirit bestows a grace, or a gift, or a truth upon us that we had not before, then is he said to come to us.

I need not now trouble myself much to find out whence he comes. "Every good and perfect gift comes from above," says S. James: from heaven it is he comes—from the Father—he "sends him;" from the Son, "he sends him" too, in this very chapter. And this is not only the place whence he comes, but here are the persons, too, whence he proceeds. So that now we have gained the knowledge, not only of his temporal, but his eternal coming too; his eternal procession, which though it be not the coming promised or intended here, yet, coming, here upon the context and coherence, relating so evidently to sending, gives us but a just occasion both to remember to whom we owe this benefit, the Father and the Son, the greatness of it, in that it is no less than infinite—the Spirit of God, God himself.

James i.17.
John xiv. 26.
John xvi. 7.

And it is but fit here and everywhere to take notice of it, that as the whence is above, so the whither is beneath, very much beneath him. But we reserve that to a fitter place, when we come to the persons that are guided by him. It is best now to suspend a while the search of the nature, to inquire into the time and manner of his coming. But the time is next: "when he is come."

III. Yea, but when is that? *Sane novum supervenisse spiritum nova desideria demonstrant*, says S. Bernard;^m you may know he is come (i.) by the desires he works in you; when those begin to be spiritual, hearty, sincere, and true to God, then is the Spirit of truth come into you; if you begin to long, and breathe, and gasp after heaven, it is a sign some heavenly breath of the Spirit, at least, is slipped into you.

(ii.) When this Spirit that pants and beats after God within, breathes out at the lips too, ere it be long, in prayers to God, and praises of him; in good communication; all bitterness, and malice, and evil speaking, and vanity too being laid aside as becometh saints. This is a good sign too, a true sign too, if it be not merely godly phrases taken up to make a show, or to deceive; if it proceed from the heart and inward spirit.

---

^m [Sane novum supervenisse spiritum certissime conversatio nova testatur.— S. Bern. in Octav. Pasch. serm. ii. p. 191 G. ed. Paris. 1640.]

(iii.) But the surest sign of it is in the hand, in the works, if they be such as are the genuine fruits of the Spirit,—" love, joy, peace, long-suffering, gentleness, goodness, faith, meekness, temperance." These are the Spirit's perpetual attendants when he comes. Boast men may of the Spirit, but if they have no love,—if they be not the sons of peace,—if patience and long-suffering be no virtue with them,—if gentleness appear not in their carriage,—if goodness and bounty to the poor abound not in them, as well as faith,—if they be not meek, and humble, and sober, and temperate—temperate in diet, in apparel, in language, in passion, and affections, and all things else; boast they while they will of the Spirit, and the Spirit of truth, that they have it, work and move by it, are guided by it, it will prove but the spirit of error, or the spirit of giddiness, or the spirit of slumber (they do but dream it), or but their own spirit, at the best; for such a one we read of, and of prophets that went according to it: "foolish prophets, that follow their own spirit, and have seen nothing;" ignorant prophets, who know nothing, yet pretend they know more than all the learned, all the Fathers that are gone; crafty "foxes" only they are, says the prophet, cunning to spoil and ravine; that seduce the people, saying, "Peace, when there is no peace;" they "build and daub with untempered morter," build up Babel, the house of confusion; and plaister up all the Scripture's texts that are against them with incoherent comments, wild distinctions and interpretations, that stick together like untempered mortar. They make "the righteous sad, and strengthen the hands of the wicked, that he should not return from his wicked way, by promising him life." And yet they there pretended the Spirit,—that he was come to them, and God had sent them, when indeed it was no other spirit from the Lord than such a one as came from him upon Saul when the good Spirit was departed from him. The Spirit of truth wants no such covering, no such mortar; makes not "the righteous sad," makes nobody sad by any oppression,—joy is the fruit of it; strengthens not the wicked in his wickedness; it is all for justice and righteous dealing. And where it comes upon any, it— as Samuel foretold it, and Saul found it—gives him "another heart," turns him into "another man." The "new man"

SERMON XL.

Gal. v. 23.

Ezek. xiii. 3.

Ezek. xiii. 4, 8, 10.

Ezek. xiii. 22.

1 Sam. x. 6, 9.
Eph. iv. 24.

SERMON XL.

S. Paul calls it, "created in righteousness and true holiness."

Indeed, there was another kind of coming of his this day. He came to-day, not only into the hearts but upon the heads of the Apostles; sat there, and thence dispersed his heavenly light into rays and flames; came down in wind, and fire, and tongues: in wind, to show that it was the Holy Spirit, the very breath of heaven; that came in fire, to signify the light of truth it brought; and in tongues, to express it to the world. But it was his inauguration day, the first solemnity of his appearance, that so both the disciples and the world might know that come he was whom Christ had promised, and be convinced by a visible apparition, who else would not have been convicted by any inward evidence which had been without it.

But thus he appeared but only once. In the effect of tongues indeed, but not in the appearance of them, he twice afterwards fell upon some disciples,—upon the centurion and his company, the first-fruits of the Gentiles, and upon those disciples at Ephesus, who knew nothing but John's baptism, that so they might sensibly find the difference of John's baptism and Christ's. They both, as soon as they were baptized, "spake with tongues," says the text; the one so honoured, to teach this truth, that in all nations, whoever doth righteousness shall be accepted, the Gentiles now in Christ as well accepted as the Jews; the other so highly favoured, that imperfect Christians might be encouraged to go on, and not be dismayed to see so many glorious professors so exceedingly transcend them.

Acts x. 46.
Acts xix. 6.

These comings were miraculous; only to found Christianity and settle an article of faith, the article of the Holy Ghost, never distinctly known to the world till Christianity arose. Christ himself was fain to confirm his divinity by signs and miracles; and the Godhead of the Holy Ghost can be persuaded by no less. But this once done, he was to lead us by an ordinary track,—no longer now by sight, but faith, that salvation might be "through faith," and the blessing upon them "who have not seen, and yet have believed."

1 Pet. i. 5.
John xx. 29.

This, I must needs say, seems the prime and proxime meaning of the words, but not the full. "When he is come," points chiefly and nearest at this his first and nearest coming, but not only at it; else are we in an ill case now, if no Spirit to come to us, no guide to lead us, no truth to settle us. It must extend beyond that his visible coming, to the ways of his coming unto us still, unseen and unheard; or however *expedit vobis*, it was expedient for them that Christ should go away, that the Comforter might come, for us it is not, I am sure, if we have none to come. Settle we, therefore, this for an article of our faith, that he comes still. I told you before how you should know it by his breathings inwardly in you, good thoughts and desires,—his breathings outwardly, good words and expressions,—by his workings with you, good life and actions; in a word, by his gifts and graces.

But if this be all, why is it now said, "when he is come?" Came he not thus before, to the patriarchs and prophets? Were not they partakers of his gifts, moved, and stirred, and actuated by him? Why then so much ado about Christ's sending him now, and of his coming now, as if he was never sent, never came before?

(1.) We read indeed in the Old Testament often of his coming, never of his sending, but by way of promise, that God would send, or of prophecy that he should be sent, and that but once neither expressly, *Emittes Spiritum et creabuntur*. Ps. civ. 30. So, though come he did, in those days of old, yet voluntarily, merely, we might conceive, never sent, never so distinct a notion of his person then; then only as the Spirit of God, now as the Spirit of the Father and the Son; then only as the power of God, now as a Person in the Godhead. This the first difference between his coming then and now.

(2.) Then he came as the Spirit of prophecy, now as the Spirit of truth: that is, as the very truth and fulfilling of it, of all the former prophecies.

(3.) Then upon Judæa, and few else besides; it may be Job in the land of Uz, and Rahab in Jericho, and Ruth in Moab; here and there, now and then one; now "upon all flesh:" upon Jew and Gentile, both alike; the partition wall, like the walls of Jericho, blown down by the breath of this Spirit, by the blast of this horn of the Most High.

(4.) Then most in types and shadows, now clearly and in truth.

214   THE SECOND SERMON ON WHITSUNDAY.

SERMON XL.
Acts ii. 1.
Acts vii. 55.
Eph. v. 18.
Judg. xiii. 25.

Acts ii. 3.
Acts xv. 28.

(5.) Then sparingly, they only sprinkled with it; now poured out, Joel's *effundam* fulfilled, a common phrase become now, —" full of the Holy Ghost," and " filled with the Spirit."
(6.) Then he came and went, lighted a little, but stayed not, *motabat*, or *volitabat*, flew or fluttered about, moved and stirred them at times, as it did Samson, coming and going; now it is he is come. He sate him down upon the Apostles, sate him down in the chair at their synod, *Visum est Spiritui Sancto et nobis*; calls us his temples now, not his tabernacles, places of a during habitation, and is to abide with us for ever.

Lastly. Then he came to help them in the observance of the Jewish and moral law, now to plant and settle an obedience to the Christian faith. For Christ being to introduce a more perfect and explicate faith in the blessed Trinity, and a Redeemer, to wean men from the first elements and beg-
[Gal. iv. 9.] garly rudiments, as the Apostle calls them; to raise them from earthly to heavenly promises; to elevate them to higher degrees of love, and hope, and charity, and virtue, and knowledge; and being besides to arm them against those contradictions and oppositions that would be made against them by the world, those persecutions and horrid ways of martyrdom they were to encounter with in the propagation of the Christian faith;—for these ends it was necessary that the Spirit of truth should come anew, and come with power, as it did at first with wonder, that by its work and power those great and glorious truths might be readily received and embraced. For
John xvi. 8. this seems the very end of his coming, to " convince the
John xv. 26. world," and " to testify of him;" and " to glorify him," in
John xvi. 14. the very next verse to the text; to evince this new revealed truth to the souls and consciences of men, that Messiah was come, that Jesus was the Christ, that the Jewish sacrifices were now to have an end, that the prophecies were all fulfilled in him, that his law was now to succeed in the place of Moses', that he justified where the law could not; that through him now, in his name, and in none other, salvation henceforth was to be preached to Jew and Gentile, and God had opened now that door of hope to all the world. To bear witness to this, and persuade this truth, so opposite to natural and Jewish reason, or so much above the ordinary reach of the one, and

the received customs of the other; thus to enhance piety and perfection, thus to set up Christ above the natural and Mosaic law; thus now to glorify God in Christ, and Christ as Christ; need there was, great need, that the Spirit of truth himself should come himself, after a new fashion, in a greater manifestation of his power than in former times, bring greater grace, because he required of us a greater work.

All this while we have given you but general notions of his coming, either when he first came in his fulness on the Apostles and first disciples; or when, secondly, he comes on any, as the Holy Spirit, in good motions and affections. We are yet to see when he comes as the Spirit of truth. To descend now, thirdly, to a distinct and particular inquiry, When the Spirit of truth is in us, or come to us,—when we have him in us?

Nor is this way of consideration less necessary than the other; though (it may be) harder far, forsomuch as we daily see many a pious Christian soul seduced into error, in whom yet we cannot doubt but the Holy Spirit has a dwelling;— many a good man also err in many opinions, of whose portion of the good Spirit we make no question; whilst some, many, others of less piety, it may be none, more fully know the truth than either of the other.

Understand, therefore, there is a double way of knowing even divine truth; (1,) the one by the way of natural reason, by principles and conclusions rationally and logically deduced out of the evidences of Scripture; (2,) the other by particular assents and dissents of the understanding and will purified and sanctified to all ready obedience to Christ.

By the first, it comes that the greatest scholars, the most learned and rational men, know always the most truths, both speculative and practick, both in their principles and inferences, and are therefore always fittest to determine doubts, and give counsel and direction, both what to believe and what to do, in all particular controversies and debates which concern either truth or error, or justice and injustice, right or wrong, the practices and customs of former times and Churches, or their contraries and disuses. And this may be done without the Spirit of sanctification, or the holy sanctifying Spirit, under that title at least, though indeed, under

SERMON XL.

1 Cor. xii. 8.

another title, it comes from him. As the "gift of tongues" or "interpretation," or "prophecy," or "the word of wisdom," or "the word of knowledge," are reckoned by the Apostle to come from the same Spirit, it may be most properly from him, as he is the Spirit of truth.

By the second way of knowledge it comes to pass, that men of less capacities and lower understandings, applying their affections as well as understandings to embrace the truth, do know and understand it more effectually, are more resolute in the defence of it, express it better in their lives, and know more sometimes of the particular ways of God in his particular providence and direction of the affairs of his saints, (for of this kind of wisdom "the fear of the Lord" always is "the beginning,") and it often happens, of the passages of the world too, as they relate to God's disposing order. Yet by reason of the inabilities of understanding, or want of the course or means of knowledge, it falls out that they oftener err in the conceits and apprehensions of things than the other. And more than so, it as often comes to pass, whether to humble them when they begin to be proud of their holiness and piety, and think themselves so much above other men—wiser, better, more holy, more righteous than they; or to punish them for some particular sin, as disobedience, curiosity of inquiring into depths above them, singularity, discontentedness, self-seeking, or the like; or to stir up their endeavours, now beginning to languish; or to make them yet more circumspect and wary in their ways; for these or some such causes, I say, it comes to pass that God suffers them to run into grand and enormous errors, foul and foolish extravagancies of opinion, which if once they trench on, practise, and are deliberate in, or might with easy industry have been avoided, even grieve and quench that holy Spirit that was in them, and expel him too; but if their errors be unvoluntary, not easy for them at that time to be avoided, or of lesser moment, stand they may with the Spirit of grace, and they good men still.

How, therefore, now shall we know what is from the Spirit of truth, when he comes so to us, is but a necessary inquiry; yet the resolution is hard and difficult. I know no better way to resolve you than by searching the nature of this Spirit of truth, as Christ has pleased to express him in his last most holy and comfortable discourse, of which the text is but a part, the several expressions of whose nature and office set together will, I am confident, assure us of a way to discern the Spirit of truth, when it is that he speaketh in us. You may turn your leaves and go along with me.

"The Spirit of truth, whom the world cannot receive;" so then, (1,) if the article or opinion which we receive be such an one as the world cannot, if it be contrary to worldly interests, carnal respects, sensual pleasures, it is a good sign at first. If it cannot enter into a carnal or natural man's heart—if "man's wisdom" teach it not, as the Apostle speaks —if it grow not in the garden of nature—that is a good sign it is "the Spirit of truth is come" that thus enables us to receive a doctrine so disadvantageous and displeasing.

Look into the next verse (ver. 18): "I will not leave you comfortless." If, then, (2,) it be such an assertion that has good ground in it to rest upon, that will not fail us in distress, that will stick by us in our deepest agonies, comfort us in our greatest discomforts, not leave us when all earthly comforts do,—then it is from above, then it is a true comfort, a truth from this "he," this "Spirit of truth," that is "the Comforter" too.

See next, verse 26: "He shall teach you all things, bring all things to your remembrance whatsoever I have said unto you." If then, (3,) it be an assertion that carries the analogy of faith along with it, that agrees with all the other principles of Christian faith,—that is, according to the rule of Christ's holy word,—that soberly and truly brings to our remembrance what he has said at any time, or done for us; that remembers both the words that he spake and the deeds that he has done, his actions and example; if it be according to his example of humility, obedience, patience, and love; if it bring us heartily to remember this Christ's pattern in our lives and opinions too, then it comes from him that should come, and is worth your receiving and remembering it.

In the same verse again, in the words just before, he is called "the Comforter," and "Holy Ghost," who is also there promised to teach us too. And if the doctrine be such, that not only comforts us in the receiving and remembrance,

SERMON XL.

but such also as becomes comforters too, that teaches us to comfort others,—the poor and needy, the afflicted and distressed, and to do it holily too, as by the Holy Ghost—that is, with good and pure intentions—and do it even to their ghosts and spirits, as well as to their bodies; if it teach true, holy, ghostly, spiritual counsel, and all other convenient comfort to them our Christian brethren; then it is, (4,) a doctrine from this Spirit of truth: he comes in it.

John xv. 26.

Turn ye now to chap. xv. 26: "But when the Comforter is come, whom I will send unto you from the Father, even the Spirit of truth, which proceedeth from the Father," &c. When the doctrine (5) is no other than what either establishes the doctrine of the Holy Trinity, Father, Son, and Holy Ghost, or contradicts it not, and in all benefits received refers thanks and acknowledgment to the one as well as the other; as from the one, through the other, by a third :—in this particular it is no other than the Spirit of truth, for no other spirit can reveal it.

Go on now through the verse: "He shall testify of me." The doctrine (6) that bears witness of Christ, that he is God, that he is man, that he is Christ, the Saviour of the world; that he came to save sinners, all whosoever would come to him, not a few particular ones only; that he is a complete and universal Saviour, such as he professed himself by entertaining all comers, sending his Spirit and Apostles into all nations, commanding them to "preach to every creature," which are no other than his own words; this is also from the Spirit of truth; a doctrine worthy him that is the Comforter that brings so general a comfort with it.

Step now into the next chapter, to which we owe the text: "When he is come he will reprove the world of sin, of righteousness, and of judgment." When the doctrine is (7) such as it reproves the world of sin; that it can do no good of itself; that it is full of evil and corruption; convinces it, and finds fault with it for infidelity and unbelief; sets up Christ's righteousness, and blames the world for neglecting it, and following its own vanity, interests, and humours; professes the prince of the world cast out by Christ, the devil overcome and brought to judgment by him, our sins forgiven, we acquitted, and the world condemned; this cannot

John xvi. 8.

be from the spirit of the world, nor from the spirit of the flesh, nor from the spirit of darkness and error,—for this were to bear witness against themselves,—but from the Spirit of light and truth.

Read the text now over again: "When he," &c. "he shall guide you into all truth." If it be the Spirit of truth that informs you, it will (8) dispose you equally to all truth; not to this only, or to that, which most agrees with your education, humour, temper, or disposition, condition, custom, interest, or estate, but universally to all, to any though never so hard or opposite to them, so they be truths. He that is thus affected towards truth, is not only probable to be directed into truth, in all his doctrines and assertions, but may most properly be said to have the Spirit of truth already come, speaking and residing in him.

Yet go a little further to the next words: "He shall not speak of himself, but whatsoever he shall hear;" that spirit (9) that does not seek itself, that opinion which renounces the glory of a leader, the ambition of a faction, the affectation of singularity, the honour of himself, that speaks not of its own head, but what he has heard with his ears, and his fathers have declared as done in the time of old; that makes not new opinions, but takes up the old, such as Christ delivered to the Apostles, they also to the Fathers, they downward to their successors; this is most probably, if not most certainly, the Spirit of truth. The spirit, sure, of humility it is, that trusts not, relies not on itself or its own judgment: and the spirit of humility is the Spirit of truth; for "them that be meek and humble, them shall he guide in judgment; and such as be gentle, them does he learn his way." Ps. xxv. 8.

Yet on a little: "And he will show you things to come." Those doctrines (10) that refer all to the world to come, which mind nothing seriously but things above and things to come, which ever and only teach us to fix there, they are surely from the Spirit of truth, because no truth like that which is to fulfil all promises, and that to be sure is yet "to come."

One more glance and I have done with this; and it is but a glance to the very next words: "He shall glorify me." Those doctrines which give God all the glory, which return the glory of all to Christ; which so exalt man only as the better thereby to glorify God; so set up Christ as that they make him both the healer of our nature and the preserver of it, the remitter of our sins and the conferrer of grace—the first mover of us to good, the assister of us in it, the sanctifier of us with it, the justifier of us through it, the rewarder of us for it, and yet all this while the accepter of us when we have done the best; which accuse not Christ of false judgment in justifying the sinner whilst he is no better, and pronouncing him just when he is no other than wicked and unjust, nor deny the efficacy of his grace to make us clean, to have a true cleansing, purifying, sanctifying power, as well as that which they call the justifying: these doctrines which take not this glory away from Christ, but give the power as well of making as pronouncing righteous to his grace, that thus magnify and glorify his justification and redemption, they certainly glorify Christ, are the only doctrines that glorify Christ truly, and according to the Spirit of truth.

So now let us sum up the matter. Those doctrines which (1) are contrary to worldly, carnal, sensual respects, not conceivable by the natural or carnal man; that (2) stick by us when worldly comforts leave us; that (3) are according to Christ's word and his example, accompanied with meekness and obedience; which (4) teach us charity and love to one another; which (5) inform us rightly in the prime articles of the faith; which (6) witness nothing more than Christ an universal Saviour, as Adam the universal sinner; which (7) reprove the sins and infidelities of the world, and show us the way to be acquitted from them; which (8) have a kind of conduct and sincere affection with them to all truths whatsoever, under whatever term or name, though never so odious, so contrary to interest or honour; which (9) seek not their own name, to get a name or set up a faction, but are consonant to the ancient Fathers and primitive antiquity, with humble submission to it; which (10) lift up all our thoughts to heaven, and (11) by all means possible can give God and Christ and the Holy Spirit the glory, deny nothing to them that is theirs, under a foolish pretence only to abate and vilify man beyond the truth;—these doctrines are truth; so much of them, at least, as agree with these rules, are from the Spirit of truth, and are manifestations that the Spirit of truth is come to that soul that embraces them: if all these together, then the Spirit altogether; if but some of these, but some, so much of that neither. All doctrines and opinions (1) that savour of worldly or carnal interests; that (2) change and wheel about according to the times, and will not hold out to the last; which (3) are not regulated by the word of God, or are any way contrary to Christ's example of patience and obedience; which (4) are not for peace and charity; which (5) deny any article of the three Creeds we acknowledge; which (6) confine the mercies of our Saviour, and bear false witness of him; which (7) advance any sin, or suffer men to live in it; which (8) love not truth because it is truth, but for other ends; which (9) seek any other title to be distinguished by than that of Christian, or glory in it, which disagree from the stream and current of antiquity; which (10) fix our thoughts too much below; or (11) rob God, or Christ, or the Holy Spirit of the glory of any good, or the perfection of their work; be they cried up never so high for truth and spirit, the new discovery of Christ, and new light of truth, and the very dictate of the Spirit, they are not so; it is not when, nor then, that the Spirit of truth is come; there is not that in them by which Christ has described the Spirit of truth.

One thing there is behind, when all these requisites before are found in any doctrine or opinion; this doctrine indeed may be such as comes from the Spirit of truth, yet accepted and entertained it may be through some other spirit, upon some sinister end or ground : that therefore it may not only be the truth of the Spirit, but have the very Spirit of truth with it, that it may be evident it not only comes from him, but that he also is come with it, it must be sincerely and intimately embraced with our very hearts and spirits out of love to truth, not any interest or by-respect, and well habituated and actuated in us, before we can say directly that the Spirit of truth is come. Some truth or other may be come, some ray and beam of his light be sent before him, but himself not yet fully come; for all truth comes along with him, though not actually altogether, yet a hearty resolute affection to all of it, all truth altogether, as God shall let it come.

SERMON XLI.

I have been somewhat long in this particular about the Spirit's coming, because I see the world so much mistaken in it, so often crying, Lo! here he is; lo! there he is; lo! here he comes; lo! there he comes; when indeed he is not here, nor there, with neither of them, nor coming to them. A word now of the manner of his coming.

IV. And that is (1) invisibly, for so comes a spirit. This is the coming we hold by; and had he not come when he came, as well invisibly into the hearts as visibly upon the heads of the disciples, their tongues, though all the tongues of men and angels, would have profited them nothing; the fire then, had it not inflamed their hearts and affections with a holy flame, as well as encompassed their heads, would have only lighted them with more glory into eternal fires. Had not this wind blown as well within as that did without them, it would have blown them little good. Tongues, and prophecy, interpretations, miracles, and the rest, are but *dona gratis data;* gifts more for others' good than for our own; they do not make us better in his sight, it is the invisible grace that makes us accepted. Nay, yet those very gifts and administrations, however the appearance was without, were wrought within by his invisible operation. So that to the Apostles as much as to ourselves, his invisible coming is the only truly comfortable coming.

That (2) is effectual too. To come truly is to come effectually; and in that he is called the Spirit of truth, it is plain he must effect what it is he comes for, or it is not true and real. It was "a mighty rushing wind" he this day came in; so mighty, so effectual, that it at once converted three thousand souls; "the Spirit of power" is one of his names; and "the pulling down of strongholds, casting down every thing that exalts itself against the knowledge of God, and bringing into captivity every thought to the obedience of Christ," is one of his works.

2 Cor. x. 4, 5.

(3.) He comes gently—that is the common pace of one that is only said to come—gently, step by step, grace after grace, gift after gift, truth after truth; leads by steps, comes by degrees; not all grace at a clap, all gifts in a trice. Nay, as hastily as it seemed to come this day, S. Peter, the chief of them, was a while after at a loss for a truth, had not, it seems, all truths together: "Of a truth now I perceive that God is no respecter of persons;" before it, seems, he perceived it not; no more did the other Apostles neither, who were all in the same error, and convented him about this new truth, and contended with him about it.

<small>Sermon XL.</small>
<small>Acts x. 34.</small>
<small>Acts xi. 2.</small>

(4.) Nay, softly too; "as dew into a fleece of wool," without noise, without clamour; no way like the spirits now-a-days; "I will put my Spirit upon him, and he shall not cry, nor lift up, nor cause his voice to be heard in the streets." He is the Spirit of meekness who is the Spirit of truth, and truth is never taught so soon, so effectually, as by softness and meekness; the meek the best to teach, the best to be taught.

<small>Isa. xlii. 1, 2.</small>

(5.) Yet as gently and softly as he comes, he is often upon us on a sudden, ere we are aware. God uses to "prevent us with the blessings of goodness," as the Psalmist speaks. He is come, sometimes, before we think of it. Our hearts are in his hand, and he suddenly turns them whither he will. Saul does but turn him about from Samuel, and God gives him presently "another heart." Samuel no sooner anoints David, but from thenceforward "the Spirit came upon him." And this note is made, not that you should always look for miraculous changes, and expect the Spirit, without so much as setting yourselves to seek him; but to make you watch continually, and wait for him, that though he come suddenly, he may not find you unprepared, the doors shut upon him; that he may not go as he comes for want of entertainment.

<small>Ps. xxi. 3.</small>
<small>1 Sam. x. 9.</small>
<small>1 Sam. xvi. 13.</small>

Yet the phrase will bear another expression of the manner of his coming. "When he is come," that is, when he is grounded and well settled in us; the tense is the aorist, a preterperfect signification; signifies not coming, but perfectly come. This is not actually always to every one he comes to, yet his intent it is in all his coming to stay and abide with us, and so he does till we drive him thence. But if we do not,—if we let him stay and dwell, and remove him not, then will he "guide us into all truth;" that is the end and intention of his coming, the next point. But I am beyond my intent and time already; I shall only sum up this last particular of the manner of his coming, and let you go.

SERMON XL.

You will peradventure understand it best by considering how the Spirit moved in the creation; the order the same in creating the new man in the soul that he there observed in creating of the world.

Now, in the first creation of the world, He first (1) moved upon the waters, then created light, and divided it from darkness; he next (2) divides the waters, and places a firmament between them; then (3) gathers the waters together and makes dry land appear and bring forth grass and herbs and trees bearing seed; then (4) makes two glorious lights to rule the day and night, and times and years; then (5) creates fowl and fish and beasts; and, lastly, makes man after his own image.

Thus does he in this new creation or regeneration. He first (1) moves and stirs us up to good, then darts in some glimmerings of light to show us our own darkness, sins, and wretchedness; then, next, (2,) divides the passions and powers of the soul, and sets them their bounds, employs some in things above, whilst some other are left beneath; then, (3,) presently makes the dry and barren soul sprout out, bring herbs, and leaves, and seeds into green flourishing desires, holy resolutions and endeavours which carry with them seed, much hope of increase; (4,) to cherish these green and tender sprouts, to direct and rule these resolutions, desires and endeavours, two lights he makes,—true rectified reason, and supernatural grace,—to guide them what to do at all seasons, days, and years, and many little stars, many glimmerings of truth begin then to discover themselves which before did not. After all this, (5,) the sensitive faculties in their course and order bring forth their living creature according to their kind, submit themselves to the command of the superior reason. And then, lastly, when the Spirit has thus totally renewed the face of the earth, of our mind and affections, is the new man created after the likeness and image of God in righteousness and true holiness. This the course, this the order of the Spirit's coming; he comes moving upon the waters of repentance, and first enlightens the darkness of our souls; he orders all our faculties and powers; he makes us fruitful to good works; he daily increases divine light and heat within us; he reforms our sense, subdues our passions, regulates our reason, sanctifies them all, comes in light, comes in grace, comes in truth, comes in strength, comes in power, that we might in his strength and power come one day all in glory.

And now, he that thus created the old world, and still creates the new, new create and make us new; and pray we all, with holy David, " Create, O Lord, in us new hearts, and renew right spirits within us." " Cast us not, O Lord," for ever, though we are now full of errors, " from thy presence, and keep not thy Holy Spirit from us," but let thy Spirit of truth come down and guide us out of our wanderings, " give us the comfort of his help again," guide us again into the ways of truth, " and stablish us there with thy free Spirit," and that for the merits and mercies of thine only Son, who here promised to send him, and this day accordingly sent him to guide us to himself, from grace to grace, from truth to truth, from truth below to true happiness above, Jesus Christ our Saviour. To whom, &c.

<small>SERMON XL.</small>

<small>Ps. li. 10.</small>

THE THIRD SERMON

UPON

WHITSUNDAY.

S. JOHN xvi. 13.

Howbeit when he, the Spirit of truth, is come, he will guide you into all truth.

SERMON XLI.

AND he this day began to guide, has continued guiding ever since, will go on guiding to the end; began it with the Apostles, continued it to the Church, and will continue it to the end of the world.

Indeed, he that looks upon the face of the Christian Churches now would be easily tempted to think that either the time was not yet come that it should be fulfilled, or that it had been long ago, and his promise come utterly to an end for evermore. For so far are we from a guide into all truth, that we have much ado to find a guide in truth, false guides and false spirits are so rife; so far from being guided into all truth, that it is nearer truth to say into all error; as if this guide had quite forsaken us, or this promise belonged not at all to us. Yet for all that, to us it is.

For the truth is, it is not this Guide's, this Spirit's, fault, but ours, that this "all truth" is so nigh none at all. "He will guide" still, but we will not be guided. And "into all truth," too, he will, but we will not; we will have no more than will serve our turn, stand with our own humour, ease, and interest; that is the reason why he guides not now as in the days of the Apostles, the first times, the times of old. We will not let him; "we cannot bear it," as it is in the verse before; or worse, we will not bear, we will not endure it; every one will be his own guide, go his own way, make what truth he pleases, or rather what him pleases the only truth; every one follow his own spirit; that is the reason why we have so little of the "Spirit of truth" among us. There are so many private spirits that there is no room for this.

Yet if into all, or indeed any truth that is worth the name of saving, we would be guided, to this one we must return, to one Spirit, or to no truth. There is but one truth and one Spirit; all other are but fancies. He that breaks the unity of the Spirit, that sets up many spirits, sets up many guides, but never a true one; chance he may, perhaps, into a truth, but not be guided to it, and as little good come of it where the analogy of Scripture and truth must needs be broken by so many differing and divided spirits. It is time we think of holding to one Spirit, that we may all hold the same truth, and in time be led into it all. The only question is, Whether we will be led or no? If we will not, the business is at an end. If we will, we must submit to this Spirit and his guidance, his manner and way of guiding; by so doing we shall not fail in any necessary saving truth; "he will guide us into all truth."

Which that he may, as I have heretofore out of the former words told you of his coming, so shall I now, by his assistance, out of these latter, tell you of his guiding; for to that intent and purpose he came to-day, and comes every day; came at first, and comes still; comes (1,) to guide; to guide (2,) into truth; (3,) into all truth; (4,) even you and all into it; yet, (5,) to guide only, not to drive or force us; to guide after his own way and fashion, not our fancy; of which, lastly, we need not doubt or make a question; he "will" do it.

So that now the parts of the text will plainly rise into these propositions:

I. That though Christ be gone he has not left us without a guide, but has sent him that shall guide us still.

II. That he that shall do it is "he," that very "he," that is, "the Spirit of truth," just before. No other can.

III. That guide therefore into truth, he will; no other will.
IV. That he will guide not into this truth or that truth only, but into " all."

V. That he will guide even us too. You, and you, and you, us as well as those that were before us; all is but "you."

VI. That he will do it yet, but after his own way and fashion; ὁδηγήσει, after the way he comes; after as he comes, so will he guide, set us a way to find the truth, and guide us after that way and no other.

VII. That for certain so it is. He " will," " howbeit" he will, though yet he has not, though yet we peradventure will not or cannot endure to be guided, yet when we will set ourselves to it, " he will guide us into," &c.; it shall be no fault or failure of his, for he for his part will, is always willing.

The sum of all is this, to assure us (1) that notwithstanding all the errors and false spirits now abroad, there is a " Spirit of truth " still ready and willing to guide us into all truth yet; and (2) to show us how he will do it, that we may learn how to be guided by him. This the sum. And the use of all will be, that we submit ourselves to him and to his guidance, to be taught and led and guided by him; to his guiding and to his truth, and to all of it, without exception. To guide and to be guided are relatives, infer one another. If we will have him guide us, he will have us be guided by him, and give up ourselves to his way of guiding. Oh that we would, that there were but a heart in us to do so! We should not then have so many spirits, but more truth; one spirit would be all, and all truth would be one; this one single Spirit would be sufficient to guide us into all truth; he would guide us into all truth. But I must from my wishes to my words, where we see, first, we have a guide; that though Christ be ascended from us into heaven, yet we are not without a guide upon the earth.

I. " I will not leave you comfortless," said he, when he was going hence. Had he left us without a guide he had so, comfortless, indeed, in a vast and howling wilderness;—this earth is little else. But a " Comforter" he sends; such a one as shall " teach us all things;" that is a comfort, indeed, none like it, to have one to guide us in a dangerous and uncertain way, to teach us that our ignorance requires, to do

THE THIRD SERMON ON WHITSUNDAY.

all the offices of a guide unto us, to teach us our way, to lead us, if need be, in it, to protect and defend us through it, to answer for us if we be questioned about it, and to cheer us up, encourage and sustain us all the way.

SERMON XLI.

II. Such a guide as this, is this "he" we are next to speak of. "He, the Spirit of truth," so it is interpreted but immediately before. He (1) shall teach you, teach you "the way," reveal Christ to you; for unless he do you cannot know him; teach you how to pray; teach you "what to say," how to "answer," by the way, if you be called to question in it; "give you a mouth and wisdom" too; teach you not only to speak, but to speak to purpose. He (2) shall lead you too, *deducet,* lead you on, be a prop and stay and help to you in your journey. He (3) shall protect and defend you in it as a guide, free you from danger, set you at full "liberty;" be a cover to you by day and a shelter to you in the night; the breath of the Holy Spirit will both refresh us and blow away all our enemies like the dust. He, (4,) if we be charged with any thing, will answer for us, like a guide and governor. "It is not you," says Christ, "but the Spirit of your Father that speaketh in you." He, lastly, it is that quickens our spirit with his Spirit, that encourages and upholds us like a guide and leader; for without him our spirits are but soft air, and vanish at the least pressure. He guides our feet, and guides our heads, and guides our tongues, and guides our hands, and guides our hearts, and guides our spirits; we have neither spirit, nor motion, nor action, nor life without him.

Rom. viii. 26.
Luke xii. 11.
Luke xxi. 15.
2 Cor. iii. 17.

Matt. x. 20.

III. But here particularly he comes to guide us into the truth. And God knows we need it; for "surely men of low degree are vanity," says the Psalmist, "and men of high degree are a lie;" not liars only, but a very lie, as far from truth as a lie itself; things so distant from that conformity with God, which is truth,—for truth is nothing else,—that no lie is further off it. Nor soul, nor body, nor heart, nor mind, nor upper nor lower powers conformed to him, neither our understandings to his understanding, nor our wills to his will, nor any thing of us really to him; our actions and words and thoughts all lie to him, to his face; we think too low, we speak too mean, we deal too falsely with him,

Ps. lxii. 9.

SERMON XLI. pretend all his, yet give most of it to our lusts and to ourselves, and we are so used to it we can do no other, we are all either verbal or real lies, need we had of one to guide us into the truth.

John xiv. 6. God is truth, to guide us to him. Christ is "the truth," to guide us to him. His word is truth, to guide us into that, into the true understanding and practice of it. His promises are truth, very yea and amen, to guide us to them, to rest and hold upon them. His way is the way of truth, to guide us into that, into a religion pure, holy, and undefiled; that only is the true one. Into none of these can any guide but this guide here. He showeth us of the Father, he reveals to us the Son; he interprets the word and writes it in our hearts; he leads and upholds us by his promises, seals them unto us, seals us again to the day of redemption, the day of truth, the day when all things shall appear truly as they are. He sets our religion right; he only leads us into that. Man cannot;—he can speak but to the ear; there his words die and end. Angels cannot;—they are but ministering spirits at the best to this Spirit. Nature cannot;—these truths are all above it, are supernatural, and no other truth is worth the knowing. Nay, into any truth this Spirit only can; we only flatter and keep ado about this truth and that truth and the other, but into them we cannot get, make nothing of any truth without him; unless he sanctify it, better else we had not known it: knowledge puffeth up, all knowledge that comes not from this Spirit: so the very truth of any truth, that which truly confirms it to the divine will and understanding, that makes truth the same with goodness, is from this Spirit, from his guiding and directing, his breathing it, or breathing into it, or upon it.

IV. Thus we are fallen upon the fourth particular—that " he will guide us into all truth."

God's mercies and Christ's are ever perfect, and of the largest size, and the conducts of the Spirit are so too, into all Gal. v. 22. "goodness;" into all "fulness;" into all truth here; into all Ephes. iii. 19. things. That we are not full is from ourselves; that we are not led into all truth, is for that all truth does not please us, and we are loth to believe it such, if it make not for us: he for his part is as ready to guide us into all as into one.

For take we truth either for speculative or practical, either for the substance against types and shadows, or the discerning the substance through those shadows; or take we it in opposition to obscurity and doubting, understand we it for what is truly to be believed, or loved, or hoped, or feared, or done,—as under these is contained all that is saving truth,—so they are all taught us by this Spirit. The signification of all old types and shadows, sacrifices and ceremonies; the things which whilst Christ was with us we were not able to "bear;" the things which when they were done we did not understand; all that we are to believe and do; what to hope and what to fear; what to desire and what to love,—this Spirit teaches. And that, first,

Sermon XLI.

John xvi. 12.

Not as other spirits teach, which teach by halves, so much only as may serve to nurse up their faction and their side, but nothing more; but all, whatever is commanded, "keeps back nothing," as S. Paul professes for himself; nothing that is profitable unto you, that is, nothing profitable to salvation.

Acts xx. 20.

Not, secondly, as other spirits, which teach impertinent or idle truths, or mere natural ones; indeed for such truths as have neither spiritual profit or command he is neither bound nor binds himself; is neither sent nor comes to teach them; such truths as appertain not unto holiness, the Holy Spirit is not promised for. Yet, all that is necessary to be known, hoped, feared, expected, desired, or done, in reference to the kingdom of grace and glory, he never fails us in.

Not, thirdly, as other spirits that never teach all truth and nothing else, whose truths are commonly mixed with error; but what he teaches is truth, "all." By this you know that it is his Spirit; it is he that teaches every part, when the doctrine is "all truth." The doctrines of the world are like those bastard children in Nehemiah, that speak half Ashdod and half Israel; one part of them is truth, the other falsehood; one part Scripture, the other a romance; one part spirit, the other flesh; one part heaven, the other earth, earthly humours and respects, and nothing else. There is not an error or heresy so gross or impudent but has Jacob's voice though Esau's hands, speaks well whatever it does, speaks fair and smooth though its deeds be rough and cruel;

Neh. xiii. 24.

SERMON XLI. with Naphtali gives good words, though with Dan it be as a serpent by the way, and an adder in the path that biteth the horse heels, so that the rider does fall backward; speaks well though it mean ill, and overthrow all that embrace it. Thus the Anabaptist says true, when he says the Apostles baptized men and women; but he says false, when he says none else, or that they baptized any twice with Christ's baptism. The Antinomian and Solifidian say no more than truth, when they say faith justifies without the works of the law, for they say with S. Paul; but they say a lie when they separate the works of the Gospel from that faith that James ii. 26. justifies, if S. James say true. Innumerable multitudes of such half-faced truths there are abroad, vented and vaunted by private spirits, such as this Spirit has no hand in. Every truth of his is truth in all its parts; all truth, though it be but one, keeps the analogy of faith inviolable, perfect correspondence with all the rest. So that now every truth of his is all truth, truth all of it; but that is not all, for, fourthly, there is not a truth necessary or convenient for us to know but in John xiv. 26. due time he reveals it to us, unless we hinder him,—"all things," says Christ, in another place.

V. But all this while to whom is all this promised? this guiding Spirit into all truth, to whom is it? To whom but you? "you," says the text. What, you Apostles only? no such matter: you disciples present then? no such matter neither. It is but a little word this "you," yet of large extent; few letters in it, but much spirit: you believers, all of John xvii. 20. you, as well as you Apostles. For "all" he prays in the next chapter, for all "that should believe on him through their John xiv. 16. word." And it is promised that he shall "abide with them for ever;" and if ever, sure then beyond their persons and their times; so that to ours, too, is the promise made, or it cannot be for ever.

To the Apostles indeed in greater measure, after a more eminent way, with miracles and wonders to confirm the truth John xiv. 26. he taught, yet to us also after our measure.
Luke xxiv. 8. To them (1) to "bring to their remembrance all things Acts i. 16. whatsoever he had said unto them." Whence we read so John ii. 22. often, "they remembered his words;" "remembered what John xii. 16. he said;" "remembered what was done unto him."

To them (2) to guide them into the understanding of old types and prophecies, what was any where said or written, or meant of him.

To them (3) to explain and manifest what they before either did not understand or made a question of.

To them (4) to teach them those things which till "he"—this Spirit—came they could not "bear," as it is just before the text.

To them (5) to settle the rites and ceremonies, the discipline and government of the Church, to take order about things indifferent. "It seemed good unto the Holy Ghost and to us," to define things not before commanded: of these Christ had given no commandment, we read of none; S. Paul professes he had received none about them, yet he determines them, and tells us he thought also "he had the Spirit of God;"—even to those truths as well as others does the Spirit's guiding reach.

^{Sermon XLI.}

^{Acts xv. 28.}

^{1 Cor. vii. 25.}

^{1 Cor. vii. 40.}

To them the Spirit came to guide them into all these kinds of truths; to us to guide us in them, or guide us after them, in a larger sense into them too. However, to one effect it comes, we and they have the same truth from the same Spirit; the way only, that is different; they immediately from the Spirit, we mediately by their writings dictated to them by the Spirit. This now guides me to the way and manner of his guiding, which comes next to be considered, and must be fetched both from the nature of the word and the manner of his coming, for after that manner is his guiding, as after he comes so he will guide too.

VI. From the word first. And the word here for "guiding" is ὁδηγήσει. Now, in ὁδηγήσει there is, first, ὁδός, and then ἄγειν,—first way, then motion in it. He first sets us down a way that will bring us into the truth, then acts or moves us in it.

The first way or means is the word of God. "Thy word is a light unto my feet, and a lantern to my paths," says holy David. "All Scripture is given by inspiration," says S. Paul, "and is profitable for doctrine, for reproof, for correction, for instruction in righteousness, that the man of God may be perfect, throughly furnished unto all good works." Inspired purposely by this Spirit to be a way to

[Ps. cxix. 105.]

[2 Tim. iii. 16, 17.]

SERMON XLI. guide us into all truth and goodness. But this may all pretend to, and every one turns it how he lists. We must add a second.

And the second is the Church, for we must know this, 2 Pet. i. 20. says S. Peter; know it first too—"that no Scripture is of any private interpretation." There are "some things so hard to be understood" both in S. Paul's Epistles and also other 2 Pet. iii. 16. Scriptures, says he, that they that are "unlearned and unstable wrest them unto their own destruction," and therefore presently his advice follows, to beware lest we be led away 2 Pet. iii. 17. with that error, "the error," as he calls it, "of the wicked," and so fall from our own steadfastness. When men unlearned or ungrounded, presume to be interpreters, or even learned men to prefer their private senses before the received ones of the Church, it is never like to produce better. The 1 Tim. iii. 15. "pillar" and "ground" upon which truth stands and stays is the Church, if S. Paul may be allowed the judge: "the pillar and ground of truth." In matters (1) of discipline when Matt. xviii. 17. a brother has done disorderly, "tell it to the Church," says Christ, and "if he neglect to hear that, let him be unto thee as a heathen man and as a publican,"—he is no Christian. In matters (2) of doubt and controversy, send to the Church, to Jerusalem, to the Apostles and Elders there Acts xv. 2, 28. convened in council, and let them determine it, so we find it done. In a lawful and full assembly of the learned Fathers of the Church such shall be determined;—that is the way to settle truth. In matters (3) of rites and ceremonies the 1 Cor. xi. 16. Spirit guides us also by the Church. "If any man seem to be contentious" about them, S. Paul's appeal is presently to the Church's customs: "we have no such custom, neither the Churches of God," that is answer enough full and sufficient, thinks the Apostle. If the Church's custom be for us, then it is good and true we think, or speak, or do: if against us, it is all naught and wrong, whatever purity or piety be pretended in it. Nay, so careful was the Apostle to preserve the public authority of the Church and beat down all private ways and fancies—by which ways only schism and heresy creep in—that he tells Timothy, though a 2 Tim. iii. 14. Bishop, and one well read and exercised in the Scriptures "from 2 Tim. i. 13. a child," "of a form of sound words" he would have even him hold fast to; and the Romans he tells of a "form of doctrine" to be obeyed," so far was that great and eloquent Apostle from being against forms, any forms of the Church,—though he could have prayed and preached *ex tempore* with the best, had tongues and eloquence, and the gift of interpretation to do it too,—so far from leaving truth to any private interpretation or sudden motion whatsoever. Nor is this appeal to the Fathers any whit strange or in the Christian religion only first to be heard of; it was God's direction from the first: "For ask now," says Moses, "of the days that are past, that were before thee." "Stand you in the ways, and see, and ask for the old paths, where is the good way," says God. As if he had said, Look about, and see, and examine all the ways you can, yet the old way, that is the good one. "For inquire, I pray thee, of the former age, and prepare thyself to the search of their fathers, for we are but of yesterday, and know nothing." See how slightly things of yesterday, new interpretations, new devices, new guides are accounted of. And indeed in itself it is most ridiculous to think the custom, and practice, and order, and interpretation of all times and Churches should be false, and those of yesterday only true, unless we can think the Spirit of truth has been fifteen or sixteen hundred years asleep, and never waked till now of late; or can imagine that Christ should found a Church, and promise to be with it to the end of the world, and then leave it presently to Antichrist to be guided by him for above fifteen hundred years together. Nor can I see why the Spirit of truth should now of late only begin to move and stir, except I should think he were awaked, or delighted with noise and fury. Nor is it reasonable to conceive a few private spirits, neither holier nor wiser than others, for aught appears, nor armed with miracles to confirm their doctrines, should be more guided by the Spirit of truth than the whole Church and succession of Christians, and Christian Fathers, especially wherein at any time they agree.

Yet, thirdly, not always to go so high. "Thou leddest thy people like sheep," says the Psalmist, " by the hand of Moses and Aaron." Moses and Aaron were the governors of the Church, the one a priest, the other a prophet; by such God leads his people, by their lawful pastors and teachers.

SERMON XLI.

Heb. xiii. 17.
1 Tim. v. 17.

The one, the civil governor, is the cloud to cover them from the heat; the other, the spiritual, is the light to lead them in the way. The first protects, the other guides us; and we are bid to "obey" them, "those especially that watch for our souls;" "such as labour in the word and doctrine." By such as God sets over us in the Church, to teach and guide us into truth, we must be guided if we will come into it. In things unlawful nor one nor other is to be obeyed: in things indifferent they always are; in things doubtful it is our safest course to have recourse to them, provided that they be not of Corah's company, that they exalt not themselves against Moses and Aaron, nor draw us to it. If they do, we may say to them as Moses did to those, "Ye take too much upon you, you sons of Levi." God leads his people "like a flock," in peace and unity, and "by the hands of Moses and Aaron." Thus the Spirit guides into all truth, because the Spirit is God, and God so guides.

You have heard the way and means, the first part of ὁδηγήσει, or the Spirit's guiding. The second follows; his act and motion.

(1.) He leads or guides us only; he does not drive us; that is not the way to plant truth, by force and violence, fire and fagots; not the Spirit's, sure, which is the Spirit of love.

(2.) Yet ἄγει there is, we told you, in it; some act of the Spirit: he moves and stirs up to it, enlightens our understandings, actuates our wills, disposes ways and times, occasions and opportunities to it; that is the reason we hear the truth more willingly at some time than other. Paul may plant, Apollos water, but the increase is this Spirit of God's; when all is done that man can do, he must have his act, or it will not be done.

Gen. xxxiii. 14.

(3.) He leads on fair and easily, for *deducet*; it is no Jehu's pace; that pace is only for an earthly kingdom, not an heavenly. The Spirit "leads softly on," like Jacob, "according as the cattle and children are able to endure;" according as our inferior powers, signified by the cattle, and our new begun piety and capacities, intimated by the children, are able to follow. It is danger, else, we lose them by the way. He that presses even truth and piety too fast upon us, is liker to tire us, and make us give out by the way, than to lead us out to our journey's end. By degrees it is that even the greatest perfection must be come to. Truths are to be scattered as men are able to bear them; Christ's own method, in the verse before. The way "into all truth" is by some and some.

(4.) This guiding is by teaching; one translation has *docebit*, shall teach; and chap. xiv. 26, it is so too; "he shall teach you,"—teach us the necessity of a teacher: "How shall they hear without a preacher?" To this purpose the Spirit sets teachers in the Church; "pastors and teachers:" pastors to rule, teachers to teach; both to guide us into the truth. Yea, but teachers we now have store, that to be sure guide not into the truth, for they teach contraries and contradictions. What teachers then are they that teach the truth? Such as "be sent," says S. Paul, sent by them that have authority to send them; if they come without authority, or from a false one, from them that never received power themselves to send others, though they were sent themselves, they are not sent by the Spirit; and though they may guide now and then into a truth, teach something that is true; into all they cannot; their very function is a lie, and their preaching of it.

(5.) Leading or guiding "into all truth" as one, *omnem veritatem*, in the singular, will tell us that unity is his way of guiding. No truth in division; we cannot so much as see our faces true in the clearest water if it be troubled; cast but a stone in, and divide its surface, and you spoil your seeing true; cast but a stone of division into the Church, and no seeing truth. It is "the spiritual man" that only truly discerns and sees the truth; the natural and carnal man, he cannot. And if there be "divisions" or schisms "among you, are you not carnal?" says S. Paul, in the next chapter. Yes, you are; so the schismatic, or he that causes rents and divisions in the Church, is but a carnal man, for all his brags, and cannot see the truth how much soever he pretend it. It were well if men would think of this, we were likely then the sooner to see truth, to be guided into all truth, if we could once keep all together; peace and truth go both together.

Thus far one word has led you: the connexion of that and the other with the former, of his guiding with his coming,

SERMON XLI.

John xiv. 26.
Rom. x. 14.

1 Cor. xii. 28.
Eph. iv. 11.

Rom. x. 15.

1 Cor. ii. 14, 15.

1 Cor. iii. 3.

will lead you further. "When he, the Spirit of truth, is come," then "he will guide you." When he "is come" is, when he is so grounded and settled in us, that we can say he is come indeed, he is in us of a truth, then all truth will follow presently. When the Holy Spirit has once taken up his lodging in us, that we also begin to be holy spirits too, then truth comes on amain. "If any man will do his will, he shall know of the doctrine whether it be of God;" till our hearts be well framed to the obedience of God's commandments, no truly knowing truth. Divine knowledge is contrary to other knowledges; they begin in speculation and end in action, this begins with action and ends in speculation— seeing and knowing God: "What man is he that feareth the Lord, him shall he teach in the way that he shall choose." When the Spirit's holiness is come into us, his truth will follow as fast as we can bear it, till we come to "the fulness of the measure of the stature of Christ," to Christ himself that is "the truth;" the way now to come to the knowledge of truth is by holiness and true obedience. Nor yet so to be understood, as if the good man only knew the truth, or that every one that has Christ, or the Spirit dwelling in them, were the only knowing men, and therefore fit only to teach others. Indeed, if you take knowledge for practical and saving knowledge, so it is; no man knows God but he that loves him; no man so knows truth but he that loves and follows it; and no man is saved by knowing, but by doing it. But that which may serve to save a man's self will not serve to save others, to bring them to salvation. It was one of Corah, Dathan, and Abiram's doctrines indeed. "All the congregation is holy, every one of them; wherefore then do you, Moses and Aaron, lift up yourselves above the congregation of the Lord?" Why do you priests lift up yourselves so much to think you only are fit to teach and rule the people? "But the earth opened her mouth," and confuted the madness of these men. Be the person never so holy, if he have no function to it, he must not presume to teach others, though he must teach himself. Holiness is one gift, the power of teaching is another, though both from the same Spirit; and no venturing upon Aaron's, S. Paul's, or S. Peter's office, unless the Spirit has set us apart to that end and purpose. It is enough for any other that he has truth enough to save himself; and it is but ambition, presumption, and sacrilege, and by that a lessening of his goodness, to pretend to that which God has not called him to, but his own preposterous zeal, or too high conceit of his own holiness and abilities; and so far from being like to guide into all truth, that our own days are sufficient witnesses all errors and heresies have sprung from it.

The way that the Spirit guides into all his truth is by the Scripture, interpreted by the Church, by the decrees, and determinations, and customs of it; by the hand of our lawful pastors and teachers, himself inwardly acting and moving in us, inwardly working and persuading us, outwardly ministering opportunities and occasions to us, leading us by degrees, preserving us in peace, keeping us in obedience, and holiness, and charity. Thus he guides into all truth, ordinarily, and no way else.

VII. And to be sure, lastly, thus he will. Christ here promises for him that he shall, for so we may render it, "he shall." And he is "the Spirit of truth," says the text. So he will make good what Christ has promised, and what he comes to be, the guide into the way of truth. We need not either mistrust or fear it. For though Christ himself must go away and leave us, because it is expedient that he should, yet this Spirit will stand by us howsoever. "Howbeit" he will. He is a mighty wind, and will quickly disperse and blow away the mists of ignorance and error; he is a fire, and will easily purge the dross, and burn up the chaff that mixes with the truth, and hides or sullies it; nothing can stand before him—nothing shall. He comes to us with a "howbeit," a *non obstante*, be it how it will; though we be blind, and ignorant, and foolish, and full of infirmities and sins, so we be willing, he will come and guide us.

Yet if now we will so be guided, to close up all,—we must, lastly, submit ourselves wholly to his way and guiding, to the truth, and to all of it.

To his way and order; (1,) no teaching him how he should teach us. "Them that be meek shall he guide in judgment, and such as be gentle, them shall he learn his way." No teaching without humility; we must be willing to be guided or he will not guide us. Men will not now; thence comes so many errors and mistakes.

To "truth" too, (2,) we must submit. If it be truth, no quarrelling against it; no seeking shelters and distinctions to defend us from it. Though we have been long in error, and count it a dishonour to revoke it, revoke it we must, be it what it will, or we endanger the loss of the whole truth,— the Spirit will not lead us.

And to "all," (3,) too. We must not plead our interest, or anything, against it, be it never so troublesome, never so disadvantageous, never so displeasing; we must resolve to embrace it, because it is truth.

With this submission, too, we are now to come to the holy mysteries; submit our hearts, and judgments, and affections here; not to presume to pry too much into the way and manner of Christ's and the Spirit's being there, but to submit our reasons to our faith; and open our hearts to Christ, as well as our mouths to the outward elements; and keep under our affections by holy and godly doing, that so the Spirit of truth may come into them all. And so doing, the Spirit will come, and he will guide us,—guide us into all necessary and saving truths,—guide us to Christ,—guide us to God,—guide us here, and guide us hence,—guide us in earth, and guide us to heaven.

THE FOURTH SERMON

UPON

WHITSUNDAY.

Acts ii. 1—4.

And when the day of Pentecost was fully come, they were all with one accord in one place. And suddenly there came a sound from heaven as of a rushing mighty wind, and it filled all the house where they were sitting. And there appeared unto them cloven tongues like as of fire, and it sat upon each of them. And they were all filled with the Holy Ghost, and began to speak with other tongues, as the Spirit gave them utterance.

THE words are the history for the day; the day the anniversary for the words. This day the text fulfilled in the ears of some of " every nation under heaven," remembered and celebrated by the tongues and voices of the Christian Church throughout the earth. The things done here the reason of the day, and the day the memorial of them. Here you may see why we keep this feast, why it is so solemn; why it is one of the *dies albi*, why so white a day; a Sunday white with the light of that holy fire that this day came down from heaven, and sate like rays of light upon the Apostles, those whitest and purest sons of light; the Holy Ghost, the third Person of the blessed Trinity, descending miraculously in it upon the disciples, as it were a sudden rushing mighty wind filling all the corners both of the place and of their souls, and so seating himself in the form of fiery cloven tongues upon each of that holy company, and thereby giving them new hearts and words to speak the wonders of the Most High.

SERMON XLII.

Acts ii. 5.

SERMON XLII.

A business we are this day to be their disciples in, to use our tongues to the same purpose, that we may testify ourselves to be led by the same Spirit, breathe by the same breath, move by the same wind, our hearts warmed by the same fire, our words framed by the same tongues that this day appeared so miraculously upon them.

We have done so in the unity of the Church several times before in the year for Christ, the second Person of the Godhead; do we so now also for the third: the benefits and glory which this day came from him, which they this day did after a strange miraculous way receive, we may this day also receive in an efficacious way, though not externally and visibly, yet internally and invisibly, from the same Spirit. For this feast is his, and our speech this day principally of him, and our praises for him.

Now the best way to keep the feast, so as to be partakers of the honour and benefits of it, is to place ourselves in the same fashion, set ourselves in the same posture, dispose ourselves after the same order with them here, both for the receiving of him, and after we have received him. For it is part of the Epistle, not the Gospel, that I have read you; and the business of the Epistle is commonly doctrine and instruction, as the matter of the Gospel is usually history. So we then to be instructed by it, how to demean ourselves for the receiving of the Holy Spirit—how to know how, and where, and when it is he comes—how to distinguish him and his coming, from other spirits—what to do also when we have received him—and when, more especially, to do the one or expect the other, by the pattern and example in the text. This will prove the best, the only celebration of the feast, the most glorious manifestation this day on our parts for the more glorious manifestation this day on God's: the manifestation of our thankfulness for the manifestation of God's goodness.

Thus, without either nicety or much art, I shall divide you the text into these particulars:—

1. The disposition of them that the Spirit comes and lights upon, them that are all "with one accord in one place," that are there quietly sitting and expecting Christ there, especially upon the solemn days, upon the day of Pentecost, a solemn festival.

2. The way, and manner, and order, of the Holy Spirit's coming, suddenly, from heaven, like a sound thence, " like the sound of a rushing mighty wind filling all the house," in the appearance of cloven fiery tongues sitting upon each on whom he comes.

3. The effect and issue immediately upon it: they are filled, all filled, filled with Ghost and Spirit, the Holy Ghost or Spirit,—begin to speak, speak strangely, strange tongues too, yet in measure and order too no other than the Spirit gives them utterance.

4. And, lastly, though first it be in the text, yet because it is but the circumstance and time of the story, and not the main business or second of it, and fittest to close up all in good time and order,—the time when all this was done, when these things came to pass, when the Apostles were so disposed, when the Holy Ghost thus descended, when this strange issue fell out, " when the day of Pentecost was fully come,"—in very good time, the promised time, Christ's time, God's own time, such as he had prefigured them in the law too, at the fifty days' feast after the Passover,—a solemn day, and somewhat more, as you shall hear anon. Thus we best join the history and the moral, the doctrine and use of Pentecost or Whitsunday; nay, the very holy Spirit of the day and our souls to-day together, that we may not be like men that only come to hear news, a story, and away, but such as hear the word and profit by it.

Which that we may, come, O " mighty wind," and blow upon us; descend, O holy fire, and warm our hearts; give me a tongue, O blessed Spirit, out of this day's number and utterance; give thy servants capacious spirits and remembrance, that thy word may rush in upon them as a " sound from heaven," and fill the houses of all our souls with joy and gladness, with holy fire of piety and devotion, that we may with one accord, one heart and mind, speak forth thy praise and glory!

The first point in the order I have set you, is the disposition of them that the Holy Spirit will come and light upon. (1.) They are of " one accord;" (2,) in " one place;" (3,) " sitting" quietly and expecting there, and that (4,) also upon the solemn day, when " the day of

SERMON XLII. Pentecost," any solemn day or occasion is presented them.

They are, first, of "one accord," whom this Spirit vouchsafes to descend into. This unity draws the Spirit to them, that keeps it with them, the house of unity is the only temple of the Spirit of unity. That soul which breaks the bond of unity, and divides itself from the Church of Christ, from the company of the Apostles and their successors, the still fathers of it, cannot hold this holy wind, cannot enclose this holy fire; they are broken and cracked, crack only of the Spirit, but are really broken from that body in which only the Spirit moves. Take and divide a member from the body—be it the principal, that in which most spirit was, the heart or the head, and once divided, the spirit vanishes from it, will not sit nor dwell in it: just so is it in Christ's body, the Church. If one of the chiefest members of it, one erst while of the devoutest and most religious in it, once grow so proud of his own wisdom or gifts, so singular in his conceits as to separate himself from his fellows, from that body whereof Christ is the head; he goes away like a member from the natural body, and leaves the Spirit behind him; that retires from him, for it is one Spirit, and cannot be divided from the body, though it work diversely in it.

If this being of one accord, of one mind, be the temper for the receipt of the Holy Spirit, as here you see it is, and in reason it can be no otherwise, it being the Spirit of love and unity; what spirit are they of, whose religion is faction, whose chief pretended piety is schism, whose business is to differ from all the world? Nothing can be more evident than that men are now-a-days much at a loss for the Spirit, however every one claim to it, seeing there is no accord, but discord; not diversities only, but contrarieties, but contradictions, amongst them that most pretend the Spirit.

Indeed were this "they" any less a "they" than the Apostles themselves and the whole number of the then disciples, or had there been but the least division among them, either about the manner of staying or expecting Christ's promise, or, which is less, about the place to stay in, it may be these men might have had a shadow for their separations; but Apostles "they" were, and "in one place" they were, too, all together, agreed in all, were all in unity, were all in uniformity; not their minds only, but their bodies too, together. Men thought it nothing, awhile since, to withdraw themselves from the houses of God, as if no matter at all for the place, they could for all that be of the same faith; but too woful experience has proved it now, that with the one place the one faith is vanished, with the ceremony the substance gone too, with the uniformity of worship the unanimity of our minds and the uniformity of our faith too blown into the air. How shall we do, O blessed Spirit, in so many cracked vessels to retain thee? Needs must the Spirit expire out of that body which has so many breaches and divisions in it, so many divided houses, so many broken churches, so many rotten congregations.

I know if it be only necessity divides us, and drives us into several dens and caves, as it did the primitive Christians in the days of those fiery persecutions, that the Holy Spirit will ransack all the crannies, and search out all the privatest corners, be they above ground or under it; but it is because the mind of all those several places is but one, and in that respect they are no more than so many several cells of the one Catholic Church: but where choice and not necessity, wilfulness and not force, singularity and not purity of truth or conscience, makes the division, and draws disciples into chambers, parlours, barns or mills, woods or deserts, "go not," says Christ, "out after them;" say they what they will of Christ or Spirit there, "believe it not." "Two in a field, and yet one taken and the other left; two at the mill, and one taken and the other left." So at the most, I fear, great hazard that any, if they be no better, no more orderly gathered when the Master comes.

Or were they yet perhaps in several places sitting as they are here, that is, quietly, and in true peace and faith, expecting the promise of their Lord, something might be said to excuse their separations; but not only actually to break the unity of the spirit and the bond of peace, but to breathe out nothing but war, contention, and dispute; to be so far from sitting down, and either suffering for Christ, or humbly expecting his time of assistance and deliverance out of their perplexities and discomforts, as to take the matter into their own hands, and prevent the coming of the Spirit of peace, by rising and raising spirits of war and confusion, they must give me leave to tell them, they know not "what spirit they are of,"—a heady, giddy, furious spirit; "zeal," I bear them witness, with S. Paul, "without knowledge," and spirit without holiness; for "the spirit of the prophets is subject to the prophets," much more to the God of the prophets, to his time and order.

And yet there is another disposition to be observed in those upon whom the good Spirit lights, to make either instruments of glory to the Church, or piety to God. It is sitting and expecting, if you mark it, till the day or days of Pentecost be fully come and accomplished; souls willing to keep a holy day or holy days to the Lord; neither to be scared from the attendance of their Master and their devotions, nor to be shortened and interrupted in their pious course of faith and piety by the now so terrible scarecrows of set feasts, as Jewish, legal and superstitious observances, as the new zealots are so wise to term them, because they understand not terms or times. The spiritual man—if they be what they boast—discerns the things of God, though hidden in darker mysteries; knows better to distinguish Judaism from Christianity, piety from superstition; and is not only content, but studies to wait upon his Lord upon any day, glad to get it too, Passover or Pentecost,—makes use of them all, and turns them fairly from their old Judaism, and consecrates them anew to his Master's service: and this doing the very Spirit himself authorizes and abets, whilst he thus seems to pick out the time for his own coming at the Jewish Pentecost, so to sanctify a new Christian Pentecost, the Christian Whitsuntide, to all Christian generations by this solemn glory of his benefits to-day, to be remembered for ever.

Thus we have the disposition he vouchsafes to descend upon, unanimous, uniform, peaceable, orderly, expecting souls; such as set apart and keep days to God with faith and patience, and in obedience and order: the contrary tempers are too rough lodgings for the Spirit of meekness, order, and peace. Be we so prepared, and he will come.

2. Now see we how he comes, the manner of the Holy Spirit's coming. Double it is, to the ear and to the eye.

To the ear first; and that (1,) "suddenly;" from heaven, (2,) secondly; (3,) like a sound thence; (4,) the "sound of a rushing mighty wind;" that (5,) "filled all the house;" yet, (6,) the house only where they sate: thus to the ear. Then, secondly, to the eye, in the appearance of tongues, cloven tongues, tongues of fire, tongues sitting; and lastly, sitting upon each of them.

SERMON XLII.

(1.) We take, first, what came first—the sound; and that, first, was sudden;—"suddenly," says the text; yet as sudden as it came, go it shall not so, not without a note or two.

"Suddenly," then, it came, (i.) to show the freeness of God's grace, so far above desert, that it is also above apprehension; it outruns that, and is upon us ere we are aware; so little probability have we to deserve it, that we commonly have not time to do it: and when we have, yet so sudden does it fall, that we may well see it comes not from ourselves, so dull a piece as earth and sin has made us.

To show (ii.) the readiness of his goodness, beyond expectation, readier far to give than we to take, comes commonly upon us sooner than we expect or wish, "prevents us with his goodness," as the Psalmist observes to us, and "runs very swiftly," flying upon the "wings of the wind." Ps. xxi. 3. Ps. cxlvii. 15. Ps. civ. 4.

To show us (iii.) the vanity of men who think it comes "with observation." "It does not," says Christ. It is not at our command. The Prophets themselves could not prophesy when they listed; it was *cecidit Spiritus*, the Spirit "fell" upon them, the common phrase in Scripture, and then they prophesied; till that fell,—and fall it did but at times, what times it pleased,—the motions of the Prophets were but as other men's. Indeed I remember Elisha, willing to prophesy to Jehoshaphat the king of Judah, calls for a minstrel, and "it came to pass that while the minstrel played the hand of the Lord came upon him." Not that either the Spirit was at the will and under the power of the minstrel or the prophet, but to show the disposition that the Holy Spirit vouchsafes soonest and suddenest to come to, a sweet and tuneable soul disposed to accord, to love and peace, and unity. And by-the-way you may take notice, music and the Spirit are at no discord, as the late spiritual men, forsooth, would have us to believe; the prophet, you see, thought it Luke xvii. 20. 2 Kings iii. 14, 15.

the only way and medium to raise his spirits into heavenly raptures, to make himself capable of new inspirations, to call for an instrument of music, and as it were to persuade the heavenly Spirit down by some grave and sober music; which may make us wonder how these great pretenders to the Spirit, and gapers for it, should be so furious enemies against the Church music, so ever employed and approved both by God and his Prophets and Apostles,—for "singing with melody," says S. Paul too,—to fit and sweeten, and raise our dull and rougher spirits to the service of heaven and the entertainment of the heavenly and gentle motions of the Spirit in those holy performances. But all this while this is but to dispose ourselves; the Spirit itself is at its own disposal for all this, and when he comes, comes on a sudden.

marginal: Ephes. v. 19.

Even to awake (iv.) and rouse us up. We are drowsy souls to heavenward, and want some sudden change to startle us; things that come leisurely will not do it. It must be a sudden turn that will turn us out of ourselves, or from our follies, or so much upward.

And sudden (v.) it is again, to show the activity of the Spirit of God, how wonderful he is among the children of men; that he can not only turn the world upside down whenever he please, but as soon as he pleases; does but "blow with his wind, and the waters flow;" casts but a sudden glance of an eye at S. Peter, and out run the waters out of his; he that was but just now afraid of the voice of a silly girl, fears not presently the lightnings and thunders of the greatest tyrants. *Mox ut tetigerit mentem docet, solumque tetigisse docuisse est. Nam humanum animum subito ut illustrat immutat: abnegat hoc* [*hunc*] *repente quod erat, exhibet repente quod non erat.*[n] He does but touch the mind and teaches it, shines into it and changes it together, forgets immediately what it was, and is what it was not. All the quickest ways of men must have time and leisure, be it but to cast an eye; but O *qualis est artifex iste Spiritus!* But how wonderful an artist is thy Spirit, O Lord, that knows not the least hindrance or delay! Ἄφνω ἐγένετο; it comes so suddenly, there is no appearance often of its coming, not so much as a whiff or shadow before it to give us warning of its approach,

[n] S. Gregory [In Evangel. Lib. II. Homil. xxx. Ed. Bened. tom. i. p. 1580.]

for this reason among the rest, lest we should attribute anything to our own preparations, yea, though they be such as God requires.

Sudden, last of all, to show us our duties not to neglect the light and sudden motions of the Holy Spirit, though we know not how or when, or whence, they rise, so we know but whither they go and lead us; if to good, catch at them, let them not go as they came, but leap we into the water while it stirs; fan we ourselves with this wind while it moves; for how long it will stay, or whether ever come again, we know not; take it in the present while we may, omit no good motion, no opportunity or occasion of any doing well; suddenly it comes, and suddenly it may be gone, if we lay not hold upon it and make use of it. Thus, from the quickness and suddenness of this Spirit's motion, God's grace and goodness, his incomprehensible power and operation, and our readiness to lay hold upon it, are preached to us.

(2.) But "from heaven" what next is preached to us, but that thence it is all holy winds and breaths, and spirits come; from heaven, not of men; no human wit can teach what this Spirit does, the "spirit of man but the things of a man," it knows no further; the things of heaven from the Spirit of heaven; *de cœlo*, from the very heaven of heavens, not any lower heavens, or any other spirits of heaven, but that which has no plural number, is but one, and is an heaven itself; not only a Spirit of heaven, but heaven that is the Spirit, the heaven in whom all of us "live and move and have our being" as in our heaven of glory. 1 Cor. ii. 11.

Yet again, "from heaven," that we may at any time know what wind blows in us; if our affections, intentions, and endeavours are only towards heaven, set upon heaven and heavenly things; if what moves us be only heavenly and not earthly interests,—then it is the good Spirit that reigns and rules in us; then it is the wind and spirit, and fire and tongue, a wind out of God's own treasury, a Spirit out of God's own bosom, a fire from that eternal light, a tongue from that eternal wisdom; but if our actions come but so much as collaterally and glancing at other respects than God and heaven, it is no spirit, no motion, no work of his Spirit, but some other's; this comes directly straight from heaven.

SERMON XLII.

(3.) Now from heaven what is it that comes here? "There came suddenly a sound from heaven"—a sound!—yes, a sound, and it is a good hearing, the best news we ever heard since Christ's departure; a sound that is "gone out into all lands, and into the ends of the world." *Sonus cœlorum*, the sound of the heavens, the very true Pythagorical harmony of the spheres, the sweetest sound was ever heard, the sound of the Gospel, of the kingdom of heaven, and the knowledge of it.

We perhaps looked, when we heard of something coming down from heaven, for some glorious host of angels, cherubims or seraphims, some or other of them at least, or for "the new Jerusalem" we read of, "coming" from above, "down from God out of heaven;" and we think much to be put off with a sound : yet I must tell you this sound sounds better in our ears, the sound of an eternal Comforter that should abide with us for ever, and bring us in due time to that new Jerusalem and those blessed spirits in heaven.

Rev. xxi. 2.

And with a fitter convoy he could not come than with a sound, who was now to send and constitute such as should sound out the Gospel over all the world, so many apostles, evangelists, pastors, and teachers.

Nor yet of all sounds with any so correspondent to him could he come as that of the wind; nothing more to express his glory and Godhead, that this Spirit "he," is that very "he" that "cometh riding upon the wings of the wind;" a fit blast to stop the idle breath of those saucy inquirers of our age, who dispute this blessed Spirit out of his Deity.

Need had he appear, it seems, (4,) as "a rushing mighty wind," to rush down these enemies of his and overthrow them. Indeed he came to-day with so mighty and powerful a blast that we might both see his power and Godhead, as well as his mercy and goodness to us; his goodness in coming like a "wind," his power in coming like a "rushing mighty" one.

The benefits we receive from the wind represent the benefits we receive from the Spirit, and so (i.) present his goodness.

The wind, first, purges and clears the air from noisome and infectious vapours; the Spirit cleanses and purifies our souls and bodies from the stinking and unwholesome steams of sins and lusts.

(ii.) The wind sometimes gathers up clouds and rains, and sometimes scatters them again. The Holy Spirit one while gathers clouds into the countenance, and brings showers into the eyes of the penitent sinner; and other while it blows away all blackness from our faces, and makes the soul look up, and the spirits smile and dance in our hearts and eyes.

(iii.) The wind cheers and refreshes the plants and trees; the blessed Spirit cheers the plants of grace within us, and makes them fructify and prosper, puts life and spirit into the root, verdure and freshness into the leaf, fineness and subtilty into the relish of the fruit of all holy actions and virtues.

(iv.) The wind cools the heat and revives the fainting spirit; the Holy Spirit does so too, allays the inordinate heat of concupiscence within us, cools the over-hotness and ardours of our passions, revives us and recovers us when we are almost choked with the fumes and flames of our own corruption, affections and lusts.

(v.) The wind, again, kindles the fire, and blows the spark into a flame; and the Holy Spirit it is that kindles all heavenly warmth and flames within us; without his breath we are all but dead coals.

(vi.) The wind scatters the chaff and screens the dust out of the corn; the Holy Spirit blows away all our chaff and dust, all our dross and rubbish, our vanities and follies, and makes us fit corn for God's own garners.

(vii.) The wind it is that drives home the ship into the haven; and the Holy Spirit it is that drives our poor torn and tattered vessels into the haven where we would be, as the Psalmist speaks; drives us up and down over the troublesome sea of this tempestuous world into the port of everlasting bliss, into the haven of heaven itself.

You see the goodness and graces of the Holy Spirit not unfitly expressed by the resemblance of the wind. See we now his power as well resembled by it, by the "rushing mighty wind."

(4.) The wind is but a thin and airy puff, so subtile that we cannot see it, yet what a rattling does it make! rattles the

SERMON XLII.
1 Kings xix. 11.

ships of Tarshish together, tears up trees by the roots, throws down houses and buildings, nay, "rends the mountains and breaks in pieces the rocks before it." But never did wind so tear up foundations by the roots, never did so strong buildings fall before that tumultuous vapour, as this "rushing mighty wind" that this day came down from heaven hath cast down before it. All the high things of the earth, wisdom and learning, and might and majesty, have fallen as easily as so many paper turrets at its breath, all have given up themselves and thrown all prostrate at the word of this Spirit, so that the whole world stood wondering and amazed to see itself so turned about by the mere words of a few simple fishermen, without force, or eloquence, or craft; to see itself so tamely submit its glory to the humility of Christ, its greatness to his littleness, its majesty to his baseness, its wisdom to the foolishness of his cross; its ease, pleasure, to the pains and patience of it. But *manus Excelsi fecit hoc;* it is the hand of the Most Highest that has done it; such a wind could come from none but God, such a Spirit can be none but his; none but he could do it, and it is marvellous in our eyes, his power as marvellous as his mercy, both of them above any created ones whatsoever.

(5.) Well may such a wind as this now "fill the house," as it follows in the fifth consideration. And yet commonly the wind fills the open air and not the houses. Common winds do so indeed, but this peculiar wind fills the house and every corner, comes in even when the doors are shut, or else opens and shuts them as it pleases; a sign it is more than air or airy spirit; it is he only that searches the hearts and reins, that can glide so into these close rooms of ours; and it is our happiness it is so, that he thus blows into the house of his own accord and power: for, Give me a ship, says S. Chrysostom,° with all its tackling, sails and anchors, spread all in order too, and let the wind lie still, let there be no gale stirring, and all its furniture and men are nothing; no more is the soul with all its preparations without the blowing of the Spirit; nay, no more is all our eloquence, all our arguments and persuasions, the subtilty of our understanding, the richness of our conceit and notion, the sweetness of

° [This passage has not been found.]

the voice, the rhetoric of words, the strength of reason, the whole tackling and furniture of the orator or preacher, unless the Spirit come and fill the sail and stretch the canvass, and so drive on the vessel. It is this *implevit* we must hold by; it is this filling our empty house, our lank and lither sails, that blows comfort to us.

(6.) And it is the enhancing of the benefit, which is the last considerable in this similitude of the wind, that it fills "the house" only "where they are sitting." It is no ordinary or common favour that God vouchsafes in filling our houses with the Spirit; he hath not dealt so with any other nation, with any other people than the Christian people. It is the Church only, and the souls of Christians in it, that this "mighty wind," as rushing and mighty as it is, does content and contain itself in. All other houses and places stand empty, cannot get this tenant. It is the property of this wind, and no other, to blow where it lists, in this house and no other, within doors all, within the Church, none without at all; or the sound of it only passes out to call others in, that they may see and wonder at the things that are come to pass this day, that Jews and proselytes, Cretes and Arabians, Parthians and Medes, and all nations under heaven may bear witness of the wonder; and if they come in, in some sort partake of it too; of the "wind," though not of the "tongues;" of some graces of the Spirit, though not of the other. Only come in they must, into the Church of Christ, which is his body, before their veins be filled with this Spirit, before they feel any motion of it.

Of the wind, I say, such a portion of the Spirit as may breathe into them the breath of life; but tongues of fire are for those only who were sitting there before, sitting as governors of the Church, to whom that baptism of fire was promised, who were bid to tarry and expect it, and when so enabled, to go abroad then and use their tongues, and blow the flames of divine love and charity through the world.

I should now proceed to these miraculous tongues, the second representment of the Holy Spirit. And methinks I am unwilling to leave them unspoken of, to which we owe our speech. But your ears are already filled with the wind;

Sermon XLII.

[1 Cor. xiv. 22.]

[Ezek. xxxvii. 7.]

yet I hope it is the proper wind of the day, and the sound of it shall not vanish as the wind, as ordinary winds and sounds, nor my words as the soft air.

So much the rather in that this point of the wind comes more home to us than that other of the tongues. Tongues were "for them that believe not," says the Apostle; but the wind, the "rushing mighty wind" from heaven, to cast down all the strongholds of sin and Satan, for them that believe, even for us all. The fiery tongues concern the Apostles, as a miraculous enabling of them to the work of the apostleship, to the preaching and divulging the Gospel of Christ; but the breath and blowing of the Spirit concerns all Christians whatsoever, under every notion. To that, our proper tenure is from this wind, nay so much the more, because it is the breath of the Spirit, not the tongue, that makes us Christian; the wind, like that in Ezekiel, quickens our dead bones into the life of Christ, and by it we live to our own salvation; by the tongues only to another's. So having gotten our share already in this wind from heaven, we may the easier bear the deferring of the discourse of the tongues thence.

And truly, if we can now get the Spirit to blow upon these dead elements, and quicken them to us into the body and blood of Christ, we shall quickly, by the virtue of that blood of the vine, speak with new tongues, the Spirit will give utterance, and we shall sing the praises of the Lord.

That should be indeed the whole business of our tongues to-day, to be as loud as the loudest wind in our thanksgivings. "O ye winds of God, bless ye the Lord!" say the three children in the fire; O ye children of the Lord, bless ye the Lord in the wind! say I, in this "mighty rushing wind;" acknowledge his goodness, admire his power, confess his praise, who thus blows the sparks of grace up in us, who cleanses our souls from all impure airs and vapours, who scatters the clouds of sorrow, shows us the fairest face of heaven; who cools and refreshes, and revives and purges us, and wafts us to our heavenly country by this holy wind; who daily does wondrous things in us, and for us, and by us, through the mighty rushings of it, and fills and replenishes us with all the benefits and comforts of it, whilst he passes by others without so much as a breathing on them!

Yet the business would be, how to catch this wind, and serve our uses of it. Why! in the word, and in the sacraments, and by prayers, we may have it, and be filled with it. Come, then, and fill your souls; you have heard the word already, treasure it up (for there are treasures for the winds), and you shall feel it blow, move, and stir in you. The blessed Sacrament is a second way to be filled with this Spirit; it is reached out and proffered to us there; we may there take it into our mouths, as before into our ears; and it will rush down all before it that stands against it—down it will into our bowels, and fill us with all heavenly fulness: and then draw it in and breathe it out we may, by devout and holy prayers; only remember always the disposition of that soul this Spirit will only abide with, peace and unity. Thus disposed you must be to receive the Spirit, thus disposed to receive the Sacrament; and then the Spirit will descend upon our sacrifice, and the wind of God's benediction upon our offering; and we shall return hence with mighty rushings in us, the rushing down of sin, the raising up of grace; mighty, mighty things will be done in us by the power of this Spirit, and this wind; and as it came from heaven, so thither will it back again and carry us upon its wings to keep a perpetual feast, an eternal Whitsunday, all in the white robes of everlasting glory.

Blow, O blessed wind, upon us this day; blow away our chaff, and dross, and dust, out of our performances; breathe into thy holy mysteries the breath of a life-giving life; rush down all our sins before thee; purify, and cleanse, and refresh, and revive and comfort us, by thy saving breath, that this wind may bring us good, all the good of heaven and earth; fill both our ears and hearts here with sounds and songs of joy, and hereafter with hallelujahs for evermore!

THE FIFTH SERMON

UPON

WHITSUNDAY.

ACTS ii. 1—4.

And when the day of Pentecost was fully come, they were all with one accord in one place. And suddenly there came a sound from heaven as of a rushing mighty wind, and it filled all the house where they were sitting. And there appeared unto them cloven tongues like as of fire, and it sat upon each of them. And they were all filled with the Holy Ghost, and began to speak with other tongues, as the Spirit gave them utterance.

SERMON XLIII. "WHEN the day of Pentecost" here "was fully come," (ver. 1,) "they were all filled," says the text, (ver. 4,) "and began to speak." Now the day is fully come again; we also are Job xxxii. 18. "full of matter," as Elihu told Job, and we must speak. For it is a day of tongues, a day to speak in, and a day to speak of too, to speak *magnalia* in it, and of it, of the great things of God, and the great things of the day, "the wonderful Acts ii. 11. works of God," which were this day wrought by the descent of the Holy Spirit. To this end the Spirit descended, to this end the tongues came, to this end both appeared—that we might learn to use our tongues and spirits to set forth his praise, every one according as the Spirit gives him utterance, according to the gift and place that God has given him : we, as the apostles and ministers of the Spirit; you, as disciples Acts ii. 37. to be taught by us; you, to ask with those hearers (ver. 37), "Men and brethren, what shall we do?"—we, as S. Peter Acts ii. 38. (ver. 38), to tell you what to do; we, faithfully to preach the word, "the remission of sins, and the gifts of the Holy Ghost" (ver. 38), you "gladly to receive" it (ver. 41); we to begin the anthem, you to make the chorus for the service of this day's solemnity; both of us to bear our parts to-day in praises and thanksgivings, for the benefits we receive from this day's business.

Sermon XLIII.
Acts ii. 38.
Acts ii. 41.

We have the last year begun to speak of it out of this text; we begin again to speak of it hence this year, shall do as the Spirit shall give us utterance. To hold our peace to-day were to sin against the Spirit, who this day gave us all our tongues to speak; and I hope nor we nor you will be silent of his glory; no such evil shall befal us.

For a day of good tidings it is, was so when it came first, will be so now it is come again, and whenever it comes about; was so to the disciples, will be so, I hope, to us to hear the voice of a Comforter, to see his appearance, or but hear of it. The text is the story of it, the relation of the coming of the Comforter, the descent of the Holy Ghost. In it, when time was, we observed these four particulars:—

I. The disposition of them the Spirit comes upon.

II. The way, and manner, and order he comes after.

III. The effect and issue that comes upon it. And,

IV. The time when it came to pass.

I. The disposition of those the Spirit comes upon is such as makes men to be of one accord, that brings them all to one place, upon such days as Pentecost, on the solemn feasts; makes them then and there sit quietly and orderly, expecting Christ; a unanimous, Church-like, orderly, devout, and religious disposition. Upon such, and such only, is it that the Holy Spirit comes.

II. The way, manner, and order of his coming, is as a "mighty wind," and like as "fire." Suddenly he came; came (1) as a sound, as a sound from heaven, as a sound of a "rushing mighty wind," and such a one too as "filled all the house." Came (2) as fire, as tongues of fire, as "cloven tongues" of fire; such fire yet as sate upon them and did no hurt, heavenly and celestial fire. Thus he came to-day.

III. The effect and issue is filling; the filling of all that then were present with ghost and spirit, Holy Ghost and Spirit; then with words, and tongues, and speech, even according to the measure or pleasure of the Spirit. This the issue of the Holy Spirit's coming,—fulness, and spirit, and ability, and utterance; new hearts and new spirits, new languages, and sobriety to use them.

IV. The time, the time of Pentecost, when it "was fully come," when all was ready, persons, and place, and time, fully disposed and fit; then comes the Holy Spirit, then came all these things to pass. I put this last, though it stands first, that I might close up all at least in good time and order.

There wants nothing now, O blessed Spirit, to go on and finish, but that thou shouldst come and order all our thoughts and spirits, that we may humbly receive the sound of thy holy word; that I, thy servant, may have utterance, this thy people give thee audience, all of us obedience, and all our hearts and tongues be so thoroughly heated with thy holy fire, that they may be filled with thy praise and honour all the day long!

That we may do so, here are tongues given in the text,— "cloven tongues, as it were, of fire;" there we left, there we begin again, at the second way and manner of the Holy Spirit's coming down to-day. And "there appeared unto them cloven tongues, like as of fire, and it sate upon each of them." Where, (1,) of the order; (2,) of the appearance; (3,) of the manner itself; and, lastly, of the continuance of it.

For the order, (i.) it is the second way of the Spirit's coming here: first in the wind, then in the fire. The holy fire within us is not kindled but with a mighty wind; the divine spark, or soul, cannot be blown up into a fire till some mighty wind has shaken all our powers, blown off the dust and ashes, those earthly, worldly affections that choked and covered it, till it has raised a tumult in all the corners of us, dispersed the vanities and irregularities of all our motions, and scattered everything that hindered it from the obedience to the Spirit; then, and not till then, the fire bursts forth, and, as the Psalmist, we speak with our tongues.

For the order (ii.) is the same between the "sound" and the "tongues." The "sound" first, the "tongues" second. We are first to hear before we speak, so the Spirit's order tells us here. Not turn teachers at the first dash; not presume to teach others before we are thoroughly taught ourselves; that is none of the Spirit's way of teaching, how spiritual soever they think themselves that do so; that speak what they have neither seen nor heard, their own fancies and imaginations, the devisings of their own hearts, such as the Christian world never heard before, whereof there is not so much as the sound, or anything sounding like it, in all the writings of the Church.

The sound too (iii.) before the fire. The Spirit manifests itself by degrees, first more obscurely to the ear, then more evidently to the eye. "I have heard of thee by the hearing of the ear," says Job; that was a favour: "but now mine eye seeth thee"—that is a greater. The Spirit comes by degrees. God's favours rise upon us in order. There comes first "a great and strong wind that rends the mountains and breaks in pieces the rocks" before him, that throws down our mountainous thoughts and projects, breaks them all in pieces, crosses our designs, thwarts them with some great affliction or some strange thing or other, breaks our very hearts, our stony hearts; then follows an earthquake in all our faculties; we begin to shake and tremble with the fear of the Almighty; then comes the fire and burns up all the chaff, scorches our very bones, and warms us even at the heart; whereupon presently there issues out "a still small voice" out of our lips, the "tongues" follow upon the "fire," or are even with it. This was signified to us thus by God's appearing to Elijah, and the same order the holy Spirit of God uses here to the Apostles; the same method still he keeps with us. For he thrusts not in upon us unprepared; he makes himself a way into us, gives us not so clear an evidence as seeing him at the first, not till the "sound" has well awakened us, and the wind well brushed and cleansed our houses for him. Yet then appear he does.

For we now presently hear of his appearance. "There appeared tongues." The "manifestation of the Spirit," says S. Paul, "is given to every man to profit withal." Not the "Spirit" only, but the "manifestation" too. No spirit without some manifestation. If the spirit be an extraordinary spirit the manifestation will be so too; if it be but ordinary the manifestation will be no more.

SERMON XLIII.

Jer xxiii. 21.

Ps. xii. 4.

[Lev. x. 1.]

1 Cor. xiv. 12.

Rom. xii. 6—8.

(i.) If God sends any with an extraordinary commission to preach or teach, he enables them with an extraordinary spirit, appears with them after some extraordinary fashion; tongues, or miracles, or some high heavenly fires come with them. They but blaspheme the Spirit, and usurp upon the office, who take it upon them without such a warrant; they "run without sending," says God; their tongues are but their own, and,—however those perverse fellows in the Psalm infer they are "they that ought to speak, who is Lord over them?"—they ought not to speak, there is a Lord over them, whatever they think, that will one day call them to account, and make them know it; their fire they bring is but Nadab's and Abihu's; their zeal, without knowledge; they have no tongue but what their mother taught them, the Holy Spirit has taught them none, made no appearance to them either by "fire" or by "tongues;" they are filled with some other spirit, the spirit of pride, of division, or rebellion, or somewhat worse; where the Spirit sends with an extraordinary commission, it will appear by some gift extraordinary and miraculous,—somewhat will appear.

But (ii.) if our mission be but ordinary, the ordinary way that the Spirit has now left in the power and authority of the Church will be sufficient; yet that must appear too, our authority appear thence; our tongues serve to it too, to "the edifying of the Church," to the building of it up, not to the pulling of it down. Every gift of the Holy Spirit is to have its manifestation, tongues, and interpretation, and prayer, and prophecy, and all the rest, yet all in order. Every one to employ, not hide his talent; he who has a ministry, to wait on that; he that is to exhort, to attend to that; he that is to teach, to busy himself in that, though "all according to proportion," all to appear to the glory of God.

Yet, even those saving graces of the Spirit are not always to be kept within, they are to appear in "tongues" or "fire," so shine that others may glorify, so speak and act that others seeing our good conversation may be affected with it, and persuaded to grace and virtue by it. The Spirit is not given to be hid under a bushel; the wind cannot, the fire will not, the tongue is not usual to be kept in so. They all appeared here after their way, the "wind" after its way, the "tongues" and "fire" after theirs; in this verse to the sight, the most certain of the senses, that we might not be deceived by pretended spirits, might have somewhat manifest to judge by, to tell us that the graces of the Spirit, whether those for edification of others, or sanctification of ourselves, are for manifestation, to appear to others as well as to ourselves; we receive them to that purpose, to profit others and to approve ourselves.

SERMON XLIII.

These may serve for reasons why the Spirit appears: but why the Spirit appears now first, and not before; now first visibly to the world, is worth inquiry. And it is, to show the preeminence of the Gospel above the Law. That stood only in "meats and drinks, and divers washings, and carnal ordinances," says the Apostle; was but "the law of a carnal commandment:" the Gospel is a law of spirit and life: the law of Moses a dead, a "killing letter," but the Gospel of Christ a "quickening Spirit;" the law a course of shadows, the Gospel only the true light. It will appear so by the next particular we are to handle—the manner of his appearing. In tongues, in cloven tongues, in "tongues as it were of fire." I shall invert the order, for the fire it is that gives light unto the tongues to make them for to appear. Of the fire, then, first, to show them the better.

Heb. ix.10.
Heb. vii.16.
2 Cor. iii.6.

For the Spirit to appear as wind or breath is nothing strange. It carries them in its name. *Spiritus a spirando*, every one can tell you. But that this breath should not only blow up a fire, but be itself also blown into it, the Spirit here appear as fire, that is somewhat hard at first, perhaps, to understand: yet you shall see many good reasons for it. Four great ones I shall give you, which comprehend more under them: (1.) To show the analogy and correspondence of God's dealings and dispensations, how they agree both with themselves and with one another. (2.) To insinuate to us the nature and condition of the Holy Spirit. (3.) To signify the several gifts and graces of it. (4.) To declare its operations also and effects.

(1.) The Holy Ghost here appeared like fire, (i.) that we might see it is the same God that gave both Law and Gospel, the same Spirit in both Testaments. The Law was promulgated by fire; "the Lord descended" on Mount Sinai then

Exod. xix. 18.

"in fire." The Gospel also here is first divulged by tongues as it were of fire, in Mount Sion. The difference only is that there were here no lightnings, thunders, clouds, or smoke, as there were there; nothing terrible, nothing dark or gloomy here; all light, and peace, and glory.

Sermon XLIII.

(ii.) Under the Old Testament, the Prophets oft were commissionated by fire to their offices; the Angel takes a live coal from off the altar and lays it upon Isaiah's mouth. Elijah the prophet "stood up as fire." Ezekiel's first vision was of appearances of fire. The commissions therefore of the Apostles were drawn here also, as it were, with pens of fire, that they might the more lively answer and the better express the Spirit of the prophets.

Isa. vi. 7.
Ecclus. xlviii. 1.
Ezek. i. 4, 13.

(iii.) That the nature of the law they were to preach might be expressed too. It was the law of love, and the holy fire of charity was it they were sent to kindle in the world.

(iv.) It was to teach them what they were to expect in the world themselves, fire and fagot, affliction and tribulation, the lot and portion both of them and of their followers ever since.

(v.) It was to teach them what they were to be, "burning and shining lights" to lead others into heaven.

Lastly. That so all righteousness, Law and Prophets, might be fulfilled, the types of the one and the promises of the other, from the first of them to the last, to S. John Baptist's, "that they should be baptized with the Holy Ghost and with fire," that the fire that Christ came to send into the earth, and was then already kindled, might now burn out into the world. And all this to show the Almighty wisdom, who thus agreeably orders all his doings from the first unto the last, that we might with the greater confidence embrace the doctrine of the Gospel which so evenly consented with the Law, and was added only to bring it to perfection, to raise up the fire of devotion and charity to the height.

(2.) But not only to manifest the wisdom of the Father, and perform the promise of the Son, but, secondly, to intimate the nature of the Holy Spirit.

Fire (i.) is the purest element. The Holy Spirit is pure and incorruptible: "Thine incorruptible Spirit," says the wise man. No evil can dwell with it. It will not mingle with

Wisd. xii. 1.

THE FIFTH SERMON ON WHITSUNDAY.

human interests; by this you may know it from all other spirits. They intermix with private humours and self-respects and great ones' fancies. The Holy Spirit is a fire, and will not mix, it must dwell alone; has not a tongue now for this, and then for that, to please men and ease itself, but is always pure and incorrupt.

Fire (ii.) is the subtilest element, it pierces into every part; and "whither can I go then from thy Spirit," says holy David; "if I climb up into heaven, thou art there; if I go down to hell thou art there also. If I take the wings of the morning, and remain in the uttermost parts of the sea, even there also will it find me out." Darkness cannot cover me, thick darkness cannot hide me, night itself cannot conceal me from thee, O thou divine Spirit! Oh keep me, therefore, that I may do nothing that may make me ashamed and hide myself, seeing thy eyes will quickly pierce into me!

(iii.) Fire is an active nature, always stirring, always moving. Nothing can be found better to express the nature of the Holy Spirit. It moved from the beginning, actuated the first matter into all the shapes we see, breathed an active principle into them all; renewed again the face of the earth when the waters had defaced it; blows, and the waters flow; blows again, and dries them up; guides the patriarchs, inspires the prophets, rests upon the governors of the people, from Moses to the seventy elders; gives spirit and courage to the martyrs. *Non permanebit Spiritus meus in vagina*,[p] says God. My Spirit will not endure to be always as in a rusty sheath; it will be lightening the understanding, it will be warming the affections, it will be stirring of the passions, it will be working in the heart, it will be acting in the hand, it will be moving in the feet, it will be quickening all the powers to the service of the Almighty; nothing so busy as this holy fire, nothing so active as this Spirit. Though the nature and essence of it cannot be fully expressed, it is thus very powerfully resembled.

(3.) The gifts of it more easily by this fire. Seven there are numbered of them out of Isaiah xi. 2: "the Spirit of wisdom and understanding, the Spirit of counsel and

Sermon XLIII.

Ps. cxxxix. 6.

Gen. vi. 3.

Isa. xi. 2.

[p] [לא ידון quasi a נדן *vagina*. Vid. Vatabl. et Grot. in loc.]

SERMON XLIII. ghostly strength, the Spirit of knowledge and true godliness, and the Spirit of holy fear," all very naturally represented to us by so many properties I shall observe to you of the fire. Fire, it ascends, it penetrates, it tries, it hardens, it enlightens, it warms, it melts. You have all these again in the seven gifts of the Spirit: for (i.) the Holy Spirit elevates our souls by the spirit of wisdom, *cœlestia* Col. iii. 2. *sapere*, as it is Col. iii. 2, to "those things that are above." *Sapientia est rerum altissimarum*, says the divine philosopher, "Wisdom is of things of the highest nature," of a high ascending strain. (ii.) It penetrates and pierces like the fire 1 Cor. ii. 11. by the spirit of understanding, understands that which the spirit of man cannot understand, the very "things of God," pierces into them all. (iii.) It tries like fire, by the spirit of counsel and advice, teaches us to prove all things and choose the best. (iv.) It hardens us against all the evils that can befall us, as fire does the brick against all weather, by the spirit of fortitude and ghostly strength. (v.) It enlightens the darkness of our souls by the spirit of knowledge, teaches us to know the things that belong unto our peace, the ways and methods of salvation. (vi.) It heats the coldness of our affections by the spirit of piety and true godliness, inflames us with devotion and zeal to God's service. And (vii.) it softens our obdurate hearts by the spirit of holy fear, that we melt into tears and sighs at the apprehension of God's displeasure, even as wax melteth before the fire. The highest, hardest, rockiest mountains melt and flow down at his presence, when once his Spirit does but cast a ray upon them. These are the seven gifts of the Spirit represented to us by so many properties of the fire.

(4.) There are seven other operations and effects of the same Spirit, as lively also expressed by it, and make the fourth reason why the Holy Ghost appears under the semblance of "fire."

Isa. iv. 4. (i.) Fire it burns; and the Prophet Isaiah calls this Spirit Luke xxiv. a "spirit of burning." It makes "our hearts burn within 32. us," as it did the disciples going to Emmaus; puts us to a kind of pain, raises sorrow and contrition in us, makes the scalding water gush out of our eyes; you may even feel it burn you.

(ii.) With this burning it purifies and purges too. As things are purified by the fire, so are our spirits, and souls, and bodies purified by the Spirit. {Sermon XLIII.}

(iii.) For purify it must needs; for it devours all the dross, the chaff, the hay, and stubble that is in us; purges our sins, burns up everything before it that offends, is a "consuming fire;" so is God, so is his Spirit. {Heb. xii. 29.}

(iv.) Yet, as it is a consuming, so it is a renewing fire. Fire makes things new again. And do but "send out thy Spirit, O Lord, and they are made;" we are all made; for so it is that "thou renewest the face of the earth," the face of this dull earth of ours, by putting into it the Holy Spirit. {Ps. civ. 30.}

(v.) To this purpose it makes, that like as fire it separates things of divers natures, silver from tin, metals from dross. *Separare heterogenea* is one of the effects of fire, says the philosopher, to distinguish and divide between things of different kinds. And *Spiritus judicii et discretionis* the prophet styles the Spirit; "a spirit of judgment" it is, a discerning spirit; teaches us to discern between dross and gold, truth and error, between good and evil, and without it we discern nothing. This the Apostle reckons as a peculiar donation of it, the "discerning of spirits." {Isa. iv. 4.} {1 Cor. xii. 10.}

(vi.) Yet, as it separates things of different natures, so it unites things of the same kind, just as the fire does several pieces of the same metal into one body. This holy Spirit is a spirit of unity. They that "separate," they "have not the Spirit." Schisms and divisions, "strife, heresies, and seditions," are the works of the flesh, not of the Spirit. "The fruit of the Spirit is love and peace," says S. Paul there. And "the unity of the Spirit in the bond of peace" we hear of too. Into one Spirit we are baptized all, for there is but one; "one Spirit, one body, one hope, one Lord, one faith, one baptism, one God," one all that are of God; nothing so contrary to the Holy Spirit as divisions of the members from the head, or from one another; a shrewd witness this against the spirits of our age, and an evidence that to what spirit soever they lay claim, they lay false claim to this, they belong not to this Spirit, which is so much for uniting all the parts of the body of Christ together. {Jude 19.} {Gal. v. 20.} {Gal. v. 22.} {Ephes. iv. 3.} {Ephes. iv. 5, 6.}

(vii.) And this it can do when it sees its time; for, lastly,

SERMON XLIII.

it is an invincible Spirit; it bears down all before it; turns all into it; like the fire, of all the elements the most victorious and triumphant. There is no standing out against this Spirit; it is an almighty Spirit, that can do what it will: it inflames the air into a fire—vain, airy spirits into celestial flames of love and charity; it dries up the water, the raw waterish humours of our souls, and fixes all waverings and inconstancies; it burns up our earth, and all the grass and hay and sprouts whatever that stand against it; it sets whole houses all a-fire, sets us all a-fire for heaven and heavenly business. Thus it burns, it purifies, it consumes and renews again, it separates and it gathers, and it carries all before it; does what it will in heaven and earth; subdues sceptres, vanquishes kingdoms, converts nations, throws down infernal powers, and turns all into the obedience of Christ. To this purpose it is that it now also here comes in tongues;—the second manner we noted of his appearance. And that for three reasons: (1,) nothing more convenient to express either our business, or him whose it is.

The tongue is the instrument of speech, the word is expressed by it; Christ is the Word; the Holy Spirit, as it were, the tongue to express him,—comes to-day with an host of tongues to send this word abroad into all the world.

Mark xvi. 15.

Nothing more necessary, for the Apostles were to be the preachers of it, had received a commission to go and preach, wanted yet their tongues, some new enablements, went not, therefore, till they were this day brought them; and a more necessary thing the Holy Ghost could not bring them for that purpose.

1 Cor. xiv. 25.

Yet they had need (2) be of fire, sharp, piercing tongues, like the little flames of fire, such as would pierce into the soul, reveal the inmost "secrets of the heart" and spirits;

Heb. iv. 12. and it seems, so they proved, " piercing even to the dividing asunder of the soul and spirit, of the joints and marrow."

Tongues of fire (3) to warm the cold affections of men into a love of Christ; every tongue is not able to do that; it must be a tongue set on fire from heaven that can do that. Tongues, and tongues of fire, sharp, piercing tongues, warm with heavenly heat, are the only tongues for the business of Christ.

Yet "cloven" they must be too. It is not a single tongue will do it. The Apostles were to preach to the world, and in the world there were a world of tongues; that they might therefore so preach as to be understood, as many tongues were necessary to be given them, as there were people with whom they were to deal.

Behold the greatness of God's goodness here. Tongues were divided for a curse at first; lo, he turns them into a blessing; then they were sent to divide the world, now they are given to unite it; then they wrought confusion, now they are given to unite it. Thus God can turn our curses into blessings when he pleases. And fit it is that we then should turn our tongues to his praise and glory.

This we may do with one tongue alone; but they who would be preachers and teach others, had need of more. Tongues, though they come not now suddenly, like the wind, yet come they must as they can come, by our industry and God's blessing. God would not have sent so many tongues, if more than one had not been necessary for his work; though not now, perhaps, to preach, yet to understand surely what we preach. It is a bold adventure to presume to the office of a teacher with a single tongue. He is not able to teach children to spell true that knows no more, much less to spell the mysteries of the Gospel to men, who understands not so much as that one tongue he speaks, if he understand no more. Unless we be wiser than Christ and his Holy Spirit, we cannot think any sufficiently endued to preach them, but such as have received the gift of tongues, more than one or two; the gift, I say, for though to speak with tongues be not given now miraculously, as it was here, yet given it is to us, it is the gift still of the Holy Spirit, as a blessing upon our labours.

But there are other tongues besides which come from this day's mercy. The tongue that speaks right things, the tongue that comforts the afflicted soul, the tongue that recalls the wandering step, the tongue that defends the fatherless and widow, the tongue that pours itself out in prayers and praises, the tongue that speaks continually of holy things, the tongue that speaks no evil, nor does no hurt, the tongue that speaks nothing but a meek and humble and obedient

SERMON XLIII.

spirit; these are the tongues of the Holy Spirit, and even from this day they have their rise; these are for all orders and sorts of men; and if those men who now take to themselves to be teachers had but learnt to speak with these tongues, they would have spoke to far better purpose, and more to God's acceptance, than now they do in speaking as they do; they had not thus blasphemed the Holy Spirit to entitle him to the extravagancy of their tongues.

Yet fire and tongues, and tongues of fire, are not all the wonders that this day produced. These fell not only like a flash of lightning upon the Apostles, but they sate upon them, or rather, " it sate upon them," says the text.

All these tongues, as divided and cloven as they were, like so many flames or tongues of fire at top, they were all united in one root below,—with " one mouth," with " one voice,"— they spake all but the same thing. They are not the tongues of the Spirit (1) that speak now one thing, now another, that agree not in the foundation, at the least.

Rom. xv. 6.
Acts iv. 24.

Nor is that fire of the Holy Ghost's enkindling, that cannot sit; for to the fire we may (2) refer this "it." The holy flame is not like the fire of thorns, that are always crackling and making a noise; it can sit quietly in the heart, and on the lips, and on the head—sometimes in the one, and sometimes on the other: it sits upon the heads, and singes not a hair; it sits in the heart, and scalds it not at all; it sits upon the lips, yet makes them not burst out into a heat: the fiery zeal that is so much cried up for spirit in the world is too unquiet, too hot, too raging, to be of this day's fire.

Yet (3) we may refer this " it " to the Holy Spirit itself. That sate upon each of them too.

It sate (i.) first upon each of them as a crown of glory, so S. Cyril.ᵠ The Apostles were the crowns and glory of the Churches; and so this installed them.

It sate (ii.) upon them as in a chair of state, to fix authority upon them, to set them in their chairs, to give them power to govern and guide the Church.

It sate (iii.) upon them so, to call into their mind the promise of their Master, that he would send one to sit in counsel with them, and be with them " always, to the end of the world;"

ᵠ [S. Cyril. Hierosol. Catechesis xvii. p. 199 C. ed. Paris. 1640.]

for sitting is a posture to denote constancy, establishment, and continuance.

It sate, (iv.) as it were, to teach us to be settled and constant too, to be established and grounded in our faith, not to be wavering, and carried about with every wind of doctrine. There is no greater evidence against error than that it is not constant to itself; no greater argument against these great pretended spirits than that they cannot sit, know not where to fix, are always moving, as if the Psalmist's curse had taken hold upon them (as it does, and will do, without doubt, upon all that "take the houses of God in possession," that usurp upon the office or portion of the Church); as if "God had made them like a wheel, and as stubble before the wind,"—that can sit nowhere, rest at nothing, but turn about from one uncertainty to another. The Holy Spirit is a Spirit that will sit still, and be at peace, continue and abide.

Ps. lxxxiii. 12.

It sate (v.) upon each, to teach each of us peace and quiet in all our passions, constancy and continuance in truth and goodness, and a settled and composed behaviour in all conditions, blow the winds never so high, burn the fires of persecution never so hot against us.

It were well now if we could say, as it follows next, concerning the Apostles, that we were filled with this Spirit, that we were "filled with the Holy Ghost," that we might arrive at that point within ourselves, though we cannot now arrive at that particular in the text.

The only filling now that I have time to tell you of, is that before us, and it is a good one, the filling us with the body and blood of Christ, which is a signal filling us with the Spirit. Go we will then about it, so to fill our souls. The tongues and fire in the text we may well apply to it, we may have use of there.

For tongues (i.) are not to speak with only, but taste with too. Oh taste we then how good and gracious the Lord is there, that vouchsafes so graciously to come under our roofs, to come upon tongues. And

Tongues (ii.) are to help to digest as well as taste; there, in the mouth, is a kind of first digestion made. Ruminate we then, and meditate upon Christ, when we have tasted him.

SERMON XLIII.

Let it be our business to spend much of our time and days henceforth in meditation of him; that is the way indeed to be filled with his Spirit, while we thus digest him and chew upon him in our spirits.

Nor is (iii.) fire improper any way to bring to that holy table. The fire of charity is to kindle our devotion there, to warm our affections and desires to it.

There (iv.) our tongues are to be warmed into praises, that they may run a nimble descant upon his benefits, and move apace to the glory of his name. Thus are our tongues to be employed, and thus is the fire to be kindled in us, that we may speak with our tongues. This is the way to be filled with the Holy Spirit, this blessed sacrament the means to it.

Come thou, therefore, O blessed Spirit, into our hearts and tongues; lighten our understanding with thy heavenly light; warm our affections with thy holy fire; purge away all our dross, burn up all our chaff; renew our spirits; separate our sins and evils from us; unite us in thy love; subdue us to thyself; teach our hearts to think, our tongues to speak, our hands to act, our feet to move only to thy will; settle thyself in us henceforward, and dwell with us; so teach us with all our tongues and powers to praise thee here upon earth, that we may one day praise thee with them in heaven for evermore!

A SERMON

UPON

TRINITY SUNDAY.

REV. iv. 8.

And they rest not day and night, saying, Holy, holy, holy, Lord God Almighty, which was, and is, and is to come.

I NEED not stretch the text to reach the time. The Τρισάγιον, "Holy, holy, holy," in it, is plain enough to teach the Trinity. An anthem sung here by the angels and saints in heaven; done so here also by four of the chief Apostles and the Bishops of Judæa, signified by the "four beasts" and "twenty-four elders;" taken up after generally by "the saints on earth," commended to us by the Church to-day as our Epistle sent from heaven with a pattern in it for our hymns and praises to the blessed Trinity, "Lord God Almighty."

SERMON XLIV.

For it is a part, I must tell you, of one of S. John's visions, presenting to us what is done in heaven, what God would have done on earth, and what should there be done ere long throughout it, beginning at Jerusalem. Glory, and honour, and thanks should be given unto God for the wonders he was doing for his servants, for the deliverance he was working for his Church, for the judgments he was bringing on their enemies; as glory had been of old given him by his saints and Prophets, was now given him by his Apostles and Bishops, so it should be given still by the whole Christian Church for ever; as he himself "was, and is, and is to come;" so was his praise, and is, and is to come; we therefore all to learn

SERMON XLIV. to bear our parts in that heavenly anthem against the time we come thither to bear them company. Example you see we have here set before us to do it by, and a form to do it in; better we cannot wish : the "four beasts" or "cherubims," Angels, Saints, and the Apostles—there is our pattern; for they rest not day and night saying it: and "Holy, holy, holy, Lord God of hosts, which was, and is, and is to come," there is the form we best do it in.

In each part we shall observe a kind of Trinity, or three parts in each.

In the pattern, (1,) the persons; (2,) their earnestness; and, (3,) their continuance. (1.) The persons praising God, and saying it, "they," the "four beasts," or living creatures, as the words tell us just before. (2.) Their earnestness in it: "they rest not saying," they cannot rest for saying it; cannot rest without the saying it, unless they say it, say it over and over, "Holy, holy, holy;" cannot rest but doing it, that is their rest they take, their praising God. (3.) Their continuance at it, "day and night" it is, and without rest and pause in it; they are continually doing it, saying and doing all to his honour and glory.

In the form of praise we have a sort of Trinity too, three things observable : (1.) The glory or honour given, "Holy, holy, holy." (2.) The persons to whom it is, "Lord, God Almighty," Father, Son, and Holy Ghost, yet all three in one; one single Lord, one only God, one alone Almighty, and no more; so there is the Unity in Trinity into the bargain. And, (3,) here are the benefits intimated we praise him for : he was our Creator, he is our Redeemer, he will be our Glorifier. So you see Trinities enough in the text to make it Trinity Sunday in it, to fill all the Trinity Sundays after it.

The sum is, that we are all to bear our parts in this holy doxology, to give "glory, and honour, and power" to the blessed Trinity, with the "four beasts," and "four-and-twenty elders" from time to time for evermore; and that which may here serve well to persuade us to it is the company; and with them we will begin. And "they," &c.

But who are "they?" The beginning of the verse tells us the "four beasts," or, as it may more genuinely and handsomely be translated, the "four living creatures," τέσσαρα ζῶα; but what, or who are they? That is the question; and a hard one too it seems, by the variety of opinions, probably to be answered rather by conjecture than resolution. We shall take the likeliest of them and pass the rest.

(1.) Some, by the "four living creatures," this "they," would have the four cardinal virtues understood; by the "lion," fortitude; by the "calf" or "ox," justice; by the "eagle," temperance; and by the "man," prudence. And then the sense will be, that God is most signally praised and glorified by a virtuous life, no way like that to praise him. To do righteousness, to walk wisely, to live soberly, to stand stoutly to God and goodness, that is the true way to give glory to the whole Trinity.

(2.) Others, by the "four living creatures," apprehend the four chief faculties of our souls to be insinuated, with which we are to praise him. The irascible intimated by the "lion," the concupiscible by the "ox," the rational by the "face of man," and the spirit by the "eagle." And here the lesson is, that we are to do it, to praise God with all our powers, set our affections and desires upon it, be moved and angry at every thing that comes in to hinder it, search all the means our reason can find out to perfect praise, and raise up our spirits upon eagles' wings, to perform it to the highest pitch.

(3.) Some, by these "four" conceive the whole world, consisting of the four elements, represented to us as praising God. The fire by the "lion," whose nature is hot and fiery; the earth by the "ox," that tills it; the air by the "man," that breathes it; the water by the "eagle," which as other fowl was made out of it. All these indeed we find called in by Gen. i. 20. the holy Psalmist to make up the song of praise, and by the Ps. cxlviii. three children in the fiery furnace to make up theirs, that we may know the fire and all the elements, beasts and all creatures, praise him as well as man; nay, better, are readier commonly to do it than he; that he is fain, even the devoutest he of all of us, to cry out to them to come in with their notes to help him out and fill up the choir.

(4.) Some think God's title of "slow to anger, and swift to mercy," is by these four here expressed by way of hieroglyphic: by the "ox," slowness; by the "lion," anger; by the "eagle," swiftness; and by the "man," mercy represented to us. And, without doubt or question, in this slowness to wrath and swiftness to have mercy, is God's greatest glory, and for them we most willingly give him glory, must not cease at any time to give him glory.

(5.) Others suppose it an hieroglyphic of Christ himself, who in his incarnation appeared in the form or face of a man; in his passion, like a "calf" or "ox" for sacrifice; in his resurrection, like a "lion," the "Lion of the tribe of Judah;" in his ascension, like an "eagle:" and if this pass, the meaning is, that by Christ God's glory is most advanced; by his incarnation, passion, resurrection, and ascension, heaven and earth is filled with his glory; and for this above all the rest, for him and his benefits, we are to give God the greatest glory; there, as it were, begins all our praise; thence the "twenty-four elders" first throw down their crowns and fall down and worship, as it were acknowledging him the beginning of all the good we receive both of grace and glory, Christ the author and original of them all.

But (6.) to come a little near. These "four living creatures," say others, represent the four Evangelists that preach Christ's life and death, resurrection and ascension into glory. The "lion" S. Mark, for he begins his Gospel, as it were, with the voice of a lion roaring in the wilderness; the "calf" or "ox" S. Luke, who begins his with the story of a Levitical priest, whose ministry was about the sacrifice of calves and oxen; the "man" S. Matthew, who takes his rise from the genealogy of men; the "eagle" S. John, who at the very first soars up on high, that we had need of eagles' wings and eyes to follow and discern him. By these four, indeed, God's grace and mercy, Christ's name and glory, is spread over the face of all the earth; and by this we learn, that to preach and teach, and publish the things of Christ, is to give God praise and glory—a singular and notable way to do so.

(7.) Some, that suppose they yet hit it nearer, conceive God here brought in in the vision sitting as the Bishop of Jerusalem, with all the Bishops of Judæa in council all about him, as (Acts xv.) it seems they did; and these "four living creatures" about the throne to be those four chief Apostles,

S. Peter, S. John, S. Barnabas, and S. Paul there present, ranked here higher than the rest. S. Peter for his primacy set first, and resembled by the "lion" for his fiery zeal and fervour. S. Paul deciphered by the "ox," in respect of his labours more abundantly than they all. S. Barnabas intimated by the "man," as being a son of consolation, humanity, and mercy, by the interpretation of his name. S. John pointed at by the "eagle," for those sublime and high speculations of the divinity of Christ above all the rest. These were the four great standard bearers of the Christian Israel, —for these "four living creatures" were borne in the standard of old Israel, and here alluded to,—these the four great champions and defenders, the planters and propagators of the Christian faith, of the blessed Trinity, of the glory of God and Christ throughout the world. And thus we see to undertake the business of the Gospel, to take pains and labour to defend and propagate it with all our might and main, is an actual and real glorifying of God and Christ.

Yet, lastly, whatever these may be imagined to represent to us, or whomsoever to point out, or what council, or persons, or judicature soever to resemble, angels to be sure they were that thus represented the vision to S. John; and as such if we consider them, we may conclude all the business with this lesson—that the business of heaven as well as earth, of angels as well as men, is to be employed in praises and thanksgivings to the Almighty—an employment, therefore, well worth our time, and pains, and study.

Now, put all these together, and I cannot give you a fuller description of the way to praise and glorify him than these have given you. For to do it as we should, is (1,) to live virtuously; (2,) to employ all the powers and faculties of soul and body to his service; (3,) to call in all the creatures to help us to do it, and to use them to it; (4,) to reflect often upon both his mercies and his judgments, and acknowledge his goodness in them both; (5,) to meditate upon the life, the death, the resurrection, the ascension of Christ, with all devotion and humility; (6,) to preach and publish it what we can; (7,) to defend and maintain it to our utmost power; (8,) to reckon it, lastly, an Angel's work, a heavenly piece of business, thus to spend our days and years in giving glory to the Most Highest.

	A SERMON ON TRINITY SUNDAY.
Sermon XLIV.	And if heaven and earth, and all the creatures else, besides sinful man, become thus the trumpets of their Creator's glory, and in all their several ways and orders ambitiously contrive themselves into the instruments of it, what strange creatures must we needs be that either neglect it or forget it! "Heaven and earth," says our Morning Hymn, "are full of the majesty of thy glory;" we can be no other than hell, then, that are empty of it, that do not resound it.
Ps. cxlviii. 7.	"Dragons and all deeps," says the Psalmist; all but the old dragon, and the bottomless deep, the deep of hell, all praise him else. You see what we bring ourselves to by our unthankfulness, what a sad condition they are in who give not glory unto God, who delight not in magnifying and praising him, who are against the hymns and anthems to that purpose. Thus you see it done in the text, by saints and angels in the heavens, by apostles and evangelists on the earth. Thus *de facto*, so it was then. But it is as well a prediction of what should be after: that not only the present age of the Apostles and holy Bishops then, but the succeeding ages also of the Church should acknowledge the glory of the undivided Trinity. And it fell out accordingly. Not only that meek and merciful "man," S. Gregory, that valiant "lion," S. Ambrose; that laborious "ox," S. Jerome; that sublime "eagle," S. Augustine,—as some please to fancy these "four beasts,"—or the four first patriarchates, as others have interpreted them, but all the "four corners of the earth" have since professed it, and, with the "twenty-four elders, fallen down and worshipped" it. The lustre and glory of that glorious mystery has shone through all the quarters of the world, and all his famous mercies to his people, and his judgments against their enemies are still daily celebrated and magnified in all the congregations of the saints. This S. John foresaw, and here foretels the poor persecuted Christians then, that how hard soever things went with them then, they should ere long turn all their sighs and lamentations into songs of praise for their deliverance and salvation.
	This they should, and we should as much: it was foretold of them they should, it is commanded us we should.
1 Cor. vi. 20.	Therefore "glorify him," says the Apostle, "glorify him in your bodies," and "glorify him in your spirits," glorify him

with the bodies that glorify him, and glorify him with the spirits that glorify him, bear them all company in so doing; do it all the ways you can, you can neither do it too many, nor too much. Put on the faces of "eagles" in the temple, and raise your souls up there and praise him; put on the faces of "men" at home, and let the holiness of your conversation praise him there. Put on the appearance of "oxen" in your callings, and let the diligence of your actions and vocations praise him. Put on the appearance of "lions" abroad in all places of temptations, and let your courage in the resisting and repelling them praise him there. Thus we truly copy out our pattern.

Yet to transcribe it perfectly well, we must now, secondly, also transcribe their earnestness: for here they not only give praise and glory unto God; but they do it earnestly, they rest not doing it, they rest not saying; that is,

(1.) They cannot rest unless they say it. And, "I will not suffer mine eyes to sleep, nor mine eyelids to slumber, neither the temples of my head to take any rest, till I have found out" a way to praise my God, till I have offered up the service of my thanks, and added something to his glory,—must be the Christian's resolution.

(2.) "They rest not saying" is, they say it, and say it again, say it over and over, "Holy, holy, holy." Ἅγιος is in some copies nine times read; "holy" nine times repeated; they think they can never say it enough. No more, it seems, did David, when he so oft repeated, "For his mercy endureth for ever," in one single Psalm. And hence it is the Church, to imitate this holy fervour, so often reiterates the Doxology, and inserts so many several hymns, and even either begins almost all its prayers and collects with an acknowledgment either of his mercy, goodness, and providence, or ends them with acknowledgment of his majesty, power, and glory; this both to imitate the glorious saints, and to obey the Apostle's injunction of being "fervent in prayers" and praises.

(3.) "They rest not saying" is, they rest not but in so doing. That is their rest, their joy, their happiness, to do so, thus to be always praising God. It would be ours too, had we the same affections to it, or the same senses of it. We could not

SERMON XLIV.

go to rest, nor lie down to sleep, could not sit down and take our rest till we had first lift up our eyes and hearts, nay, and voices too, sometimes, till we had first paid our thanks, and given him praise for his protections in our ways and labours until then.

(4.) But to be thus eager and earnest at it is not all. So we might be for a start, and give over presently; but it is "day and night" that angels and good men do it. There is no night indeed, properly, with the angels; it is with them eternal day: yet all that time which we call day and night they are still a-saying it. The morning comes, and they are at it; the night comes, and they are at it still. "Let me go, for the day breaketh," says the angel that strove with Jacob. And I must sing my matins, adds the Chaldee paraphrase;[r] as if he had said, I can stay no longer; I must go take my morning course in the heavenly choirs. And in the depth of night we find them by whole hosts and multitudes at their *Gloria in excelsis*, "Glory be to God in the highest."

Gen. xxxii. 26.

Luke ii. 14.

The first fervours of Christian piety were somewhat like this of the Angel's. You might have seen their churches full at midnight; all the watches of the night you might have heard them chanting out the praises of their God, and all the several hours of the day you might have found some or other continually praising God in his holy temples, as well as in their closets. Nay, in the Jewish temple they ceased not to do so. "Ye that by night stand in the house of the Lord, praise him ye," says holy David; for indeed ye stand there to praise him; and the temple itself stood open all the day for all comers, to that purpose, when they would. "Therefore shall every good man sing of thy praise without ceasing," says the Psalmist; "it is a good thing" to do so; "to tell of thy loving-kindness early in the morning, and of thy truth in the night season;" so good that David himself resolves upon it: "Every day will I give thanks unto thee, and praise thy

Ps. cxxxiv. 2.

Ps. xxx. 13.
Ps. xcii. 1,2.

Ps. cxlv. 2.

---

[r] [Targum Jonathan. Ben Uzziel in Gen. xxxii. 26. ואמר שדרני ארום סלק עמוד קריצהא וכביא סיתא דמלאכי מרומא משבחין למרי עלמא ואנא חד מן מלאכיא משבחייא ומיומא דאיתברי עלמא לא מטא זמני לשבחא אלהן אלא הדא זמנא. Et dixit; Mitte me, quoniam ascendit columna aurorae:

et advenit hora qua Angeli excelsi laudant Dominum mundi: ego autem sum unus ex Angelis laudantibus; et a die quo creatus est mundus non advenit tempus meum ad laudandum nisi hoc tempore.]

name for ever and ever;" prays also that his mouth may be filled with God's praise, that he may "sing of his glory and honour all the day long," from morning to night, and from night again to morning, he would willingly do nothing else.

<small>SERMON XLIV.</small>
<small>Ps. lxxi. 7.</small>

Nay, be the night and day taken either in their natural or moral sense, either properly for the spaces and intervals of light and darkness or, morally, for the sad hours of affliction and adversity, and those bright ones of jollity and prosperity; good men praise God in them both—do not cease to do it; if sorrows curtain up their eyes with tears, and put out all their light of joy and comfort, yet, "blessed be the name of the Lord," cry they out with patient Job. Again, if their paths <small>Job i. 21.</small> be strewed with light, and the sun gild all their actions with lustrous beams; if heaven shine full upon them, they are not yet so dazzled but they see and adore God's mercy in them; and in the midst of all their glories and successes they are still upon his praise, and render all to him. Neither the one night, nor this other day, make them at any time forget him. A good *item* to us hence, (1) not to suffer our pleasures and vagaries, our mirths and vanities, our successes and prosperities, to steal away the time we are to spend in giving God thanks and glory for them. Nor (2) to permit ourselves so much time to the reflection upon our griefs and troubles as to omit the praising God that they are no worse, and that he thus fatherly chastises us to our bettering and amendment,—does all to us for the best. Yet not to cease praising him day and night, seems still to have some difficulty to understand it. The angels, perhaps, that neither eat nor drink, nor sleep nor labour, they may do it; but how shall poor man compass it?

Why, first, (1) imprint in thy soul a fixed and solid resolution to direct all thy words and actions to his glory. Renew it (2) every day thou risest, and every night thou liest down. Renounce (3) all by-ends and purposes that shall at any time creep in upon thee, to take the praise and honour to thyself. Design (4) thy actions, as often as thou canst, particularly to God's service, with some short offering them up to God's will and pleasure, either to cross or prosper them; and when they be done, say, God's name be praised for them. And, lastly, omit not the times of prayer and praise, either in public or in private, but use thy best diligence to observe them, to be constant and attentive at them. Thus, with the spouse in the Canticles, "when we sleep, our hearts awake;" and whether we eat or drink, or walk, or talk, or whatsoever we do, we "do all to the glory of God," and may be said to praise "him day and night," and not cease saying, " Holy, holy, holy, Lord God Almighty, which was, and is, and is to come." And so I come to the second general—the form here set us to praise him in; in which, first, we have to consider the glory itself that is expressly given him; " Holy, holy, holy."

To speak right, indeed, the whole sentence is nothing else; yet this evidently referring to that of Isaiah, where the seraphims use this first part in their hymn of praise, I conceive this the chief and most remarkable part of, which may therefore bear the name before the rest.

Now this saying, " Holy, holy, holy," is attributing all purity, perfection, and glory, to God as to the subject of it himself, and the original of it to others, thereby acknowledging him only to be worshipped and adored. So that saying thus, we say all good of him, and all good from him to ourselves.

Thrice it is repeated, which, according to the Hebrew custom, is so done to imprint it the deeper in our thoughts, and may serve us as a threefold cord, which is not easily broken, to draw us to it.

But another reason the Fathers give. And it is, (1,) they say, to teach us the knowledge of the holy and blessed Trinity. Indeed, why else thrice, and no less or more? Why follows "Lord God Almighty;" three more words? Why ὁ ἦν, ὁ ὤν, ὁ ἐρχόμενος, three yet again, and yet but three, " who was, who is, who is to come?" Why do the seraphims in Isaiah say no more, yet say so too? Why have we in the following verses, "glory, and honour, and thanks" (ver. 9), and "glory, and honour, and power," so punctually thrice, and thrice only offered to them? How came it to be so universally celebrated throughout the world, and put into all the Catholic Liturgies everywhere? Words fall not from angels and angelical spirits by chance or casually; the holy penmen write not words haphazard; nor is it easy to conceive so hard a doctrine, so uneasy to reason, should be so generally and humbly entertained, but by some powerful working of God's Spirit. This may be enough to satisfy us, that the blessed Trinity is more than obscurely pointed out to us here.

And (2) to be sure, the Fountain of all holiness is here pointed to us, that we may learn to whom to go for grace; that we may see we ourselves are but unholy things; that nothing is in itself pure or holy, none but God.

And (3) it points us out what we should be: "Be ye holy, as I am holy," says God. No way otherwise to come near him; no way else to come so near him as to give him thanks; for out of polluted lips he will not take them. For, in the second place, the Lord God Almighty it is we are to give this glory to.

The three persons here, methinks, are evident however: God the Father, the Lord the Son, and the Almighty Spirit, that made all things, that does but blow and the waters flow, that does but breathe and man lives, that with the least blast does what he will.

Yet these three, it seems, are still but one, "one Lord," and "one God," and "one Spirit"—all singulars here; nouns, verbs, articles, and participles—all in the singular number here; ἅγιος, and Κύριος, and Θεὸς, and παντοκράτωρ, ὁ ἦν, ὁ ὤν, ὁ ἐρχόμενος; that we might see, though a Trinity there be to be believed, yet it is in unity; though three personalities, but one nature; though three persons, but one God.

All the scruple here can but arise from the setting Lord the Son before God the Father; but that is quickly answered when they tell you, there is none here afore or after other, none greater and lesser than other, and therefore no matter at all for the order here, where all is one, and one is all, Lord God Almighty.

Yet now, to encourage us the better to our praises and thanksgivings, see we, in the last place, the benefits they here praise him for, and they are intimated to us in the close of all, "who was, and is, and is to come."

In the first, we understand the benefit of our creation. God it was that created us.

In the second, we read the benefit of our redemption; the Lord it is that redeems us daily, pardons and delivers us.

In the third, we have the benefit of our glorification still to come, the Holy Spirit here sealing us, and hereafter enstating us in glory.

In them altogether we may, in brief, see as in a prospect, that all the benefits we have received heretofore he was the Author of them; that all the mercies we enjoy, he is the Fountain of them; that all the joys or good we hope for, he is the donor of them; he was, he is, he must be the bestower of them all; without him, nothing; he was, and is, and will be to us all in all.

And now, sure, though I have not the time to specify all the mercies we enjoy from this blessed Lord God Almighty; and indeed, had I all time, I could not, and all tongues, *Si mihi sint linguæ centum, sint oraque centum*, I could not; yet we cannot but in gross, at least, take up a song of praise for all together, say somewhat towards it.

"Holy, holy, holy, Lord God Almighty;" holy in our creation, holy in our redemption, holy in our sanctification; holy in heaven, holy in earth, holy under the earth too; holy in glorifying of his angels, holy in justifying his saints, holy in punishing the devils; holy in his glory, and holy in his mercy, and holy in his justice; holy in his seraphims, and holy in his cherubims, and holy in his thrones; holy in his power, and holy in his wisdom, and holy in his providence; holy in his ways, and holy in his laws, and holy in his promises; holy in the womb, and holy in the manger, and holy on the cross; holy in his miracles, and holy in his doctrines, and holy in his examples; holy in his saints, and holy in his sacraments, and holy in his temples; holy in himself, holy in his Son, holy in his Spirit; holy Father, holy Son, and holy Spirit.

Therefore, with angels and archangels, and with all the company of heaven, and all the saints in heaven and earth, we laud and magnify thy glorious name, evermore praising thee, and saying, Holy, holy, holy, Lord God of hosts, heaven and earth are full of the majesty of thy glory; glory be to thee, O Lord most high, Lord God Almighty, which was, and is, and is to come; glory, and honour, and thanks be unto thee for ever and ever. *Amen, amen, amen.*

THE FIRST SERMON

UPON

THE CALLING OF S. PETER.

S. LUKE v. 8.

Depart from me, for I am a sinful man, O Lord.

A STRANGE speech for him that speaks, to him it is spoken, from S. Peter to his Saviour. One would think it were one of the Gadarenes, who thus entreated him to depart the coasts. Strange indeed, to desire him to depart, without whom we cannot be; stranger to give such a reason for it, a reason that should rather induce us to entreat him to tarry than to go; for being sinful men, we have most need of him to stay with us; but strangest of all it is for S. Peter to desire it, and upon his knees to beseech it. To desire Christ to go away from us, to go from us because we have need of his being with us; and for such a one as S. Peter, and that so earnestly to entreat it, is a business we well skill not at the first dash.

SERMON XLV.

Yet if we consider what S. Peter was when he so cried out, or what made him to do it, or how unfit he, being a sinful son of man, thought himself for the company of the Son of God, we shall cease to wonder, and know it is the sinner's case for ever so to do,—to be astonished at miracles,—not to bear suddenly the presence of our Lord,—and when we first apprehend it, to cry out to him, with S. Peter here, to withdraw from us for a while, for that we are not able to endure the brightness and terror of his splendour and majesty.

It was a miraculous and stupendous draught of fish (after

SERMON XLV.
they had given up all hopes of the least) suddenly came to net, which thus amazed S. Peter and his fellows. They had drudged and "toiled all night," and not a fish appeared; but when Christ came to them, then came whole shoals, and thrust so fast into the net that they brake it to get in, as if the mute and unreasonable creatures themselves had such a mind to see him by whose word they were created, that they valued not their lives so they might see or serve his pleasure. And yet S. Peter makes as much means that he might see him no longer, whom if he had not seen, and seen again, notwithstanding his desires to the contrary, it had been better he had never seen, nor been at all.

But such is our mortal condition, that we can neither bear our unhappiness nor our happiness: unreasonable creatures go beyond us in the entertainment of them both, according to their kinds; though it may be, here, S. Peter's humility speaks as loud as his unworthiness or inability to endure the presence of his Lord.

S. Peter, we must needs say, was not thoroughly called as yet to be a disciple; this humble acknowledgment of his own unworthiness to be so was a good beginning. Here it is we begin our Christianity, which, though it seems to be a kind of refusal of our Master, is but a trick to get into his service, who himself is humble and lowly, and receives none so soon as they that are such, none at all but such, whom by the posture of their knees, and the tenours of hearty and humble words, you may discern for such.

And to sum up the whole meaning of the words to a brief head, they are no other, nor no more than S. Peter's profession of his own humble condition, that he is not worthy that his God and his Redeemer should come so near him, and therefore—in an ecstasy, as it were, at the sight of so glorious a guest—desires him to forbear to oppress his unworthy servant with an honour he was not yet able to bear.

Yet we cannot but confess the words may have a harder sense upon them, as the voice of a stupid apprehension, or an insensibleness of such heavenly favours as our Saviour's company brings with it. We shall have time to hint at that anon. It shall suffice now, at first, to trouble you only with two evident and general parts.

A SERMON ON THE CALLING OF S. PETER.

Christ's absence desired; and The reason alleged for it. — SERMON XLV.

I. Christ desired to be gone,—" Depart from me;" and,
II. Why he is so,—" For I am a sinful man, O Lord."

The desire seems to be the voice of a threefold person, and such is S. Peter's now:—
1. Of a " man."
2. Of a " sinful man;" and yet,
3. Of an humble man, " me;" that me here, confessing myself a sinful man.

The reasons equal the variety of the desires, or desirers. Three they are too.
1. For I am a man.
2. For I am a sinful man.
3. For thou, O Lord, thou art God, and I am man.

It is a text to teach us what we are, to whom we speak, and how to speak to him. And if you go hence home without learning this, you may say, perhaps, you have heard a sermon, but you have learnt nothing by it. It shall be your faults if you do not.

And unless we cry in a sense contrary to S. Peter's meaning, " Depart from us, O Lord," out of a kind of contempt and weariness of his word, and not out of the conscience of our own unworthiness of so great a blessing; then, though our words be somewhat indiscreet, though we sometimes speak words not fitting for our Saviour to hear, though they seem to show a kind of refusal of him, yet being no other than the mere expression of the apprehension of his glorious presence, and our own unworthiness, Christ will comfort us, and call out to us presently, as he doth to S. Peter, not to fear; we shall *Luke v. 10.* not lose by his word or presence, nor by our so sensible apprehension of his glory, though we be but a generation of sinful men.

That our desires, first, may be set right, though peradventure not always speak so, the desires being the hinge upon which good and evil move on their courses, I begin to examine S. Peter's desire under a threefold consideration: Of a " man," of a " sinful," of an humble man. For all these S. Peter at this time was capable of; and in which of these he speaks most feelingly will be perhaps anon the *quære;* and how far they may pertain to us, be used or not used by us, will be the business we are to speak of. If we take all, we are sure to be right.

Then, first, of the desire, as it is that of man or human nature, considered simply in its own imperfection, unable to bear the presence of a supernatural honour.

Nature sometimes desires God to depart from it; it loves not to be forced out of its course, to be screwed up beyond itself. Miracles are burdens to nature; and however it be ready to serve the will of the Supreme Mover, yet when it is diverted from its own way, and strained to a service or quickness, with which its innate slowness is unacquainted, it does even by its hasting back to its old wont, in a manner desire to be freed from the present command of its great controller.

It is so with man, who being of a corruptible make, cannot endure the presence of an incorruptible essence. Angels and spirits bring affrightment to it when they come; we are terrified at the presence of an angel, though he bring us nothing but tidings of the greatest joy. Nay, if we do but think we see a spirit,—as the disciples did when it was no other than their beloved Master,—we are wholly frightened and amazed. There is so great a distance between our corrupt mortality and their immortal conditions, that we desire not to see them.

Yea, the body itself is so little delighted with the presence of its own best companion, the incorruptible soul (though it enjoy all its beauty and vigour by it), that by continual reluctances against it, and perpetually throwing off the commands of it, and so daily withdrawing its imaginations from the thoughts of, or converse with, that nobler part, it seems to wish it gone, rather than to be bound to that observance which the presence of that divine parcel requires at our hands.

And if it fare no better with these natures of angels and our own spirits, which are nearer mortality and imperfection, and have more affinity to us, and full natural engagements upon us, because their excellences breed either a kind of envy or terror to us, that we, in a manner, say to those that we cannot sunder from us, our very souls, Go away, trouble us not with these spiritual businesses; how is it otherwise likely than that we should be ready to avoid the presence of that Eternal Purity, in whose sight our best purities cannot stand at all?

We love not to see our own imperfections; that makes us unwilling to endure the presence of any thing that shows us them. Now, the divine excellences, above all the rest, being that which by its exactness discovers the most insensible blemishes we labour with, you cannot wonder that a creature so much in love with itself, should desire the removal of that whose nearness so much debases it.

Nor is this all; there is terror besides at the approach of the Almighty. When God drew near to his people upon the mount, and "the people saw the thunderings and lightnings, and the noise of the trumpet, and the mountain smoking," conceiving him to be at hand, whose voice is terrible as the thunder, at whose presence the mountains smoke, " they removed and stood afar off; and they said unto Moses, Speak thou with us, and we will hear, but let not God speak with us, lest we die:" thus, at least, entreating God to withdraw somewhat farther from them, even lest they should die for fear, if he should come nearer them. *Exod. xx. 18, 19.*

We cannot always say such desires are orderly and good, yet such there are, we may say, in the best created nature. Indeed, we commonly desire what is worst for us; as if we knew not our own good, or did not study it.

Certainly, God's company can do us no harm. " In his presence is life," says the Psalmist, yet say we, we die if we see him. " In him we live, and move, and have our being," says the Apostle; yet say we, if he come too nigh us, or depart not from us, we shall be no more. Thus our thoughts and desires run counter to him. *Acts xvii. 28.*

Nay, there is a generation that the Prophet complains of, that say plainly unto the Lord, Depart from us, we will have none of thy laws, we desire not thy precepts, thy word is a burden to us, thy solemn worship we cannot away with, we are weary of thy sacraments, we are sick of thy truth, thy priests are a trouble to us, thy holy days take too much time from us, thy holy service and thy holy things they are too chargeable for us; take them away, and depart from us; we will have none of them any longer. This is more than the *Isa. xxx. 11.*

voice of nature's imperfection; it is the voice of sin and rebellion added to it. But take we heed, lest while we thus thrust God from us, he go indeed and come no more,—go away, and leave us in perpetual sin, darkness, and discomfort. It may please God, peradventure, to construe what we have done hitherto as the rash, hasty words only of affrighted or disturbed nature, not knowing which way to turn itself upon a sudden, being amazed at the things that (we know not how) are come to pass in these days; but if we shall persist to desire him to depart (which of all sins has most unthankfulness and impiety, I may add atheism also in it), he will go, and he will not return; then shall we seek him early, but we shall not find him; we shall seek him sighing, and weeping, and mourning as we go, but we shall not find him; we shall "eat of the fruit of our own way, and be filled with our own devices," but we shall see him no more for ever; then shall we beg for what we have rejected, but he will not hear us, he is departed from us, and will not come again.

Thus it was not S. Peter's desire. He was not tired with Christ's company, nor glutted with it, as the Israelites with their despised manna; only Christ, by showing a miracle, had so amazed his wits, that he knew not how, on a sudden, to recollect his spirits to entertain so great and holy a guest,— does therefore, not well considering what to say, desire him to divert a little somewhither else, where he might be more honourably entertained, or to stand off a while, and give him breath, that he might recover his spirits, and be able more worthily to entertain him.

But there was somewhat else which made S. Peter so express himself. He was not only sensible of his mortal lot, but of his sinful condition too. Thus we are to consider it as the voice of "a sinful man," of human nature corrupted with sin.

Though all created substances contract a kind of trembling or drawing back at the approach of God, the very seraphims "covering their faces with their wings," yet did not sin and folly cover them with a new confusion, the weakest and poorest of them would draw a kind of solace and happiness from the beams of that majesty that so affrighted them. It is sin that speaks the text in a louder key, that more actually cries to him, not softly and weakly out of weakness, but aloud and strongly, out of wilfulness, to depart.

It does more than so. It drives God from us; not only bids him go, but forces him. It is not so mannerly as to entreat him; it discourteously and unthankfully thrusts him out of doors. *Exi a me,* Get you out, says the sinful soul to God; no *Obsecro,* no entreaty added; not, Go out, I pray thee; or, Depart, I beseech thee. We should do well to think how uncivilly we deal with God; we are not content to put him out of his own house and dwelling, the temples of our bodies, the altars of our souls, by our sins; nay, and his holy temples by sacrileges and profaneness; but sometimes in ruder terms we bid him begone, and thrust him out by wilful and deliberate transgressions, by solemn and legal sacrileges and profanenesses, which we commit and reiterate in contempt of him, as if expressly we said to him, Go from us, we will have nothing to do with thee any longer; thou shalt not only not dwell, but not stand, or be amongst us. The people of Gennesareth besought Christ to depart out of their coasts. These sinners will out with him whether he will or no; and though he come again, and knock to be let in, and continue knocking till "his head be wet with the dew, [Cant. v. 2.] and his locks with the drops of the night," yet can he hear no other welcome from us than, Depart from us, we are in bed, well at ease in our accustomed sins, and we will not rise to let thee in; we will not be troubled with thy company, with a course so chargeable or dangerous as is thy wonted service.

Strange it is that we should thus deal with God, but thus we do; yet no man lays this unkind usage to his heart, never considers how he thus daily uses God. If good motions arise within us, we bid them be gone; they trouble us, they hinder our sports or projects, our quiet or interest. If good opportunities present themselves without, we bid them go, we are not at leisure to make use of them, they come unseasonably. If the word preached desire to enter in, if it touch our consciences and strike home, we bid that depart too; it is not for our turn, it crosses our interests or our profits, or our pleasures; we will not therefore have it stay any longer with us. If God, by any other way, as of afflictions or of deliverances, by blessings or curses, or any other way come to us, they are no sooner over, nor these any sooner tasted, but we send them* gone to purpose, and think of them again no more; our sins return and send them going, make us forget both his justice and his mercies.

This is the course the sinner treads to Godward. From whence it is, that the soul thus ill apparelled with its own sins, dares not look God in the face without the mediation of a Redeemer. She has driven God from her by her sins, and having thus incensed him, flees away when he draws towards her. Thus Adam and Eve, having by sin disrobed themselves of their original righteousness, when they hear the voice of God, though but gently walking towards them, and calling to them, they run away and "hide themselves from the presence of the Lord amongst the trees of the garden." They felt, it seems, they wanted something to shelter them from the presence of God, into the thickets, therefore, they hie themselves, as if they then foresaw they had need of the "rod out of the stem of Jesse," the "branch out of his roots," as the Prophet calls Christ, to bear off the heat of God's anger from them.

Under the leaves of this branch alone it is that we are covered, sheltered from the wrath to come. His leaves, his righteousness, it is that clothes our nakedness; the very garments which our first parents were fain to get to themselves, before they durst venture again into his presence. There is no enduring God's presence still, no coming near him, unless we look upon him through these leaves, from under the shelter of this "branch of Jesse."

Tell the sinner, who keeps not under this shelter, that lies not at this guard, of God's coming to him, of his looking towards him, of his approach to judgment, and with Felix he trembles at it, puts off the discourse to another time, refuses to hear so terrible news as God's coming is, if Christ came not with him. Such a one has sin made him, that he desires not to see him, whose eyes will not behold sin; "Depart from me, O Lord," instead of "Thy kingdom come," is his daily prayer.

Yet, as hardly or unadvisedly as nature or corruption may

* [So in old edition.]

deliver this speech of S. Peter's, it may be delivered in a softer, sweeter tone, and so it was by him. It may be the voice of the humble spirit, casting himself down at the feet of Jesus, and confessing himself altogether unworthy of so great a favour as his presence.

{SERMON XLV.}

If we peruse the speeches of humble souls in Scripture, by which they accosted their God or their superiors, we shall see variety of expression indeed, but little difference in the upshot of the words. "I am but dust and ashes," says Father Abraham. Now, how can dust and ashes, with their light scattering atoms, endure the least breath of the Almighty? The Prophet Isaiah "saw the Lord" in a vision, "sitting upon a throne," and presently he cries out, "Woe is me! for I am undone, because I am a man of unclean lips, and I dwell in the midst of a people of unclean lips: for mine eyes have seen the King, the Lord of hosts." What! undone, Isaiah? Yes, "Woe is me, I am undone; for mine eyes have seen the Lord of hosts," who certainly cannot but consume me, for so boldly beholding him. "I am not worthy," says the centurion to Christ, "that thou shouldest come under the roof of my house: speak the word only;" as if his presence were so great he might not bear it. And S. Paul, as soon as he had told us that he had seen Christ, tells us he was "one born out of due time;" was "the least of the Apostles," and "not meet to be called an Apostle;" as if the very seeing of Christ had made him worth nothing. Indeed it makes us think ourselves so, of whom we ever think too much, till we look up to God. Then it befalls us, as it fell out to Job, "I have heard thee by the hearing of the ear,"—but that was nothing,—"now mine eye seeth thee: wherefore I abhor myself, and repent in dust and ashes." Hither it is always that the sight of God depresses us, to think humbly of ourselves, that we profess our just deserts to be no other than to be deprived of his presence.

{Gen. xviii. 27.}

{Isa. vi. 5.}

{Matt. viii. 8.}

{1 Cor. xv. 8.}

{Job xlii. 5, 6.}

There are like expressions of humble minds towards our superiors too in Holy Writ. "When Rebekah saw Isaac coming towards her, she lighted down from her camel, and covered herself with her vail;" as if either her humility or her modesty would not suffer her suddenly to look upon his face, who was presently to be her lord. But Abigail's compli-

{Gen. xxiv. 65.}

mental humility surpasses. When David sent to take her to him to wife, "she arose and bowed herself to the earth, and said, Behold, let thine handmaid be a servant to wash the feet of the servants of my lord." And Mephibosheth, though not so courtly, yet as deeply undervalues himself in the sight of his lord and king, when he thus answers David's proffered kindness, "What is thy servant that thou shouldest look upon such a dead dog as I am?"

Sermon XLV.
1 Sam. xxv. 41.
2 Sam. ix. 8.

Now if Rebekah descend from her camel, and vail her face at the sight of her designed husband; if Abigail term herself the servant of the servants of David, even to the meanest office, to wash their feet; if Mephibosheth count himself a dog in the presence of King David, each of these thus expressing their humility, it is no wonder if S. Peter, at the presence of his Saviour, it is but just that we, in the presence of our God and Saviour, descend from our camels, from our chairs of state, from our seats of ease, from the stools whereon we sit, and bow down our eyes, our hearts and bodies in all humility, as unworthy to look up to heaven, to look him in the face whom we have so offended, willing to wash the feet of his poorest servants, to serve him in anything, in the poorest, meanest way or office, ready to profess ourselves amongst the vilest of his creatures, who cannot so much as expect a good look from him.

You may surely guess by the frame of speech,—though nature and sin may sometimes use some of the same words, —that the tenor of them altogether is no other than the expression of S. Peter's humble acknowledgment of his own vileness.

He confesses plainly he is "a sinful man;" how could he more depress himself? ἀνὴρ ἁμαρτωλός, a man that was nothing but a sinner, a very sinner.

Thence it is that he thinks himself unworthy that he should stay with him; therefore desires him to quit his ship, but much more his company, as far unfit to receive him, or be near about him.

And whilst he thus confesses himself to be a sinful man, he speaks somewhat doubtfully, at least, to him, as if he conceived him to be the Lord his God. Thus much however: he acknowledges so great a disproportion between himself and Christ, that whilst he knows what to call himself, he knows not well what to style him: to be sure knows not how to speak; speaks indeed, but knows not what he says; whilst humbly desiring him to depart, he unwittingly parts with his own happiness, not knowing what he desires or does in this distraction.

These three, an acknowledgment of our own wretchedness; a sensible apprehension of our own unworthiness and Christ's greatness; and a kind of troubled expression of them, without art or study, are the signs and effects of true humility, and are here caused by the consideration of God's miraculous dealing with us, which commonly shows us God's goodness and grace, his glory and majesty, our own weakness, sinfulness, and misery, and by so setting them so suddenly together, render us unable to express either.

In some perverse natures there arises, we must confess, sometimes a pride upon the receipt of divine favours, so that we may say S. Peter's behaviour after so great a miracle showed towards him, makes his humility the more commendable. A great and wonderful draught of fish he had taken, and he had laboured hard for it; somebody would have given at least part of the glory of so good success to his own labour, or at least triumphed and gloried highly in it, as if he had been the only favourite of heaven, the only saint for his good success; but S. Peter saw by his lost labour all the by-past night, and the uncouth multitude of fishes now against hope taken up, that his labour did but little here; there was one with him in the boat he saw at whose command the fish came to it in such number; so that now he sees little, by himself or his own endeavour, but that he was not fit company for the Lord that was with him, neither worthy of that miracle nor of that Master.

Thus, good men are humbled even in their prosperous successes, whilst nothing but miraculous miscarriages can humble the ungodly, and not then neither, to think ere a whit the worse of themselves or the better of others; or understand but that God himself is, notwithstanding, bound still to tarry with them before all the world besides. He is truly humble whom prosperity humbles, who, in the midst of his accomplished desires, casts himself below all, acknowledging he is less than the least of God's mercies, or gracious looks towards him any ways.

There is yet a way that perfect souls—souls elevated above the height of ordinary goodness—have spoke these words. There is sometimes a rapture in heroic souls, overborne, as it were, with the torrent of the contemplations of the divine beauty, and the delights flowing in abundance from it, that some glorious saints in their several times have been heard to say sometimes, Depart from us, O Lord; we have enough, we have enough, oppress us not with pleasure which our earthen vessels are not able to bear.

There have been those that have died with excess of joy, but it was temporal joy; spiritual joy is not so violent to rend the body, yet it even sometimes oppresses the soul into a kind of death, and wraps it beyond itself into an ecstasy, and after that it is in danger to be strained into another excess of pride or vain-glory. S. Paul was near it: "Lest I should be exalted above measure," (it seems there was great fear of it,) there was given him something to humble him, to bring him down from so dangerous a height. It is necessary, it seems, sometimes, if not such a desire, yet such a condition to the most perfect souls, that Christ should depart from them now and then, lest they should be "puffed up with the multitude of those revelations" by which Christ reveals his presence in them and his favour towards them.

There are delights in heavenly joys which these old bottles are not yet able to hold; and hence it is, that some have desired God to depart a while, to hold a while, lest they should overflow at least and lose so precious a liquor, if not break in pieces and lose themselves in so vast a depth, or at so forcible a pouring in of heavenly pleasures upon them.

But I am too high now for that lean, meagre, creeping goodness, which is only to be found among the sons of men in these latter days, where we meet with this desire in a lower key, if at all. Our souls, you know, are the vessels of divine grace, old crazy ones, God wot, and there is a danger lest the new liquor of celestial grace should cause them to crack and break at its approach. There is something which we are not able to bear away at first. Christian profession must come in to us by degrees. Christ must come a little and go a little, or come a little and hold a little; "line upon line, precept upon precept, here a little, and there a little," not all at once; no, go away a little, turn aside a little, O Lord, and require not of us all at once, but by degrees visit us and bear with us. With this kind of entreaty we may desire him to withhold now and then in mercy from us, for we are sinful men, and not able to endure other fuller dealings with us.

And, lastly, in humility we may desire God to depart from us, when he approaches to us in thunder and lightning, when he comes armed like a man of war: then we may cry, and not without cause, Oh, come not to us! or, Go from us, for we are sinful men, O Lord; have thou therefore mercy upon us, and forbear us.

We have seen by this time how we may use S. Peter's words and how we must not use them. We may in humility desire God to withdraw his judgments, to proportion his mercies, and to distil them by degrees, to forbear to overthrow our nature or overwhelm our souls with a happiness above our mortal capacity. We may, lastly, by such a kind of speech declare the sense of our own unworthiness to receive so glorious a guest home to us, so even wishing him to choose a better house to be in, or make ours such. But we must not, through natural imperfection or impatience, draw back ourselves from the service of God, or desire him to draw back from us; nor must we at any time, by sin, cause him to depart, or by perverseness and iniquity thrust him out of doors; nor yet, lastly, grow weary of the gracious effects and tenders of his presence, in his sacraments, word, and worship: for so we do not so much confess, as profess, and make ourselves to be sinful men; in humility you may sometimes use the words, in impatience never.

We cannot, now you see, say always he does well, that, with S. Peter, says to Christ, "Depart from me, for I am a sinful man, O Lord;" yet there is something to make the desire at least seem reasonable, and often be so, when he says it as S. Peter did.

And the first reason why S. Peter desires Christ to depart here, is for that he is a man; and the first reason why we are all so willing to have God gone from us is because we are men. Firstly, mutable and inconstant pieces, which are neither well when God is with us, nor when he is from us. If he be with us, then presently, *Fac cessare sanctum Israel a nobis:* "Cause the Holy One of Israel to cease from before us." We cannot away with that strictness and exactness he requires of us, his ways are not pleasing to us. As soon as he is departed then we are at another cue, "Thou turnedst away thy face, and I was troubled." "Why art thou absent from us so long?" "Why hidest thou thy face from me?" and the like.

Secondly. Man is a mortal nature, a piece of clay. Now earth cannot contain heaven. We cannot endure the thunder as it roars, or lightnings as they glister, much less him whose presence is more terrible, whose voice more dreadful, who even shakes the wilderness with his breath, at whose presence the earth removes, and hailstones and coals of fire tumble down.

Thirdly. "Flesh is grass," we are but hay and stubble, and "God is a consuming fire;" well may mortality, then, desire him to depart, lest it should consume it in a moment.

Fourthly. It was the opinion of the Jew that man could not see God and live, as appears by Manoah's speech, in Judges xiii. 22, and several other places. S. Peter, it may be, had such an imagination, whence it is he desires Christ to depart from him, being no other than God himself, after whose sight he was perhaps afraid he had seen his last.

Thus (1) man, as man, thinks he can spare the presence of his Lord, as feeling his earthly cottage altogether unable in itself to entertain him. But (2) reflecting upon his sin, whereby he is yet made far more unfitting and undeserving such an honour, he desires the absence of God by reason of his sin.

(1.) He loves his sin, and is loath to forego it, and knows God will not be content to dwell with it, so he wretchedly chooses rather the company of sin than of his God; this is the way that men of the world only speak the text. (2.) Sin even bids defiance to the Almighty, and turns him out of doors, that is the reason men so readily bid God depart from them. (3.) Sin so disenables the powers of soul and body to any handsome attendance upon heaven, that neither of them know how to receive him if he should come; and besides such a stench and filth there is from it in all the soul that the divine purity cannot endure them. Thus sinful man bids God go from him, because he is a sinful man.

Now comes the last reason why God is entreated to depart; because he is the Lord our God: a reason not readily conceived, yet this it is. Thou art the Lord, a God of pure eyes, a strict Master over thy servants, a person far above the reach and quality of thy vassals under thee; they are, therefore, no fit company for thee, thou so infinitely transcendest them. These are the reasons which S. Peter seems to allege, to persuade Christ from his poor wretched company, because both his natural imperfections and his sinful weaknesses made him unfit for the company and unworthy the favour of his Saviour's glorious presence.

If we consider the same reasons they will serve to humble us as low as S. Peter did himself, to think ourselves unworthy of the least glance of our Saviour's eye: we will confess, if we remember that we are but men, that our frail, inconstant, corruptible nature is not answerable to the glory of so great a blessing; we will acknowledge, if we recollect we are sinful men, that we are not worthy that those eyes should look upon us, that infinite beauty come near our polluted ugliness. We will, in a word, profess, if we believe he is our Lord, we can no less than even desire him to depart, lest he should see too many errors and miscarriages in his servants. Indeed, the whole sum of all is, but to teach us humbly to confess ourselves unworthy of such a Lord and Master, not worthy of his miracles, not worthy of his mercies, not worthy of his presence, and ways or methods of his presence, being no better than sinful men. This if you carry home, and lay it up, and practise it, you carry enough for once, and this well done will be a sure foundation for all Christian virtues.

Yet I will not bid you say, with S. Peter, expressly, "Depart, O Lord:" or at least when you have said so in humility, say presently again with faith, rather "Tarry with us, O Lord, for we are sinful men." Say to God, as Jacob did to the angel that wrestled with him, "I will not let thee go unless thou bless me;" or else, Lord, if thou wilt depart,

Sermon XLV.

yet come again and take me with thee, though I be a sinful man; or, depart, O Lord, as thou art angry with us, let thine anger go, but turn thyself again in mercy, and be pleased to stay. What though we be sinful men, O Lord? Yet we are men, thy creatures, the work of thine own hands, the price of thine own blood. Spare us, therefore, good Lord, and though thou hast departed from us, for a long, too long a season, return again and save us, for we are sinful men, people that have need of thy presence, never so much as now, who cannot be without it, who though we are not worthy to be with thee, yet we cannot but desire to be with thee for ever and ever. Turn thee then, O Lord, and be gracious unto thy servants, cleanse us from our sins, free us from our iniquities, fit us for thy presence, compass us with thy mercy, and visit us with thy salvation; salvation here and salvation hereafter, where we may enjoy thy blessed and glorious presence for evermore.

THE SECOND SERMON

UPON

THE CALLING OF S. PETER.

S. LUKE v. 5.

Master, we have toiled all the night, and have taken nothing: nevertheless at thy word I will let down the net.

THE words are a complaint for labour spent in vain, yet not quite without hope of better success. And they are S. Peter's to Christ, at whose word, notwithstanding so much pains already lost, he fears not to fall to his work again.

And the words have both their history, their moral, and their allegory. They tell us what was and what will be; what was S. Peter's and his fellows' lot, and what will be ours, both in moral and spiritual employments; to lose all our labour if Christ, if God be not by us, if our Master look not over us, if his word be not with us, both to direct us what to do and to bless us in the doing. They, here, "toiled all the night, and took nothing;" that is the history. Men often toil and labour day and night, and catch as little; that is the moral. Nay, God's own labourers, his fishermen, fish and fish, labour and take pains, and catch nothing; that is the allegory. Now what is the reason, but because God is absent all the while? For that, as man lives not, so he thrives not, but by every word that proceeds out of the mouth of God. All we prosper or profit is by the power and virtue of his almighty word, and in the power of that word we must let down our nets, if we look for a draught;

SERMON XLVI.

SERMON XLVI.

and though we have laboured all this while and caught nothing, or but little, or though it must be still our lot to labour still and get nothing, yet, in confidence of that word we must "let down again,"—and now we do,—yea, though it be his pleasure that our net return again both empty and broken.

I will not meddle now with S. Peter's story, as he was a fisherman; what he sometimes was it matters not, "God respecteth no man's person." I shall consider him only under these two notions: as a man, one of the same common fortune with the sons of men; and as a "fisher of men," one selected by the great Master of the world to ensnare the souls of men, to bring them to his own table, and in this sense I divide the words into generals:

I. S. Peter's and his partners' ill success, that they "toiled all night and took nothing."

II. His conclusion yet to go to his work again upon Christ's command, and confidence of better issues: "Nevertheless at thy word I will let down the net."

I. In the first, whether we consider S. Peter under the common condition of men, as a man, or under the nature of an Apostle, as a man separate to a holy function, to deal with bringing other men to the kingdom of heaven through his ministry and office, we have these particulars:

1. That all our labour by itself is but toil and misery, if Christ be not in it to lighten those words, "We have toiled."

2. That it is uncomfortable, as being in the night, a sad dolesome time, if Christ be not by to enlighten it.

3. That it is vain and unprofitable; we get nothing by it all, if he be not with us to direct and bless us: "We have toiled all night, and taken nothing."

4. That be it whose it will, how seasonable soever, be we as wise and politic in it as we can, be we never so industrious in our trades or works, so it will be: We—we men that well enough know our trade, we who have toiled, and omitted no pains—we who have "toiled all night," failed in no point of art or time, we yet, even we, have "taken nothing" all the while that Christ was not with us.

5. That of this we may and must sometimes complain, with S. Peter, to our Master, "Master, we have toiled," &c.

Complain we may, yet not be discouraged for all that, or lay down our work, for in the second general we have several particulars against it.

II. Not to leave off work, but to resolve to set to our work again, and hereafter to direct it better, to guide and set it by his will and word that so it may thrive and prosper.

1. To do it at his word, that is, readily, whensoever, or as soon soever as he commands.

2. "At his word," that is, obediently, for his word's sake, upon his command and word.

3. "Nevertheless at his word," that is, confidently, notwithstanding all that flesh or reason can say against it.

4. And lastly, resolutely, to resolve, come what will upon it, we will do it. "Nevertheless at thy word I will let down the net."

I. I begin with S. Peter's ill success, and that is no comfortable beginning; but it is the beginning of the text, and I love order everywhere, though it cost never so dear to keep that.

(1.) Well then, "We have toiled all the night," says S. Peter for himself and his partners, " and have caught nothing." So say I first for me and my partners, my partners and fellows in nature, for all, or most of the sons of men, and my partners and fellows in office and ministry, the ministers of Christ, "We have toiled," &c. I am to speak of all our labours that all of them, even the best of them, are first but toil and misery.

For the labours of the sons of men that have nothing else to sweeten them but earth, that they are toils you need ask nobody but yourselves. Your very pleasures are toils and weariness: tell me the sweetest and easiest of your delights and recreations, if they do not quickly weary you, and grow toilsome to you? Let it be hunting, or hawking, or running, or walking; let it be any other exercise of the body, let it be your more quiet and sedentary recreations, let it be but talk and discourse, you are weary often before the day runs out, and out of wearisomeness change your seats and stations and postures and discourses too.

And if your pleasures prove in effect but toils, what, think you, do your labours do? To rise up early, and go to bed

SERMON
XLVI.

late, and eat the bread of carefulness—to break your rests, to wear out your bodies, to consume your spirits—is it not a toil somewhat more than labour? Yet, thus is all our labour under the sun, when Christ is absent from us; for what is there to sweeten any of our labours when God is gone? Call up the choicest of those aims you propound as ends to your pains and rewards to your labours, and tell us, if you can, whether they be able to take off the sorrow and trouble from your work, or make amends for them at all. Riches, they are some men's aim, and are not they as troublesome as the ways you got them by?—do they not afflict as much in the keeping, and disposing, as they did in the getting? Pleasures are others' aims, and I have told you already what they are, whose very pursuit or enjoyment is as wearisome as your work. Honours are other men's aims; and what has honour in it that is not burthensome, but a name? Nay, even that too sets a man upon the rack to behave and demean himself with a kind of niceness and scrupulous observance of a respect due to such a title or place, in which he is as much pained sometimes as in Little-ease, or a narrow prison. These ends, then, not being able to take off the nature of toil from the means and endeavours by which they are pursued, there can be nothing said to quit our labours from the true titles of toils and miseries.

Miseries, indeed, as well as toils, if God be not with them; for without him we cannot but be miserable, we, and all we do,—we, and all we have. Samson, grinding at his mill, is in more ease and happiness than we without Christ. All our works are like spiders' webs, good for nothing but to catch flies; that is, impudent and importunate desires, which are the daily issues of our ill-spent hours; for our desires and lusts increase with our labours, and add to their toil; they suffer us to take no rest, neither day nor night; even upon our beds they trouble us, and make our downy feathers as hard as rocks and marble; the covetous man cannot sleep for the importunate buzzings of his desires, nor the ambitious man for his; nor the luxurious man for his; their eyelids cannot sleep, nor can the temples of their head take any rest, for the swarms and hummings of their inordinate passions.

The case is somewhat better with him whose labour is for

God; but it is somewhat alike when it finds no success, a mere toiling of the spirit's. Our studies, and pains, and preachings do but wear out our bodies and afflict our souls, when we only go round, as in a circle, without fastening any where, when we effect nothing with all our pains. Men think the ministers have an easy life of it; but if they knew their down-sittings and their up-risings, the travail of their pains, even to a sickness,—the labour of their minds, even to distraction,—the perplexity of opinions that molest them,— the hard task of reconciling differences, that daily lies sore upon them,—the diversity of judgments that distracts them,— the care of their pastoral charge, that night and day tortures them,—their toilings whole nights, even without a figure, that wear them out; the little esteem, after all this, of all their pains and persons that dejects their spirits; the less success of their endeavours, that grieves them to the souls and heart; if men would but understand the sad toil of these labouring thoughts as well as labours, together with those indispositions of body that usually grow upon them, and those forced retirements, or debarments from those just pleasures and recreations that men of other conditions lawfully enough indulge themselves, they would confess freely that our labour too, if we abstract it from the relation it has to God, is but toil and misery.

And (2) as uncomfortable too as yours, as any else can be; for what more uncomfortable than to see so many years of preaching and praying, reading and studying, return back upon us without success? And yet it is common; to have employed all our time, and means, and industry, many years, and to come at last to our Master with this heavy account, "Master, we have fished all night," all fishing time, and " have caught nothing;" and yet it is usual.

Yet thus uncomfortable is all our work, when God pleases to withdraw from us. Hence it is that Moses draws back so fast, and would fain avoid God's embassy. He foresaw it would prove but an uncomfortable piece of work. Hence Isaiah cries out so complainingly, "Who has believed our report?" Hence Jeremiah grows sad and out of heart, and bemoans himself, " Woe is me, my mother, that thou hast borne me a man of strife and a man of contention to the

SERMON XLVI.

Exod. iii. 11; iv. 10, 13.
Isa. liii. 1.
Jer. xv. 10.

SERMON XLVI.

whole earth! I have neither lent on usury, nor have men lent to me on usury; yet every one of them doth curse me." Here is something indeed to make our case less comfortable than any others, that do we never so well, live we never so justly; if, with Christ, we live like other men, after the ordinary fashion, then Behold friends of publicans and sinners; if somewhat strictly, with S. John Baptist, in fastings and rigours, then Behold, they have a devil,—we are superstitious and popish; nothing pleases them; use we people never so fairly, we are always sure to be opposed, to be contradicted, to be evil spoken of, even in those things wherein we deserve not; and, which is sadder yet, to have those which are committed to our care seduced from us easily, and by troops, and seduced from God, even by those who care not for their souls, but for their fleece, and for the glory of making proselytes, and by that, children of hell, at least, as much as themselves; all this, notwithstanding the painfullest of our endeavours.

Thus, of all kind of labours, the minister's (i.) if God's word be not by to comfort them, is in natural reason the most uncomfortable. Yet, (ii.) there is no comfort in any, where he is not. All men's labours have something of night and sad darkness with them, where that eternal sunshine does not come and clear up the coasts. The wicked man, he toils and moils, but finds no comfort; the blackness and horror of his own sins continually affright him. The natural man, he works and labours, but he finds no comfort; none of his works can open him so much as a window into heaven, either to be received in, or even to see into it: without faith it is impossible to see comfort thence. The Jew, he labours, and sees no comfort of his work; it is high night with him; Moses' veil is upon his eyes, the shadows are still upon him, and he sits down in darkness. The ignorant man, he sees no comfort in his endeavours, for he goes on, and toils and moils, and sees not, minds not heaven at all. Nor is there any labourer in the world, but he that works upon Christ's word, in his presence, and by his assistance, that meets any comfort in anything he does. The strong man has no comfort in his strength, nor the rich man in his riches, nor the great man in his honours (all of them but a discontented crew), if this sun of righteousness make it not day unto them. All these men's labours are in the night, the night of ignorance, where there is no light at all, or the night of nature, where it is but star-light, or the night of the law, where it is but moon-light, or the night of sin, where all these little lights are dimmed, and the great one of grace put out quite. There is no light in any of these to comfort us, wherein to rejoice; nay, all the goods of the world, all that we daily strive and strain and spend ourselves for, cannot afford the least true comfort or refreshment to an afflicted soul; for get we what we can, catch what catch we may, we do but toil all night and catch nothing, if Christ or his grace be absent from us. Our labours also are, thirdly, unprofitable, where the darkness either drives out, or admits not the bright sun of glory; where our toil and labour is in the night.

(3.) He that works in any of the aforesaid nights, his labours profit not; he shall take nothing. To run through them particularly: The Gentile, (i.) he is the first night-worker, he toils, and labours, and works indeed, but can neither find out the knowledge of the truth, nor attain the practice of true virtue; finds no benefit of all his labour. He walks on, says S. Paul, in "the vanity of his mind, his understanding being darkened;" their "imaginations vain," and "their foolish hearts" hardened. They neither know wherein consists happiness, nor how to come by it. Their wise men are divided in their opinions about it, and themselves wholly estranged from it; "alienated from the life of God," says the Apostle. They can catch nothing, with all their busy inquisition, but a mere "profession to be wise," and professing they "become fools;" a pretty catch of it.

(ii.) The Jew, he labours much to as little purpose; and, indeed, he labours in the night too, for his day is done, his time is past; Jewish religion dead and gone, and nothing now to be gained by that. When it was at the best with them, they "received not the promise;" they laboured indeed, but caught little in hand; the full promise, that was kept for us, "that they without us should not be made perfect." Their burnt-offerings and sacrifices for sin could not truly purify them one whit; all were but figures, their whole religion but one great type of ours, their brightest day but

SERMON XLVI.

Eph. iv. 17, 18.
Rom. i. 21.

Eph. iv. 18.

Rom. i. 22.

Heb. xi. 39.

Heb. xi. 40.

VOL. II.   X

night to ours. At the descending of this eternal Word was all to be perfected, nothing to be obtained but from him and by him, at whose arriving only first appeared the day, and with him the only draught worth drawing up.

(iii.) When any man is involved in the night of his own sins, all his works also will prove unprofitable whilst he is so. God will not hear him; his sins they cannot profit him,—whatever they pretend, how fair soever they promise him; for "what fruit had you then in those things whereof ye are now ashamed;" no fruit, but much shame. Nay, his good works in that estate, how fair soever they seem, will do him as little service: "Though I bestow all my goods to feed the poor, and though I give my body to be burned, and have not charity, it profiteth me nothing." "His prayer shall be turned into sin;" his fastings shall not be accepted. His very tears shall be neglected, as Esau's were. He shall get nothing by all his works, all his labour, but grief and sorrow; for without this heavenly flame of divine charity—which is put out by sin—to enlighten that night, even good works themselves will gain us nothing; all of them together will do us no good, but as done in the faith of his word, whose word is in the text; in the efficacy of his command, at whose command Peter again lets down his net. Without his word and presence too, to quicken us out of our sins, it is but toiling all night; all our labours nothing else.

(iv.) No man's labours or endeavours at all can avail anything as from themselves; not only as to the gaining of an eternal reward—to which they carry no proportion—but not of a temporal happiness neither. "Except the Lord build the house, their labour is but lost that build it." A man's trade cannot help him : "Except the Lord keep the city, the watchman waketh but in vain." A man's vigilance will not keep him: it is " but lost labour that thou hast to rise up early and go to bed late, and eat the bread of carefulness;" no care or pains can gain that man anything whom God does not vouchsafe to prosper. "The race is not to the swift, nor the battle to the strong, neither yet bread to the wise, nor yet riches to men of understanding, nor yet favour to men of skill; but time and chance happeneth to them all;" that is, God's providence, that by changes of times, and intermixing of accidents and contingencies, disposes all, says the wise man; and it is "the blessing of the Lord" that "maketh rich," says the same good man; it is uncomfortable being rich without that blessing.

Sermon XLVI.
Prov. x. 22.

(v.) But, above all, the blessing upon our labours, the ministers' labours, is from God. We may "be instant in season and out of season, reprove, rebuke, exhort, with all long-suffering and patience;" "though we should speak with the tongue of men and angels," words of life and spirit; though we should every day preach, with S. Paul, even to midnight, and call out to you to hear and obey, till we were hoarse with speaking, and can speak no more; yea, though we should speak with that passion, as if our own souls were melted into it, and were distilling with our words, and so continue from day to day, till our day were overclouded in everlasting night; yet it might be, with all this pains, we might catch nothing. It is what I need not stand to prove; Moses, and Elijah, and Jeremiah, and all the prophets, are sufficient witnesses, some time or other, of vast labours spent in vain. And the times our own eyes have seen, and do yet behold, are too unhappy an evidence of many men's whole lives and ministries thus spent in vain, where Christ pleases to withdraw himself either from the minister or from the people.

And indeed, this is the least wonder of all the rest: the gaining of souls being God's proper business; and therefore never like to be done without him. We fish but in the night, as if we knew not what we did, nor saw how to cast our nets to any advantage without him. At his word only the net is rightly spread; at his word only the waters flow and bring in apace; he calls, and the fishes come amain; and till he himself either calls or comes, we catch nothing.

(4.) Nay, to come to the fourth particular, though we omit no pains, but even toil and labour what we can, nor slip no time, but even break our sleep, and take in the nights; nor fail of any opportunity, but take every hour of the night, ready all the night long, upon the least occasion; nor neglect any policy or art to help us, but make it our whole labour and business every way to gain our intentions, though we be never so great or good, so wise or subtle, so many or so

SERMON XLVI. powerful, we shall gain nothing but labour and sorrow by the hand, unless God be with us.

(i.) Toil itself, and labour, catches nothing; "We have toiled all night and caught nothing;" all our labour is but as the running round of a mill, or the turning of a door upon the hinges, never the further for all its motion. "Consider your ways," says the prophet, "you have sown much, and bring in little;" "he that earneth wages earns it to put into a bag with holes." He gains somewhat, as he thinks, and lays it up; but when he looks again for it, it is come to nothing. He that gave his mind to seek out the nature and profit of every labour under the sun, returns home empty, only with this experimental saying in his mouth: "What has a man of all his labour, and of the vexation of his heart, wherein he hath laboured under the sun? for all his days are sorrows, and his travail grief." A goodly catch for all his pains.

Hag. i. 6.

Eccles. ii. 22.

(ii.) All the attendance upon times and seasons will effect no more, if you separate from God's special benediction; "We have toiled all night and yet caught nothing." Let a man serve seven years for a fortune or preferment, as Jacob did for Rachel, and in the morning his fair and longed for Rachel will prove but blear-eyed Leah at the best. Whatever it is he gets, it will be but misery to him, or a false happiness. Or let him lie waiting with the bed-rid man at the pool of Bethesda eight and thirty years for the moving of the waters, he will always be prevented—be never able to get in—till Christ come to him; yea, let him wait out all his years, and draw out his days in perpetual expectations and attendances for some happy planet, some propitious hour;—he will never see it, unless God speak the word and command it to him. These fishers, in the text, had even chose their time and spent it out to the last minute—the best time to fish; when the eye of the sporting fish could not see the net that was spread to entangle them, nor perceive the hand or shadow of him who subtilly laid wait to take them, —the time of night; and they pursued their labour till the day came on, "All the night," says the text, yet nothing they could catch; they lost their labour and their hope. Just thus it is, when men having, as they think, diligently made use of the opportunity, and expected it out, having never thought of God all the while, find themselves at last no nearer the end of their desires than they were at the beginning. Your own eyes see it by many daily experiences that it thus oft falls out.

(iii.) Policy comes ever and anon as short of its aims where God is set aside. Though men be oft so cunning in all the arts of thriving, that nothing seems to escape their reach; though the net seem full with fish, their fields stand thick with corn, and their garners full and plenteous with all manner of store; yet draw up the net when the night is gone, when the clear day appears to show all things as they are, and, behold, in all these they have taken nothing: their souls, the best fish, are lost and gone by their unjust and wicked gains; the true fish is slipt away, and there is nothing but the scales and slime, a little glittering earth, or slimy pleasure left behind. Thus mere policy, I mean such as God is not remembered in, proves ever at the last. But it is ofttimes seen, that such policies even deceive them of their own intentions too, and they fall commonly by what they had determined as steps to rise by. Laban, thinking to enrich himself by his covetous bargain, changes Jacob's wages ten times, but still changes for the worst. If Laban says to Jacob, "the speckled shall be thy wages, then all the cattle bare speckled; if he say, the ring-straked shall be thy hire, then all the cattle bare ring-straked:" because God was with Jacob, and not with Laban. These men here, cunning sure enough at their trade in which they were bred up, having picked out their time, and cast on every side of the ship, tried all their art, all their tricks and sleights, (for we cannot but think that being so often disappointed they used all their skill,) yet for all that "they caught nothing," for Christ was not there. "Thy wisdom and thy knowledge," saith the prophet, "it hath perverted thee." And "thou art wearied in the multitude of thy counsels." These are of no power if once God leave us. Nay, they serve all to nothing but to pervert us if Christ be not in them; all our wisdom and counsels but ignorance and folly without the presence of this Eternal wisdom, this great Counsellor.

(iv.) We, be we never so great, never so good, never so

Gen. xxxi. 8.

Isa. xlvii. 10.
Isa. xlvii. 13.

SERMON XLVI.
Ps. lxxvi. 5.

many, never so wise, may toil and trouble ourselves, and all for nothing. "All the men whose hands are mighty have found nothing." Great men may fail as well as others. Nay, more, Peter here and his partners were good and honest men, yet success does not always answer such men's labours

John xxi. 3, 6.

neither; here they fish, and after Christ's resurrection again. They fish all night, but catch nothing till Christ came to them: there is good men labouring and catching nothing. And many they were together; they join hands, and heads, and all their implements, yet it is all to no purpose.

Prov. xi. 21.

"Though hand join in hand, the wicked shall not be unpunished." And though hand join in hand to bring matters to pass, the issue and event comes from above. A multitude is nothing against the Lord of hosts; no, nor without him. There is many joined together and effecting nothing. And then, again, there is Solomon, a wise man—the wisest of the earth—after all his search and labour, coming back with nothing but "vanity of vanity; all is vanity and vexation of spirit." He found it not scientifically only, but experimentally, not only by happy knowledge, but unhappy experience also, too sad a truth. And all this to inform us in this one truth, that there is neither skill, nor labour, nor strength, nor policy, nor time, nor opportunity of any prevalence, not only against the Lord, but without him too.

We must not, after all these men, think much, nor must you, that men of our order should toil and labour day and night, and catch nothing. The text says, "We:" it is a common misery; that is some comfort, that it is not a personal lot, but a common condition to others with us. And in this "we" there is a better we than we ourselves; S. Peter and his fellows must be reckoned. It is S. Peter's, the greatest fisher's fortune, to be sometimes disappointed of the end of his labours. It may be so much the rather his, and such as he, Christ's skilfullest, greatest fishers, such as with him here fish in the deep, even because they do so; whilst a company of petty fishermen, that stand by the shore and fish in the shallows, catch fish enough. Will you know the reason?

S. Peter and his followers lay deep in the depth of heaven, and catch few fish, because the fish are of the world, and therefore savour not heavenly baits; care not to leap so high; they are for watery, fading, transitory pleasures. But others, that fish upon the shore, that stir not from the earth, that stand up and preach nothing but earthly interests and respects; who fish with flies, vanities, and follies, or earthworms, earthly arguments; or cast into the shallows of vain fancies and inventions; who make religions of their own every day new: these catch fish enow, because perhaps the silly fish, the fry at least, are most delighted with such baits.

We might have thought it had been these men's faults, that having fished all night they took nothing; but that they were fishermen by their trade, expert in the art, such as were brought up to it, and lived by it: there is, therefore, something more in it than so. The great Governor of sea and land would not suffer those inhabitants of the water to come at that time, as at others, into the net. It is God's disposing hand that thus deceives the net of its expected prey, and we must be content. Noah was a good man, and Lot was a good man, and great men both, yet Noah preaches repentance to the old world, and Lot afterward to the men of Sodom, without any success; the one preached one hundred and twenty years, the other all the time he stayed in Sodom, yet not one soul gained by all their labour. Many wise men and prophets have had as sorrowful success. Miserable is the case the while that the devil thus out-fishes us. Yet so it is; take we what pains we can; though we were more thoroughly read in S. Paul's practice than we are, in fastings often, in watchings oft, in hunger and thirst, in fears and anxieties, in cares and painfulness; watch we our times never so punctually, and fish we never so studiously in the night, when the passions are at rest, and the deep silence of the night upon them, no noise or distractions, as we would think, to hinder the distinct hearing of the word of Christ; use we never so much art and policy, so much rhetoric and argument to persuade, so that one would think we could not possibly but take: yet even thus our hopes may be deluded, because nothing comes to God's net but what he brings.

(1.) We may, then, first comfort ourselves, if we have done our utmost, if we have discharged our duty, that however

SERMON XLVI. this unhappiness betide us, yet we are not alone; nor is it our fault, though our misfortune. Paul may plant, and Apollos water, yet both be in the same lot with us, if God give not the increase. Nay, God himself seems to be in the same case, whilst he complains : "All the day long have I stretched out my hand to a disobedient and gainsaying people." And you all also may cheer up your souls in your honest and painful labours, though peradventure they succeed not; however that you have done your duty, and rest now only upon the hand of God to second you, and give success: which if it do, you presently grow up and prosper; if not, God's overruling providence, and wiser disposing goodness, well thought upon, will easily teach you to be content.

And (2) remember, this taking nothing may prove at last more profitable than the greatest draught you ever did or could expect. S. Peter and his fellow-fishers, by catching nothing caught everything,—because Him, who is all in all, who thus called them to himself by the occasion of their ill success. And when the worst of casualties betide us, let us think, that though all our hopes and expectations fail us,— all our labours languish away in utter despair,—and we be left confounded with the miscarriages of all our pains; yet God can so order it, that out of nothing all things, all good things, may one day after happen to us; and though he will give us nothing else, yet he will give Himself at last; and upon this not only be comforted, but rejoice in our miscarriages.

And (3) that we may descend to the last particular of S. Peter's ill success. Though we may comfort ourselves a little in the frustration of our hopes, that it so pleases God to order them, and must therefore well be pleased because it is his pleasure, and rejoice sometimes too that we are by such means drawn to God ere we are aware: yet we may complain to him also, lastly, of the same business, and cry out, with S. Peter, "Master, we have toiled all the night and taken nothing."

It is a usual thing to complain of a misery, or miscarriage, and it is as usual to complain to those whom it either does not concern to know it, or who cannot help us. But this complaint here is set right; to Christ it is, and he is our Master, to whom we are to account for the works of our calling, for the works both of day and night.

And therefore to thee, first, Master, we complain that we are no better servants, that we are not worthy to call thee Master, that we are unprofitable servants.

Next we complain that we have wearied ourselves in the ways of vanity, in the works of darkness, and have loved the night too well, and the works of darkness more than light.

Then we complain that all our labours are but toils and sorrows.

Then, again, we bemoan our sad condition, that we, even the best of us, that we, even all of us, can say no better for ourselves.

Yet, lastly, we complain again, that, notwithstanding all our toil and labour, notwithstanding thou art our Master, and we thy servants, for all our hours and pains spent upon our work we have caught nothing. Were it never so little gain, it would not grieve us; were it but a few little fishes, (they might serve for thousands), yea, but one, something, any thing, it would not so afflict us: but this [nothing] is of [So in old edition.] hard digesture; this [nothing] in every thing troubles us, every way perplexes us: so much the more in that it comes often from our own fault, or we may justly fear it, that we thus miscarry. However, it is a thing we may well complain of, as by such complaints even desiring him to give us better success in the rest of our labours.

But whether he will do that or no, if he command us to go on, we must do so still, all other businesses notwithstanding, whatever success past or to come, "nevertheless," at his word we must let down the net; which is our second general; to resolve, notwithstanding all former lost pains and labours, to fall yet, upon his word, to our work again.

II. The net, in moral businesses, is all those several ways and means by which our actions catch their several ends and take effect; and to let down these nets is to apply ourselves to the pursuits of our desires and intentions by ways and means probable to effect them.

In spiritual employments, the net to fish for men is, commonly, the word truly preached; the threads are the words of persuasion; the knots, the arguments of reason; the plummets are the articles and grounds of the faith. This net is to be wove by study and pains, to be let down and loosed by preaching, to be gathered up by calling men to account of what was heard, what they have done upon it; it is washed and cleansed by our tears and prayers, and spread and dried by our charity and mortified affections. And this is the net that we must let down, though we catch nothing. And at his word it is to be let down; his word to be the length and breadth, the whole rule and measure of all our sermons, all your actions. Leave off our work we must, not because it does not answer us with success, but to our work again, and see where we erred, and mend it; find what was the occasion of our ill success, our taking nought, and avoid it. If we prided ourselves too much in our own skill or wisdom, or trusted too much upon the goodness of our own works and labours; or, through the darkness of ignorance, could not well see what to do; or, through the thick night of sins, miscarried in it; or, for want of God's implored assistance, missed of our success; let us now mend all, by ruling ourselves and all our actions according to his word. His word will teach us that art which shall not fail us; his word shall give us humility to cast deep enough; his word will be a lantern to enlighten our night, that we may see our way, and what to do; his word will bring us near himself, that we may the better hear his counsel, and obey his voice, and bring him nearer us, that he may bless us. And so certainly he will, if, with S. Peter here, whatever has befell us, or is like to do, we "nevertheless" at his word again let down the net: (1) readily, without delaying; (2) obediently, without murmuring; (3) confidently, without disputing; (4) resolutely, without wavering.

And indeed, at his word to do it, is to do it (1) readily, for a word speaking, not to expect command upon command, with S. Peter, even to be grieved to be bidden again and again, to have our love or duty called so much in question as to hear a second or third injunction to it. Our former hard hap must not make us to demur, but rather hasten us to our work again, to make amends for our former losses. Abraham leaves his country and his father's house for a word speaking: God did but speak, and away presently goes the father of the faithful. "Whatever thy hand findeth to do, do it instantly," says the wise man; but if God speak to thee once to do it, let the word be no sooner heard than thy hand in action. Do what thou art to do readily, do it cheerfully. That first.

_{SERMON XLVI.}
_{Gen. xii. 1, 5.}
_{Eccles. ix. 10.}

(2.) At his word to do it, is to do it obediently; to do it for his word, for his speaking, because he commands it, "At thy word." Actions are then only done in obedience when they are done for his sake who commands, and because he commands them. He that here pleads his own respects, that preaches for his own ends, or does any thing only to satisfy or content himself, that frames his actions for gain or pleasure, he aims at nothing but himself, and does not those labours at Christ's word, or in the power of it. He does it properly at Christ's word that looks for no other reason of his actions but his command and will, nor propounds any other intention to himself but a full submission to God's will and pleasure; that is reason enough to the truly obedient soul, that God commands it.

(3.) And upon this it is that we expound, "Nevertheless at thy word," to be in confidence of the truth and virtue of that word above all words besides, above all reason besides. S. Peter with his company had fished and toiled in fishing all the night, the fittest time to fill their nets, and yet nothing would be caught. It was against all reason and experience to expect anything now, they themselves, too, being over-wearied with their toil; yet he disputes not with his Lord; but, as if he confessed he could teach him better, he (i.) calls him "Master;" and (ii.) as if his word were of more power than all their skill and experience far, he rests himself wholly upon that. And yet more; as if the very loosing or letting down now of the net upon his bare word alone were enough to bring up a full draught of fish, he makes mention no longer of his own pains or labours, as if they could anything avail, but professes only to "let down the net," confident now by the power of his word only to obtain what neither his art nor labour could procure before, nor reason persuade him to at any time, nay, what all they persuade him now against. This is the right rule of faith

SERMON XLVI.

Rom. iv. 19.

and obedience, even against hope to believe in hope, to believe his word above our reason, to neglect all petty under scruples, to rely wholly upon his authority. It was Abraham's glory that "he considered not his own body now dead, nor the deadness of Sarah's womb;" considered not the strength of nature when God's promise came above it; that he was so ready to offer up Isaac, in whom God had promised him to call his seed, as if he believed God could raise him up again being dead, or else some way or other make good his promise, which was made in Isaac, and that he would do it too though Isaac were made a sacrifice, and so no natural or reasonable possibility left him for any such hope: yet nevertheless do he would as God commanded, offer up Isaac at his word as readily here as S. Peter let down his net.

"Nevertheless," lastly, "at thy word we will;" whether, that is, he please to bless us according to our wish or not, whether we shall bring up fish or no, whether he will have us take or not, we will let down the net because he bids us. To the former confidence is to be added resolution. As we know and are confident he can by his word do what he will, so whether he will do it, yea or no, yet for his word, because it is his will that we should still continue on our labours and work, we will do so, "We will let down the net," come what will come of it. Whether they will hear, or whether they will forbear, preach we must; for "woe is me," says the Apostle, "if I preach not the Gospel;" the command is hard upon us. And whether your works be like to prosper in your hands as you desire, or whether not, labour still you must, and not be idle. To toil all night and catch nothing is uncomfortable, yet to toil all night and catch nothing, and yet to toil again, is constancy and resolution, and may challenge the reward of no petty virtue at his hands, who so esteems and accepts it. You show as much daily in temporal affairs: ye work, and toil, and lose your labour, yet you try again; you plough and sow, and sometimes bring home little, yet you plough and sow again. Be we but as resolute in our spiritual affairs, and work, and they will succeed at last to purpose, to make a recompense for all former misfortunes. If your prayers after a whole night return empty, if your endeavours to repentance and amendment, if your wrestling with temptations, or struggling for mastery with your passions and sins, be not presently answered with success, but you yet groan under the dominion of them, not yet fully able to resist temptations, nor to leave off your sins or break off your transgressions, if you cannot by some nights and days of exercise and endeavour obtain yet those graces and virtues you desire, endeavour yet again, strive and pray, and labour yet again, and in his name and word pursue your work. In his name you cannot miscarry at the last, your net will come at length full fraught with grace and glory.

You see the very Apostles of Christ are in the like condition: many nights and days toil and labour brings them nothing home, yet they still fish again, and so must we, if at last we may gain but one poor soul into the net of the kingdom, nay though but save our own. And if none but that, yet we must let down the net for more, not despair of more; there may come more at length: we must preach, and you must hear, again and again, "line upon line, line upon line, here a little and there a little," cast on this side, cast on that, in season and out, night and day "with all patience and long suffering," as the Apostle speaks, if so be at last that Jesus will deign to come unto us, that he will vouchsafe to speak effectually to his servants, and make them hear, that he will please to stand by and call the fish into the net.

"Master, we have now at thy word let down the net," Oh speak the word only and thy servants shall hear thee and hasten to thee, and obey thee, and be wholly taken by thee. Our labours are vain without thy blessing, nothing in them but weariness and toil; have mercy upon this our sad and uncomfortable condition, and relieve us, both the fishers and the fish, and lift us up out of this sea of misery, this depth of iniquity, catch us all together in thy net, and us unto thyself into thy kingdom, where there is no more toil or labour, no more night at all, no more tempestuous seas or weather, where we are sure to catch that which is above all our labours, all our toil—a full and sufficient recompense for them all, the overfull, infinite and unspeakable rewards of eternal glory.

A SERMON

UPON

THE TRANSFIGURATION.

S. LUKE ix. 33.

And it came to pass, as they departed from him, Peter said unto Jesus, Master, it is good for us to be here: and let us make three tabernacles; one for thee, and one for Moses, and one for Elias: not knowing what he said.

SERMON XLVII.

AND S. Peter, when he thus said he knew not what, was in the mount with Jesus, Moses, and Elias, and saw their glory. One cannot blame him for crying out, it was good being, good building there; though somewhat there was in it that was amiss, it seems, when S. Luke tells us "he knew not what he said." But methinks the words would sound nothing amiss at all, if they had been taken up by us upon our late being with Christ in the holy mount, at the holy table, or if used still in reference to that good meeting, "Master, it is good for us to be here," in thy holy presence; let us build tabernacles, tarry here, go down no more henceforward in our affections to earth or earthly things; let us build here tabernacles for thee, for Moses, and Elias, that neither thy gospel, law, nor prophets may go from us, never henceforth depart out of our hearts and mouths. Sure there is no error in such a speech of ours, whatever was in S. Peter's.

Indeed somewhat there was faulty in S. Peter's, as there is commonly in the most of our best words and actions, somewhat more or less, at least, than should be in rigour, if God should enter into judgment with them. The sudden apprehension of unexpected or extraordinary joy or happiness, be it spiritual or be it temporal, makes many affections and expressions arise in the best of us somewhat irregular sometimes. Our business at this time, and upon these words, is to rectify them, by considering what was here short or over in S. Peter's, what to be left, and what followed in them, that we may learn how to bear our happiness, the great favours of the Almighty, the extraordinary dignations and discoveries of Christ, and besides also all temporal felicities, how to proportion them to others' benefit as well as our own, how so to regulate our judgments, counsels, expressions and affections upon any such occasions, come they when they will upon us, that we may safely say with S. Peter here in any of them, "Master, it is good for us to be here," let us now build tabernacles; this condition is good we now are in, let us still be here; and yet not incur S. Luke's censure, that we know not what we say.

The sum, then, both of the text and sermon will be but this: S. Peter's and our common judgments, advice, affections, and expressions, in any kind of extraordinary content and happiness, spiritual or temporal, what they are; usually they are we "know not what;" and are, therefore, so branded here by the Evangelist, that we may henceforth consider and know what judgments, counsels, affections, and expressions, pass from us in any such conditions, before we pass them. So that our work is to be this, to examine all these in S. Peter's speech, and show you how far it may be said by any of us, and how it must not, and that in these particulars:—

1. How far his judgment may pass, that "good it is to be here;" how we may say, "It is good for us to be here," think and say so, and how we may not.

2. How far his advice is good to build tabernacles, how we may say, " Let us build three tabernacles; one for thee, and one for Moses, and one for Elias," and how far it is not good to say so, wherein we may not say so.

3. How far his affections to his own, or his Master's ease and safety and present glory may be allowed; how we are

SERMON XLVII.

to relish Moses and Elias their departing, or desire their staying, and how we may not; "as they departed," Peter said unto Jesus, as if he would needs be staying them, that he might stay where now he was.

4. How far expressions, sudden and unwary, such as for haste or passion and amazement slip sometimes from us, as this did here from S. Peter, may be borne with, how far we may be tolerated to say sometimes we know not what, and when we may not be allowed it; "Not," &c.

By this limiting and dividing the particulars of the speech and text, and giving the several ways and senses it may be spoken in, we shall neither wrong S. Peter nor S. Luke, but give both their due, S. Peter's saying and S. Luke's censure: his saying, "Master, it is good for us to be here, let us build," &c., and that S. Peter's speech was not altogether to be disapproved; and that yet notwithstanding some fault there was in it, and that therefore S. Luke's censure just, and S. Luke's saying upon it, that "he knew not what he said." Say with S. Peter, and say with S. Luke both, and yet say well with both, when we know what they both said, and in what sense to say it. S. Peter's authority will not in this point bear us out against S. Luke's; but if we say it as S. Peter did, with all the circumstances, S. Luke will say of us what he said of him, that we know not what we say: but if we say the words as they may be said, he will not say so. Begin we then to sift the saying, and the first part first: "Master, it is good for us to be here." S. Peter's judgment of the condition he was in, and how we may judge and say so.

And it may be good to be so and good to say so; good really in several senses; a right judgment and a right saying.

For, first, this here was in the "mount," a place of solitude and retirement, "apart by themselves," says S. Mark. And it is good sometimes to retire ourselves from the world and worldly business, to think and meditate upon heaven and heavenly things, especially having lately tasted of those dainties, that we may chew and relish them; nothing so good and convenient then presently as some retirement, to sit down a little and bethink ourselves of the sweetness we have so lately tasted, the covenant we have so lately renewed, the resolutions we have so lately taken up, and the ways to perform them.

SERMON XLVII.

2. It was "a high mountain" too, says S. Matthew. Nothing henceforth should serve our turn but high thoughts and resolutions; we must do nothing mean after so high favours and dignations: fix our thoughts, "set our affections" now henceforward "upon things above;"—"good to be here."

Matt. xvii. 1.

3. It was "the holy mountain" too, so styled ever since from the authority of S. Peter. And it is good to be holy, better than to be high. High contemplations of God and heaven are not so good as holy conversations. It is good indeed, very good, to be also in the "holy mount," in holy places, at holy work, where Christ is to be seen or heard in beauty and glory, in the Church, at his word and sacraments.

2 Pet. i. 18.

4. For "into a mountain to pray," says our Evangelist. So, "to be here," is to be here praying; Christ went up to that purpose, as he tells us there,—often went up to that purpose, as we find it,—so it must needs be good; nothing does us so much good at heart as praying. It fills it with joy and gladness, fills our mouths with good things, fills our hands and our barns and our coffers; all our filling comes from thus opening of our mouths. Be we in sickness, or be we in health; be we in prosperity, or be we in adversity; be we full, or be we empty, nothing does us so much good in any of those conditions as our prayers. Prayer—why? in sickness it cheers us, in health it strengthens us, in prosperity it fastens us, in adversity it comforts us, in our fulness it keeps us from oppression, in emptiness from fainting, in all it does us some good or other. It is good indeed to be here, that is, to be praying, especially to give ourselves to it, to go aside on purpose for it, to ascend the mountain in it, to go to it with raised thoughts and elevated attentions; take good how you will, for honest, profitable, or pleasant,—prayer is all of them. To be with Abraham in the mount, entitles us to be called with him for it, the friends of God; and there is *honestum*, honest, even in the honourable sense. To be with Moses in the mount is profitable against Amalek, to beat down our enemies. To be here with S. Peter in the

Luke ix. 28.

mount gives us the most pleasant prospect that mortal eyes ever beheld or saw; gives us a prospect of heavenly glory. *Bonum est esse hic*, it is every way good thus being here.

5. To be here is to be with Christ, and Moses, and Elias, with the Gospel, Law, and Prophets in our hands, reading and comparing them, meditating as well as praying. And it is good being so, good spending our time in such employments. "Search the Scriptures, for in them ye think"—and ye think right too—"to have eternal life;" "Profitable they are," says S. Paul—and that is good,—"for doctrine, for reproof, for correction, for instruction in righteousness: that the man of God may be perfect, throughly furnished unto all good works," thoroughly good that serves to make a man so thoroughly good: good to be thus in the mountain here, upon the tops of our houses, in our closets and highest rooms, where we have most leisure, less avocations, that we may the better attend so holy a work, especially since our late holy work; good to keep the scent and relish of those heavenly dainties in our souls.

6. To be here is to be with Christ, and Moses, and Elias, S. James, and S. John, and S. Peter; to be in good company. Nothing better to make or keep us good. Oh, how good, yea, and joyful or pleasant a thing it is to be together with such! Nothing drives away sad and heavy thoughts like such good company, where the discourse is heaven, where the entertainment is heavenly, where we eat and drink with Christ, where there is nothing but sweetness and meekness, and goodness to be learnt; where there is nothing harsh or horrid, or unseemly; where the news we talk of is what is done in heaven, where our meat and drink is "to do the will of our Father which is in heaven," where our talk is not the vain talk of the new fashions of men and women of the world, but the fashions of angels and saints, and martyrs of all ages; where we talk not of other men's lives, but mend our own; where our music is the praises of our God, and our whole business salvation; where we shall hear no idle words, see no unseemly gestures, meet no distempers or distastes, but those things only which become law and order, Prophets and Apostles, or scholars and disciples of so good a Master; good it is to be here, to be with such.

7. But above all, it is good being with Christ. S. Paul would fain be dissolved and gone to be with him; would die when you would, to be with him. "Far better," says he, it is; far better than to be anywhere or with any body else. Nothing comparable to it, be it in life or death, be it upon the mount with him, (1) in a place of safety—it is, no doubt, good being there with him; or, be it with him (2) talking with Moses and Elias about his passion, about "his decease, that he should accomplish at Jerusalem," as S. Luke relates him, in the saddest discourse of his sufferings, or the saddest sufferings themselves, it is good being with him still; or, be it with him (3) "in shining and glistering garments," in a condition of glory; either when his face shines, the heavenly light of his countenance shines out upon us, when eternal glory encompasses him and us; or (4) when only "the fashion of his countenance is" only "altered" towards us, when spiritual contentments flow upon us; or (5) when "his raiments" only "are white and glister," when outward blessings glister about us, it is at every turn good being with him. Yet more particularly:—

Sermon XLVII.
Phil. i. 23.
Luke ix. 31.

It is good for us (1) to be with Christ in safety and security, if we may so, as S. Peter thought he now was here, that we may serve the Lord without distraction. Good to "lead a quiet and peaceable life in all godliness and honesty," says S. Paul.

1 Tim. ii. 2.

It is good (2) again for us to be with him also in his passion; to suffer with him; good to be with Moses and Elias ever and anon, thinking and speaking of the death and passion of our Master, all his bitter sufferings, affronts, reproaches, whips and scourges, sweats and faintings, nails and thorns, and spear and scoffs, and tears and sighs and exclamations, and giving up the ghost; good to be made partakers, too, of his sufferings with him, to "fill up what is behind of the afflictions of Christ in our flesh," as the Apostle speaks. "It is good for me," says holy David, "that I have been in trouble;" good above what David thought, to be with Christ in trouble, to be troubled for him, to suffer persecution for his name. Blessed are they that do so, and that is good to be blessed; and they that are not yet arrived to that, to suffer and be troubled for him, it is good they in

Col. i. 24.
Ps cxix.71.
Matt. v. 10.

the meantime be troubled with him, troubled that he should be so troubled and afflicted for them. It is good to be with Christ in either of these conditions.

It is good (3) to be with him in his glory; that to be sure needs no proving, the only good, the only true and perfect happiness to see his face in glory; all good is concentred here, no good beyond it.

And yet (4) it is good, too, to be with him, so as to enjoy some glimmerings of that eternal light in the meantime whilst we are here, to enjoy the happiness of his gracious presence in our souls, to have him shine comfortably into our hearts. "This is eternal life," one ray of it, "to know Jesus Christ whom thou hast sent;" to be sensible of those inexpressible comforts which he oftentimes vouchsafes to give us; to be partakers of those sensible delights of piety which he sometimes allows us. It is good, the sweetest good this life can yield us, to feel the sense and sweetness of his presence, and walk in it; good to be in grace, and good sometimes to see the glory of this grace, to feel the joy and comfort of it; so "good to be here," that it is not good to be anywhere else, if we may be so.

Nay, and (5) "it is good" sometimes to have our raiments white and glistering with him, to enjoy outward satisfaction and prosperities from him. They are not always the portion of the wicked; they are often happy instruments of grace and glory, and when they are so it is good to have them. "It is good" so also "to be here," to be under some of the fringes of these shining garments, when God pleases that we shall.

But, last of all, "it is good to be here," be that "here" where it will, so it be where God would have us; "it is good to be here," because God would have us here. So this "here" is anywhere with God and Christ; good for David to be in trouble; good for S. Paul to be under the thorn and buffeted; good for Manasses to be in fetters; good for some to be in clouds and sorrows, as good as for others to be in safety and ease, plenty and prosperity, continual light or gladness. But, above all, in all these "it is good to hold me fast by God," says David, to cling close to Christ; good so to be here, to be, to hold so here, and everywhere, in all conditions, not to stir from him, to keep always by him, in his ways, under his protection. And yet, as good as it is, and as we may say it is, we had best know what we say. For we must know sometimes, for all this, it is not good to be here, nor good to say so. "Not knowing what he said," says S. Luke of S. Peter, for saying thus. Let us therefore now know why he said so; when it is we say amiss, when we say, with S. Peter, even upon the mount, in Christ's company, and the presence of his glory too, that "it is good to be here."

1. We know not what we say when we say, "It is good to be here," that is, in the mount only and no more, in honour and high places. They may prove the worst places we can be in. *Summos feriunt fulmina montes;* when the lightnings are flashing and the thunders roaring, they are nearer the storm and danger than the low valleys.

2. Nay, even the mountain of righteousness, high speculations are not always good to be in; we must be sometimes in the plains of action as well as in the mount of contemplation. Nay, and even our own righteousness proves too often an offence; when it is at the height, we are in continual fear of falling, fear of being proud of our graces and goodness; as good as it is to be highly righteous, it is not always safe; it is good at least to come down a little out of the mountain, to humble ourselves a little to the practice of ordinary and common virtue now and then, lest we grow proud of some extraordinary performances.

3. And more than so. It is not good always, in all senses, that Christ be with us, or that we know it. "It is expedient for you," says he himself, "that I go away;" and expedient is always good, and both it is that he should sometimes withdraw his presence, the heavenly gusts and ravishments, lest we should grow proud, and slack, and negligent. It is not good always to be here in perpetual and uninterrupted sensible heavenly comforts. It is good that Christ, and Moses, and Elias, all should draw sometimes behind the cloud; good the sweetness of Law, and Prophets, and Gospel too, should be curtained up from us for a while, that we might see our wants, increase our longings, advance our endeavours, and grow more earnest to seek, more careful to pursue after them.

John xvi. 7.

4. But it is not always good to be in continually bright shining garments, in the region of joy and glory, in daily and hourly happiness. It will make us forget Christ when we are just by him, and not know what we say though the eternal Word stand by us, scarce know how to look or speak. Such things too often do so.

5. But especially it is not good, because it is not fitting whilst others are all in sadness, others all in the vale of tears, for us to be then in the mount of joy, all afloat in mirth and pleasure. Fit it is, and therefore good, to have some fellow-feeling of Joseph's irons, of others' miseries, infirmities, and calamities, not good to be here without such compassions.

6. It is not good, however, to cry out *Bonum est*, though we be in such a condition, either of goodness or greatness, grace or happiness, above our fellows; it is not good to hug and please ourselves in either of them, but especially not in temporal successes; no good crying it up, or ourselves for it.

7. Not good, to be sure, to cry it up as the only good, to be in any worldly glory or security. The Transfiguration will not always last. Christ's face will not always shine like the sun upon us, nor his garments glister beyond what any fuller of the earth can give them; he himself will back again ere long to lower ground, and have less splendid clothing. Yet should this continue, it were not yet the only good that we should cry out nothing but *Bonum est esse hic;* this very being here is enough to allay the goodness, to tell you it is not all, nor will be so for ever.

It is good (1) neither to be in honour, nor prosperity; nor alone, (2,) nor with others; neither in high contemplations, (3,) nor sensible consolations; neither in high mountains, (4,) nor high company,—swallowed up in any of them, or so taken with any of them, to conceit any one of them is the only good, nothing good but that, no good being but being there. To say so of any of these is merely to say we know not what—an ignorant judgment and sentence upon it.

II. And, secondly, to advise to make tabernacles for Christ, and Moses, and Elias here, is to advise we know not what. Yet, to give the great Apostle but his due, see we first in our propounded method how we may be allowed to say it or go about it.

(1.) It is no ill advice to take or give, to raise us such tabernacles as our Saviour tells us are to be raised with the "unrighteous mammon;"—" habitations " or " tabernacles "—for the word is the same, σκηνὰς, both here and there—that will not fail us when all others do; it is good making everlasting habitations, eternal tabernacles with temporal goods, with good works and almsdeeds; rearing tabernacles, by building alms-houses or endowing them.

(2.) It is no ill counsel neither to make tabernacles here, so they be but tabernacles, so we place not our minds and dwellings here; if we make them but tabernacles, not houses; tabernacles to lodge in for a night, or stay in for a shift by the way, have our abiding city somewhere else, have that above, look for that to come; if we only build us inns or shelters as for strangers, make all our buildings, all our contrivements, only to help and shelter us in our way. Then it is good.

Especially (3) if we make them here, that is, upon the " mount," not in the low and dirty valleys. If, in the midst of all our projects, building and making fortunes, fortresses, and securities, we place them not in human confidences, in worldly strength and riches, in that thick muddy soil; if our refuges be in the "mount," as near heaven as we can come, upon Christ, according to Moses and Elias, as the Law allows us, and the true Prophets teach us, we may make tabernacles here, and do well in doing it.

If (4) we build them here, here where there is such good company to live with, Christ, and Moses, and Elias, good rulers, and good priests and prophets, good government, and true religion, upon such grounds we may have leave to fix our habitations, and desire to stay and dwell among them. So we pitch not our tabernacles among " the tents of Kedar," nor choose to dwell in " Mesech," if we can keep out of the streets of Gath and Askelon, our stay a while upon earth may be desirable.

And (5) " three tabernacles" we may make also in particular: one for Christ,—make all the provision we can for Christ to stay with us, use all the ways and means we can imagine to keep him among us, his presence, his grace, his Gospel, his sacraments, his administrations, his ministers, his religion, his worship still among us; good advice it is, and a good thing it is to build tabernacles and houses, churches and chapels, that Christ and his may tarry with us.

Nay, and (6) "one for Moses" too; some room we must make for works as well as faith; the obedience of faith is the only faith of the Gospel, to live according to God's precepts and commandments; this part of Moses' law "Christ came not to destroy," or dissolve, "but to fulfil" himself, and to give a new command, and grace to us also to fulfil it.

So, lastly, "one for Elias" too. The prophets must not be shut out of doors; a "chamber, a bed, and a candlestick" for them, as the noble woman of Shunem provided for Elisha, that as they pass by they may enter in and bless us. A place for the old prophets, that we may confirm our faith out of their writings; a place for the prophets of the Gospel, that we may increase it by their preachings; a place, too, in all our houses for Elias' zeal for God's worship and service, that that may be restored and advanced in all our families and dwellings, in all our habitations, a tabernacle at least in our hearts for the zeal for God's glory to reside in, provided that it be not so heady that it speak it knows not what.

Thus it is no ill, but good counsel to say, "Let us build here three tabernacles," if (1) they be only prepared for here, but raised in heaven; if (2) they be only for inns and shelters here, and not for mansion houses; if (3) they be set upon high ground; if (4) among good neighbours; if (5) made for Christ, and (6) Moses, and (7) Elias, for to keep Christ and his religion, faith, good works, zeal and piety among us. Let us make such tabernacles as fast and as much as we will or can, we need not fear S. Luke censuring them for the sacrifices of fools, or the actions of men that know not what they do.

Yet now, secondly, there is a making "tabernacles," and a counselling to do so, that will deserve that censure, several such making "tabernacles."

1. When we would make the everlasting tabernacles to be here, when we raise them no higher than Mount Tabor, seek heaven upon the earth, living as if there were no other

world, building our hopes and fortunes here, as if we were to continue here for ever, then we know not what we do.

2. When we will have nothing here but tabernacles to shelter us, when we think much to descend out of the mount to suffer with our Saviour, would not willingly part with any point of honour, safety, or advantage, for him, would have Christ glorified before he is crucified, contrary to his Father's decree upon him and us, that we should both first suffer, and then enter into glory; when we thus shun the cross, and will have nothing but the comfort; all for Mount Tabor or Mount Olivet—peace, and quiet, and glory, and triumph; nothing for Mount Calvary, any kind of suffering; all for being "clothed upon," not being unclothed or disrobed at all,— 2 Cor. v. 2. would avoid even death itself, which we cannot avoid; when we can brook no article of the faith but the ascension into glory,—then "you know not what you ask," as Christ said to the sons of Zebedee at another time; you know not what you would have, ye know not what you say.

3. When we speak of making tabernacles only for our own interests, that we may be in them, and consider not our brethren; when we will be engrossing Christ only to ourselves, shut all others out, or pass by them, or at least never think of them, or care what becomes of them, so we be safe, we then also speak we know not what. Christ came to redeem the world, and not that little pittance of it in the mount, Moses, Elias, S. Peter, and his two fellows; not any only pittance in any mount, a few particular elected mountaineers, and leave all the rest in Adam's dirty mass. He was to be an universal Saviour, and pay a general ransom; to preach not only in the mountains of Judæa, but in the Cabul, the [1 Kings ix. 13.] dirty vale of Galilee; to be "the God of the valleys" as well as of "the hills," of those that sate "in the vale of the shadow of death," Gentiles and sinners, as well as those that dwelt in "the hill countries," in the land of light, the Jews and other righteous. S. Peter knew not what he said, nor know they that say thus after him, that would be keeping him always in the mount, make tabernacles, bars, and fences, to keep him from doing his office to all the world besides. To talk of such tabernacles, so cooping up Christ to our own sect and company, is to talk we know not what.

SERMON XLVII.

Numb. xxxii. 6.

John x. 16.

4. When we speak of making tabernacles to retire ourselves from doing our own office too, from performing those duties we owe our brethren, which God has designed us to, and requires of us, we talk not wisely. *Quid dicis sancte Petre?* says S. Augustine,*ᵗ Mundus perit, et tu secretum quæris?* "What sayest thou, blessed Peter? The world is ready to perish, and dost thou withdraw from helping to uphold it?" Dost thou, that art to feed Christ's sheep upon the plains, and defend them from the wolves, seek only to keep thyself secure in the mountains? Nor pastor nor people must so retreat into any tabernacles to desert the charge that lies upon them of their brothers' souls. " Shall your brethren go to war," says Moses to the children of Gad and Reuben, " and shall ye sit here?" No, surely, we must down among them, and not think of tabernacles for ourselves till we have also made some for them. If our retirements hinder us not in our Christian duty, we may retreat into our tents; if they do, we say and do we know not what, to pitch upon any tabernacles, solitudes, or retreats.

5. If we think of making tabernacles several for Christ, and Moses, and Elias; one for Christ, one for Moses, and another for Elias; think of severing the Gospel, Law, and Prophets, it is we know not what; they all dwell in one together, all say the same thing, will not be severed. *Unum est tabernaculum evangelii in quo lex et prophetæ recapitulanda sunt,* says S. Jerome;ᵘ there is but one tabernacle for all those, all agree in one together, all preach Jesus Christ the Saviour of the world, though each in his proper way and fashion.

6. No talking of " three tabernacles," at any hand. There is but " one sheepfold" and " one Shepherd." The sheep that were " led by the hands of Moses and Aaron;" the sheep that were seen in a vision by Micaiah, " scattered upon the mountains;" the sheep which the prophets led, or fed, in any of their times, as pastors sent by God; the sheep and lambs that S. Peter and all the pastors of the Church are to feed, from time to time, are all to make up but " one fold," under " one Shepherd," all to come into one Catholic Church, to be

---

ᵗ [This passage has not been found.]
ᵘ [S. Hieron. Comm. in. Matt. cap. 17. tom. ix. p. 42 G. ed. Franc. 1684.]

gathered all into one mountain, into the same everlasting tabernacles at the last. No tabernacle against tabernacle, no altar against altar, no Church against Church, no schism to be made in the " mount of God."

<small>SERMON XLVII.</small>

7. To place the beatifical vision in Christ's corporal presence, or think that the blessed want tabernacles and tents to dwell in, with S. Peter; or, which is the same, in fine, to place Christ's kingdom upon earth, and dream of the millennary's happiness, Christ's reigning with his saints in all temporal pleasures and satisfactions upon the earth for a thousand years, is mere talking in our dreams. Let us make no such tabernacles in our brains—they are mere castles in the air, raised in the mount of our own fancies and vain imaginations; if we say so, we know not what we say.

No building our thoughts then upon (1) worldly confidences; (2,) no making tabernacles to shelter us from all storms, even from suffering for our Master; (3,) no building them only for ourselves; (4,) no raising them to keep us from our Christian duty; (5,) no making them to separate between Law and Gospel; (6,) no making them to divide the sheepfold, to set up schism in the Church of Christ; (7,) no making them to anticipate heavenly happiness, to keep Christ upon the mountains of the earth, as if our business were wholly here, or wholly for ourselves, or our affections carnal and earthly still. Let us make no such tabernacles, preach no such fancies, believe no such imaginations; for if we do, S. Luke will tell us, were we as good as S. Peter, we say and believe and advise we know not what.

III. Now that we may know whence it is that the same words have thus different senses, why they may be spoken well or ill, we are in the next place to examine the divers affections with which they may or might be spoken; either out of fear or out of joy; out of fear for his Master and himself, of future sufferings, which he heard them talking of, and a desire to avoid them, or out of joy in the contemplation of his present enjoyment, and a desire to continue it. <small>Luke ix.31.</small>

Consider the words spoken, as proceeding out of fear of death and suffering, and a desire to avoid it, to disturb the method of redemption by a new kind of *Propitius esto tibi,*

SERMON XLVII.

a subtle new device to persuade Christ to favour himself and his followers, *Non ita fiet tibi,* to turn off the cross, to keep with Moses and Elias in the mount; or at least, if he would go down, keep them from departing, keep them however with him,—Moses with his wonder-working rod, Elias with his commanding fire to defend him. Consider them thus, and he and his fellows may well be answered with a *Nescitis cujus spiritus,* " Ye know not what spirit ye are of," what you are to look for in the service of your Master; Christ's cross the chief lesson they were to learn.

Consider them, secondly, as words issuing out of excess of delight and joy, either in the present glory, as the all he wished for; in Christ's corporal presence, as the whole he expected; in temporal felicities, as the sum of his desires; or in sensible consolations, as the only pieces of devotion: so also he is but *nesciens quid diceret,* he says he knows not what.

But consider them now again, (1,) as arising out of a moderate delight in spiritual or temporal contentments, with S. Matthew's *si vis,* submitting all to his will and pleasure: " It is good to be here," Master, " if thou wilt ;" and " let us make tabernacles here," Master, " if thou wilt;" if thou thinkest it good, if thou knowest it fit, (for so S. Matthew relates S. Peter's words, and) then they may pass without reproof; they are the words of knowledge, of " truth, and soberness."

Or, (2,) consider them as spoken in the very rapture of joy and high delight in the contemplation of heavenly glory, of God's glory and his Master's, and great hopes of his own desiring what he can to promote and advance it, the words are the expressions of much love and piety, not the speech of a "mad fellow," as Jehu's captains styled the prophet; he knows what he says, and what he desires; or, if through the excess of joy he said he knew not what, more than he could well express, there was no fault, but that which such heavenly joys necessarily cause in human language by their inexpressible greatness, that if we say anything, we must needs say more than we are able to express, they are so great that we know not what to say; and so S. Mark, S. Peter's

Mark ix. 6. disciple, tells the story: " For he wist not what to say, for they were sore afraid,"—almost stupified and amazed.

And if now, lastly, that be the passion too to be added to the other two, and S. Matthew says the same, there will be at least an excuse for any indiscretion in S. Peter's speech; though withal a caution to us for ours, that we speak no more than we understand; that we meddle not to settle conditions, to pitch places, to erect buildings, to give counsels, or pass our judgments in things we have no knowledge of, lest S. Luke tell us we are to blame, we say we know not what.

Sermon XLVII.
Matt. xvii. 6.

IV. Yet now, in the last place, we are to see how far sudden and hasty expressions may be borne with, and when they may not, without rebuke.

1. If they rise out of any sinful passion, sinful they are, and have no allowance.

2. If they rise out of any wilful heedlessness and indiscretion, they are sins of indiscretion, and the words of folly, foolish words.

3. If they proceed out of natural infirmity and shortness of wit, they are at the best but to be excused; faulty they are; for why do they venture on what they do not understand?

But (4) if they proceed merely out of the excess of holy joy, or any passion unblamable, they are no sins; we may well bear with them, seeing we know not how to better them. There is a kind of spiritual and heavenly drunkenness, when ravished and overgone with the sweetness of some inward, spiritual, and heavenly joy,—made drunk with the spouse's "flagons" of wine, in the holy Canticles, with "the drink of thy pleasures," says the Psalmist, "as out of the rivers;" overborne with the strength of this celestial liquor, we say we know not what, do things beyond the ordinary course of action, seem mad though we be sober, as the prophets did sometimes—when the Spirit came upon them—lay down naked; use strange gesture, or speak words, with Caiaphas, which at the time we understand not; run like madmen with some martyrs into flames and fires, to blocks and halters, upon the sudden, powerful, and miraculous motion of God's Spirit or grace within us. These, for all that, not to be looked for now.

[Cant. ii. 5.]
Ps. xxxvi. 8.

Yet, it is ever to be noted here, that how strange soever the expressions of some holy saints have been in such excesses, though they have not understood themselves, yet

SERMON XLVII.

others have; they never spoke nonsense by the Spirit, never blasphemy, never contradictions to holy Scripture, never anything against Christian patience and obedience. We have heard of late of the pattern in the mount, a Church talked of to be formed according to that pattern. Indeed, it seems to have somewhat of S. Peter's *bonum est*, of his desire to be with Christ without the cross, to build tabernacles here for him, a new kingdom upon earth, to set up King Jesus, a phrase much canted; but to this S. Luke gives his dash; it is a *nesciens quid diceret*, that neither he nor they know what they say, what they would have; it is mere fear of I know not what, "a fear where no fear is," a mere stupor, as S. Mark, and a desiring what is not to be desired, an expectation of what is not to be expected, of nothing but ease, and pleasure, and glory, in Christ's service. Their present condition and successes make them say and wish they know not what.

For, if we truly examine it, we shall find this saying what comes next—we heed not what—comes from present contentments and successes; when all things succeed to our mind, then we begin to forget ourselves, or not to know ourselves. Worldly felicities commonly so transport us, that we know not, care not, what we say or do; our greatness, we think, shall bear us out. "We say in our haste" too, with David, "we shall never be removed;" so care not what we say, how we behave ourselves to God and man, only *bonum est esse hic*, we set ourselves to enjoy our pleasures, and build houses for them that shall come after.

Yet it is worth the noting, that whilst we are thus speaking, we speak often against ourselves when we do not intend it. We call all our great buildings, all our great hopes, but tabernacles, with S. Peter; so, as it were, presaging their remove, that they are of no long continuance and abiding. How many have we heard of in their times who have, by some sudden word, some unexpected expression, been the presages of their own ruin, and by the slip of some unlucky syllable or two, doomed the period, and foretold the shortness, of this mountain of glory! Of so unhappy speech are we, when we begin to talk of any glory or continuance upon the high places of the earth, we pitch a word instead of a tabernacle, that takes away all our *bonum est esse hic* on a sudden, even whilst we mean no such matter, whilst we know not what we say. And as no holy company, Moses, nor Elias, nor Christ's own, can keep us from all indiscretion in our speech no more than they did S. Peter, so neither do they keep us from undoing ourselves often with our own language. We in a passion say we know not what; enough to throw down all our tabernacles, remove all our *bonum est,* all our goods. The more need then, with the Psalmist, of " setting a watch before our lips," and " a guard before our mouths, that we offend not in our tongues;" that we consider what we say before we say it; that we learn to speak before we speak it; that we keep our mouths " even from good words," as the same holy prophet has it; that we do not take up every word that seems good and godly, but weigh and ponder it in " the balance of the sanctuary," by Christ's rule and precept, before we utter it.

And so doing and so speaking, we may, in all conditions, high and low, in glory and ignominy, in prosperity and adversity, in all companies, in all places, say merrily and cheerfully, without danger, " Master, it is good for us to be here," and " make tabernacles " here, for Christ, and Moses, and Elias, to keep them with us; we may build in the mountain or in the valley, without fear of this censure—not knowing what we do. All will be good unto us, all will work for good, if we temper our words and speak them soberly, and place them rightly, and direct them every one to his *hic et nunc,* to his proper object and circumstances; and Christ will tarry with us, and Moses not forsake us, and Elias not depart away out of the mountain from us, till we come to the "everlasting hills," to " eternal mansions," " houses not made with hands, eternal in the heavens," to dwell with Christ, and Moses, and Elias, and all the patriarchs and prophets, see them " face to face," be transfigured, and " clothed in bright shining garments," and " shine like stars for ever and ever."

THE FIRST SERMON

UPON

ALL SAINTS.

Psalm cxlix. 9.

Such [This] honour have all his saints.

Sermon XLVIII.
So the text, so the day—a day dedicated to God in honour of "all his saints." "Such honour" has God allowed them, "such honour" has the holy Church bestowed upon them. Because they are "his," and as his here they are had in honour; because his holy ones, *sancti ejus*, as his saints, or holy ones, honoured with a holy day; or, if you will, God honoured in them on the day. For this honour also have all the saints, that all the honour done to them, all the honour done by them, by the saints in earth to the saints in heaven, all the virtues of the one, all the praises of the other, are to the honour, and praise, and glory of God, in all the "congregations of the saints," whether in heaven or earth.

It is not fit, therefore, any of them should be forgotten, from whose memories God receives so much; not reasonable to deny them any honour that so redounds to God's. The Psalm gives them it, and the day gives them it; God says they shall have this honour, and the Church this day pays it, and we must pay it, if we honour either him or her, God or the Church, or father or mother; pay it to them all—to all to whom it is due, all honour that is due. This is a day for us to meet all together to pay it in, for them all together to receive it in. We cannot do it to all severally, they are too many, we may do it to all together. We profess a great article of our faith, the Communion of Saints, by doing it; are therefore, surely, not to blame for doing it, having so good authority, so good a ground, so good a profession for it.

For say our new saints what they will, unsaint they whom they please, dishonour they all the old saints how they list, (I.) God has "his saints," says our text, and, "saints in glory," saints in "their beds," or in their graves; "his" they are, and "saints" they are, though there. His saints (II.) have, and shall have, honour. A signal special honour (III.) it is they have; "this honour," such honour as the former verses spake of. All of them (IV.) have it. All his saints have it (V.) from him, are to have it from us;—*gloria sit,* so some read. Let this honour be given to all his saints; that is the last; and all five so many parts of the text. I go on with them in their order.

I. God has his saints. "Saints" in heaven; "saints upon earth," "saints in glory," and saints of grace. Saints at rest in their beds of honour, and saints in the bustle of noise and trouble. The stranger men they that engross the title to themselves, strike all the saints out of the calendar, and will not call them so whom God has called so. Yet, if to be "saints" be to be holy, the title is their due that are in heaven, they are the holiest: if to be "saints" be to be called effectually, they are called to purpose that are already there; if to be "saints" be to be separate to God from the drossy multitude, they are of the highest separation; if to be "saints" be to be established, if *sancti* be *sanciti,* there are none so sure, so established, as they who are in heavenly glory. And dare men be so bold to rob them of this honour so proper and peculiar to them, that it is but a kind of an impropriety to give it to any here below, which yet both Scripture and their own tongues give to some below, yet to none but such as are in communion with those above, and as far only as they are in it. God has a "chosen generation, a royal priesthood, a holy nation," a separate or "peculiar people;" a people to show forth his praise, called out of darkness into his marvellous light to do it, says S. Peter. S. Paul, and the rest of the holy epistlers, say as much, call believers saints ever and anon; and these have "fellow-citizens;" saints in "an inheritance of glory," worth

Sermon XLVIII.

Ps. cxlix. 5.

Matt. xxvii. 52.
Ps. xvi. 3.
Ps. cxlix. 5.

1 Pet. ii. 9.

Eph. ii. 19.
Eph. i. 18.

the knowledge, says S. Paul, and now worthy honour too.

II. For "his saints have honour," are persons of honour; "kings and priests;" "heirs of a kingdom;" "sons of God;" "children of the Most Highest." So that if the sons of kings, or kings themselves; if men in highest office, or the nearest relation to the highest princes, be men of honour, the "saints" are they who are so honourably related to and so highly employed by the "King of kings;" who are (1) first honoured by him with such titles as his "friends," as his "anointed," as his "sons and daughters;" who (2) are so his that he reckons what is done to them is done to him; receive them and receive him, despise them and despise him, the very least of them not excepted; who, lastly, are so entrusted by him that he admits them into his secrets, makes them of his privy council, an honour, without question, of the first and highest rank.

Enough, however, to teach us (1) not to despise them whom God thus honours, though they here walk in rags and are fed with crumbs, and look desolate, and though they are covered with poverty, and encompassed with afflictions, and had in derision, and a proverb of reproach whilst they are here, and when they depart hence seem to die, and "their departure is taken for misery;" they are honourable for all that, such as the great King delights to honour, and must not be despised.

Sufficient (2) it is to teach us not to dishonour ourselves with any unworthy action or behaviour. It is not for persons of honour to do things base and vile, indeed to live or act like men of ordinary and mean condition. Nor is it for any of them that are "called to be saints" to employ themselves in the drudgeries and nastinesses of sins, in the low poor businesses of the earth, to work in mines and metals, or make that our business here.

For (3) this honour is to teach us to do honourable things, higher thoughts, and higher works; to live like saints, like such as are to "inherit the earth," to reign and rule in it, not to serve it; like such as are to inherit heaven too, and are therefore to have our conversation there, to do all things worthy of it, nothing but what becomes the kingdom of

Christ, especially seeing it is not only mere honour, ordinary honour, but a signal special honour that is here given to the saints. *Gloria hæc est,* or, *Gloria hic est omnibus sanctis ejus,* "This honour have all his saints," or "He is the honour of all his saints." What it is we shall best gather by the context, out of the foregoing verses.

III. (1.) "The Lord taketh pleasure in his people." There is the honour of a favourite. (2.) "He will beautify them with salvation," in the same verse; there is the honour of his salvation; as David speaks in another place; there is a second honour. (3.) "Let the praises of God be in their mouth, and a two-edged sword in their hands to be avenged of the heathen," &c.; there is the honour of conquerors, that is a third. (4.) "To execute upon them the judgment written;" there is the honour of judges, that is a fourth. (5.) Look back again, "Let the saints be joyful in glory;" there is the honour of glory, of eternal glory, that is a fifth. (6.) "Let them rejoice in their beds," or sing aloud upon their bed; there is the honour of eternal peace and security, or the security of their honour. (7.) Lastly, *Gloria hic est,* for the pronoun is masculine in the Hebrew, "He is the honour of his saints," God is their honour, so the text may well be rendered; there is the infinity of their honour, *honor infinitatis,* or *honor infinitus,* "their infinite honour," that is the last. So here is the saints' honour, like wisdom with her seven pillars, strongly built, firmly seated, magnificently set forth upon them. They have the honour of being favourites; the honour of being ever and anon honourably saved and delivered; the honour of being victors; the honour of being judges; a glorious, secure, infinite honour the saints have.

1. This "honour" that they have is the honour of grand favourites. God (i.) is well pleased in them, taketh pleasure in the prosperity of his servants; his delight is placed in them; "the Lord's delight is in them that fear him;" he deals with them as Pharaoh did with Joseph; puts his ring upon their hands and espouses them to himself, makes them the keepers of his signet, and grants petitions by them. He arrays them (ii.) in vestures of fine linen, that is, "the righteousness of the saints," says S. John; clothes them with

the best robe too, the royal apparel of his Son; (iii.) he puts a gold chain about their necks, obliges them with the richest blessings; (iv.) he makes them to ride in his second chariot, carries them in the clouds, and sets them all at his right hand; (v.) cries before them, Bow the knee; such honour have all his saints; (vi.) he makes them rulers over all the land of Egypt, makes them "to have dominion over the works of his hands;" gives them all the blessings of the land; gives them their heart's desire, and fulfils all their mind, all at their disposal; (vii.) he does more than Pharaoh: he entertains them at his table, feeds them with the bread of heaven, embraces them in his arms, receives them into his bosom, counts them as the very apple of his eye, reckons them as his jewels, compasses them continually with his loving-kindness, "prevents them always with the blessings of his goodness," and "crowns them with glory and worship;" puts crowns upon their heads as well as robes upon their backs; crowns them with this favour above the rest, as to unbosom himself unto them, to grant them secret conferences and discourses with him, as to his only favourites in the world.

2. That this may appear the better, "their honour," secondly, "is great in his salvation;" they do but cry to him and they are saved; they do but go to him and they are delivered. "He preserveth the souls of his saints," says holy David. "He preserveth the ways of his saints," says David's son. Nay, says the father again, he gives his very "angels charge over them;" makes them tarry all "about them," that they "hurt not so much as their feet;" that they "break not a bone;" that they "lack nothing." This is an honour to some purpose, and a huge one for God to descend to do it for us; not like the honours of the earth, that lay us open to wind and weather, that cannot shelter us from danger and ruin, but raise us up commonly to throw us down with the greater violence. No; he lifts up his meek ones to salvation; lifts up his Son upon the cross to save them, a high honour this; we would count it so if a king should venture himself to save us, an honour we knew not how to value; and such a one this is, you will see it clearly by the next, honour and salvation both exalted, which is the honour of victors and conquerors granted also to his saints.

3. For, though the heathen rage, the saints shall be avenged; though the people imagine a vain thing against them they shall rebuke them; if the kings of the earth stand up, and the rulers and nobles take counsel together, the saints shall bind them all in chains and links of iron, all together; the gates of hell shall not prevail against his saints; against his Church all the counsels and devices, all the strength and power, all the subtilty and malice of earth or hell shall do no good. Come life, come death, come angels, come principalities, come powers, come things present, come things to come, come height, come depth, come any other creature; come tribulation, come distress, come persecution, come famine, come nakedness, come peril, come sword, come all the kings and princes of the earth, all the heathen and infidels under heaven, all the violence and cunning of hell, and all the inhabitants of that dismal dwelling; come what can come, come how they can, come all that can, as good come nothing, nothing will come of it, of all their fury;—in all these, says S. Paul, "we are more than conquerors, through him that loved us." "Thanks be to God," says he, "he always causes us to triumph in Christ." We may erect our trophies, we may hang up our spoils, the spoils of these our enemies, and dance about them, "praise his name in the dance," as we are called to do, as certain of our victory "through Jesus Christ," for through him "this honour have all his saints."

4. Yet not the honour only of the triumph, but of the judgment-seat besides, to pass sentence and execute judgment upon the conquered enemies. "Know you not," says S. Paul, "that the saints shall judge the world." Are you ignorant of the honour God has promised them? "Know you not that we shall judge angels" too? Much more, then, the potentates of the earth, who have oppressed the Church, gainsayed the truth, stood up against Christ, and for a while trampled down the saints. The time will be, the day will come, when those great princes, such as Antiochus, Herod, Nero, Diocletian, and the rest of those persecuting furies, shall be brought before the great tribunal, and receive their sentence from the mouths of those poor saints whom they so tyrannically raged against, to be bound hand and foot and

SERMON XLVIII.

Isa. xiv. 9.

cast into utter darkness. And how great an honour, think you, must this needs be, to sit judges over those great men who made the earth tremble still before them, and even "hell at their coming thither to be moved" at them, as the prophet speaks. How great an honour, I say, for such poor scrubs as we, for the very poorest saints to be made judges of such men! yea, and judges too not here, not in earth below, but in heaven above; yet such also "is the honour of the saints."

5. And greater yet; for it is not *honor* but *gloria* here—*et Ps. cxlix. 5. sancti in gloria*—a glorious honour that the saints are honoured with. All earthly honour reaches not to this title; glory that we may be joyful in is more than earth affords. The honours here are so full of fears, so farced with troubles, so stuffed with cares, so amongst thorns and briers, so blasted with envies, so justled at by rivals, so assaulted by enemies, so undermined by neighbours, so suspected by friends, that there is little true mirth or joy to be had in them; it is only the honour of the saints in glory that is troubled with none of these, but surrounded with uninterrupted joys and songs of joy. And were the saints' lives here but so many days and years of affliction and vexation, ignominy and dishonour, this crown of honour at the last were a sufficient, abundant, superabundant recompense for them all. And this is so properly the saints', that none else have the dream

Col. i. 12.
Eph. i. 18.
Luke vi. 23.

of a title to it; it is their "inheritance," it is their "reward," the reward of their inheritance both together. The greater honour to be so honoured as to have glory itself called their reward; strange honour to them, to have honour entitled to them as their due.

6. But honour, joy, and glory given to them "in their beds," to have joy and glory conferred upon them "in their beds," to have it, as it were, with ease, with lying still, and to enjoy it with security, without fear of rousing from it, and in the very beds of dust, the dark chambers of the grave, the mansions of death itself, to have this light and glory shine upon them, to have security and peace, ease and pleasure established on their glory, and those melancholy rooms that are hanged with worms and rottenness enlightened with the beams of perpetual joy and comfort, is a vast addition to

their glory. Yet this they have, not only an immarcescible and incorruptible "crown of glory," laid up for them, but their very "bones flourish out of the grave;" and even the lodgings of their very ashes seem to exult with a kind of joy to be made the receptacles and cabinets of those jewels of the Almighty, and their sepulchres and memorials are blessed for evermore. The very places where they come are joyful at their shadows as they pass by; miracles have been done by their shadows whilst they passed by; and when their bones have lain awhile silent in the grave, the dead have yet been raised by them to life again. Thus his saints have honour in life, and death, and after death, then when they seem to have been some while, nay, a long while raked up in dust and quite forgotten.

<small>Sermon XLVIII.
1 Pet. v. 4.
2 Tim. iv. 8.
Ecclus. xlvi. 12.
Ecclus. xlix. 10.
Acts v. 15.
2 Kings xiii. 21.</small>

7. Nay, lastly, *Gloria hic est*, their honour is infinite, too, it is a masculine glory; all other glories and honours are but feminine, weak, poor things to it. God is their glory, honoured they are with his blessed presence, honoured with his sight, with his embraces; they see him and enjoy him. This is the very glory of their honour, the height and pitch of all, for "in thy presence is joy, and at thy right hand there is pleasure for evermore;" honour advanced into eternal glory; and "this honour" also "have all his saints," some *in spe*, and some *in re*, some in hope, and some in deed, all either in promise or in possession. "All his saints," some way or other, more or less, are partakers of it; that is their honour at the full extent, an honour wherewith this day is great, which is a great considerable also in the text, that this honour of the saints, as special a one as it is, is yet also universal, some way or other belonging to all the saints.

IV. Some way or other, I say; for this honour, it is to be confessed at first, is not equal to them all. "One star differs from another star in glory." One saint differs from another in his honour. There is a sun, and moon, greater and lesser stars, in the firmament of saints. There are celestial and terrestrial saints; saints wholly busied in the work of heaven, and saints who intermeddle also with the works of earth; contemplative saints and active saints. There were saints before the law, there were saints under the law, and saints still after it. Patriarchs and prophets, martyrs and apostles,

<small>1 Cor. xv. 41.</small>

all were saints; Jews, and Christians, and Gentiles too, have saints among them.

And all have their honour : the Jews literally, to the very words; the Christians mystically, to the higher sense and meaning; greater honour these, because more abundant grace than they. The Gentile proselytes, they come in also for their share. Beloved and favoured by him all, delivered by him some way or other all; conquerors, at least over their ghostly enemies, all of them ; to be judges all, at last, and prepared to glory and honour, and God's presence after all. There are false saints many, as there are false gods many; and false honour there is too, that is by some men given to both the false and true ones ; yet this no reason to scrape the true ones out of the calendar, nor deny the true honour that is due to them. If God say the saints have honour, *est et erit*, for ἔσται the Complutensian Bibles read it, as others ἐστί, that they have, and shall have. I cannot but think that man too bold that dares contradict it, that dares annul the festival or memorial of All Saints, of any saints, together or asunder, or rob them of the honour that God has given them. Holy they are—saints is nothing else; and the Scripture so often calls them holy that it is infidelity to doubt it,—impudence to question it,—and atheism to deny it; and, therefore, sacrilege it must needs be too, to violate their honours, or plunder them of that which God has given them ; for this "honour," says he here himself, or his Spirit for him, "have all his saints."

V. Have it from God, (1) first, are therefore (2) to have it from us too. Have it from God, for he has promised it. " Those that honour me I will honour," says he; and honour them he does: (i.) He speaks of them with honour throughout the holy page, and tells forth their praise ; builds there, as it were, a lasting monument to their memories. (ii.) He gives them titles of honour : calls Abraham his friend; Enoch, in a manner, his companion, one that continually walked with him ; Job, his servant, with an emphasis, with a *Quis similis* in all the earth ; David, his dear heart, as one would say, " a man after his own heart;" the true Israelites, " the precious sons of Sion ;" and all his saints his "jewels;" jewels "made up" and laid up in cabinets, in the cabinets of the highest heaven. (iii.) He gives them high and honourable employment: to Moses, to be faithful in all his house, his high-steward there; to Joshua, and Jephthah, and Gideon, and David, to be generals of his wars, and fight his battles; to Solomon to be his master-builder, and the overseer of his works; to all his saints to be his courtiers, and tread his courts; honourable all. Nay, (iv.) he makes them all, as it were, masters of his requests, grants petitions often upon their score. Thus, "for Abraham my servant," "for the oath I sware unto Isaac," "for my servant David's sake," at the petition of "my servant Job," and the like, says God, I will do this or that. Many, many things God did for Israel for their sakes; many times withheld his judgments, and bestowed his mercies, for their only sakes; and with us he deals so too, grants us many favours and blessings for some of our holy forefathers' sakes, which he would not give us for our own. (v.) He so honours them that he seldom discovers any of their faults, or but easily glances at them, or but favourably speaks of them, as in that remarkable expression, where he calls David's murder and adultery the "matter" only "of Uriah the Hittite;" yet recounting of their virtues he is alway full and large. Lastly, he sometimes honours them with miracles, even at their sepulchres, as he did Elisha; makes napkins and handkerchiefs from their bodies, nay, their very shadows cure diseases; and—unless we will believe nothing but what we see done before us in our own days—many great miracles have been done at the sepulchres of the martyrs, God so honouring the memory of their faith and patience, to the glory of Christianity, and the glorious propagation of it through the world; and there have been thousands of witnesses to attest it.

And now, if God so honour them, as if he delighted to honour them, it cannot seem strange if I now go on to tell you we are to honour them too. It cannot be a sin in us to do that which God does before us, that we may do it the better.

I must confess there has been a fault, and still there is some, in giving more honour to saints and martyrs than their due; not robbing Peter, as we say, to pay Paul, but robbing God to give to S. Paul, S. Peter, S. Mary, and other saints. Yet there is a fault in others too, to rob the saints under

Sermon XLVIII.

1 Kings xv. 4.
Job xlii. 7.

1 Kings xv. 5.

2 Kings xiii. 21.
Acts xix. 12.
Acts v. 15.

SERMON XLVIII.

pretence to give to God. But is there not a mean between them? Sure, sure, there is. We may give each their due; God his, and the saints theirs, and all will be well.

For "praise God in his saints" (the beginning of the next Psalm, as we may read it, and some understand it, and may so without offence, it coming especially so close to this honour of the saints) may seem to call upon us to give this honour to them. And, Ps. lxviii. 35 may be as well "God is wonderful in his saints," as "God is wonderful in his holy places," for aught that I can guess by the sense or context, and a good reason to praise him for them, and in them too, as well as in his sanctuary; we may praise him, I hope, for all the wonders that he does for the children of men, be they in heaven above or in the earth beneath. And, indeed, there is an honour due in both, to "the saints that dwell on earth," as it is Ps. xvi. 3, and to "the saints that dwell in heaven." Distinguish we but the honour as the Scripture does, and find out the several senses of it there, and we may know to give each their own. We shall begin below, see how we are to honour "the saints that are in the earth."

Ps. lxviii. 35.

Ps. xvi. 3.

To honour is (1) to esteem and value one; good men are to be valued, be their condition never so mean or poor, that is one duty we owe the saints whilst they live here; and there is good reason, for they are very "pillars" of the earth, and bear it up. "Ten righteous men," you know, would have saved even Sodom and its four neighbour cities. It is good we should prize them high that are more worth, one of them, than half a city.

Ps. lxxv. 3.

To honour one (2) is to perform the offices of charity unto him: thus we are bid to "honour all men," to go one before another in giving "honour," especially then to do it to "the household of faith," men of piety and religion.

1 Pet. ii. 17.
Rom. xii. 10.

(3.) To honour is not only to value, or to love, but to delight to be with, to seek their company: *honorare timentes Dei*, "to make much of them that fear the Lord," never to think ourselves so well as in their company. "All my delight," says the same Psalmist, "is upon the saints that are in the earth, and upon such as excel in virtue;" he was never pleased but when he was with them. Nay, even Saul, as bad as he was, yet "Honour me," says he, "I pray thee," to Samuel, "before

Ps. xv. 4.

Ps. xvi. 3.

1 Sam xv. 30.

the elders of my people, and turn again with me;" his company he must needs have, and an honour he acknowledges it to have the company of such a man, a holy priest or prophet. The world now is of another opinion; no company so contemptible; men are never well till such a one is gone; never merry till these holy men are out of doors, so far are men from thinking themselves honoured with their society, or willing to honour them with theirs; any company rather than such as they; they make us melancholy, say they; they make us sad and dull; they trouble us with discourse we do not like—with God, and heaven, and virtue, and religion, such hard businesses, and we know not what. But for all that, it is a duty we owe both to ourselves and them, to give them this honour, be they never so poor or despicable; and David, you hear, made it his delight as well as Saul his honour, to receive this honour from or give this honour to such men as they.

(4.) To honour is to maintain them too, when they have need. "Honour widows," says S. Paul; that is, maintain them out of the Church's stock; and they that labour in the ministry are to be honoured with "double honour;" maintenance and respect out of the Church's stock and out of ours. Honour is thus taken too in the fifth commandment; and we sin against the commandment both of God and men, when we deny this honour where it is due, or whensoever the poor saints stand in need of it. Thus you see what it is to honour, or how you are to honour the saints below, to set a high value and esteem upon them, to perform all offices of love and charity unto them; to seek their company, and take pleasure to be in it, and, as occasion serves, to express the honour and respect we bear them, by some outward real testimonies and effects. We will see now how we are to honour the saints above.

To honour, then, as it may relate to them, is to give them a respect above other men, to look upon them as the courtiers of heaven, as persons in highest place, as the inhabitants of glory, as such as are always praying for us, such as are "following the Lamb whithersoever he goeth." Nebuchadnezzar himself, at the hearing of the interpretation of his dream, could not refrain himself, but he must even worship

Sermon XLVIII.

1 Tim. v. 3.

1 Tim. v. 17.

Rev. vi. 9; vii. 14, 15; [xiv. 4.]

Dan. ii. 46.

SERMON XLVIII.

Daniel, in whom he saw the wisdom of God so eminent. We cannot hold ourselves sometimes, but that we must needs express some especial respect or other to some who either amaze us with their stupendous abilities of nature, or works of grace. And is it only strange and irregular to give honour to those glorious saints whose excellences are so great, whose virtues have been so full of wonder? I cannot see why their memories may not live in honour—why, being departed hence, they should be forgotten, when their virtues and good works,

Heb. xi. 4. as S. Paul says of Abel's faith, "though they be dead, yet speak" unto us.

And if they yet speak we may speak too, speak of them to their praise; for to honour them is to commend them: so

Ps. xxii. 22. God is said to be honoured; so Christ to receive honour from
2 Pet. i. 17. his Father; so men are said to be honoured; that is, praised
Prov. xiii. 18. or commended. To this purpose it is that the holy Scripture
Prov. xxvii. 18. relates their histories; to this intent S. Paul reckons up a whole
Heb. xi. catalogue of them, and would do more but that the day would fail him. After the same sort he honours Lois and Eunice,
2 Tim. i. 5. the grandmother and mother of the blessed Timothy. And an ancient custom it was among the saints of God, it seems
Ecclus. xliv. 1. by the son of Sirach, to "praise famous men, and the fathers that begat us," to make a solemn commemoration of them. The primitive Church was not behind in this duty neither, but in the prayer for the holy Catholic Church recited the names of the most famous saints and martyrs, and gave God thanks for their good examples, even at the altar itself; nay, brought
1 Tim. ii. 1. in the command of the Apostle for "intercessions and giving thanks for all men" for the preface of it, as a text to authorize their so doing. Evidences these sufficient to honour the saints with all our praises.

With our praises, I say, but not our prayers; our praises of them, not our prayers unto them; that is a piece of honour God has no where in Scripture any way allowed them. Prayers I find not that they are to have; praises I find they may.

And which yet makes more to their honour than such prayers could do, that they should be the conduits of God's honour to convey it to him; God is now to be praised for them. He praised in his saints; he honoured in their honour;

honor servorum redundet ad Dominum, so S. Jerome.[x] God to have the honour of their honour; he who bestowed so excellent graces upon them, so excellent examples in them unto us, he to be blessed for them. Blessed too for the honour he has done to take them hence, out of this vale of misery, to himself, to glory and honour; this is to season the saints' honour right, to give it as we should when the Author of it is thus honoured by it.

But there is an honour still behind, that makes up all. We are said to honour those whom we follow with our attendance. He that is highest in honour has the most followers, the greatest attendance. If we will therefore honour the saints indeed, we must honour them by following their virtues and examples. This is that the Church principally intends by all the saints it sets before us, by all its festivals and holidays, to put us in mind of the patience of S. Stephen, of the repentance of S. Paul, of the faith of S. Peter, of the purity of S. John, of the holy chastity and humility of the Virgin Mary, of the ready following of our Saviour in S. Andrew, of the leaving and forsaking all for Christ in S. Matthew, of a holy boldness to profess the truth in S. John Baptist, and so of the rest; and of the love, and charity, and communion the saints ought to hold together in this day's feast; where they are all, as it were, joined together, that we might learn never to make a separation from this communion, never to break off from " the doctrine once delivered to the saints," nor leave one single virtue unpractised which we find in any of them. This is truly honour to them to have a multitude of followers, the "honour of all his saints."

And it will be our honour too, to follow them, and do like them; to make ourselves honourable by these virtues, patience, obedience, chastity, holiness, great piety, which have rendered them so renowned through the world; so famous in this, and so glorious in the other.

And all these together are all the honour, lastly, the saints expect or require from us, besides that of our prayers for their consummation, that they with us, and we with them, may in due time obtain the fulness of this honour,

[x] [This passage has not been found.]

the completion of this glory at the resurrection of the saints.

By this "honour," this reverent esteem of them, by this honourable mention of then., by the devout praises of God for them, by our diligent imitation of their virtues, and our prayers for their perfection and consummation, and our own —for "they without us shall not be made perfect"—by thus "giving honour where honour is due," as the Apostle speaks, we shall give God his honour, the Church her honour, ourselves honour, and one day be made partakers of that honour and glory which "all his saints" that are departed hence in his faith and fear enjoy already, and reign with him and them in honour and glory for evermore. *Amen.*

THE SECOND SERMON

UPON

ALL SAINTS.

HEB. xii. 1.

Wherefore seeing we also are compassed about with so great a cloud of witnesses, let us lay aside every weight, and the sin which doth so easily beset us, and let us run with patience the race which is set before us.

"SEEING we also?" What, we also "under the cloud?" Indeed, "our fathers were," yea, "and were baptized in the cloud." Christianity, then, in clouds, in shadows. But when the sun displays his mid-day glories, the clouds vanish out of sight: what then means this *nubem tantam?* How comes this cloud? Is it because that Majesty is yet too glorious for our weak eyes to look upon without a veil? Is it still *videmus tanquam in speculo?* See we nothing here but through this watery glass? It is so. *Viatores,* they, and we; and the sun in a cloud fittest for travellers. Thus distinguished from the saints in bliss, "we" for *nubem,* "they" for *lumen,* we compassed about with clouds, they with light.

^{SERMON XLIX.} ^{1 Cor. x. 1.} ^{1 Cor. xiii. 12.}

And as *nubem* makes the difference between *viator* and *comprehensor,* so *circumpositam* (for so is περικείμενον), between *viatores legis* and *evangelii,* those pilgrims of old, and our travellers. They were ὑπὸ, the cloud above, they under it; so under it that they could not look up to the end of that which was to come. This περὶ, about us, we in it, and so see the easier through it. The Apostles, by a figure, first entering it at the Transfiguration, when Moses and Elias, law and prophets, were departed, not before.

Yet should we grant them *circumpositam*, to be in it too, it would prove but τὴν νεφέλην, "a little cloud," to this τοσοῦτον νέφος, or but a dark one, to νέφος μαρτύρων, a "cloud of martyrs," whose flames outshine the brightness of the sun.

The truth is, our cloud and theirs are not alike;—ours but analogical at the most. The Apostle had to speak to Hebrews to persuade them to the race of Christian faith, and to them he was to fit his speech. They would not so soon from their beggarly rudiments. A cloud they always had in all their journeys, and a cloud they would have now, or they would not stir a foot. S. Paul raises up a cloud in the preceding chapter, yet a little to wean them from sense, though a cloud he calls it, it will prove no such cloud as their dull eye gazed after, but a cloud of saints.

Indeed, need he had to tell them of a guide from heaven, that a few verses before had told them of so ill entertainment upon earth; stoning, sawing in sunder, deserts, dens, and caves, nothing but torment and affliction. *Ideoque* had been a poor inference, could expect but a cold welcome, without a *nubem tantam*.

And yet what avails a guide, though sent from heaven, if this same ὄγκος, some weight about us overwhelm us, or the way be so bespread with τὴν εὐπερίστατον ἁμαρτίαν, such snares that every step we stumble and fall into inextricable dangers? Were it not for ἀποθέμενοι, that he shows us how to quit ourselves of all, the cloud might walk alone for all the Hebrews, καὶ ἡμεῖς, and for all us too.

For, as they, so we pretend often we would run, but that we have no guide,—here is a cloud to conduct us; then, we have no company,—here are saints to go with us; nobody to encourage us,—here are witnesses to behold us. Then we are too pursy and unwieldy for the course,—why, off with that superfluous weight; yea, but the way is full beset with briers and thorns,—down with them too; well, but the way is tedious, —let us "run with patience," no more than so; but we have nothing to run for,—yes, there is something set before us that is worth the running for; we shall easily find that too in *propositum.* So then here is—

I. The guide of our way: "a cloud of witnesses."

II. The companions of our course: "a cloud of witnesses that compass us,"—*habentes nobis,* having it with us, or being compassed with it.

III. The spectators of our course: "a cloud of witnesses about us,"—*habentes circumpositam.*

IV. The impediments of our speed: (1,) one, that hinders us from setting forth, " every weight;" (2,) the other, that entangles us by the way, " the sin that doth so easily beset us."

V. The removal of them both, by laying aside, or casting away.

VI. The running of our course: " let us run with patience."

VII. The race to be run: " the race set."

VIII. The crown of our labours: " set before us."

IX. The influence of the cloud upon all, or the inference from it, *ideoque curramus.* Seeing "a cloud" we have, and such an one, "a cloud of witnesses," that will not lead us about as that cloud did Israel in the wilderness, but *breve per exempla,* the shortest cut, without staying now by the way at *lugens in infernum,* or *sinus Abrahæ,* but hence immediately into Canaan. Seeing the cloud so great, the guide so good, the company so full, the spectators of so high account, the hindrances so easily put by, the course so facile, the race so short, the prize so glorious, how can we but run like lightning after them? You see the parts.

It is fit the guide should lead the way; the cloud first.

I. When time was, there was *columna nubis;* Moses his cloud, Israel's guide to Canaan. Canaan is gone, and *nubem non habentes,* we have no such cloud, we.

There is another, *ut nubem iniquitates,* Isaiah's cloud, " a thick cloud of transgressions," a winter cloud that sticks by us, a morning cloud that rises with us, at the first dawning of our days, and God make it too as a morning cloud to pass away. I would I could not say here *habentes nubem,* that we had not this neither; but this I can, *ideoque habentes,* it is

I. The cloud.

Isa. xliv. 22.

not no good[y] conclusion thence, we have it not to follow, it sets in darkness.

What cloud, then? Why, *nubem testium*, S. Paul's new cloud, " a cloud of witnesses," of holy saints, who by the glory of example lead us more happily to heaven than theirs did them to the land of promise. A cloud, for their multitude; but that we let alone till we come to *tantam*. A cloud, for the likeness of their production, their seat, their nature and effects.

1. Their production, first. Clouds, though heaven's near acquaintance now, are (i.) but refined earth, or water divested of its grosser body; and were not the departed saints, a while since, prisoners in these clay houses, now bereft of their happy tenants? one of the best of them, in his own esteem, no better than dust and ashes.

(ii.) Why, then, how got they up so high? The clouds, they get not up themselves; it is the sun that draws them upward. And, *Trahe me et curram post te*, is the voice of the spouse. Some celestial influence we must have, the best of us; something without us, from above, to lift us up to heaven; nature cannot reach so high.

2. Like they are in their seat and situation. (i.) Clouds are above the tops of the mountains; and the highest pinnacles of the earth are too low for an habitation for these sublime spirits. Nor earth, nor all the mountains, the high places and preferments of the earth, could content them; nothing under heaven, nothing but heaven. You know the desire, " Bring me into thy holy hill, into thy dwelling."

(ii.) But if we look upon the saints of Judah, they were clouds indeed, and types of Christ, who in them appeared as the sun under a cloud, the cloud between the eye and him. His birth in Isaac, his name in Joshua, his death in Samson, his reign in Solomon. *Omnia hæc illis contigerunt in nube;*— still a cloud between.

3. There is a third analogy between their natures and effects. (i.) Clouds, they do not move themselves; it is *spiritus spirat*, the wind that drives them. And the saints, they do not move themselves neither; it is *Spiritus spirat*, the Holy Ghost.

[y] [So in the original edition.]

(ii.) But, which is more to us: Clouds they keep off the sun from too much sweltering, too much parching us. This we get, at least, by the examples of the martyrs, that however the heat of persecutions and afflictions scorch us, we are refreshed in this, that no temptation takes us but what is and has been incident to the most beloved darlings of the Almighty. As comfortable this to an oppressed soul as a cloud of rain in the time of drought, as a cloud of dew in the heat of harvest.

(iii.) And as they comfort, so they teach us too. "The clouds drop down and distil upon man abundantly," says Elihu; and the doctrines of holy lives drop as the rain; their speeches even yet distil as the dew, whose blessed spirits now inhabit those everlasting hills.

SERMON XLIX.

Job xxxvi. 28.

To put all together. Thither they ascended up like clouds, by the secret and spiritual operation of divine grace; there they dwell like clouds, their souls like the upper part of the cloud, light and glorious; though their bodies, like the lower, darkened in the grave. There they move like clouds, in heavenly order; thence they descend like clouds, in the still showers of their happy examples, that in them, as in a glass, we may see the power of faith, the glory of their Lord, who has made earth ascend beyond its nature, and dwell above it.

And yet for all this, is it but *nubem* still, "a cloud," not a star. "The saints shall shine as stars," and methinks it being *nubem martyrum*, the martyrs' flames should rise better into stars than clouds. Should and shall in the resurrection, till then *nubem* still, some degree of darkness, at least a less degree of light. And whatsoever to themselves, for us perhaps it is necessary it be a cloud.

Dan. xii. 3.

For had we not need of this dark word? When, did not God on purpose cloud their glories from our eyes, were it not for this *nubem*, this "cloud" that covers them, man, as subject to superstition as profaneness, would quickly find out some excellences for δουλεία and ὑπερδουλεία, to fall down and worship.

Or if not necessary, yet more convenient far: for (1) a star would only guide us, a cloud both guide and refresh us.

Why not a star.

And (2) guide us better: for stars only appear in the night. Clouds night and day we can see them, so best follow them.

SERMON XLIX.

The sunbeams put out star-light. Prosperity cannot see a star, so small a glimmering ray. A cloud, come it night or day, in prosperity or adversity, we perceive that presently; so a cloud to teach us in all estates how to demean ourselves like devotion in its ancient innocence. Abraham's cloud, when the days are calm and clear: Job's, when the day is swallowed up in a tempestuous night. So never destitute of a cloud.

(3.) Clouds, not stars: they are none but the Magi, wise learned men, can follow the stars and their courses, but every peasant sees which way the clouds move. So if stars, they had been for none but wise learned men to follow: now the poor countryman has a cloud to run by.

Why *nubem* in the singular.

And yet how easily soever we perceive the track of the clouds, yet if there be a scattered multitude, we are as easily distracted. It were best to have but *nubem* in the singular, but one cloud,—it is so. Many drops, but one cloud, though the materials fetched from several quarters. The martyrs all one cloud, to show their unity, all and each confessing, witnessing one and the same truth, for truth is but one. So not S. Jude's clouds, they not only empty, no *stillicidium doctrinæ* in them, no good to be learned from them, but clouds too in the plural; some moving this way, some that way; no constant course. In division, too, one coursing against the other, at such enmity is evil with itself. It is only good, and good men that keep together *in nubem*, in peace and unity, and by that you shall know them.

Nubem.not *nubeculam*.

Be it a cloud, and but one cloud, the more probable still too small it may be to command the eye, and then what are we the nearer? *Nubem*, not *nubeculam;* no diminutive. Will that do it? If that will not, *tantam* will. "So great a cloud." Why, how great? So great that S. Paul tells them, the day "would fail him" to show them it all, as if "so great a cloud" could not but shut up the day in darkness.

Heb. xi. 32.

Tantam.

Our first fathers of the world had no cloud to guide them, nothing but nature's dusky twilight. This cloud began to rise in the time of the patriarchs, but to appear in the time of Moses like Elijah's cloud at the Red Sea, went before him thence into Canaan, covered the whole land of Judæa in the time of the prophets. So these Hebrews had cloud enough; yea, but καὶ ἡμεῖς, we have more.

Even those Hebrews, to whom this Epistle was sent, they are in the cloud. About that time this cloud, rising in the east, spread its wings presently into the west, and had almost in an instant filled up the corners of the world: so that if you now ask again, how great?—so great I cannot tell you.

Primitive Christians they in the number, you will not wonder at μαρτύρων, if it become a cloud of martyrs. Indeed the law of Moses had its martyrs too: witness Isaiah's saw, the three children's fiery furnace, the emptied skins of the tortured Maccabees. But since the time of Christ his servants have engrossed the name—as if they only were the martyrs—and filled up *tantam* to the brim; their multitudes tiring the wit of cruelty, and their patience overcoming it, as if from the streams and rivers of their blood heaven might now enscarf itself in a scarlet cloud.

Well, talk we may of *martyrum* what we will, yet if *nubem* be not first, they will be but *stultæ philosophiæ* all this while, no better. It is the order in the text, *nubem* first, then *martyrum*. First, clouds, lifted up to heaven in their thoughts and conversations, and all in one, the sons of peace and unity; if you can see Christ in the cloud, then martyrs if you will. Schism, and faction, or discontented passion yield no martyrs. You shall know a martyr by *nubem* if that go first.

But taking martyrs thus, all are not martyrs. All died not for their faith, but all are *testes*, "witnesses,"—witnesses of the power, witnesses of the mercy, witnesses of the justice of God;—of his power in delivering them from sin, of his mercy in saving them from punishment, of his justice in rewarding them with glory.

Witnesses to this *curramus*, (1) to witness the possibility that this "race" we are to speak of by and by may be run; this *propositum*, the prize won; for *ab esse ad posse*, run the one they have, and won the other long ago. (2) To testify the easiness, that even the weaker sex, Sarah and Rahab—the weakest age, the three children, the army of Innocents, have run it. (3) To testify the dignity that both king and priest and prophet, David and Samuel and Daniel thought it worth the pains. (4) To testify the universal necessity, all ages, young and old; all sexes, men and women; all degrees, high and low, to run this race, none excused.

And that you may not mistrust their testimony, what is required to the best witness, you have in them. (1) That he knows what he speaks:—and what knowledge like theirs that speak by experience, that now feel the reward of truth? (2) That he will and dare speak it:—and these have feared no torments for it, they are martyrs of it. (3) Witnesses should be men of rank and quality, their worth has placed them above the clouds. (4) They are authentical:—*habentes circumpositam*, the Spirit has set them round about us to that intent, and he is the Spirit of truth. So far now from doubting of our guide, that we wave *nubem* and pass to *habentes*, the second relation they have to us, not only to direct us, but to bear us company.

II. And, indeed, what is *nubem* and *nubem tantam*, and *nubem martyrum*, and *nubem testium* to us without *habentes*, except it be ours; yea, and *habentes nobis*, if we have it not along with us? What are the glorious angels themselves to us but flames and two-edged swords without this *habentes*, if we have them not for ministering spirits? What are the triumphant saints to us, however dazzled with their own glories, without *habentes*, if they be none of ours, if they be not members of the same Church, of the same religion with us? Cast off your religion quite if you can claim no portion in the saints, if you have no martyrs.

What is it, then, that some so often ask, what have we to do with saints? It is well, besides the *habentes*, that we have an *impositam* from the Vulgar Latin, that it is imposed upon us, some necessity of it sure; and that we have a *circumpositam* from the Greek περικείμενον, that not only we have this "cloud," but that we have it "put about us," not of our own putting on. *Habentes* it might be, we might have it of our own choosing or fancying—we know who have so, clouds of their own making, saints of their own canonizing—but *impositam* or *circumpositam* it cannot be except somebody put it on us; and who is it that makes the clouds a garment for this earth, but he that makes the clouds his chariot? Who can dispose of the saints but the King of saints? So then a sufficient excuse we have for *habentes*, God it is that compasses us with this "cloud of witnesses."

SERMON XLIX.

III. And if they compass us they will be near about us by and by, that they may behold our doings, to be spectators of our course, and witnesses to that too, to rejoice at our speed, to congratulate our success, to receive us with the triumphs of glory.

III. The spectators.

And yet methinks the Apostle mentions saints that are gone before; how come they now to be round about us? Angels, indeed, "are ministering spirits," perhaps some of them may be pitched about us. *Angelus Domini in circuitu timentium:* "The Angel of the Lord tarrieth round about them that fear him:" but how can the saints be said to compass us about?

Ps. xxxiv. 8.

May it not be a metaphor to show their multitude, because there are so many that we cannot turn our eyes anywhere about us but we see them? The phrase is David's in another case, "The sorrows of death compassed me;" at every hand, on every side, at every turn. I cannot avoid them.

Ps. xviii. 4.

Or is it that they guard us round with their *Quousque, Domine, quousque?*—their earnest prayers for their afflicted brethren?

Or is it that being " there is joy in heaven over one sinner that repenteth," and they with the Angels make up the choir, and heaven itself encompass us, they therefore are said to compass us?

Luke xv. 7.

Or is it that their graves and sepulchres are round about us, and we as it were still encompassed with their bodies, and they as it were did still encompass us in their bodies? The word may seem on purpose as it were. Κεῖμαι is *jaceo*, and περικείμενον is *circumjacentem*, "lying round about us." The sepulchres of the saints do so this day. As if S. Paul had meant that from the sight and nearness of the resting-places of their sacred ashes we should every day be put in mind with thankfulness to acknowledge the riches of God's goodness in our deceased brethren, and learn those virtues whereby their bones now flourish out of their graves, and their memorials live for evermore. Lest, as Abel's blood from the earth, so their dust from their silent dormitories should cry out against us.

Sermon XLIX.	Not *suppositam* now; no supposed cloud; it is true, it is real, if it encompass us. Such saints there are without a supposition, they die not all when they go hence, something there is still to make the God of Abraham the God of the living.
Not *suppositam*.	
Not *superpositam*.	Περικείμενον it is, and *circumpositam* it should be, not *sub*, nor *super*, not *superpositam*, not set over us, they as lords and masters of our faith, to make what articles they list, but *circum*, "about" us, as fellow-witnesses and companions.
Not *præpositam*.	Once more, not *præpositam*, not set before us to run to either for mediation or intercession. He that regards the clouds thus shall not reap, no thanks I am sure. "The prayer of the humble pierceth the clouds,"—flies higher. It is the prayer of the self-conceited, however it seem a voluntary dejection and humility, that is stifled in the middle region: and if you mark it there is no *aspicientes* here; no looking up to them; *habentes* is all that is here, *aspicientes* is kept till the next verse for *Jesum*. For if this cloud dim our eyesight, and we, instead of being compassed about with them, compass them about by pilgrimages, adoration, or invocation, our best way is to the next words, *deponentes pondus*, to cast off that heavy mist that sits upon our eyelids; or to the next verse, ἀφορῶντες εἰς Ἰησοῦν, turn our eyes from them, and "look to Jesus the author and finisher of our faith."
Ecclus. xxxv. 17.	
Application.	I hope by this time we know what to do with *nubem*, what use to make of this cloud of martyrs, for *habentes* it is, and we have it not for nothing.
Habentes.	Are they clouds? why *habentes* first? Let us have them in account for such, for something more than earth. *Habentes in honore*; let us think and speak reverently of those happy spirits, have their virtues in remembrance, their remembrances in honour, them in our thanksgivings, their monuments and ashes in so much respect; to keep them from the profane scattering hand, to put us in mind of their exemplary piety and a resurrection.
Habentes nobis.	*Habentes nobis* next, to have them to ourselves, to apply them home for imitation, to ascend up in our thoughts like clouds to heaven, in our affections to inhabit there, to live and move there in all our actions, that Christ may be seen

in all our doings. To learn from *habentes nubem* good company; from *nubem* something heavenly; from *nubem* in the singular, peace and unity; to learn the degree from *tantam*; from *testium*, the open profession of our faith; and from μαρτύρων, courage and constancy.

<small>SERMON XLIX.</small>

To do all this, *habentes circumpositam* is the way, to place them round about our thoughts, to fix our eyes upon their piety and reward. You know what the imagining a heathen Cato present has done with some to fright them into honesty, and shall not the presence of those blessed souls shame our dulness into piety, if we would but suppose those stupendous patterns of unconquerable goodness always cheerfully busied in beholding us, encouraging us, and rejoicing with us?

<small>*Habentes circumpositam.*</small>

IV. But we must not stand too long gazing into heaven. There are blocks and traps in the way, and we may chance to stumble; we must look about us. There are two impediments sufficient to hinder any man from running: when he cannot go for weight, nor go on for snares. We will handle each with his removal, first apart, then together, and begin with the weight.

<small>IV. Impediments of running.</small>

And yet, peradventure, *pondus* were little, were it not for *omne*, were it not a collective, a collection of all, of infinite weights. Infinite in weight, infinite in number, above the sand of the sea, and that you know can be nothing else but sin.

<small>1. *Pondus.*</small>

Sin, *Sedet in talentum plumbi*, "as heavy as lead." A weight, right, for it (i.) burdens as a weight. How does the repentant soul groan and break, *conteritur*, is ground to powder under it! (ii.) It wearies as a weight. How tired is S. Paul with it! Who, oh "who shall deliver me from this body of death!" (iii.) It presseth down as a weight, down from the joys of heaven, down from the throne of grace, down to the chambers of the grave, down to the bar of judgment, down to the depth of hell. David found it by his deliverance: "Thou hast delivered my soul from the nethermost hell."

<small>1. *Quid peccatum.* Zech. v. 8. 2. *Quare pondus.* Rom. vii. 24.</small>

Every sin is a weight, but there are some heavier than other. Some (1) *gravamina spiritus*, weights with a powder,[z] such as even weary the Holy Spirit, and grieve it, and make him leave his dwelling with us:—mortal sins. (2.) Some

<small>3. *Quotuplex.*</small>

[z] [So in the original edition.]

SERMON XLIX.

heavier yet, that so oppress our own spirits too, that with a sad, heavy eye, they cannot see anything but those dismal dungeons, hell and desperation :—sins of despair. (3.) Some, on the other side, that look too high, weigh up, *ut lapsu graviore*, to fetch down with a vengeance :—sins of pride and presumption : it is one signification of ὄγκος, a weight that hoisting up the rebel angels above their pitch, as speedily pulled them down from the highest palaces of their new-created glories to the lowest prisons of damnation. (4.) And yet some sins there are of a lesser bulk, such as some call venial, yet heavy enough to lay us low enough :—sins of infirmity and ignorance. Dispose they do, at least, to the more grievous : *Peccatum quod mox per pœnitentiam non deletur suo pondere ad aliud trahit.* S. Gregory. The least, the pettiest sin, if it remain a while unrepented of, is a weight to draw us to another, that to a third, so downward till we can go no lower.

The removal.

And think you now we had not need of an ἀποθέμενοι to remove it? Can we know it to be a weight, and not deal with it as with a weight? Either cast it away, *abjecto pondere*, Beza translates it; or lay it aside, *deponentes*—so the Vulgar.

Both together.

Cast it away, nay, first cast it out, for it is a weight within us. Out of the heart : (1,) by the mouth in confession; (2,) by the eyes in the tears of contrition; (3,) ἀπὸ, from us, far from us by the hand of satisfaction.

Abjecto pondere.

Abjecto ; there is some violence and passion in the word. We use not to cast away things from us but out of some sudden (1) fear, (2) shame, (3) anger, (4) joy, or the like. They are the passions that enliven a repentance. (1,) Fear of judgment; (2,) shame of sin; (3,) anger at ourselves; (4,) joy and delight in God and goodness. (1,) The tremblings of fear (to begin with) will shake sin off; (2,) shame lay it down; (3,) anger cast it from us; (4,) joy and love, the love of God, put it quite out, lay it aside out of the way; for if that holy fire once enter, the house will be too hot for sin to dwell in.

Deponentes pondus.

But violent motions are but short, and passions momentary. *Abjecto* does well at first, but it must be backed with a *deponentes*, a resolved and deliberate laying down of sin. It is to be feared *abjecto* cannot do it alone; sin has too deep a root to be cast off utterly on a sudden. That is *deponentes'* office, to lay it down, down by degrees. First, (1,) those *gravamina spiritus*, then that ὄγκος, that pride in sin, or as the word may bear it, that dominion of it, lay it aside as a tiresome burden, grow weary of it; (2,) or, as we do our clothes when we go to bed, not sleep in it; (3,) at least the weight of sin, that is, the guilt of sin, by confession and absolution,—the spots and habits, by contrary resolutions and endeavours,—the great weights, the little ones, all. *Omne pondus*, every one; *omne* and *pondus*, both in the singular, to tell us "every weight" to be cast off, not one single weight to be left hanging on.

^{SERMON XLIX.}

No; not the weight that is no sin, not that, for such an one there is. *Pondus terrenarum possessionum*, says S. Bernard. What say you by riches? Pluto, the god of riches, feign the poets, dwells below; hell is his kingdom. And riches, from the caverns of the earth they come, and, like waters to the sea, thither they naturally return; down they carry us. Not but that if you look up, your eyes may behold a rich Abraham above in heaven. Riches are as they meet with owners. The pious hand makes himself wings of these golden feathers, to fly to heaven; the wings of the Psalmist's dove, that is "covered with silver wings," and "her feathers like gold." And if I must needs have riches, *Quis mihi dabit pennas columbæ?* Oh that they may prove the wings of this dove, "that I may flee away and be at rest!" The churlish fingers frame themselves fetters, to chain them faster to the lowest pit. Indeed, nothing more knits us to the earth than our wealth; we are loth to use it in our life, loth to leave it at our death, though for a kingdom. "Sell all;" you know he startled at it that thought he had "kept all the commandments from his youth."

2. *Pondus divitiarum.*

I love not impossible tasks to persuade any amongst us now-a-days to that; yet emperors, and kings, and saints have done it; and *Qui capere potest*, &c.: for I would not have you think but honourably of those magnanimous heroes, such as we read of,—those prime constant heirs of grace and glory.

Abjecto omni. The first remove.

Acts iv. 34.

It is but a counsel this, and counsels, it seems, are out of date. Well, all of us to cast off riches, when they come to *pondus*, no necessity till then, keep them you may till *pondus*

Abjecto pondere.

SERMON XLIX. come; ὄγκον first, then ἀποθέμενοι; that is the order, then it is a precept. If the "weight" be ready to hurry you headlong into sin, then off with them. Better lose ὄγκον πάντα, them all, every farthing; the world and all, than your souls.

Abjecto pondere divitiarum. Or yet better that they come not thither so far; cast off the "weight" of riches, that is, the superfluity of them; cast that away upon the poor. Cast away, said I? Pardon me; *deponentes,* lay it down, lay it aside for them; or *recondentes, reponentes* (it is no straining of ἀποθέμενοι), lay it up in the bosoms of the poor, lay it down at the feet of Christ, lay it out upon God, lay it up in heaven.

Deposito reposito.

3 Depositis honoribus. And say we not as much for honour too? Ὄγκος is a word peculiar for majesty and honour. Lay them down too, in *deponite;* there is a *de,* that is, down; lay them down upon the ground, descend even thither by humility, if your honours puff you up, overpoise you. Sins, riches, honours, "every weight;" away with all.

Omni pondere non onere. And though "every weight," not every burden yet. "Bear you one another's burdens," says S. Paul; and Christ's burden is no weight. *Leve meum,* that is, light and easy; and *tollite meum,* take up that. Besides, everything in this world is a burden; this body we carry about us; *Corpus mortale degravat,* we are a burden to ourselves; our necessities, our pleasures, our meat, our apparel, our life, are burdens; and all we cannot cast away; he must go out of the world that can do that. But take heed they come not, any of them, to ὄγκος, *pondus;* if they do, πάντα ἀποθέμενοι, "every weight," be it what it will, that keeps our spirits from rising to those eternal dwellings,—pleasures, profits, preferments, cares, desires,—off with all if they begin to solicit us to sin.

2. Impediment. *Peccatum circumstans.* Deut. ix. 21. Rom. vii. 7. Before I was aware, I have told you what is *peccatum circumstans* too; what is this "sin that does so easily beset us." The occasions and temptations to sin. So the golden calf is called "*peccatum vestrum;*" the Israelites' sin; that is, the occasion of it. So S. Paul: "Is the law sin?" that is, the occasion or cause of sin. So here, by *peccatum circumstans,* the sin that does so easily beset us, I see not to the contrary but may well be understood all things about us

whose only presence become temptations, which are *tentationes objectivè*, or *materialiter*, the objects of temptation, and of these already. Or, more properly, the temptations themselves, which rising from those things about us, do besiege the soul, and are *formaliter tentationes*, formally temptations. And if you please to mark either the mutual opposition, or the correspondence of the words, it will be no great mistake, however, to think this sense most native and genuine.

There is a double " cloud " in the text, S. Paul's and Isaiah's,—his of saints, this of sins;—the one opposite to the other. Εὐπερίστατον ἁμαρτίαν to νέφος περικείμενον, in opposition right; and a cloud of temptations that are without us, σύστοιχον too, in the Apostle's phrase, fitly "answering" to the "cloud of witnesses " about us. Opposed (1) in *pondus*, that is heavy, to *nubem*, for its lightness. (2.) In *peccatum*, sin, that is black and ugly, to *testium*, saints beautiful and glorious. (3.) In *habentes*, that to *deponentes*, the one to be put on, the other put away. And that it might be fitly opposed, fitly answering it is in *omne* to *tantam*, for the quantity, in *circumstans* to *circumpositam*, *circum* and *circum*, *extrinsecum extrinseco*, for the same external relation that is in both alike.

(i.) Only with a double difference. *Circumpositam* passive, that belongs to *nubem* : *circumstans* active, that to *peccatum*. God puts the one about us, not the other; not the sin nor the temptation. *Nemo dicat.* " God tempts not any man." *Habentes* indeed properly the one, the sin we have of our own ; and *circumstans* the temptation, that rises of itself and besets us round, but no *circumpositam* to either; God no author of the one or the other.

(ii.) There is a second. In εὐπερίστατον there is εὐ, that is, *facilè*, to show how ready the temptation is to entangle us. We had a "cloud " of saints, and that had a περὶ, but no εὐ, no *facilè* there. Sin and its occasions are a great deal more welcome to us, do more easily wind about us, and work upon us, than any examples of the saints can do.

I know there are, that would have εὐπερίστατον ἁμαρτίαν be understood that fruitful soil of sin within us, our innate corruptions and propensions. But περὶ here, *circum*, is without,—that within us. Ἡ οἰκοῦσα ἐν ἐμοὶ ἁμαρτία : " Sin that

Sermon XLIX.

Gal. iv. 25.

Rom. vii. 17.

SERMON
XLIX.
dwells in us," says S. Paul; not that dwells about us, as temptations do; ἐν ἐμοί, not περὶ ἐμοῦ; and then ἀποθέμενοι must be no participle for τὴν ἁμαρτίαν. *Deponentes concupiscentiam?* It cannot be; we are not commanded impossibilities. I would it came within a precept. The sin that came with it into the world is gone in baptism: we have washed off that; concupiscence stays still; wash off that we could not, and yet we cannot lay it away. The thoughts that thence arise, arise they will, we cannot hinder; the sins we may.

Acts xxii. 16.

For between that inordinate proneness to sensual good and the motions that take rise thence, there is a difference. That cannot well be said to be without us which is the bent of nature. But these, though they are within, yet produced by the presence of external objects, and being acts really distinct from that natural disorder of inferior powers, do, as it were, environ and ensnare our souls no less than the suggestions of the devil do. That we can nor hinder, nor lay off these, though sometimes we cannot hinder from rising up, yet we can cast them down again; and these now we style temptations.

The devil, or our own corruption, (1.) suggests them. (2.) Then they are delighted in by the flesh. (3.) Forthwith consented to by the spirit. (4.) After that approved by both, and with the first unhappy opportunity put into execution.

Ἀποθέμενοι.

Answerable to these four degrees of temptation I find four several significations of ἀποθέμενοι, besides those you heard;—four ways to remove them, to each his way, as if the Apostle had meant in one word to furnish us for all.

The first is *rejicere*, to reject or refuse. The second *exponere*, to expose, as they do infants when they cast them out to the mercies of the wilderness. The third *differre*, to defer or delay. The fourth is the Syriac interpreter's *solvamus à nobis*, to untie ourselves, for that we use to do when we are entangled, as εὐπερίστατον intimates we are; or, if you please to take the verb to the participle, *deponentes curramus*, to lay it aside and run away.

Εὐπερίστατον, ἀποθέμενοι.

So then, when a temptation at first presents itself clad in adulterate beauties, (1.) reject it, bar it out. (2.) But if it have got in before thou be aware, give it no entertainment, fix not thy thought upon it with curiosity or delight, but presently cast it out of doors. (3.) If thine unhappy negligence have won thee to a delectation, delay at least thy consent, withdraw thyself a while and divert thy thoughts to some other object; death, judgment, hell, or heaven. But if thou be fallen to consent too, the only remedy left thee is (4.) to untie thy resolutions, to unravel thy thoughts,—thy admitting, thy delighting, thy consenting,—to undo all and fly away.

In brief thus :—Temptations thus to be avoided. (1.) The suggestion by repelling. (2.) The delight by casting out the thought. (3.) The consent by withdrawing. (4.) The defence by flying.

(1.) The surest way, when all is done, is to take these untimely brats, and "dash them against the stones," against that " corner stone, Christ Jesus." (2.) The safest way, to hide thee in the holes of that Rock, the wounds of his side : ἀποθέμενοι, *reponentes*, laying your souls up there, and *recondentes*, burying your sins in the meditation of his passion and sufferings. (3.) The surest way, *exponere*, to lay them open to thy ghostly counsellor;—thou shalt find them vanish in the air. (4.) The wariest way, to flee all opportunities whatsoever. Indeed, if the devil fight against thee by troublesome and piercing thoughts, stand to him and resist him; ἀποθέμενοι, thrust him from thee; if he besiege thee with delights, *deponentes curramus*, run away from him. It is not cowardice, but wisdom; he that fights against pleasures may overcome, he that runs from them is sure he does.

Take this, lastly, for a general rule. If temptations rise so many that they swarm about thee like bees; fight not against all at once, they are too many, but τὴν εὐπερίστατον; —the principal, that single, hand to hand.

Τὴν εὐπερίστατον.

Nor is this all. This τὴν, this article, seems to point at some special εὐπερίστατον, something yet more adequately opposed to νέφος περικείμενον. The "cloud," a cloud of martyrs, good company, what more answers to it than a dark thick mist of ill companions? What more opposed than good and bad examples? What temptation more deserves an ἁμαρτίαν, the name of sin, or sooner brings us thither? or a τὴν εὐπερίστατον, the title of " easily besetting" us?

SERMON XLIX. What hangs more fast upon us? What clings more near us? What more ensnares us? And what more needs a τὴν, an article, against it?

We will sum up all in the advice of that mighty Counsellor: "If thy right hand,"—thy counsellor on whom thou leanest,—"or thy right eye,"—thy friend by whom thou seest,—"offend thee,"—(give me leave to make a parenthesis to go on with the interpretation,)—"if thy right eye offend thee,"—if thou canst not look upon a woman (though with no ill intention) but lust will arise; if the eye of thy reason dim thy faith; if thy right eye of contemplation become an offence, and puff thee up,— *erue et projice*, out with it, cast it from thee. Better it is to go into heaven lame, and blind, and ignorant, and poor, and friendless, and alone, than to go down to hell with company. Remember ἀποθέμενοι here, and then as I have now done with *peccatum circumstans*, so shall you; that you may answer your Lord in S. Peter's phrase, *Ecce nos reliquimus omnia*, "Behold, we have left all," our sins, possessions, honours, pleasures, occasions, our dearest friends, our very thoughts, *et sequuti sumus*, "to follow thee," to run after thee. *Curramus per patientiam*, that is next to *deponentes*, to cast off sins, then run from them.

VI. *Curramus*. VI. And can we less? "I will run the way of thy commandments," cries holy David, "when thou hast set my heart at liberty." Set him but at liberty from these weights and snares, and you cannot stay him.

Yet why so fast? No less than running? Give me but a man once thoroughly freed from these heavy chains, he will tell you so. No haste enough from these miseries, says he that felt them.

VII. *Certamen*. VII. And it is but just, for run we did before; the wicked his feet are swift, but that is down hill; ours is a race, upon even ground that.

Well, but the world has its *certamina*, its races too, and such as are *abjecto pondere*, cast away all, riches and possessions. That is for gallants:—ours ἡμῖν ἀγῶνα, a race for Christians.

How is that? Please but to join it to several words within the verge of the text, and you shall see.

Join ἀγῶνα to the words before, ἁμαρτίαν ἀποθέμενοι, such a race that is a running from sin, *certantes contra peccatum,* and it will prove *certamen justitiæ,* "the race of righteousness;" S. Paul's ὑπωπιάζω μου τὸ σῶμα, "the keeping under of his body" by fasting and abstinence, οὕτω τρέχω, so ran he.

<small>SERMON XLIX.
Certamen justitiæ.
Heb. xii. 4.
1 Cor. ix. 26.</small>

Match it with the words that follow, ἀφορῶντες εἰς Ἰησοῦν, that it be such a one that "looks to Jesus," then you have *certamen fidei.* S. Paul calls it the "good fight," where he tells us he has "finished his course," he has "kept the faith;" and it seems the very intent of S. Paul here, who had reckoned up so many *per fidems* in the chapter next before, to which this seems but a conclusion.

<small>*Fidei.*
2 Tim. iv. 7.</small>

Yet, you may lay it to μαρτύρων, and then it will be the race of martyrdom. *Certamen fidei* ofttimes proves so. *Nondum certastis,* sometimes turned to *certastis usque ad sanguinem.* Per patientiam so close shows some affliction towards; and δι' ὑπομονῆς ἀγῶνα together cannot well be less than to an agony. A race, this, that crowns the victor with a diadem, the brightest of all created glories, brighter than the sun.

<small>*Martyrii.*
Heb. xii. 4.</small>

VIII. And yet even this, if *propositum* be wanting, will be thankless. If it be taken up of our own heads, and not proposed. Nay, if it be proposed in general to be good, if it be not *propositum nobis,* so to us; if God propound it not to us, as most convenient for the time, the cause, the persons. Else "when they persecute you in one city, flee to another;" it was his counsel whose the martyrs are; but if it be at any time *propositum nobis,* set before us, so propounded, then good luck have you with your honour, ye blessed of the Lord, run on, and your right hand shall teach you terrible things.

<small>VIII.
Certamen propositum.
Propositum nobis.
Matt. x. 23.</small>

But yet, if you would fain be martyrs, you may be martyrs without dying. "I die daily," saith S. Paul, a living martyr. Would you know how that is? There is a spiritual martyrdom that sometimes equals the other torments with its own difficulties. (1.) Abstinence in the midst of swelling plenty. (2.) Humility in the pride of rising glory. (3.) Meekness in the confluence of domineering injury. (4.) Chastity in the flower of blooming youth, of sparkling blood. (5.) Bounty in the depth of poverty. (6.) Joy in the abyss of misery.

SERMON XLIX.
Per pa-tientiam.
Quid.

[2 Kings vi. 32, 33.]

Per pa-tientiam curramus.

(7.) Charity to our enemies in the height of their insulting cruelty. (8.) Obedience in the hardest precepts that most cross our own opinions and desires. This the race, without which the other is but a naked title, an airy name. This is always *propositum nobis*, the race of them that seek thy face, O Jacob.

And now I speak of martyrdom, I should not forget *per patientiam*, patience, the proper virtue of a martyr.

Patience hath pain for her object. So then to "run with patience" is to fear no pains so we may finish our course, to undergo all for faith and righteousness' sake. It is no small thing to cast off all delights and pleasures; we have been at that in *deponentes*; it is much more to endure evils too, that is in *curramus per patientiam*. The Christian's life is a very race of patience. He suffers all.

And patience is cheerful. He does not only suffer evil, but welcome it. It is more: it is ὑπομονή, not ἀνοχή, μένειν ὑπό, to tarry, stay, abide under it, not to be weary of it presently. It was but a desperate speech of the "son of a murderer," so Elisha styles him, "Why should I wait for the Lord any longer?"

More: ὑπό is "under:" then keep thyself under still; let us have no pride in patience; under afflictions,—then think they come from above, and take them so, with all submission, as not worthy, but below the mercy of punishment.

Not tarry under only, but tarry till the end too. Ὑπομονή is as well perseverance as patience; and *per patientiam*, *per* is "through,"—so run through, not part of the way. Patience runs the race, but perseverance keeps the goal.

Neither is this enough. Patience has been long mistaken for a heady daring and braving of deserved punishment. It were well we would remember *patientia* comes from *pati*. Passive we must be only here; suffer evil when it comes, not thrust ourselves upon it.

Running indeed is *agere*, not *pati;* and the primitive Christians upon some secret inspirations (who knows?), perchance to daunt the fury of their persecutors by their cheerfulness, have run to torments. *Vos autem non sic*, we have not that warrant; and yet we may be active too. *Curramus per patientiam*, let them be companions, never without *per* or *cum* between them, never severed. Patience is a dull, heavy virtue without *curramus*, without faith and righteousness, without life.

<small>SERMON XLIX.</small>

Active enough we may be, but not in seeking crosses. They will come fast enough themselves. There is time and place for *curramus*, when in the midst of injuries we run to heaven for succour. Thus also *curramus per patientiam*, both joined do well together, patience and prayer.

That patience may have her perfect work, and we all with joy finish our course, it will not be amiss to tell you how the very words would have you run, what the very words would have you observe in running.

<small>Quomodo currendum.</small>

1. Running is our swiftest course: such must your speed be here.

2. Running is a motion that actuates every part. Our running must be so; total, universal, soul and body, not a member idle.

3. It is the likelier so to be if we do *certamen currere*, that is, *currendo certare*, strive to do it. It is a race, and in a race there run many; strive who shall run fastest. Do it emulously.

4. Strive, yet not so strive as the sons of strife, " to provoke but to love," says S. Paul. One *curramus* joins us all together, and let us keep so;—in " us," not " I " and " you,"—but let " us " run unanimously.

<small>Heb. x. 24.</small>

5. That it may appear so. Remember ἀγῶνα comes from a and γωνία, " without corners." Such let your course be, open to the world. Run not, separate not yourselves into corners. *Veritas non quærit*. Let the Donatists to their conventicles; for by the way I cannot pass but tell you that ἀγὼν in profane writers signifies *templum*, a " church," sometimes, as if our course could not be right if it bent not thither.

6. To run into corners, as it separates from others, so it breaks the bond of charity; as it entombs our works in darkness, so it eclipses the divine glory. It is but to hide the talent in a napkin, or a sign we are ashamed of our religion, when we closet up all our piety and devotion.

7. Not into corners, not aside; neither on the right hand nor on the left, no way of your own finding out, but τὸν

SERMON XLIX.
Proposi-
tum nobis.
The crown.
Heb. xii. 2.

IX.
Ideoque.

[Isai. lx. 8.]

προκείμενον, the way that lies before you: the king's highway, you cannot miss it.

Yea, but if we miss of a happy end, it were all one as if we missed of the way. Yes, but "set before us" it is. Who set it? He that is our crown and glory: it is before us; we then to look forward. Whither? Unto Jesus; to the "joy that was set before him," the same verse; unto the "throne of God," the last words of that verse, and the last of our desires. He that proposed the race proposes the prize and sets on the crown; ye cannot now fear lest you should run in vain.

Now, therefore, so "run with patience," cheerfulness, humility, courage, constancy, with all your speed and powers; emulously, and yet all together; openly, yet not to be seen; straight on, yet upward, and all the way your eye thither; "so run that you may obtain."

IX. I have now almost run myself out of breath, and you out of patience. Give me leave to run out my text too, for I am come to the conclusion. "Therefore run."

It is a "cloud" of saints, therefore away with sins, that other cloud. It is a "cloud about" us, then off temptations too. It is a "cloud," *et qui sunt illi qui ut nubes volitant*, the quick-flying cloud; "therefore run" at least. It is a "cloud of martyrs," therefore "run with patience." It is a "cloud" that God has "set about" us, and it is the "race" he has "set before us;" both set, that this may be run.

Had we not a guide it might seem unreasonable to force us to an uncertain journey; or were it not a guide from heaven we might as easily fear misguiding; or were it a star, our eyes might dazzle into blindness, and we lose our guide; could we fear the sad melancholy of a solitary way, we might pretend it uncomfortable. Should we want the quickening eyes of beholders, we might fear to falter by the way for want of encouragement; were we to run through the furies of flames we might startle at the hardness of the employment; or should we be commanded to disavow the pleasures of a convenient life for all the austerities of a penitential rigour, we might stand confounded at the task; were the way full of circling labyrinths we might fear our erring inevitable; or were the race voluntary, not set before us, we might then use the freedom of our choice; or were it of an uncertain length, not set out, to run *in infinitum*, we might account it vain; or were there no crown to run for, despair might kill the life of our affections: but having a guide, and that from heaven; a cloud to compass and defend us that nothing harm us, not the sun look too hot upon us and discolour us; so great that the wandering eye cannot lose it; so near encircling us that the weary step may almost rest upon it; a cloud that cleaves itself into an ample theatre, where you find both company and spectators; where by the examples of a world of saints surrounded; where by the steps of tender virgins and little children, taught the easiness of the way; where by the crowns, and robes, and palms of martyrs too transcendently glorious, assured of our reward; seeing we are to bid adieu to nothing but our misery and our sin, to leave only the courting of our own damnation; when it is no more than an easy run to heaven, no studied torments in the way, no tedious or eternal journey, a plain certain way, directed by him who will as well help us forward as command us— what colour of excuse for the least remissness?

Say no more but that we had a guide; a guide is not given to go alone, and a guide from heaven deserves not so to be disrespected; but guide and company both thence to be neglected, what name shall I style it by? "Run" while you have the "cloud." The time may come when we shall have no *habentes*, when we shall not dare to look upon this "cloud" for shame; when our sins shall stand so thick about us that we cannot look through them, nor up for them; when we shall strive to run, and this weight and snares so hinder us we cannot stir; when these "witnesses" shall turn to be witnesses against us; when we shall desire this "cloud" to cover us, and it will not be; when we shall not have so much as *cum patientia* left to help us; but weary of ourselves, run from hill to dale to hide us, and cannot run out of sight; and were it not better now to run for something than then to run in vain?

Great, certainly, is the force of example: will that do it? It is here to the full. Did the Jewish saints, who had not so clear a light to run by, nor so clear or full promises to run for, nor so skilful guides to run after, nor so full a glory

SERMON
XLIX.
to run into, cheerfully fulfil their course? And shall we, whose knowledge as much excels theirs as theirs did ignorance, who do not so much see as enjoy the promises, after so fair a troop, into so perfect glory, move on heavily? How oft have royal virgins met the terrors of a long and subtile death with the same countenance they would have met their wedding joys, and children run to torments as to play! How oft have kings and princes—fifty of our own within the space of two hundred years—changed their kingdoms for the house and bread of poverty! O blessed spirits, how lamely do we halt after you! How do we dishonour your aged glories by us so often boasted of, and scatter, as it were, your sleeping ashes in the wind by our degenerate Christianity! How do ye even hide yourselves in clouds, and blush to see us call that religion which ye would not have called by so honourable a title as profaneness!

What if without example? Is it not enough that God propounds it? Had it been some greater matter ought we not have done it? Will reward? But why stand I upon any when we have all? And may I not then well add, " therefore run?"

We have set the *ideoque* upon *nubem*, upon *tantam*, upon *habentes*, upon *martyrum*, upon *circumpositam*, upon *pondus*, upon *peccatum*, upon *circumstans*, upon *curramus*, upon *certamen*, upon all; and being now at the end, I shall leave it upon the last, *propositum nobis*, the reward of our pains.

That when this *pondus mortale*, this body, be laid aside, and we have done our race, we may sit down with Abraham, Isaac, and Jacob, where for this cloud we may dwell in light; for this sin put off, be clothed upon with long white robes; for that sin which did beset us, be circled with cherubims and seraphims about us; for this *deponentes* find a *depositum*; for laying off, a crown laid up; and for this " weight," an " eternal weight of glory." And in that last great day, when for this casting away, this earth also now about us shall then cast off its heaviness into lightness and agility, shall we ourselves be caught up together with these saints in the clouds, to run and meet the Lord in the air, where though to others it be a day of clouds and thick darkness, yet shall this cloud, and we in it, shine like the sun in the kingdom of the Father. SERMON XLIX.

To which he bring us, who going hence, ascended up in clouds with triumph, and shall one day come again in clouds with power and glory, to dispel all clouds and darkness into an everlasting day, Jesus Christ. To whom, with the Father and the Holy Ghost, be all power, and praise, and honour, and thanksgiving, and worship, now and for ever. *Amen.*

A SERMON

UPON

S. ANDREW'S DAY.

S. MATT. iv. 20.

And they straightway left their nets, and followed him.

SERMON L.

Ps. cl. 1

IT is well, say I, that Sundays and holidays sometimes meet; that it is as well Sunday as holiday to-day, that so the Lord may be sometimes hallowed in his saints, as here followed by them. David's "praise God" in his saints (for so it is to be rendered), may by this means be sung still, and preached yet sometimes, in spite of that peevishness and malice that has so impudently and ungraciously unsainted all the saints; not so much as an Apostle allowed that name; not a saint left in the whole Christian calendar, if I may call it Christian, that so uses the saints of Christ.

Well, though the course of the times has thus robbed God of his glory in his saints, and the saints of their honour, and of (if it could be) their very " rejoicing in their beds ;" yet the course of the years, as it were to confute that frowardness, will bring it about ever and anon that the Master and the disciple, the Lord and his saints, shall rejoice together upon a day; and if they may not be allowed their several feasts, will yet sometimes feast together, be remembered together, as S. Andrew and his Lord to-day, do what they can to hinder it.

For this day, as it now falls out, is solemn both for Lord and saint.

And amongst the saints S. Andrew is the first in order, for here the Christian Church begins her festivals (I know not what or whose Church to call it that has none), and fitly too does she begin with him who was the first that followed Christ from Galilee, says S. John. Fit, sure, that he should lead the rank that there begun it, that brought the great S. Peter as his second, though afterward, for that excellent confession of his, made the first. Yet just certainly it is that S. Andrew too should have his primacy, and so the Church has given it him, to begin the army of saints and martyrs in her calendar, that we may see no man shall lose anything by his speed to Christ; the more haste to him, the more honour for it.

I shall not yet, this day, though it be the first of Advent, much meddle with that, or primarily or very particularly set myself to speak of Christ's Advent or coming. I shall be content (because we are not like to meet many such opportunities as this day in conjunction brings us) to speak this day of the disciple, and only glance at his Lord. We shall have many occasions to speak of the Master, few, now a-days, to take notice of the disciples. Yet for all that cannot we well speak of the one without the other. The honour of the servant will redound always to the glory of the Master. It is for that that we commemorate the saints, that we may so magnify the King of saints, both by acknowledging his greatness and goodness in them, and by doing gloriously to the honour of our Master by their examples.

And indeed we cannot separate them; and as the text falls out, it ends as all the praises and commendations of his saints should end, in him, αὐτῷ. And it begins with a conjunctive particle, which will refer us to him. And with an also, or an οἱ δὲ, which, to make the text to be understood, will make us look back to an Ὁ δὲ, περιπατῶν δὲ ὁ Ἰησοῦς. This Οἱ to that Ὁ, this δὲ to that δὲ, this "and" to another "and," this their following to Jesus walking, this "and they left and followed," to "and Jesus walking and calling them to follow," in the two immediately foregoing verses.

We shall then, for the full sense of the text, and the honour of the day, not quite separate the Lord and his saints, but join the Ὁ and the Οἱ together, speak somewhat of Christ's coming as well as of their following; though more fully of this, it being expressly in the words, the other but implicitly

Sermon L.

John i. 41.
John i. 42.

Matt. iv. 16.

Matt. iv. 18.

Sermon L. or implied, yet referring this wholly to the glory of that, their following here to Christ's coming before, S. Andrew's *exit* to Christ's Advent; join them both, as the day does for us.

For in the words are both, though just as in the day; the one swallowed up by the other, the holiday in the Sunday; only with this difference: S. Andrew's feast in the Advent, in the day; the Advent in S. Andrew's, in the text. The day more evidently for the Lord's day, the text for S. Andrew's.

We will forget neither, but must follow the text, where we are to consider two particulars; the one expressed, the other implied. (1.) S. Andrew's festival; and (2.) the feast of Advent, or the grounds of each; the ground of S. Andrew's festival expressly, his leaving his nets and following Christ; the ground of Christ's Advent implicitly, that it was "straightway" done, that is, presently upon Christ's coming and calling to him. You see Sundays and holidays are at no such variance but they can stand together; their grounds, too, both scripture grounds; both from the same text too. Our new reformers may as well deny the one as the other; and no doubt if they stand but in their way a little, they will too. Only some day must be kept up a while to preach the cause; when that is done, " Ye observe days, and months, and years," will be as good a text against the Lord's day as his saints'.

But not to trouble you with the division of days, we will afford you another division of the text.

I. St. Andrew's, and together with him his brother's obedience express: " They straightway left their nets, and followed him."

II. The ground of it in δέ and αὐτῷ, in the first words and the last, intimated and applied. Jesus came first, and walked by the sea, and looked upon them and spake to them. And— and what then? "And they straightway followed." Followed whom? " Him," says the text. Who is that? One that was worth all their nets, one that would make them fishers indeed— Jesus; for him it is they leave their nets, and him they follow.

Matt. iv. 18.

In their obedience there are three particulars: (1,) the readiness; (2,) the sincerity; (3,) the rightness of it.

1. It was " straightway;" there is the readiness.

2. It was to the "leaving of their nets," their very life and living, all the poor living they had; there is their sincerity.

A SERMON ON S. ANDREW'S DAY.

3. It was "to follow him;" there is the right placing and bestowing their obedience.

In the ground of it we shall see their obedience was not groundless; for that it was,—

1. Not without a just and lawful call: Jesus called them first, and then they followed, and not till then.

2. Not without a powerful, effectual, and enabling call, which so soon and suddenly could make and enable them to leave their whole course and means of life, and very "straightway" follow him.

3. That it was not any but Christ; not any thing, or hope, or interest, but only "Jesus," the true Messiah, him they followed, whom, you shall see anon, they had good reason to conceive was worth all they could leave or do. The ground of their obedience was neither rash, nor light, nor sinister. It was discreet, and wise, upon just call; it was powerful, upon a strange, sudden, powerful change of their affections; and it was right and due to him they paid it, Jesus the Christ.

I begin with the express parts of the text, with S. Andrew's and his brother's great and ready obedience to Christ's command and call, which is the lesson you are to learn upon S. Andrew's day, that which you are to learn now particularly from him, as upon the days of other saints, their particular virtues and graces, which is or should be our holiday business; and if it had been but so taught and learned, we had never seen profane calendars for Christian, these unhallowed days, or our holidays unhallowed, God deprived of the glory, or we of the examples, as much as lies in these men's power, of his saints.

Two there are in the text, S. Andrew and S. Simon, though but one in the day. Christ calls by couples, that the one might help the other, if the one should fall the other might help him up; that S. Andrew's fortitude—for that is the interpretation of his name—might strengthen S. Simon's obedience, which is the English of his; and a courageous obedience, the meaning of both together, the proper lesson for the text and day.

Three points we promised you to consider in their obedience—readiness, sincerity, and rightness; we now prosecute them in order; and their readiness first: "And they straightway followed him."

Verus obediens nescit moras. True obedience, says S. Jerome, knows no delays. He that stands disputing with his Lord, or bargaining and conditioning with his Master, or long consulting with flesh and blood, will scarce deserve the name of obedient, even when he after so long does what he is bidden. The temper of the obedient soul is far other. S. Paul tells us, when it pleased God to call him, and reveal his Son in him, that he might preach him among the heathen, he did not immediately " confer with flesh and blood," nor go up to Jerusalem to the Apostles to be resolved, but into Arabia, and so again to Damascus, about the work that God did send him. When God sets us about his business, our own fleshly interests, or carnal friends, are not to be consulted with, lest they hang upon us and hold us back; nor are we to stay the calling of a council, even of spiritual friends, before we set to our obedience in things so evident as God's commands; but into Arabia the desert rather; that is, to throw off all delays, to desert those petty demurs that rise always upon a change. After that, indeed, after we have first broken the threads that held us, and made worldly affairs and relations stand off a little, we may return to Damascus, with S. Paul, to that *succus sanguinis,* as it is interpreted, to the juice of our blood, to consider and weigh our strength to particular points of our obedience; but we must thence to Jerusalem to the Apostles, and such as have been before us, and such as are set over us, to confer about the ways and means to correct and purify our blood, to refine our flesh, to get strength of counsel and direction how to break through all lets and obstacles, and obtain strength against our weakness; and so return again to Damascus, after the other interpretation of the words, *incendii similitudo,* to burn up, as it were, the stubble of our affections, to purify and inflame them with the divine love, with holy charity, which with its active flame will enliven and quicken us, that we shall " straightway " follow our Lord whithersoever he will, without delay, demur, or disputation.

The young man that proffered fair to follow Christ, but first desired to go and bury his father, was forbidden it.

Even an act of charity, such as is the burial of the dead, must not be preferred before obedience. Indeed, with Elisha, peradventure we may have leave to go kiss our father and mother at our parting, to use civilities to our friends, and with some little solemnity leave the world and them. God's work does not make us unnatural or uncivil; it is none of his, whatsoever is pretended, that makes us unnatural, that makes us disrespective of our friends, or uncivil to them, or utterly renounce the bonds of nature and relation. It only requires that they should not hinder us, that they should not stay or let us from our Master's business. Kiss them we may, but kiss and part, not stay long upon ceremonies when we are about our Master's business, much less defer our following him till they are dead and buried, till they forsake us first. We must first be of the parting hand, and let nothing keep us from him any longer than necessities and just civilities do exact.

Nay, for these too, we are to ask his leave. And if he answer us, as Elijah did him, "Go back again; what have I done unto thee?" Go, but consider what I have done; Go, but consider;—*Quod meum erat feci tibi*, I have done my do; thou must make haste if thou wilt find me, or overtake me; thou must not look for a second call: then go back we may, and slay our oxen, and boil their flesh with their instruments, and give unto the people that they may eat; dispose of our affairs, but with what haste we can; not stay the resting or fetching so much wood to boil it, but with their own instruments at hand; boil them all in haste, take the quickest course we can imagine to despatch; to give away much of our substance also to the poor and needy to make more haste; and then arise and go after him, and administer to him of the rest.

But if he answer us, as Christ did the young man, "Follow me, and let the dead bury their dead," there is no striving then. If, as sometimes he does, he calls us in a nick of time, where the opportunity of doing good is now in prime, and if we stay but a little it will be gone; then "let the dead bury their dead," let even that natural charity be performed by somebody else; go we whither we are sent; do we what we are bidden, and think we that Christ says to

SERMON L. us what he said to S. Peter upon some such like dilatory
[John xxi. query, What is that to us? follow we him.
22.]
Let us always think, when we hear him calling us to his service, whether the call be inward or outward, within us by his Spirit, or without us by his minister, that we cannot make too much haste to follow him. It may be he has called his last, and will call no more; or he will be gone if we make not haste, and we shall then at least have much ado to find or overtake him. It is no easy overtaking him that "rides upon the wings of the wind," if he be once gone out before us. It is not safe to loiter by the way for fear of temptations that may prevent our good purposes and quite overthrow all holy resolutions. It is an unworthy usage and unmannerly to stand talking to anything else when God is speaking to us to come to him. It is dangerous to play away our precious time in excuses and follies, in other business, nay, even in good business of our own, even in an act of private charity or devotion, when God calls us to his public service and obedience. Christ calls even Judas to do his business quickly; you may well think he would have S. Simon
Matt. iv. and Andrew be as quick in theirs; nay, they were, for in
18.
the midst of their work he called them, and in the midst they leave; away with nets, come Christ; fish who will, for them, they will follow Christ, not so much as stay to draw up their nets, be what will in them they care not; let all go so they may catch him. Nay, more, and if the Spirit of Christ be in us, we will, with him, be pained and straitened till his business be accomplished, though it be such a baptism as he was then to be baptized with, even suffering and dying for his name. There can be no excuse from our attendance upon him with the first, who will not at all stay with us if he be not the first in all our thoughts, if we prefer anything before him, or any business before his; nay, if we leave not, secondly, our nets too, all our own business for his.

Regnum Dei tantum valet quantum habes, says S. Gregory, "The kingdom of heaven is worth all we have," must cost us so, be it what it will. And alas! what have we, the best, the richest of us, as highly as we think of ourselves and ours, more than S. Andrew and his brother, a few old broken nets? What are all our honours but old nets to catch the breath of the world, where the oldest is the best, and that which has most knots, most alliances and genealogies, the most honourable?

What are our estates but nets to entangle us? It is more evident now than ever; to entangle us in strange knots and obligations, in vexations and disquiets, in fears and dangers; to entangle silly souls beside in vanities and follies.

What are all our ways and devices of thriving but so many several nets to catch a little yellow sand and mud? and if you will have it in somewhat a finer phrase, a few silver scaled fishes, in which yet, God knows, there are so many knots and difficulties, so many rents and holes for the fish to slip out of, that we may justly say they are but broken nets, and old ones too, the best of them, that will scarce hold a pull, all our new projects being but old ones new rubbed over, and no new thing under the sun.

What are all those fine catching ways of eloquence, knowledge, good parts of mind and body, but so many nets and snares to take men with? It may be finely spun, neatly woven, curiously knotted, but so full of holes, vanity, and emptiness, that no net is fuller than these things we take so much pride in, so much delight in. Nay, this very body itself is but a net that entangles the soul; and the rational soul itself, too, we too often make but a net to catch flies, petty buzzing knowledges only, few solid sober thoughts; at the best but a net for fishes of that watery and inconstant element, watery, washy, slimy notions of I know not what, of flitting worldly things; so full of holes, too, that all good things slip out of them.

Our very life, lastly, what is it but a few rotten threads knit together into veins and sinews: the strings and powers of a thin and immaterial soul knit to the threads of a feeble body, so slender and full of holes, and the knots so loose, that the least stick or stone can unloose it or break it all to pieces.

And are not these pretty pieces, think you, now to stand so much upon the leaving, that we will rather leave our Master's service than these broken nets that will bring us up nothing but slime and mud, a few fins and scales, a few sticks and weeds, a few stones and gravel, things only that will dirty us, or delude us, or run into our hands and pierce

SERMON L. them, or into our feet, like gravel, and race[a] them; or, at the utmost, but a few fish, slippery or watery comforts, that will either quickly leave us, or but slenderly comfort us whilst they stay? Are not these fine things to quit heaven for? Oh, blessed saint of the day, that we could but leave these nets as thou didst thine, that nothing might any longer entangle us, or keep us from our Master's service!

Not that we must presently quit all honours, estate, and ways of gain, bodies, and souls, and life, and throw ourselves into dishonour, poverty, and death, in that instant we propose to follow Christ; but that we must know we cannot follow him if we cast not off our inordinate affections to all of these, use them as if we used them not, enjoy them as if we had them not; so humbly bear our honour as if we sought none else but God's; so manage our estates as to give an account to him for every farthing; so use our trades as if our whole business were to trade for heaven; so feed our bodies as if their chief food were the bread of heaven; so employ our understandings as if they were to mind nothing but heavenly things, and so live as if we had nothing else to do but die; so cast away our nets as if we had nothing now to do with them, now we had caught Christ, or but to catch and hold him.

Worldly honour may consist with Christ's; our greatest estates with the true riches; our lawful busiest vocations with his service; our secular learning with heavenly knowledge; the care of our bodies with the salvation of our souls; our lives with his death : only they must not stand in competition for time and place, but be all left to his disposing; and when at any time they cannot either stand with his service, or will hinder it, then leave them all we must to follow him, as occasions and opportunities shall require the forsaking any of them, be it life itself. Alas! he loves not Christ at all that loves anything above him, anything equal with him, that prefers anything to him, or will not readily leave it for him.

We have read of many who have left their thrones and cast away their sceptres; many who have thrown away their riches, and deserted their estates; many who have given over all their thriving ways; many who have bid adieu to all

[a] [So in the original edition.]

secular studies; many who have in strange austerities and mortifications neglected, nay, crucified their bodies, and others that have run to death as to a wedding, that so they might the easier follow, or the more happily attain to their Master's steps: but these are singular and particular heights; the ordinary course of Christianity is by a lower way. Yet is the way good too. *Et omnia deserit qui voluntatem habendi deserit*, says S. Jerome; he also verily forsakes all that desires none, nothing but Jesus Christ; who "has crucified the flesh with the affections and lusts," as the Apostle speaks, Gal. v. 24. the world with all the desires thereof; who though he has all he can desire, yet desires nothing but what God will have him.

Sometimes it may fall out that we must leave our callings to go after him, when they be either truly sinful or evidently dangerous; and our wealth, when it is unjustly gotten or unrighteously held, we must restore and leave to the right owners of it. Sometimes again it may be lawful for us to leave both estates and callings, though we be not bound to it; as when we plainly see we can thereby serve our Master better, and he seems to point us to it; when we perceive we cannot else perform the task or calling he has designed us to, or the business he has already set us upon. Otherwise, "Let every man," says the Apostle, "abide in the calling wherein he is called," and stir not from his station but when he may lawfully and orderly be made free from it. It is not presently from the counter to the desk, from the loom into the pulpit, from the shop into the church, from our nets to our books, from secular trades to the holy function, that we are to run: there is something more than so when the Apostle bids men stay and continue in their callings. And to follow Christ is not only to be apostles and teachers,—for who then shall there be to be taught? And to satisfy all from the example in the text, this is the third time of S. Andrew's being called. To the knowledge of Christ he was called, S. John i. 38; to his familiar acquaintance, S. Luke v. 10; and here, thirdly, and S. Mark i. 17, to the apostleship; so many steps even these here made ere they came to be apostles, and not till now threw they quite away their nets to return no more unto them. It is no such hasty business

SERMON L. to become apostles or succeed them in any point of their office. Yet truly, when Christ shall give any of these hasty heads power to do wonderfully, to show miracles, to manifest their calling, and to do extraordinarily, as he did to these, then we were much to blame if we would not allow them that God has extraordinarily called them to it; and what were we that we should oppose against it? But in the meantime let us see them leave their "nets,"—their private interests and hopes of gain, and repute, and fame,—that we may have reason to think they follow Christ, and not their own bellies, fancies, and humours.

Yet we can tell them too of those who have done more than the most they dare pretend, have left all, expressly all, and yet no followers of Christ. Heathens have done it, Socrates, and Bias, and Thales, and Crates the Theban, and Fabricius the Roman, yet Christ not followed by it. And I know they will say as much of the hermits of the desert, and the brethren of the cloister, that—though they have done what they dare not think for Christ—yet they have not followed him. And could these great confidants show what they have done or suffered, or lost or left for Christ, yet by the same argument, their own, they cannot prove they follow him the while. But, alas! they have left nothing but what they should not, their proper callings wherein S. Paul would have them abide with God. And it is not Christ but the loaves they follow, not God's glory but their own. For if we but examine what was their following in the text, and the grounds of their so doing,—as we shall anon,—it will appear quickly whom they seek, what they follow too, who pretend only, or rather only pretend, so much now-a-days to follow Christ. Let us next see whom S. Andrew followed when he left his nets, and how he followed.

Christ it was he followed, for this "him" is "he." (1.) Not his own profit sure; he could hope for little from him who had not where to lay his own head. (2.) Not his ease and pleasure in his company, who was always hungering and thirsting, and yet had scarce bread to eat or water to drink, or time to do either, watching, and walking up and down about his Father's business till he was faint and weary, and yet nor place nor time to rest in, not to sleep but he must be awaked as soon almost as he is laid down. (3.) Not his own honour certainly under a Master who was the most rejected and despised of men, as the prophet styles him; called "wine-bibber," and a friend of sinners, and deceiver of the people, and a worker by the devil. Not his own humour or fancy, but Christ's powerful call that so straight transformed his mind, and raised him to a faith that could so suddenly part with all without murmuring, reasoning, or taking care for a future living. In a word, not anything but him. But him, then, how did he follow?

1. He followed him with his body, gives himself to be one of his menial servants and continual attendants, content with such coarse fare and clothing as his poverty would allow him; partaker of his fastings, and watchings, and journeyings, and hard lodgings, and painfulness, and weariness, and reproaches, to teach what our bodies must be content to endure for his service, and in following him.

2. He followed him with his mind, gave up his understanding to be informed, his will to be directed, his affections to be ordered by his doctrine and precepts; for to follow Christ is to resign up our understandings to the obedience of faith.

3. He followed him in his life in patience, and meekness, in humility, in poverty of spirit, in mercifulness, and doing good, in the life and practice of Christian virtues, lived an admirable holy life; went up and down from country to country, into Macedonia and Achaia, into Scythia and Ethiopia, preaching Christ, and following Christ whithersoever he called him; and this is properly to follow Christ, to imitate him. And

4. He followed him in his death too, was also crucified for him; followed him so cheerfully to that, "that," says S. Bernard[a] and the story of him, "he seeing the cross afar off thus joyfully saluted it, *Salve crux diu desiderata et jam concupiscenti animo præparata! ecce gaudens et exultans ad te venio;* 'Welcome, sweet cross, so long desired and wished and longed for, and now come at last; I come rejoicing, I come leaping to thee; I come, I come.'"

Thus I have showed you how S. Andrew followed Christ;

[a] [S. Bernard. De S. Andrea serm. ii. p. 327 K. Ed. Paris. 1640.]

SERMON L.
how we also are to follow him; to throw away our nets, not only all unlawful ways of gain and preferment; nor all things that stay and hinder us from the service of our Master, but anything, everything, that may entangle us, or keep us from the readiness and exactness of our attendance; and having so prepared ourselves, to conform ourselves presently, after his example, to humility, to patience, to meekness, to doing good, to obedience, to acts of mercy, to fastings, to watchings, to praying, to any hardship or affliction; no more now to seek ourselves, but him; not our own praise, but his glory; not our own profit, but the profit of our brethren; not our own private fancies, but Christ's precepts and the saints' examples; so to follow in their track, in the ways, and orders, and obediences that they have traced us, and to be content to part with anything, with all our own magnified imaginations, all our own desires, our goods, and estates, and repute, and ease, and quiet, and life, and all, whensoever he pleases to call for it. This is truly following Christ. And whatsoever else we have in S. Andrew, following him as an Apostle is particular, and concerns not any at all but those who by some signal outward visible call are commanded to a more immediate attendance on their Master. To thrust ourselves into that without that ground is both impudence and presumption; to follow our own proud hearts and giddy heads, and not him that they here followed, who followed him not either as disciples or apostles without good ground. Let us else examine it.

He came himself, and publicly and professedly called them
John xviii. 20.
to him. "In secret," he tells Pilate, "he had said nothing." All the people could bear witness to his doings, that his followers might know for ever he would have none to enter into such offices without a solemn and public calling. To his doctrine, to be his scholars and disciples, perhaps he will admit us in private, or by night, as he did Nicodemus, or in the crowd and multitude together; but to be apostles and preachers of that doctrine, not without a public and particular ordination and authority, that shall equivalently say, as he did to these brothers, in the verse before the text, "Follow me, and I will make you fishers of men." Nay, more, he picks them out
Mark iii. 13, 14.
that he calls apostles; does it with great solemnity. Goes

up into a mountain,—that was then, as it were, his Church,— and calls unto him whom he would, not who would themselves; and they came unto him, they, and none else. And them he ordained,—the very word the Church uses still. He ordained twelve, that they should be with him, and that he might send them forth to preach. Lo here, what a solemnity Christ makes of it, of making ministers, who certainly, had he intended any should make themselves or any ministers but those teachers and preachers who from him and his Apostles derive their power, the Bishops and Fathers of his Church, would not with so much solemnity, so ceremoniously, so publicly, so punctually have thus ordained those whom he intended should be in nearer attendance to him than others, to whom he would commit the preaching of his Gospel, and the dispensation of his ordinances to the world.

This is not all: they had another ground of their calling, a second reason of their following; they were enabled to it by a strange and sudden change within them, whereby they found they could now already do what he called them to. They were now become quite other men, merely spiritual, no longer seculars; away with temporal business, they minded worldly things no more, but straightway to him without delay. This inward call, though alone it be not sufficient, yet joined together with the outward, is good ground indeed to follow Christ any whither soever. And unless thus God either on a sudden, or by time, by extraordinary or ordinary means, shall enable any man for his service and ministry, and by the outward power also call him to it, he shall bear his sin that undertakes it, whoever he be, that he did not send; he is one of those that God complains of, that runs when he is not sent; and though the pretence be to stay the falling Ark—the Church—from perishing for want of teaching, his sin is Uzzah's, that touches holy things without this double commission. Perez-Uzzah is his place; a breach he makes in the Church, and God will one day break out upon him that thus breaks into the Church, not by the door, but some other way; that neither being enabled within, nor from without, or within and not from without, or without only and not from within,

[2 Sam. vi. 8.]

SERMON L.

whom God has not given both inward abilities and outward calling to the handling of his holy mysteries and dispensations.

They have a third ground yet why they leave their nets, and it is, to follow Christ. They know and are assured who it is they do it for, and why they do it. "It is the Messias, John i. 41. it is the Christ," says S. Andrew to his brother Simon. And so stands the case; they can no longer tend his business and their nets together. This is the third time they were called, we told you. To the mere knowledge of him they were called first in that place of S. John; to a nearer familiarity, S. Luke v., where, though they leave their nets, yet it is only for a while; but here being called to follow him to the apostleship, they wholly leave them altogether. They saw his power before in the miraculous draught of fishes, which made them leave their work for a time to follow him: but now they feel it warm within them, they cannot stay, shall I say? to draw up their nets, or to cast them in, though they were now casting and about it, but "straightway,"—the word no sooner out of his mouth but they at his heels. When we are sure it is Christ that calls, that him we follow, no haste too much, no leaving too much, no following too much for him. For him if it be, we may leave all without danger; but if we be not sure it is, it would do well to have a net to take to. I speak this for that too many leave their nets, their business, their work, and bestow themselves and theirs upon things that are not him, nor his; upon false Christs, upon deceivers, upon such as, whatever show they make, will be found upon examination to seek their own and not Jesus Christ. It is fit we should look it be Christ indeed, not our own ends; not leave catching fishes to go lead silly women captive, laden more with sins than ever S. Andrew's net with fishes. If it be for some new device of late, which our fathers have not known, which Christ's Church has not received, some new-sprung pattern in the Mount, it is some new Christs, not the old ones, some false ones, not the only true ones, who being God blessed for ever is always like himself. He that leaves anything to follow those new calls or callers, either to be a teacher or a follower of them, had better keep his nets, though broken ones.

The sum is, we are to have good ground for what we do, an "and" to begin with, and a "him" to end in, good authority (1) to go upon, and the right end to go to; sufficient abilities, and lawful authority to send us if it be as labourers into the vineyard, and a true Christ to serve with them: good reason too (2) we must show for all our actions in Christ's religion and worship, though we be but to follow only as disciples; just power to commend it, and the infallible glory of Christ and his Church to design it to. So our obedience to be ready, sincere, and upright, when we can perform and are required it by Christ, and those that under him have the commission to call us to it, or command it for his service, or his Church's; and we not to undertake it till we find ourselves truly enabled, rightly called, and uprightly intending in it.

To join now the two points of the text together, to know our right grounds, and settle our obedience right upon them, that we may know what we undertake, when we undertake to follow Christ, and do accordingly, not pretend above our strength, but keep Advent and S. Andrew both. We are (1) to provide, by S. Andrew's obedience, for Christ's Advent, that he, when he at any times comes to us, either in his Spirit or in his Word, in humility or glory, in our lives, or at our deaths, may find us ready straight to follow him. No so acceptable entertainment for him, no so fit preparation for him, as a ready, entire, well guided obedience; none so fit to receive him as S. Andrew, the soul so fitted and resolved to all obedience. Thus we are to make our way for Advent by S. Andrew.

And (2) to keep S. Andrew's feast, to give ourselves up to this obedience, we must remember Christ's advent to us, that we cannot follow till he first come to us,—acknowledge all our motion is from his. Look he first upon us, and speak to us, and we straightway run; but if he come not, there is no following to be expected, much less haste to do it. All is from him; to him therefore be all the praise, if at any time, or wherein at any time, we follow him; it is his grace that does it, that comes first before we follow.

And then, thirdly, to keep time, to join both feasts together in our hearts all the days of our life, as well as in this day of the year, magnify we him in his saints, follow we S. Andrew as he did Christ; follow him to Christ, cheerfully without delay, to-day, whilst it is day, begin our course; let us not think much to part with anything for him; lay our honours, riches, souls and bodies at his feet, and with pure and unmixed intentions study we wholly his service, not our own.

Let not any be discouraged, that perhaps he has nothing worth the leaving, nothing but a few old broken nets. Be it never so little we have left, if we have left ourselves nothing, but given ourselves and all to Christ, we have given much; he that, with these saints here, leaves nothing but a few knotty threads, if he has no more to leave, has left as much as he that leaves most, for he has left all, and he that leaves most can do no more. It is the mind, not the much, that God values. Remember the poor widow's mites accepted by Christ above far greater gifts, for they were all she had, and who could give more? The poor man's all is as much to him, and as much *all* to God, as the rich man's all; his tattered nets as much all his living as the other's lands and seas are his; and the poor man can as hardly part with his rags and clouts, his leather bottle, his mouldy bread, and clouted shoes, as the rich man with his silks, and state, and dainties; so much perhaps the hardlier in that they are more necessary.

Yet that I may not seem to leave you upon too hard a task to scare you from following Christ, I shall now tell you, you may keep all, and yet leave your nets. You may keep your honours, you may preserve your estates, you may enjoy your worldly blessings, only so keep a hand upon them, or upon yourselves, that they be not nets and snares unto you; let them not take your hearts, or ensnare your affections, or entangle your souls in vanities and sins; let them not hold you from following Christ—and keep them while you will. Cast but off the networks, the catching desires of the flesh and world, and so you also may be said to have left your nets. And having so weaned your souls from inordinate affections to things below, let Christ be your business, his life your pattern, his commands your law. Be ye followers of Christ, and let S. Andrew this day lead you after him into all universal obedience, ready, pure, and sincere: think not much to leave your nets for him that left heaven for you; you will gain more by following him than all the nets and draughts of the world are worth. You may well throw away your nets, having caught him in whom you have caught glory, and immortality, and eternal life, and by following him shall undoubtedly come at last out of this sea of toil and misery, where there is nothing but broken nets, and fruitless labours, or but wearisome and slippery fruits of them, into the port and haven of everlasting rest, and joys, and happiness.

And that it may be so, let us pray with the holy Church in the two Collects for Advent and S. Andrew :—

"Almighty God, which didst give such grace to thy holy Apostle S. Andrew, that he readily obeyed the calling of thy Son Jesus Christ, and followed him without delay; grant unto us all, that we, being called by thy holy Word, may forthwith give over ourselves obediently to fulfil thy holy commandments; that we may cast away the works of darkness, and put upon us the armour of light, now in the time of this mortal life, in the which thy Son Jesus Christ came to visit us with great humility, that in the last day, when he shall come again in his glorious majesty to judge both the quick and the dead, we may rise to the life immortal, through him who liveth and reigneth with thee and the Holy Ghost, now and ever."

A SERMON

PREACHED

AT S. PAUL'S.

Col. iii. 15.

And let the peace of God rule in your hearts, to the which also ye are called in one body; and be ye thankful.

SERMON LI.

How little or much soever the Colossians needed this advice, I am sure we do more than a little, and much need there is to press it close. For I know not, but methinks, as much as we talk of peace, and write it in the front of our petitions and projects, I am afraid our hearts are not right to it—it rules not there. And as much as we pretend our thankfulness to God for bringing us again into one body, we see but slender expressions of it. And yet we have the same arguments both for thankfulness and peace, to be thankful for our late recovered peace, and to be at peace if we would be thought to be thankful, as the Colossians had or could be imagined to have here; our being called again into one body, who were not long since in several ones; united now under one head, who were of late under many; God's call, and our own callings—God's present mercies, and our late miseries, calling to us—to persuade both.

There wants indeed some S. Paul to mind us of it, to preach it home; that we would be what we pretend, that men would be honest once, and either say no more than they mean, or do what they say; be content at least to be at peace, and not disturb it, but let it rule (so the Apostle would have it, and so it should rule) in our hearts and rule in our lives; rule in our hearts, and make them unanimous; rule in our tongues, and make them thankful; rule in our hands, and keep them quiet; rule in our actions, and make them peaceable; rule us all into one as we are called into one; rule us all into one mind, and one heart, and one soul, as we are in one body; rule us as a rule sent from God to rule us. For it is the peace of God we speak of, and we ought, every way we can, to be ruled by it, and be thankful for it.

It is S. Paul's request here in the text, or his command, rather, to the Colossians; yet the better to commend it home to you, I shall divide it into two parts:—

I. The motion for peace and thankfulness; and
II. The arguments to persuade them.

If you will draw the motion into smaller parcels, for six things the motion is: I. For "peace;" II. for "the peace of God;" III. for the "rule" and dominion of it; IV. for a place for it to rule in, "our hearts;" V. for the manifestation and expression of it in εὐχάριστοι, by being gracious and compliant, as εὐχάριστος sometimes signifies in Scripture, and may do here, and does, so say S. Jerome and S. Chrysostom;[b] VI. and lastly, for our being εὐχάριστοι again in the common sense, that we would be "thankful" for it. "Let the peace of God rule in your hearts," and be ye mild and gracious, or "be ye thankful."

And the arguments for these are full as many in number as the motions.

I. You are called; you are Christians, that is, the sons of peace; let peace therefore rule among you. II. It is that also which "ye are called" to, and let it therefore "rule." III. "In one body" ye are too; let it therefore "rule your hearts" into one also. IV. Into this body ye came not by chance, came not of yourselves; ἐκλήθητε, ye were "called" into it, God brought you lately to it. For this goodness' sake of his be ruled a little, now ye are once again called together, be at peace one with another. For, V. unthankful ye will be else, the proof of your thankfulness lies upon it, and therefore let this "peace of God" be in "your hearts," that ye may show yourselves to be "thankful." Nay, VI. and lastly, gracious ye cannot be, but graceless and perverse creatures you will seem if ye stand out now, and therefore whatever

---

[b] [S. Hieron. Comm. in Ephes. (ad Paul. et Eustoch.) v. 4—tom. ix. p. 185 C. ed. Francof.—But S. Chrysostom *in loco* interprets εὐχάριστοι in the sense of "thankful."]

has been hitherto, let "the peace of God" now really "rule your hearts" at last.

Thus I have given you the text in parts, which all together give you this in the sum, that it lies as a duty upon us all to let peace rule among us, to endeavour by all means that it may, to use all arguments for it that we can, both to ourselves and others, and be thankful that it does so much as it does, that it does in part, and let our thankfulness more and more increase as that increases.

II. But I pursue the parts, and make my first motion for peace itself.

I. And truly, it is worth the motion, worth the moving for. *Pacem te*, Thee, O peace, says the poet with an apostrophe, who would be without thee? *Te poscimus omnes*, every body would have peace; all but the ungodly, "no peace to the wicked;" indeed they have, they would have none; they have none among themselves, would have none among us. They fish best in troubled waters. All else are for peace and quiet. God is for it; he is the "God of peace." Christ is for it, he both commanded and bequeathed it. The Apostles are for it one after another; S. Paul, S. James, S. John, S. Peter, S. Jude; they all commend it. The Prophets before them were for it; they proclaimed it. The Angels are for it; they bring and sing it. All good men are for it; their daily prayer is, "Give peace, O Lord," though it be but "in our time" only; so, rather than not at all. Nay, though with Hezekiah, in other things it go hard with them, yet that is "good" for all that; "good and pleasant" also. Many good things are not so: fasting, and watching, mortification, repentance, and many other virtues, good they are, but they are not pleasant; peace is both; to dwell together in unity pleasant as well as good, very pleasant, and very good. *O quam!* so good and pleasant that he is fain to leave it upon the question, he cannot answer it; or leave it with an exclamation, *O quam!* leaves us only to admire it, at the goodness and sweetness of it. The messengers that bring but the tidings of it too, "how beautiful" are their very "feet!" Yea, even afar off, "upon" the tops of "the mountains," says the Prophet, afore they come near us; as far as we can see them we adore them; they are the only evangelists that preach peace; they bring the Gospel, their words no less whose words are peace.

And no wonder; for peace is a word of that vast latitude, that all God's blessings are folded up in the very name. It signifies all the temporal, and all the spiritual, yea, and all the eternal goods we can expect; glory and honour, grace, and mercy, and truth, life, and plenty, and joy, are in their several turns joined with it; you may so read them ever and anon. To wish us peace is to wish us all; to pray for peace is to pray for all; to give peace is to give all.

<small>Sermon LI.</small>

<small>Rom. ii. 10. Tit. i. 4. Jer. xxxiii. 6. Zech. viii. 16.</small>

But the notion being so large and general, we must distinguish it to understand it the better here. There is an outward, and there is an inward peace. There is a spiritual, a temporal, and an eternal peace; or if you will, there is peace the blessing, and peace the grace, and peace the reward. Our hearts, I hope, are for them all; but that which is here to rule them is peace the grace or virtue, the study and pursuit of peace; the other are our happiness, this our duty.

And of this, two kinds we have in the text,—the particular, and the public peace,—both to be endeavoured. The particular, among ourselves, of one member with another: the general, of the members with the body. The first is with our brethren and neighbours; the second is with the Church itself. "Peace among ourselves," that must be had, says S. Paul. And peace with the Church, as the whole body, there must be too; for "there should be no schism there," says the same Apostle. And, here, to speak of peace, and make the "being called into one body" the motive to it, must needs mean the union and agreement both of the members with one another, and with the body itself.

<small>1 Thes. v. 13.</small>

<small>1 Cor. xii. 25.</small>

II. Yet, for all that, there may be a body with which there is no joining, and men to whose "assemblies our honours may not be united;" the motion therefore now, secondly, for peace, is no farther for it than it is "the peace of God," or as some copies read it, the peace of Christ; that is, such a one (1) as God commands; such a one (2) as Christ wrought; such a one (3) as Christ practised.

(1.) Such a one as God commands. Now what is that? A peace it is, (i.) that is joined with "righteousness," in which "the fruit" of righteousness is sown. Not such a peace, or

<small>Rom. xiv. 17.</small>
<small>Isa. iii. 10.</small>

Sermon LI.

Prov. i. 11, 12, 14.

combination rather, as that we read of, where they all agree so far as even to have but "one purse" and one "lot" among them, but the business is to "lay wait for blood," and "lurk privily for the innocent without cause," that they may "find their precious substance," and "fill their houses with spoil;" we have had enough of that. The "peace of God" is peace that will do righteousness, not that peace that devours the righteous and all.

Heb. xii. 14.

A peace (ii.) it is that is joined with holiness, if it be God's. So we find them together, Heb. xii. 14. No sacrilegious peace, then, where the Church's patrimony must be shared among them, or they will not be quiet: that were to sell God to buy peace; or indeed to sell them both; to sell God out of doors, and peace out of doors, and all out of doors, ourselves at last, we know it well enough: but I know not how to call it, whether worldly peace, peace only upon worldly interests; or the devil's peace, that is only for "Thou Christ," or "thou anointed of the Lord, why didst thou come to disease us, to disquiet us, to turn us out?" We were well enough at peace before thou camest; let us alone in our usurped possessions, and then perhaps we will be content with peace; but for this peace of God and Christ, this holy peace, it is not for our turn, we skill not of it; our spirits are not made for it.

Eph. iv. 3.

(iii.) Nor are they for the third sort of God's peace neither, that which is "in the unity of the Spirit:" and yet it is not "the peace of God" that is not so. When we pray, and preach, and prophesy, and say *Amen* with one heart and mouth and spirit; when we do all things with decency and order, after one fashion, with uniformity, unite and agree so; then our peace looks like "the peace of God," who is not "the author of confusion, but of peace," even such a peace:—"the peace of God" is the peace of order and uniformity.

1 Cor. xiv. 33.

Rom. xv. 13.
Eph. iv. 13.

And his peace (iv.) is "peace in believing" too, where we all agree "in the unity of the faith, and of the knowledge of the Son of God." Diversities of faiths and of opinions, however they may seem to knit sometimes in an outward community, cannot yet challenge to that external agreement the title of "the peace of God." There must be among us an unity of faith as well as an uniformity of order to make up this peace. Men are not left to believe as they list, nor take up what opinions they please; as there is but "one Lord," so there is but "one faith," says our Apostle; where there is more, "the unity of the Spirit" will not be kept;" "the bond of peace" (whatever is pretended for the prophesying liberty) will not hold them together, when opportunity is presented to break it with advantage.

[Sermon LI. Eph. iv. 5.]

(2.) But I remember I told you some copies read "Christ" here instead of "God." The matter is not much, the business but the same. The peace of God is the peace of Christ. For (1) between God and us Christ wrought that peace, which is the ground of all the rest; and such a one also now (2) as he wrought between God and us, would he have us see what we can do to work one with another. That was between persons at the greatest distance, the greatest enemies; so must ours be too, if it be Christ's peace. Peace between friends, if they jar a little, is soon made up; no greater a business than the religion of a publican will reach to: the Christian's peace takes in enemies too; sends us from the very altar even to seek a reconcilement with them; then also when, for aught we know, we have given them no offence, though they have taken it;—sends us the world throughout to make peace, even "with all men," says S. Paul. This is Christ's peace; such a one he wrought, and such a one it is that we must follow.

[Matt. v. 24. Heb. xii. 14.]

One point yet higher, from his practice. Such a one it must be (3) as he practised, not only to love our enemies, and be at peace with them, if possible, but to hold our peace if they reject it, and revile us for it. There are spirits in the world (and they would fain set up for Christ's more than any) that pretend they are for peace as much as any, but they cannot hold but they must open their mouths, and extend their lungs, and let loose their pens to enlarge the breaches;— Micah's prophets, such as God complains of, that "make the people err, that bite with their teeth, and cry, Peace;" that bite, and backbite both king and Church, and all that truly endeavour peace; that, with him in the Proverbs, throw abroad their firebrands, wherever they come, among the people, and yet cry, "Is it not for peace?" But let these men remember there was one, both the author and example of our peace, that being reviled, reviled not again, that could

[Micah iii. 5.]

hold his peace before the shearers, and murderers;—though they fly daily in the faces of them that seek their prosperity and peace, and " by the bowels of Christ" beseech them now at last to be " reconciled to Christ" and the Church, to unite with us "in the bonds of peace." It is but a righteous, a holy peace, a " unity of faith " and order, a general reconcilement, and peaceable language and deportment, that we desire of them. "The peace of God" you have heard is such, and our request is but the Apostle's, that this peace now may rule among us. That is our third motion, the third particular of the text for the rule of peace.

III. The word that is here translated "rule" has much more in it, several senses. And peace itself being of so large a notion, and so general a concernment, I may, I hope, take the liberty to use as many of them as will serve my turn.

Let us take our own translation first, $\beta\rho\alpha\beta\epsilon\upsilon\epsilon\tau\omega$, *moderetur*, let it "rule." Wars and dissensions have ruled long enough, let peace rule now. Many passions there are that bustle in us for supremacy when there rises any contest between us and our superiors, or between us and our equals. Envy would carry it, anger would overbear it, discontent would order it, pride would decide it, honour would dispose it, interest would drive the trade, lust would sway it, covetousness would have all, peevishness would have more; but "let peace," for all that, and none of them, "rule" the business, says the Apostle. What we do let it not be to gratify our envies, nor to satisfy our spleens, nor to humour our discontents, nor to court our prides, nor to exalt our repute, nor to drive on our interests, nor to fill our purses, nor to fulfil our lusts, nor to soothe our peevishnesses, but to promote peace and unity among all we have to do with. The unruliness of these passions are the things that hinder it; whilst we give way to them, to any of them, we are nothing but combustion. These are to be laid down at the foot of peace, nothing done by us upon their account, and then we shall be quiet.

Nay, not only over the passions let peace bear rule, but even among the virtues; there $\beta\rho\alpha\beta\epsilon\upsilon\epsilon\tau\omega$ in the second sense, *palmam ferat*, let her wear the crown, bear away the prize; $\epsilon\pi\grave{\iota} \pi\hat{\alpha}\sigma\iota \delta\grave{\epsilon} \tau o\upsilon\tau o\iota\varsigma$, this above them all. Bowels of mercy, kindness, humbleness of mind, meekness, long-suffering,—put them on all; but this above them as a robe of honour. Excellent graces all; but the bond of all that ties them all together—the bond of perfectness, which perfects all; why! it is this; for ἀγάπη there is but εἰρήνη here; "love," in that verse, is "the peace of God" in this. [For εἰρήνη is from εἴρειν, to knit together, and so fits σύνδεσμος, the bond, there, as well as does ἀγάπη; and τοῦ Θεοῦ here fits τελειότητος, as well as love does there also: God being all perfection, and his peace a knitting or binding God to man, and man to man, and man to God, so perfecting all.] Where this is wanting we are but imperfect; nor is our virtue nor our felicity complete. He is the perfectest Christian that is most for peace, and he only conquers (what side soever at any time prevails) who makes peace, or does most for it.

But as peace must rule our passions and crown our virtues, so it would do well to decide our controversies, the third sense of βραβευέτω, *dijudicet*, or *determinet*. If controversies or differences arise among us (as rise they will), let us first consider calmly on them, weigh them without passion, discuss them without noise, treat of them without heat; and if they chance to be so troublesome that they cannot easily be decided, either by reason of the eagerness of the disputers, or the interests of the parties, or the abstruseness of the question, the spirit of peace will quickly do it. Keep thy faith and opinion to thyself; trouble neither thy weak nor thy strong brother with them; disturb not the peace of the Church about them, but sit down, and rest thyself in the decision of the Church; be content with general terms of agreement, and draw not out controversies into nice expressions; the peace of the Church is commonly (I may say always) more considerable than the question, and he determines best, that either determines, or is determined, for peace. Rom. xiv. 22.

To do this the better I shall give a fourth signification of βραβευέτω, Μεσιτευέτω, (*Hesych.*) *Medius sit vel arbiter;* Let there be a moderator or mediator made to moderate the contention. This does well, we find, in all particular contests: cannot but do so surely in the Church's. We must not always be our own judges. Best refer it, and then either our superiors or our laws will be the fittest for it. But whatever

SERMON LI.

may be perhaps objected against superiors in particular, the law and canon they stand always impartial judges; they cannot be accused to lean either to the one or the other, they are akin to neither, and not capable of flattery or a bribe; let them then be umpires between us, and decide the matter.

Yet, to be sure to keep the peace, let there be order kept: so βραβευέτω fifthly signifies *ordinet;* let peace set some order now among us. The Apostle S. Paul was very careful of it when he spent two several chapters to the Corinthians, the 12th and 14th of his First Epistle, to prescribe it. Indeed, peace cannot consist without it; where there is no order there can be no peace; where there is confusion there can be no quiet; that body must needs be torn in pieces where the members draw several ways; that Church into more, where the members of it do what they list, go which way they please. No keeping rule for peace without keeping order.

After all these readings the Vulgar comes in with an *exultet*. And though I can scarce guess how it came to be the interpretation of βραβευέτω, yet it comes not amiss to tell us that God's peace does not make dull and heavy hearts. It makes us merry, it makes us glad, stills all the grudges that rise within us, all the quarrels that rise without us, everything that would disturb our quiet. Nothing so glad, so merry, as the soul that dwells in peace, where peace keeps court, which is reconciled to God; at odds with no man, in amity with all. Thus all the triumphs of the world are much below the garlands of peace; and the Apostle may not only well say *moderetur*, "let it rule," but *exultet,* "let it triumph;" and let us triumph when it does.

And now to sum up the severals, that you may know at once what it is to have peace rule. If the peace of God rule truly in us, it must overrule our passions, it must advance our virtues, it must decide our differences, it must compose our quarrels, it must work us into order, and it must make us cheerful under its commands, in our obedience under it. So it will infallibly, if it once be seated where it should be, in our hearts. That is the place the Apostle would have it exercise its rule and dominion in, the fourth motion he makes here to us in the behalf of peace. Let "the peace of God rule in your hearts."

IV. And were it once but sincerely there, it would rule our words into a milder key, our actions into a smoother dress; we should hear no whispers against the government of Church or state; no feigned jealousies of superstition coming in; no talk of, I know not what, persecution coming on; no canting of sad times at hand; no suggesting of vain fears; no fomenting all distastes; no reviving those wretched principles and pretences that first ruined all our peace and quiet; no scattering libels and wonders up and down to amuse the people, so to hinder them from reunion with the Church, and keep them in perpetual discontent for they know not what. These are not the words of such as seek the peace of Sion, or heartily pray for the peace of Jerusalem. They are not the words of peace, my brethren, not the ways of it, nor do they become the messengers or servants of the God of peace. To raise needless scruples, to canvass every word and tittle, to make a noise and pother about every trifle, to flutter and keep a stir as if we had much to say, to make it out in number where it wants in weight, to write and scribble over old objections answered over and over a thousand times, to talk of peace and thus make ready for the battle, if it must pass for peace, it is a " peace that passeth all understanding" in another sense than the Apostle meant; we cannot conceive it, we cannot understand it.

Would we but lay down our interests, our envies, our animosities, our prejudices, our pride, our humours, the justifying ourselves and doings, the glory we take in a false constancy, that magisterial conceit we have of our own judgment, and that popularity that undoes all,—were these out of the heart, peace would be quickly in. But if we stand upon punctilios, and will not pray but in our own words, will not worship God unless we may do it in what form we list ourselves, will not appear in the congregation unless it be in one of our own gathering or choosing, will quit the Church rather than an humour; if the Church music and harmony must drive all concord and agreement out of doors; if the garments and emblems of peace and purity affright us, if order scare us, if uniformity drive us out of the Church, if kneeling at the altar and feast of peace must go for a reason to keep us from it, if the very sign of the cross of Christ, by which we were reconciled—for by his cross it was, says the Apostle—must needs be made an argument against all reconcilement,—it is a sign we have no hearts for peace, our hearts are not at all for it, who may have it at so easy a rate, upon so handsome terms, and yet thus rudely thrust it from us, as if we had sworn and covenanted against it, and all the ways that can lead to it. Fain would we see some better expressions of it, if it be otherwise. Let us try the Apostle's in the next particular, examine it by our ordinary deportment and behaviour, whether that be εὐχάριστος, mild and gracious as it should.

V. What our common translation here renders *grati*, "thankful," S. Chrysostom and S. Jerome, I told you, and from them Erasmus turns *gratiosi*, "gracious."[c] In this sense we find εὐχαριστία, and εὐχάριστος. Both senses the word may bear, and the connexion will bear them too. And to do both right we will balk neither, we will take both;— *gratiosi* first. Be we mild and gracious, kind and amiable. The Apostle says it fuller in ver. 12, 13, beseeches us to be tender and compassionate, meek and humble, patient and "long-suffering," "forbearing" and "forgiving." These are the best symptoms and expressions of peace's ruling. The words of peace are smooth and sweet; they are no swords: the looks of peace are mild and cheerful; they are not sour or dogged: the hands of peace are soft and open; they are not rugged or close; they are easy and stretched out to all that come into them. These are the ways of peace, and the best means to draw it on. To look always austere and muddy, to carry scorn and superciliousness in the countenance, to be unsociable and untractable, to run as far contrary as is possible, to receive or join with none but upon our own conditions, and reject all that look, and speak, and understand not just as we do ourselves, is so far from the paths of peace, that I shall not stick to call it an open defiance of all the world. Yet such men there are; and some that add to all a renunciation of all the forms, and words, and signs of civility, and make it religion to be unmannerly and sullen. I know not what sense these men can have of peace, who come not so near as the salutation of it, addresses to it.

[c] [Erasm. Comm. in loco. See above, p. 395.]

And truly I have but little to say for them neither, who after so many condescensions from their Sovereign, so great compliances, so long forbearances, so much forgiveness, so fair a time given them to consider and come in, and resolve all petty scruples,—for there are no other,—are not yet composed for peace; who the more is yielded, the less they are satisfied; the more graciously they are dealt with, the more averse and froward they are to a reconcilement; the nearer we come, the further they fly from us. Only I know I am bound by S. Paul here to be εὐχάριστος, to think and speak as mildly and gently of them as the thing will bear. I would they would do so too.

Yet methinks if they like not *gratiosi,* they might do *grati;* if they like not to be gracious, they might however to be thankful,—thank God, and thank the King, and thank the Church for their graciousness and forbearance; be εὐχάριστοι in the second sense, in that of thankfulness. It is the last motion I have to make out of the Apostle's, that ye would be thankful.

VI. It is a duty, I will assure you, that lies upon us; for "it becometh well the just to be thankful." I cannot tell you anything more becoming: no, not more becoming us in regard of the mercies mentioned in the text, "the peace of God," and the calling us to it in one body. Each of them so ample subjects for our thankfulness that we cannot show thankfulness enough for either.

Ps. xxxiii. 1.

Peace, so great a blessing, that *Nil dulcius audiri, nil delectabilius concupisci, nil utilius possideri,* as one under S. Augustine's name expresses it; A blessing than which there is none more pleasant to be heard, none more delightful to be desired, none more profitable to be possessed.

And God's calling us to it in one day,—calling us into one Church,—calling us then, when we were almost out of call, some of us in very remote parts of the earth; some of us in dark corners at home; some of us in dungeons; some in dust almost, ready to go down into it, and be covered with it,—calling us all together out of our several graves, as it were, into a new life, restoring us our "head," and uniting it to the "members,"—is so transcendent a mercy to us, that we can never be sufficiently thankful.

Yet that we may be somewhat thankful though, what is it to be thankful? I shall give you it in brief—for I cannot be long—and leave you to enlarge it.

To be thankful, then, is (1) humbly and heartily to acknowledge God's infinite goodness to us, and our own infinite unworthiness of it. He that thinks light of peace and unity, that undervalues God's calling us into one body, or thinks he did anything towards it to deserve it, either understands not God's goodness, or is not thankful for it.

(2.) To be thankful, is openly and publicly to confess God's mercies and our own engagements; to be telling of them all the day long; to make hymns, and praises, and panegyrics daily for them. I need not be so impertinent to tell you it was David's business commonly to do so for mercies that were not like these, or quote the Psalms wherein he does. But words are not all.

(3.) To be thankful, indeed, is by our deeds to show it; to present ourselves and all that is ours henceforward daily to his service; to offer up our souls and bodies, and what else is ours, as peace offerings and sacrifices of thanksgivings: never to fear we can do too much, never to hope we can do enough for what God has done for us, in thus reinstating us in our Church and our religion; thus bringing home our Prince and our peace; and that not with thunder and lightning to punish or upbraid us for our former sins; not in a storm and tempest, to fright us with a mercy; not with fire and sword, to embitter the blessing; but in a calm, with a still voice, with joy and melody, with no other noise than that of Hosannas and Hallelujahs. Be we therefore thankful unto him, and bless his name for ever and ever; for ever, I say again, for we have no time here limited to do it in; only be thankful, still be thankful: "For a good thing it is to give thanks unto the Lord;" yea, "a joyful and pleasant thing it is to be thankful."

II. Methinks I should need no arguments to you to persuade you to it, either to thankfulness or to peace. Yet so many being in the text, I must not be so injurious to you or it to pass them by. Six I find in it to persuade to peace. Ye are, I. called; called, II. to it; ye, III. are one body; called, IV. into that too; can neither be, V. *grati*, nor,

VI. *gratiosi*, can neither be thankful, nor appear gracious, if ye be not for it, for the rule of peace. And to be thankful and gracious you have good reason too; for your being called, for your peace, for the body you are of, and your calling into that, to be members of it, are all motives to persuade it.

I. The first argument is your being "called," and it is a good one. To be "called" is to be Christians in effect. Κλητοὶ, the adjective from ἐκλήθητε is so taken, and the verb itself in several places may bear it too. Now to be Christians is to be the sons and servants of the God of peace; a very good reason that, that the son should be like the Father, the servant be as his Master is. It was Abraham's argument to Lot to end all differences: "Let there be no strife, I pray thee, between me and thee, or between my herdsmen and thy herdsmen, for we be brethren." It is the same for us, but with some advantage: let there be no strife between thee and me, for we be brethren, for we be Christians; for if the servants should not disagree when their masters are brethren, because they are so, much less should they when they all have but one Master, and themselves are brethren. The meanest herdsman should not by this reason—none of the people; but the chief shepherds—the great pastors—however, they should think upon their callings better than to fall out one with another. "As the elect of God, dearly beloved," says S. Paul, you must not: you must "forbear," you must "forgive." It is the best way to make your calling and election sure, to assure yourselves and the world, after all this, that ye are Christians. All are not that pretend to it. The servant that fell a-beating his fellow-servants was but an hypocrite. I am sure he had his portion given him among them; was "cut asunder" because he would join no better. For peace and true holiness go together; no holy men, however so called, who are not peaceable; false and hypocritical only is that holiness that is not joined with peace, and those Christians no better; called so, perhaps, but not, in the Apostle's sense, true Christians indeed. The truly called ones are all for peace.

II. But they are particularly called to that. So the Apostle, "Ye are called unto peace." Why, then "let every man

SERMON LI.

1 Cor. i. 2.
Rom. i. 6.
Eph. iv. 1, 4.
Gal. i. 6.

Gen. xiii. 8.

Col. iii. 12.
Col. iii. 14.

Matt. xxiv. 49.

1 Cor. vii. 15, 20.

SERMON LI.	wherein he is called therein abide;" even in this sense too, every man stick to his calling, for it is a "holy one," we
2 Tim. i. 9. Heb. iii. 1.	told you so just now; it is a " heavenly one," peace dwells for ever there; no jars, no discords among the saints or angels. And seeing God has thought us worthy to call us to it, I hope we will bethink ourselves and walk worthy of it.
Gal. v. 13.	"Called" I know we are "to liberty," but "not to use it for an occasion to the flesh, but by love to serve one another."
Gal. v. 15.	Mark the end of it, else, says the Apostle, for "if ye bite and devour one another, take heed ye be not consumed one of another." Indeed ye will; a strong argument to persuade to peace.

Yet III. we have not only our general calling,—the being Christians, and our particular designment to it after that,—but our interests public and private, both to persuade us to it: "we are in one body." Now, it is neither for the interest of the body, nor of the members to be at difference one with

1 Cor. xii. 26. another. "If one member suffer, all the members suffer with it." And the body cannot be torn or rent but every member is concerned; the least scratch with a nail, or the prick of a pin, or the touch of a thorn, may, by the ignorance or cunning, neglect or ill managing of a heady chirurgeon, be improved into a gangrene, or a wound that may make the heart ache, and all the members rue it. We lose our health ere we are aware, and the very neglect of a little air at a cranny, or the slighting the pettiest stirring of an humour, sometimes endangers life and all. There is nothing to keep us safe but order and peace, to keep the humours quiet, and the several members in due order. How has the body of Christ, the Church of God, of which we all are members, by the ill managing of a petty controversy, through the negligence or ignorance sometimes of the managers, or the sly cunning of an undiscerned or unminded adversary, or the peevishness of a party, been often thrown into a confusion, and almost brought to desolation! If we love the Church—and we pretend it,—nay, if we love our ourselves—and that we commonly do too much,—we must agree together. We cannot hope our houses shall escape, if the city be all on fire at every corner. Or it is but a poor comfort when we see Polyphemus devour our fellows, to think only

we shall be the last. And a vain confidence it is to suppose, when a mutiny is once begun, that we can stop it when we please. Diseases and ill humours once let loose run insensibly through all the parts; we cannot retrieve them as we list, or fix them when we will. Our very hopes of a recovery are lost in a moment; we have betrayed ourselves by opening the way to confusion by our own contests, and the whole body drops into a carcass, and all is gone. If we would but consider our own bodies, and learn thence from our own senses, as the Apostle would have us in the forecited chapter, we could not be so stupid, so senseless, to draw on our own ruins by our divisions. Methinks I cannot speak more sensibly to all the purposes of peace, nor you understand them more feelingly, than by this metaphor of the body and the members. Yet the argument is much advanced by ἐκλήθητε, by our being called into it, by the favour that God has done us in bringing us into it.

IV. That God has brought us into the Church, made us to be a body of Christians, is (1) a blessing we too seldom think of, yet it is a great one, and a great motive too to be at peace with our own happiness, and not disturb it. No man would divide his happiness who may enjoy it whole, much less divide it when he must lose it whole, divide from it and divide it from himself, lest as "for the divisions of Reuben," so for this, there should come nothing of it but grief of heart. Judges v. 15.

Again (2) we are "called into one body," says the text, certainly not to make it two, or tear it asunder into more; we are called into one, to keep in one, to love, and live, and die together; this "one" is an argument to hold unity.

(3.) I may raise a third argument, if I read the words exactly as they are, without the indulgence of construing ἐν into εἰς, read it as we do, "in" one body ye are called, called all at a lump, all in a body at once. However it was with the Colossians, whether called all together, or by parcels, I am sure with us it was lately *in uno corpore*, the whole body of the nation were called into one at once; our happiness came all at a clap, and shot from east to west, from north to south, like lightning, in a moment. The land came not in by pieces, was not won in, as lands are, by conquest, one town or country after another. And will we then now tear off ourselves by pieces into our late confusions? Who has bewitched us that we should think to do it?

(4.) If we add for a fourth, as we may do well in a reflection upon ourselves, that we were called who a little before seemed cast away; called into a body who durst not for many years before appear in any; called into one, who were then scattered into many; called into one Church, into one government, under one head; then, too, when we scarce had any name but by-names to be called by, and had made ourselves unworthy of any by our sins; to be then called, and so called as we were, was even a calling us out of worms and dust, out of nothing, to an anticipated resurrection. And can we so far forget ourselves as to undo our happiness, and divide again? Have the miseries of our late dissensions so clearly slipped out of our memories, or are the squadrons and divisions of armed troops so blessed a sight within our quarters? If so, God has done us an injury to call us into one, to cease our wars, and bring home peace and safety to our doors, and we do as good as tell him so, whilst we either run ourselves into divisions, raise them, or continue them. For unthankful, fifthly, miserably unthankful, too, as well as foolish and inconsiderate we must needs be thus to contemn, to throw away our peace.

V. And shall we add unthankfulness to the bulk of our transgressions? I trow not. And yet we shall if we oppose the rule of peace. To be thankful is to return somewhat answerable to the favour that is received. Now what more answerable to peace than peace itself, to the peace of God than peace with our brethren? And he that returns not this, returns nothing. He can no more have peace with God than love to him whom he has not seen, if he have not peace with his brother whom he has seen. To be sure he cannot be thankful that kicks God's favours back again into his face, and unmannerly bids him take them again, he cares not for them. And yet we do no less when we despise and cast away the peace to which he has called us; we say plainly enough it is not worth the having whilst we do not think it worth the keeping. Nay, and all the blessings of peace, all God's calling and recalling us first and last out of sin, out of misery, out of confusions and destructions;

the very name of Christians, and the uniting us again under one King and Church, are certainly no blessings in our judgments and opinions, if we thus wilfully and contemptuously tear all in pieces rather than peaceably submit to their determinations for unity and order, where we have nothing to object, but that they are in things indifferent, which is in all men's reason else the greatest reason we should comply with them. And no man that truly thanks God for them can do otherwise.

VI. I am loth to say what I must needs say now in the last place too, that they must needs be churlish and sullen, as well as unthankful; no εὐχαριστία at all in them in the other sense neither, no mildness or softness, who after all S. Paul's arguments for peace and union, will not be persuaded unto it: for when God, that here calls us unto peace, shall one day call us to an account, how gracious and thankful we have been for his calling us to it, what we have done or not done towards it; consider, I beseech you, whether you think seriously in your hearts that it will there pass for true endeavours for peace to answer thus: Lord, we have been all for peace, and we petitioned for it, but we could not have it upon our own conditions; we would have agreed for a public service, but we could not have it of our own making; we could well enough have condescended to an uniformity, but they would not let us, that were the inferiors, set the rule; we yet agree in the Articles of the faith, only for indifferences we kept still off; we are all saved, too, we confess, by the Cross of Christ, but the very sign of it we thought enough to keep us still asunder; we were zealous for thy worship, but we would not be confined to it by any imposed rule of reverence and order;—we could indeed have yet submitted to it ourselves, but we, some of us, had taught the people otherwise, and were ashamed to unteach them; we might perhaps have easily come in at first, but now we have so long stood out that it is not for our honour to retreat; they will call us turncoats and apostates, and we shall lose the people quite: gracious and kind notwithstanding we have been in our deportments, but it was only to our own party; thankful besides to God, though we kept not indeed any solemn days of thanksgivings, or as perfunctorily as we could, we would go no further. In the sum, we have done all we could to have peace upon our own terms, but we could not obtain it, unless we would submit to decency and order; and so it stands.

And when our governors and superiors, called to the same account, shall be content to stand to our own confessions, that they imposed nothing but things indifferent for unity and order: think soberly, I beseech you, on which hand lies the true plea for the endeavour of peace, where lies the perverseness, where the compliance. And if this be the business, as I fear it is too near it, I shall leave the whole world to judge whether peace truly rule in the hearts of those who upon their own terms only seek it,—whether they answer their callings or are thankful.

I say no more; I have said too much, perhaps; yet I wish I had said enough to make up the peace: I shall only rally up the Apostle's arguments, and dismiss you hence, however, in peace.

You have heard the Apostle's and our motions and motives to peace. And now if we have any respect to our Christianity, any thoughts of our vocation, any love to unity, any consideration of God's goodness, any kind of gratitude for his mercies, or would be gracious in his eyes, let the meekness of Christians, the remembrance of our vocation, the obligations to unity, the endearments of God's kindness, the reasonableness of gratitude, the hope of God' sfavour, and our endeavour for the common happiness of the world, engage us to peace, to God's peace, to the Church's. To this we are called. And God that calls us to it, work us to it, work it in our hearts, and in our practices, by the same power by which we are called into one body make us of one mind, through him who, &c.

A SERMON

PREACHED

AT S. PAUL'S CROSS.

SIR RICHARD GURNEY BEING THEN LORD MAYOR.

JER. xxxv. 18, 19.

Thus saith the Lord of hosts, the God of Israel; Because you have obeyed the commandment of Jonadab your father, and kept all his precepts, and done according unto all that he hath commanded you: therefore thus saith the Lord of hosts, the God of Israel; Jonadab the son of Rechab shall not want a man to stand before me for ever.

THE text, you hear, is the word of God; "Thus saith the Lord," whatever the sermon be like to be; and if the preacher stir no further from the text than the Rechabites in it from the command of their father, the sermon is like to be no less, and to be heard accordingly. I know whose work I am about, *Sic dicit Dominus;* I shall keep to that. "Thus saith the Lord," begins the text; and it shall run through and end my sermon.

SERMON LII.

And I could wish I could begin it, as Christ did his at Nazareth, "This day is this Scripture fulfilled in your ears." Luke iv. 21. But then, I fear, I must leave out *dicit Dominus:* nor God, nor his prophet can say so for that they call the greatest part of city or country; or for the success we expect upon it.

I cannot therefore say the text is fit for the time, but I am sure it is needful,—a text of obedience never more. A little of that, well practised, would make us understand one another, set all together again. It is needful for that: and that is as much as peace, plenty, and religion is worth.

SERMON LII.

Yet, as needful as it is, it is well we have a *dicit Dominus* for it; one above that dares commend it. *Non dicit homo;* nobody beneath had best to do it : or, if he do, this too will be popery and innovation, the doctrine of the popish clergy; words as common in the people's mouths, for all they dislike, as ever *dicit Dominus* was in the prophets'.

Well; be it what they will; say man what he please, " Thus saith the Lord;" and so, by God's blessing, will we. Say it, and say it as he says it, by way of commendation. *Eò quòd.* Make obedience the cause of our speech, of a set commendation.

Yet we had best take heed what we do. *Sic dicit Dominus.* His for the Rechabites, that shall guide us. And what is it he commends them for?

Because they "obeyed;" for their obedience. But to whom that? Obeyed "your father;" obedience to man. What was he? " Your father Jonadab," saith the text. What power had he? All: natural, civil, ecclesiastical. Jonadab was the father of their family; had (1) *jus patrium*, the power of a father over them,—he disposed of their kind of living, their estates, and civil affairs; had (2) *jus regium*, the civil power, over them,—contrived all to a religious course of life, to the freer service of heaven; had (3) *jus ecclesiasticum*, the spiritual power, over them.

He hath not more of authority than they of obedience. Obedience formal, to his command; universal, to all; punctual, according to all that he commanded them. This, then, is the obedience that God here commends; a formal, an universal, a punctual obedience to natural, civil, and spiritual parents.

Commends them for, commends to us; rewards to them, will reward to us. Likes them so well upon it, that he loves to look upon them for it; will not, therefore, endure them out of his sight; promises to keep them there for ever; will do as much for us upon the same performances; passes his word upon it, " Thus saith the Lord;" engages his honour, as he is " Lord,"—his power, as he is " Lord of hosts,"—his mercy, as " the God of Israel," to make it good.

You see the text in its full dimensions. It will now fall easily into parts; evidently into two:—

I. God's approbation of the Rechabites' obedience.
II. And his reward upon it.

I. In the approbation you have, (1) the form and style of it, "Thus saith the Lord of hosts, the God of Israel." (2) The grounds of it, "because you have obeyed," &c. Obedience commended upon some grounds: commended, (i.) from their persons: ye, Rechabites,—ye, your wives and your children; because ye have obeyed. (ii.) From the expression of it, by a threefold act, *obedistis, custodistis, fecistis*: you have obeyed, kept, and done. (iii.) From a threefold object: the commandment of their father, all his precepts, and according to them all. (iv.) From the power or person whom they obeyed, Jonadab their father.

II. In the reward, first, for their triple obedience, we shall find a triple blessing: (1.) The blessing of a posterity still to succeed them: "Jonadab, the son of Rechab, shall not want a man," *Non deficiet vir de stirpe Jonadab*. (2.) Of an honourable and pious posterity: "not want a man to stand before me;" such upon whom God will always cast an eye of favour and honour. (3.) Of a lasting, everlasting posterity: not want a man "for ever."

Then, secondly, the certainty and assurance of it. "Thus saith the Lord of hosts, the God of Israel;" and you may take his word—he will perform it.

And because we come not hither only to commend others, but to learn ourselves,—and God therefore sets the Rechabites' obedience upon record, that we may know what he likes, have a precedent to follow and do accordingly,—we will, in the close of every several point of their obedience, examine our own; see how near or short we come; where, if I chance to say you have not done so much, pardon me that person all the way; it is the person in the text, and I therefore use it. I mean not you, nor you, none of you, unless your actions apply it. I know not; if they do, you must forgive me if I strike home. I come not so far to flatter you; and the times require a sharper physic.

Yet if I may persuade you by the approbation, example, or reward of obedience in the text; or the punishment of disobedience by the rule of contraries implied there, I shall so conclude in full desires, that what God here says of the

Sermon LII.

Rechabites, he may hereafter say of you: "Because you have obeyed the commandment of your father, and kept his precepts, and done according to all that he commands; therefore thus saith the Lord of hosts, the God of Israel; You shall not want a man to stand before me for ever."

I. You see my method; I begin with the approbation: the style of it, " Thus saith the Lord :" and that is a good beginning.

(1.) And is it God indeed that speaks for obedience? Who is it then that speaks against it? What spirit are they of?

1 Cor. vii. 23.

They pretend S. Paul's, " Be ye not the servants of men ;" it is true, that : not so theirs, as to forget to be Christ's : but to remember withal, you are the children of men ; some of whom you must obey as fathers, if you mean to be Christ's servants.

Matt. xxii. 21.

He tells you so, " Render to Cæsar the things which are Cæsar's," as well as " to God the things which are God's." He puts Cæsar first too, to show they talk vainly who say they serve God, when they leave out the king. First, thy father "whom thou hast seen," then "God whom thou hast not seen," is the Apostle's rule for us to judge by; and his is God's.

Well, then, we have God on our side, whoever be against us; him speaking for it, and speaking of it; and they are words of commendation, while he so well likes obedience, that he cannot forbear to speak of it.

It is no small matter that, that can command the eye or tongue of the princes of the earth; it must be more that even forces a panegyric from the Lord Almighty; something sure worth commendation.

Man indeed makes great matters of little or nothing. "God sees not as man sees;" man may be deceived, God cannot. He says the Rechabites have obeyed; commends them for it, say who dare against it. And I am afraid we shall find too many in the upshot that neither like their obedience nor God's commending them ; say all they can against it.

It is no matter what they say : God doth more than say it; says it with delight; goes with it over and over again; *obedistis, custodistis, fecistis;* thrice in a breath; takes notice of every tittle, fills the whole chapter, almost every verse with it ; loves to speak of it, it so much contents him.

Says it encircled with his glories; talks of it amidst his

hosts; tells them, as it were, of it. For he had told his prophet and his people of it before. Now he even tells it his angels; would have them take notice of it.

He goes further; almost forsakes his Israel to look on them: is now become the God of the Rechabites; they are they that shall now stand before him for ever.

He goes on still; is so well pleased, that he tells it to themselves; commends them to their faces; a thing not usual with God, but to the very chiefest of his saints and children: at least, then only when he is most highly pleased with any. "Ye have obeyed."

Lastly. Says it not in the form his other speeches go: not *dixit*, but *dicit*, in the present. Is still saying it: said it then, and says it still: said it to them; says it to us, that we also might say it after him,—say it in our actions, that he might have some ground to say of us what he does of them, "Ye have obeyed." Which brings me the parties into sight, whose obedience is the ground of all this approbation. And the first is from their persons.

Ye Rechabites. Every verse almost tells you it. They, Kenites, some say, descended from Jethro: Midianites by original, strangers from the covenant; yet even they obedient to their father, taught to be so by the law of nature; commended for that.

Abulensis is loth to derive them from so poor beginnings. He makes them of the family of Caleb, of the tribe of Judah, the royal tribe; that even princes too, as well as people, might know obedience to their father sometimes in those commands that seem to divest them of that honour; but that obedience is the greatest honour, greatest in such persons.

Whether they were such or no, they were the sons of Jonadab. He was a devout man. *Spontaneus Domini*, says S. Augustine;[d] "One that would serve God, though it were for nothing." Some of our age would have told them, they might have excused them being the seed of the godly. It is a part of their commendation that they thought not so.

It is another, that they excused neither age nor sex. "You." Who? "We, our wives, our sons, and our daughters." Jer. xxxv. 8. Oh! happy family, where obedience is thus taught by autho-

[d] [S. Aug. In Psal. lxx. Conc. i. tom. viii. p. 270 G. ed. Col. Agr. 1616.]

SERMON LII.

rity, learned from example, sucked from the breasts; where the wife learns it from the husband, hers to him, from him to the magistrate; the children from both.

Time, yet, lifts their virtue higher. Three hundred years had Jonadab been gathered to his fathers, while yet his sons persist in his commands, with as much constancy as integrity, that we might prescribe no time against obedience.

This, then, is the sum of that part of God's commendation from their persons, that Rechabites, princes by their tribe, holy by descent; women and children, after so many ages past over Jonadab, neither pleaded their descent, nor their honour, nor their claim to the covenant, nor their age, nor their sex, nor the abrogation of laws for antiquity, but without any contrary plea whatsoever generally submitted to all obedience.

Thus says God for them.

What say we for ourselves?

In civil affairs, laws, they say, are cobwebs. Great men, great flies, that easily break through them; mean men, little enough to slip out at any hole; women do what they please; children are not old enough for any thing, but sin and disobedience.

In ecclesiasticals it is worse. Though it be a matter of reverence enjoined to God himself, great ones are too good, others too perverse, women too tender, children not of age, all too weakly to bend the knee or bare the head in God's service; so that what was said of Moses, that "God talked with him as man doth with his friend," I may invert, and say, Man now talks with God as man doth with his friend; so fellow-like, that, though our fathers had not commanded the contrary, all the world would say, There is nothing like reverence or obedience in this.

Let me ask now, Had the Rechabites the law of nature to guide them, and have not we? Were not they a righteous offspring as well as we? Had not they the tenderness of wives and children to plead for weakness of constitution and complexion (greater hindrances to their strict kind of life) as well as we? Could not they have pleaded antiquated laws, as truly we? Yet says God, "You have done all that was commanded you;" done it, when others have not; not mine own people; he may add now, not my Christian people. Thus our negligence commends their obedience. We that have no more to excuse ourselves than they; not so much, our task being easier, our helps greater; yet we have not—they have. Let that be an addition to their first commendation, raised a little by comparison with us. You Rechabites,—I may almost say now, You only—have obeyed.

I pass now to the second ground of the approbation: the expression of their obedience.

Three acts there are of it: (1.) *Obedistis.* (2.) *Custodistis.* (3.) *Fecistis.* You have obeyed, kept, and done what was commanded you. The first belongs to the inward, the two other to the outward man.

I begin with the inward. For without that, outward obedience is of short service, no continuance. Four acts flow from it: To (1) hear; to (2) hearken; to (3) submit to; to (4) acquiesce in the commands of our superiors. All point blank against those four grounds of disobedience:—(1.) Untractableness; (2.) Impatience; (3.) Pride; and (4.) Murmuring. To hear, that against untractableness, that will not so much as endure the hearing; to hearken, that against impatience, that will not take pains to hear it out; to submit, that against pride, that will veil to none; to acquiesce or rest in, that against murmuring, that is never content with any thing imposed upon it.

Let me but ponder the word as I go, I shall find all those, and not go from the word.

In all three languages, the word, whence comes obedience, comes from hearing. *In auditu auris obedivit* is King David's. Ps. xviii. 44. The first duty God ever requires, " Hear, O my people." The Rechabites stumble not here. They hear their father speaking even out of his dust; they are far enough from untractableness, that hear so easily. *Promptitudo obedientiæ,* that is the first commendation of their obedience, the readiness of it.

Yet he will give you little that will not give you the hearing. The son in the Gospel that did not mean to go, and the son that meant not to go, both went thus far—heard their father: שמע signifies more—to attend and listen with a desire to it. How this is, you may understand out of Psalm xlv. 11, "Hearken, O daughter, and consider." Hearken first, then consider, weigh and ponder the words: then "forget thine own people and thy father's house," thy kindred and companions, that alliance that uses by a kind of faction to draw too often from obedience; those private and mutual interests, that, under a pretence of obedience, beguile us of it. To hearken then is to assent to, in God's own phrase, to leave all private relations and intentions, out of the mere desire of obedience. Thus the Rechabites hearkened neither to the tenderness of their wives, nor the cries of their children, nor their own commodities and conveniences, to hearken to their father. This is *obedientiæ patientia*, the approbation of their obedience by their patience.

This is a ready passage to the next, to submit their judgments, affections, persons, and estates to the will of their father. It is a hard theme; and I had best prove it to be obedience, before I venture to approve them for it.

The Latin and Greek words [to obey] sound nothing more than *sub*, and ὑπό, all 'under;' ὑποτάσσεσθαι, ὑποκεῖσθαι, ὑπακούειν, *subditi estote, subjicimini*; the soul itself under; that submitted. "Let every soul be subject:" as if S. Paul had foreseen the distinction—the body, not the soul. The soul, says he, not the body alone, and therefore "put them in mind" of it: as if every body knew it well enough; no, nobody were, nobody could be ignorant of it, only want one to remember them. Put them in mind, therefore. Wherefore? We may gather something from the reason he adds: "For we ourselves also were sometimes foolish, disobedient, deceived, serving divers lusts." First foolish, then disobedient; none else are so, how wise soever they think themselves. Yea, and deceived; for just it is that he that will not trust his superior's judgment, (especially, where his own is as well inferior as himself,) should be deceived by himself, or those who have no power over him but to deceive him. And he that will not obey their will, just it is he should be given up to serve his own lusts. And so they are, mark it when you will, "natural brute beasts," says S. Peter. None more "sensual, proud, devilish," so S. James finds them, than those that thus proudly cast off the yoke of submission and obedience. Their bodies then and passions scorn to obey them, who by their own disobedience have taught their inferior powers to rebel. It is no wonder then if that follow in the verse, "Living in malice, envy, hateful, and hating one another." I need call nothing else but the dismal experience of these last tumultuous, rebellious times to witness it, wherein tongues, and pens, and actions too have so horribly expressed it.

And give me leave a little to reason with you. Authority used to be a logical argument to guide our reason: and have we lost our logic too, as well as our obedience? The consent of wise, grave, learned fathers, (till you know where to find better,) with any man not too high in his own conceit, is certainly of a value somewhat above his private imagination. For, who tells you they are deceived? Your private minister? And are you sure he is not? And are they deceived? And is it not as likely that you and he should be? Were they not as wise as you—as just as you—as devout as you? Have you reason, and had not they? Do you use Scripture, and did not they? Had they interests, and have not you? That all should be deceived, till you, and your new ministers came into the world, is morally impossible. That they should purposely deceive you, you have nor ground, nor charity to imagine. To think then that you may not as easily be deceived, does it not look like pride? And is not pride enough to blind you from seeing truth? It is true, your governors are not infallible; no more are you. Yet certainly there is more certainty in their united judgments, than your simple fancies. And I am sure many might with less hazard have erred with them, (suppose they erred,) than sometimes gone right. That they might at any time in simplicity of heart; this seldom without faction, schism, or pride.

You mistake me all this while, if you suppose I require a blind obedience. No; I know God would not be served with a blind sacrifice. His service is a reasonable service. Clearsighted as you will, but no curious, inquisitive observance. Know you must, if possibly you can, that it is not ill you go about, and the power just that commands it; but to inquire into every circumstance, as it is beyond the power of most, so it is more than the duty of any. It is this creates you so many difficulties, suspicions, controversies, till you have lost your reward, your Church and country, the profit of your virtue.

Were the judgment thus once submitted, our affections would the sooner follow; though they indeed are the cause commonly that we submit not our judgments. Our affections set so strongly upon honours, profits, liberty, pleasure, make us take up opinions to keep them. Yet nature will tell you thus much, *partem patria, partem parentes.* Your king and country, and Church too, claim a portion in your affections, persons, and estates.

I leave now *de jure* for *de facto*, the justice for the practice of it: to show you all this done by the Rechabites. How easily else might they have vied reason with their father? What! drink no wine? All creatures are good; nothing to be refused with thanksgiving? No houses neither? Must we thus be made the talk of the world—turn heirs to Cain's malediction—"vagabonds upon the face of the earth?" Must our wives and children too suffer all the hardships of a kind of perpetual banishment? No mercy to be had of ourselves, none of them? What, no lands neither—no caring, nor harvest? Must we leave our children beggars, our wives unprovided for, purchase nothing for them? Thus, and more they might have argued; but all these notwithstanding, how harsh soever they conceived it, they rather trusted their fathers' judgment than their own.

But is their reason only submitted? are not their affections too? They neither contend for honour, nor stickle for riches, nor grudge at any inconvenience; but submit their desires to their fathers; tread under their own natural propensions to obey him. Would he have them drink no wine? They will not drink, though the prophet bid them. Would he have them poor? They have no lands. Would he forbid them houses? They will have no abiding place; be everlasting pilgrims. What would he have them do, that they will not do?

They submit judgments, affections, estates, persons, their own and their posterity's, as much as in them lies, that they may satisfy their father's. This, if any thing, is *obedientis summa humilitas*, the exceeding humility of their obedience, with so much approbation so oft reiterated through the chapter.

They go one step higher. Not only submit to his authority, but resolve into it. Make no further queries upon it, nor murmur at it, but, as the Hebrew root sometimes signifies, *acquievistis*, rest fully contented with it. You may call this *obedientiæ hilaritas;* their cheerful delight in their obedience.

Thus far the Rechabites; now again to ourselves.

And, first, have we heard the king, our father? Have we not rather, with the deaf adder, stopped our ears? one with the earth, that is our profit; the other with our tail, that is our pleasures; that we might not hear him, charmed he never so wisely.

The fathers of the Church have had less at our hands.

Next, how have you hearkened? Much that way given. Hearkened to find fault, to cavil at, to plot against, to undermine. This hath been the people's course of late, so to destroy those by whom God would save them. The civil magistrate hath not been in much better case.

Your judgments, they have been submitted too. But to whom? To the factious and discontented decisions (shall I call them, or ravenings rather) of ignorant and malicious teachers; who have exercised more tyranny upon your consciences, than the most clamorous can prove ever bishop did, durst ever accuse him to do; while they thus both belie God, and abuse you, by exacting an infallible assent to their unreasonable, seditious, unchristian frenzies, under the name of the Word of God. Thus, while you refuse to submit your judgments, where you are bound, you captivate your reason to them who have lost their own; and are therefore angry that others should have any.

How in the interim you have believed the sincere declarations of your sovereign; how submitted to what he thought best or fittest for you; how to the entire intentions of your right spiritual fathers,—let the general slighting and undervaluing their judgment we hear in every shop, as we pass along, testify for both.

In a word, how you delight in the laws and statutes of State and Church, and rest contented with them, I would the general practice and countenance of disobedience and profaneness did not even "tell it in Gath, and publish it in the streets of Ascalon."

Thus we serve again to exalt the Rechabites, while our sins condemn ourselves; for while our untractableness, impatience, pride, and murmurs banish obedience, they have heard their father readily, hearkened to him carefully, submitted humbly, and rested contentedly in his sole authority, without the least reluctancy or contradiction.

And by the way I may point out the reason: they lived temperate, mean, and humble lives; had no thoughts of raising houses, but in heaven. Now, the riots, riches, pride, and a desire of raising families, have made many of you forget ὑπὸ in ὑπακούειν, to keep under. Yet, let these men take heed, lest while, with Corah and his company, they cry out to Moses and Aaron, "You take too much upon you," keep us under, keep us down too much, they go down with that cursed crew into the pit. He that will not bear this ὑπὸ, keep under here, must go under there; and better ὑπὸ here, down here, than down for ever.

We have now done with the inward virtue of obedience. Now for the exercise of it outward. You have obeyed. How shall we know it? As S. James of faith, so we of obedience. Show me that by thy works. You have obeyed. Have you kept statutes then? God is the Rechabites' witness, and the prophet Jeremiah is their witness, and the land of Israel is witness that they have.

1. Kept them diligently; obeyed them carefully; even watched to keep them: it is the very word that God gives them.

2. Kept them without intermission, kept them "all their days."

3. Kept them from violence and misconstruction; added no new senses of their own: kept them, that is, broke them not by subtle distinctions, but *observantes fecistis*, says Tremellius; did it with all observance, and due honour to them; never seemed to entrench the least upon them by any seeming breach, till fleeing from the Chaldeans they entered Jerusalem, stayed a little till the storm was over, and likely rather pitched their tents there, anywhere in the streets, or upon the house-tops, as the Israelites themselves did at the Feast of Tabernacles, than dwelt in houses.

This kind of keeping statutes was a doing of them. *Cus-*   SERMON
todistis, fecistis. Not that keeping statutes which some talk   LII.
of, when they tell us they keep laws, while they are willing
to undergo the penalty it demandeth of them. S. Paul certainly was of another mind: "Not only for wrath," says he,   Rom. xiii.
"but conscience' sake." Makes obedience a matter of con-   5.
science, not of punishment. Not the punishment, but conscience makes up that. And, I believe, these men themselves
would think it greater tyranny to exact the penalties, than
the law. That the true obedience, then, that doth not keep
laws with the tongue, but with the hand. The doing, not
the talking of obedience is the Rechabites' commendation.

    Yet, had they lived by our later distinctions—for now we
are to compare them with our times—they would have told
us they obeyed their fathers, and kept no precepts; been
obedient sons of the Church, and kept no canons; loyal
subjects, and denied Cæsar's due when they list. All might
have been done in spirit; the body and estate saved quite;
done enough, to say they were humble and obedient subjects.
Laws too interpreted how we would, to our own ends and
purposes. Now this meaning affixed, now that; turned and
wrung which way we please. This, you know, the ordinary
practice of the people of the age.

    But, if this be keeping and doing the commands of our
fathers, it is beyond the wisdom of man to make such laws
which some senseless distinction cannot elude, and then what
becomes of all obedience? Whatever we see among our own
people, we see no such matter among the Rechabites. Here
again God reproves us, while he approves them, and the
sincere simplicity of their obedience.

    We are now next door to see it fully by what they did—
what they kept—what they obeyed. Obeyed the commandment of Jonadab their father; kept his precepts; did according to all that he commanded them.

    The first object of their obedience is "the commandment
of their father." His commandment, not their own wills.
It is a usual thing now-a-days to direct their governors,
what to do, what to teach, what to command; then, forsooth,
they will obey them. This is not to obey the father's command, but their own wills. And you know how the world

SERMON LII.
Judges xvii. xviii. xix.

went when every one did his own will, "what seemed good in his own eyes." Parents, then, could not keep their goods from the fingers of their own children. Micah will steal his mother's money. Men could not keep themselves from violence, nor their wives from ravishment, nor the Levite his. Men could not keep their own priest; he is taken away by force. The priest could not tend his cure; he is fain to wander about, to seek a place to live in, to play the idol's chaplain instead of God's. Pray God it prove not so with us. The king cannot keep the prerogative of his crown: "There was no king in Israel." God cannot keep his own; they lived as if there were no God in Israel. This the case where every one neglects commands, to do what is good in his own eyes; either hath or acknowledgeth no father to obey but his own arbitrary power. Happy Rechabites that obey command, prescribe not; petition not for commands to their father, but obey theirs, for it is *mandato* in the singular, as if that singly were the rule of their obedience, the command of their father.

Thence it is an easy passage to all his precepts. Resign once themselves to his command, they stick at nothing of his precepts. Interests prevail no longer. *Omnia* is good doctrine then: obedience universal. Active in all just commands; passive, where they are not such. These were just; God would not else reward them for doing them. Will you see what they were?

Jer. xxxv. 6.

1. "You shall drink no wine, neither you, nor your sons for ever." And it is not likely their fare was dainty. A hard task, you will say. Measure it by what our days would think of it, wherein we so much study our palates. How does a little restraint in diet afflict us! What a burden is it now to be denied excess!

Were it to be denied us for ever, how would we rather die than admit it! A few fish-days trouble us above measure: and it shall go for superstition, rather than not be cried down. How far are we from the sweet temper of their obedience!

2. Their keeping this first command shows that: the next will show their courage. "Neither shall ye build houses." The foxes have holes, and the birds of the air have nests;

but the sons of Jonadab have not where to lay their heads, but in a tattered tent. Many conveniences they must needs want there; suffer many inconveniences, both in their abode and in their removal. This especially be exceeding troublesome to their wives and children; subject in the interim ever and anon to storms and tempests; to be burnt by the heat of the day and the frost of the night; full every way of trouble, uncertainty, and hazard: yet this they are content with too, to show the courage of their obedience.

3. Yet to have neither field, nor vineyard, nor seed, nor harvest, nothing to delight in; a kind of common want; nothing to leave their children but an hereditary poverty: thus to give back at no inconveniences; so cheerfully to cast off any superfluities, so continually to trench upon necessities, to renounce all the glories which we place in earthly accommodations, only to obey their father; I now call you to witness who want nothing of worldly things, whose greatest care it is to digest your pleasures into order, to enjoy your honours and estates, and to dispose them, to keep yourselves from being oppressed with too many enjoyments, whether these valiant Rechabites may not yet deserve a third commendation, for the constancy of their obedience.

This *omnia*, these all you see expressly kept. If there were more, some lighter precepts, as certainly there were, all of them too; it is not *omnia hæc*, but *omnia* indefinitely; "all whatsoever were commanded them."

Their obedience is yet completer; not only all the precepts, but *omnino prout*, just according to them. Not all for substance only, but all for circumstance too. Omitted not a ceremony. God, as he loves not blind, so loves not lame sacrifices, nor blemished. And if it once be arbitrary for any one to neglect a ceremony, to dispute an inconvenience, *perit obedientia*, farewell obedience. "According to all" was the Rechabites'—was good doctrine then, hath been ever since till these unhappy days. And they gained by the hand God's approbation of the punctuality of their obedience. They failed not in a tittle; no more must we, if we look either to *dicit Dominus*, what he says, or what he commends; and he truly is commended, not whom men, but whom the Lord commendeth.

But though God said it, and commended them for it, now we draw it home, we had best prove it good.

It is that, then, which God requires of your children to you: "Children, obey your parents in all things." Of your servants: "Servants, obey your masters in all things." Of all subjects: "to every ordinance of man."

Indeed, so it may be, that the ordinances are not just. If so, then, if the power be, you have a passive obedience to supply you. Submit willingly to the punishment, but do you must not. All other must be done.

Yet, I must confess, while we dispute how far our governors are to be obeyed, in what, whether God or man, it oft comes to pass we obey neither. That God must be obeyed, not man when he commands an evil, is too plain to make a question.

But this is a true rule too: unless you are certain it is truly evil you are commanded, you ought to obey. If you be only doubtful, I should think in reason, as you would answer God for doing your uttermost, you should more rely upon his wisdom under whose command you are, than on your own, or any private engaged judgment; especially if it seem to carry anything that contradicts your private liberty or interests, in which case we are seldom competent judges.

If, indeed, you are fully certain of his ignorance, or general indisposition to all honesty and goodness, whom you are to obey, you are not debarred from better counsel: but the surest—and that you ought to look to—is men of the like authority and condition, at least of no known contrary resolve, no private, discontented, engaged affections of whose wisdom and honesty, and care too of your souls you are as justly confident, as of the other's malice and indiscretion.

Else I cannot tell you but any other may as well misguide your private respects, as much mislead both them and you, and you be left with less excuse. Whereas the condition that God hath set you in, the authority under which—and in that the gift of government, for certainly such a thing there is, which may be excellent sometimes in the worst men—may plead something for you at your last account.

You may pretend liberty, but they that promise you it by

disobedience are "themselves the servants of corruption." You may pretend conscience, but it will prove pride. And does it not appear so? For while you determine that in something you must, in other you may choose, is it not as if you thought you only knew what were best? Your fathers, they old doting fools. You pretend wisdom; but every ordinance, says S. Peter, is, for no other cause, for that he gives, "to put to silence the ignorance of foolish men:" they only are against it. And there are, too, that pretend the Spirit; these are they that go so far upon their own heads, that at last they separate themselves: and what are they for it? " Sensual, having not the Spirit," says S. Jude. Where is now the Spirit you so much boast of? ^{SERMON LII. 2 Pet. ii.19. 1 Pet. ii.15. Jude 19.}

All precepts therefore must be our rule to walk by: "all," though harsh and hard ones; " all," and more than all sometimes, more than law will give them. *Ne offendamus* is Christ's rule; "lest we should offend them:" them and others too, by teaching them by our example at other times to disobey.

S. Paul stretcheth it further, *dicto obedire;* to obey at a word speaking; a command by word of mouth, when it is not express law. For, when all is done, something will still be left to the interpretation of the lawgiver, in the breast of the judge, to which we must submit. ^{Tit. iii. 1.}

We are not yet at the uttermost: " all" is not enough, unless our obedience be " according to all;" *Omnino prout*, says Tremellius; just as they would have it to a tittle, in every circumstance.

You find this requisite in your several corporations; where the omission of a punctilio draws after it intolerable defaults. The hedge is easily passed through, where but one bush is wound aside; and the breach of one circumstance is but the disposition to another. Things that in themselves seem of no considerable moment, within a while appear considerable by the neglect; as the error that appears not at the first declining line of the workman, a while after manifests an irrecoverable deformity. " According to all;" that is the surest rule to go by. You know it yourselves in your own corporations; you know it in your own families, if you know anything. Give an inch, they'll take an ell, is your own proverb. And cannot you judge as equally for the Church?

I am sure not there; where had this rule been kept, we had never met these distracted times. But so long have some omitted this, some that, that all at last is thought innovation. One likes not this, another not that, another not something else; so it is come at last they like nothing. Rubrics and canons have been so long played with to please the people, or I know not who, that nothing but the ruin of the whole will now content them. I would we saw it not by the misery of these (however some call them) truly sad, distressed times.

Yet take this caution with you, *Quæ præcepit*: not according to every humour, what this man or that man fancies decent, but according to all that is commanded.

Now, two things there are which have the force of precepts—laws and customs.

1. Laws; and they according to the letter, not the equity; that is for no private power to go by. A privilege indeed, sometimes, for the supreme lawgiver and the judge.

2. Customs; that they bind like laws and precepts, you all tell us in your tenures, in your lands, in your corporations. How comes it about they do not in the Church? I am sure you plead them on all sides strong enough against it.

And has the Church none; or hath it none to plead? Yes, both. It was S. Paul's plea; no meaner man's: "We have no such custom, nor the Churches of God." Many indecencies were then crept into the Church of Corinth; about prayers, about preaching, about sacraments, about gestures and ceremonies. The rule that he confutes them by is, they had no such, nor the Churches of God; the contrary then they had: and that he thought conviction enough for Christians; yea, for the contentious too. "If any man be contentious," will hear no reason, this the way to answer him.

It was so then; it is so still. They, the Apostles, and the Churches of God, customs they had, and made this use of them; so may we; customs we have, and we may plead them.

Some derived from them; so high: others later, yet of age enough to speak for themselves. Such as, only directing all into order and beauty, stood still unquestioned, till of late a subtle profaneness creeping in, under a pretence of law, though obeying none, would fain accuse for illegal tyrannies.

But let me argue it with this kind of man. May not I as lawfully serve my God in a reverent posture, as thou in a saucy and irreverent garb? Is it superstition in me to stand, because thou sittest or leanest on thy elbow? Is it idolatry in me to kneel, because thou wilt not foul thy clothes, or vex thy knees? Strange must it needs be, that sitting, leaning, lolling, must be law and canon, where no set behaviour is expressed, and my reverence only be against it; made innovation which law never forbad, custom has retained. When you can bring me law against my standing, bowing, kneeling, which yourselves know custom hath observed, where uniform order has been kept, I shall either submit or answer. Else I must ask by what law I am bound to sit or lean, and not to stand, or kneel, or bow; though I urge thee only to charity and reverence.

This for some reverent customs, which hadst thou any equal to, for age or reason, in thy civil affairs, thou wouldst plead against the law. I here only wish it, where there is naught against them, that they may stand still, if not under the notion of obedience, yet far enough from innovation or disobedience. And, I believe, in cold blood it would be found so.

Well now: "all," for the matter, though never so hard. "According to all," for the manner, though never so troublesome and inconvenient; if commanded by good law or custom, must be the compass of your obedience. "If any man teach otherwise," says S. Paul. Otherwise than what? Than "all honour;" that is, obedience in all things. What then? "He is proud, knowing nothing," how much soever he seems to know, "doting about questions and strife of words, whence cometh envy, strife, railings, evil surmises, perverse disputings of men of corrupt minds, destitute of the truth, supposing that gain is godliness." You see the times, and you may see the place. *1 Tim. vi. 3—5.*

How these rules have been kept amongst you towards the command of your king and Church, I leave to the scrutiny of your own bosoms; if you find it otherwise, as surely you will, let it be mended or get S. Paul and S. Peter made

Apocrypha, and scrape out *dicit Dominus* here, God's approbation of the Rechabites for observing " all," for doing " all."

I have been so long about ourselves, I had almost forgotten them. But I return, and now inquire upon their last commendation,—whom they obeyed? " Jonadab their father;" their father by nature, he from whose loins they descended: their civil father and prince; he that had power over their estates; so it appears by his ordering their temporal affairs, their new kind of commonwealth: their spiritual father, by his decrees disposing all for the freer exercise of their piety and religion; by commanding abstinence from wine and the delights of sense, to refine their understandings for heavenly thoughts; by forbidding them houses, putting them in mind of better dwellings; by the oft removal of their tents, to keep them in continual thoughts they had "here no abiding city;" by a voluntary resignation of all earthly accommodations, to teach them the contempt of worldly things; a total vacancy to their religion and order.

So you have them here, lastly, commended for three kinds of obedience to three kinds of fathers,—their natural, civil, ecclesiastical father, which is the right directing their obedience.

Yet I meet here three other commendations from the words, " your father."

1. That they obeyed their right father; " your father;" sought them out no new ones, neither in Church nor State; kept, as you would say, to their own king, to their own bishop, their own priest; wandered not out of their diocese, gadded not out of their own parish to find one of their own choosing.

2. That they acknowledged him for a " father," and so used him, with all honour and respect; not a word against him for all the difficulties of his injunctions.

3. That they obeyed him under that name, because a father, upon no other ground, though he was but one man. This indeed is that which formally constitutes obedience, when we do anything for no other reason, but because " commanded by our father." To do it for other ends, for the justice, equity, or goodness of it, may bring it under the title of some other virtue; this only, because " commanded by our father," makes it obedience.

You have seen the last part of the Rechabites' obedience. Shall we see whether you have any better luck in this than in the rest? — whether you can here say anything for yourselves, that you have obeyed the command of your father?

Yet we must see, first, what fathers we acknowledge; take heed we are right, lest God answer us as he answered those by the Prophet, "Ye have set up kings, but not by me; ye have made princes, but I knew it not."

To begin then right. Kings, they are our fathers, κατ' ἐξοχὴν, nursing fathers; God hath set them over us; *Per me reges*: made them supreme too; it is S. Peter's, "To the king as supreme." Mark that: no earthly power above him; nor Pope nor people. Be not we fallen into strange times, in the interim, that God must be driven to recant, and we learn a new supremacy? The king's preeminence is expressly a part of your oath of allegiance. And "for the oath of God," says Solomon; so think of him, so obey him.

Next to him, those "that are sent by him," says S. Peter; of nobody's sending else, of whosoever's choosing; not so properly fathers, as hands and fingers of that great father, *pater patriæ*: those to govern under him, not above him, so we pray in our Common Service.

Every magistrate, that is, every governor of a country— every mayor of a city—every master of a company—every father of a family. Some of these have their statutes to be kept; all of them their commands to be obeyed.

These are secular powers: you have besides spiritual; such as take order for your souls, as the other for your bodies and estates, your bishops and clergy.

Bishops are fathers by their title, the fathers of the Church; so the first Christians, so all since, till this new unchristian Christianity started up. Fathers in God, it is their style; however some of late, sons of Belial, would make them fathers in the devil, antichrists; perhaps, that they might make them like themselves. Strange antichrists to whom Christ hath left the governing of his Church these 1500 years!

1. If you value them by their antiquity, they are fathers for that, "their enemies being judges;" who would fain

SERMON LII.

Hos. viii. 4.

Prov. viii. 15.
1 Pet. ii. 13.

Eccl. viii. 2.

SERMON LII.

distinguish between their offices and their names, that they might have some pretence to disobey them; though more commonly they fill their mouth with scoffs and calumnies, the language of the devil, than their books with the language of antiquity truly understood.

2. Fathers, secondly, for their authority. Time was when their commands, their councils, and canons were laws to Christians; none of the least neither, when their breach inferred the greatest punishment, spiritual malediction.

3. Fathers, lastly, for their tenderest care over the tenderest part, your consciences. Such who would quickly set all in order, would you not listen too engagedly to by-respects; such whose commands you cannot complain of when you have examined them. A hat, a knee, a reverent posture of the body, are no such tyrannies, as some please to fancy them. You would do more in a great man's presence, more for a small temporal encouragement. A habit, a hood, a cap, a surplice, a name, are wonderful things to trouble a devout conscience. You have more ceremonies in your companies and corporations, and you observe them strictly. You will find it if you compare them.

If thus fathers now, their precepts then certainly are to be obeyed. Yet with this rule ever both for them and all other inferior magistrates beside: So far as they contradict not the supreme authority. It is a rule in natural reason, In two contrary commands the superior's is to be obeyed. Now, "to the king as supreme," we told you out of S. Peter, "to rulers as sent by him;" that is, as far as they are sent by him; no further; no further than their commission from him. Else obedience can find no bounds, nor consciences no rest, if the supreme be not enough to terminate and guide all obedience into your father.

There is an argument in that word may make you obey him above all the world besides;—the tenderness of a father. Never could any challenge this name with greater justice; never any so far condescended to his children: to part with his own privileges, maintenance, conveniences, provision, attendance. He hath done as much for his sons as the Rechabites for their father; left all, even his houses for them, lest, by the insolence of some tumultuous spirits, he should be forced to punish them. What natural father like this father?

But whether he hath been used like a father, (indeed you used him lately, in your entertainment, like a conqueror, and are justly honoured for it, but whether by others like a father,) let the affronts at his own palace-gate, the saucy language in every rascal mouth, the rebellious sermons, the seditious libels cast abroad, his own words, where he is fain to proclaim to the world he is driven from you,—let these speak; I say nothing.

Your inferior magistrates have, almost everywhere, found disrespect. And whether your bishops and clergy have been used like fathers, if the usage they have had of late, the tumults about their houses, the riots upon their persons, the daily insolences the whole clergy have met with in your streets, never seen till now in a civil commonwealth, in any ordered city, upon the most contemptible men; if the injuries done their persons in the churches, at the very altars—once sanctuaries against violence, now thought the fittest places for it—in the very administration of the sacraments, in their pulpits, both among you and abroad the kingdom: in a word, so many slanderous, malicious accusations without ground, entertained with pleasure, besides the blasphemies upon the whole order;—if these cannot tell you, after-ages will determine, and in the interim let the world judge.

Our fathers' imperfections are not to be divulged, though true; much less false ones to be imposed upon them. This is a reverence but due to fathers. It was cursedly done of Cham, and he paid for it, he and his, with an everlasting curse, to uncover his father's nakedness. It was wretchedly done of Absalom to tell the people there was no man deputed of the king to hear them, no justice in the land; and he thrived accordingly. And "Let all the enemies of my lord the king be as that young man is," says Cushi.

Yet say we, it were well it were no worse. How is all this made religion too! Oaths and protestations (intended certainly to better purposes) abused, to maintain rebellion and profaneness; construed so in pulpits, and professed by their scholars in the face of God and man; pray God it go no higher. And dare you, after all this, look for a blessing?

SERMON LII.

Alas! you must lay by those thoughts till you have learned the Rechabites' lesson. They used their Jonadab like a father; so reverenced his memory, so preserved his name, so obeyed him in all his several authorities, so punctually, so constantly, so courageously, so sweetly, so universally, so sincerely, so really, so carefully, with that contentedness without grumbling, that humility without disputing, that patience, that readiness, that full content of every age, sex, and condition, no weakness, tenderness, or privileges pretended against it, that God himself presently upon it promiseth a full reward. "Therefore, thus saith the Lord of hosts, the God of Israel," &c.

I am now at the reward; and it is a full one: full of (1) honour, full of (2) proportions, full of (3) blessings.

Full of (1) honour at the first; "Therefore, thus, &c.," as if their obedience deserved it, or God at least would seem so far to honour it. He had promised length of life, in the commandment, for it; and God is not unjust. It deserves therefore by the covenant of his promise, yet by the interpretation of his mercy.

And (2) full of proportions it is. Proportionable to the three acts and objects of obedience. You have obeyed your father; therefore you shall want no sons—there is one. You have kept his commandments; therefore shall your sons stand in them, and by standing in them, stand before God—there is a second. You have kept all, and done according to all, that hath been commanded you, failed in nothing; therefore shall you have a reward, all of you; not a man of you fail for ever. This last, indeed, is beyond proportion; eternity for time; all blessings for a few precepts; the wine of angels, for abstinence from the blood of the vine; for want of houses upon earth, eternal dwellings in the heavens.

You see the reward is full of blessings. I shall observe their triple proportion in running over them.

(i.) Such then, first, is the reward of their obedience, that it lengthens days. The world thinks it shortens them, if by it you take away any thing from your flesh, bate any thing of your diet, either in quantity or quality, when the king or Church commands to do so. It was not so here; and without doubt it is not. Obedience hath the promise of length of days, in the commandment. It was the reason that Jonadab gave his sons to obey him, "That you may live many days." It was a blessing of long days upon themselves. That is the first.

<small>Sermon LII.</small>
<small>Jer. xxxv. 7.</small>

But it ends not so. Upon their children too; reaches to them, is a blessing of succession. This is to live beyond ourselves, to sprout afresh out of the dust, to have posterity.

And a posterity that shall not fail, wither, or crumble away, that is more.

If it be a male succession, it is more still. *Non deficiet vir,* not a man fail you. Female generations lose the name; and so the succession fails even while it lasts.

It does almost so, when it passeth into a collateral line. This fails not that way neither. Not *vir de stirpe,*—it continues in a direct line from the root.

Tremellius's translation sets it higher. *Non exscindetur vir.* Of all this progeny there shall not so much as a man be cut off. Die they must by the necessity of nature; but not a man cut off by violence; that, however it fared with the captive Jews in Babylon, not any of these should fail there, but return to their tents in peace; that a fair and even succession it should be, that, after many days, pass on calmly and quietly to their fathers' tombs—in peace gathered to their fathers.

It is well this; such a blessing upon posterity. But when not only succeeding generations participate the blessing, but Jonadab and his father Rechab too, past ancestors, receive a new accession of glory by it, this is a blessing not upon the sons only, but upon deceased fathers too. And all this you may look for upon the like obedience. A long life, a lasting, a continued, a male, a lineal, an unblemished posterity; all redounding back again to your own glory. This the first proportion; that which is given for your obedience to your father.

(ii.) The second is greater, *stans in conspectu,*—a posterity high enough to be seen, placed in the eye of the world; men famous and renowned in their generations. This is but to stand on high before the kings and princes of the earth. *In conspectu meo,* is higher: that stands before God,—a posterity as virtuous as honourable.

SERMON LII.
2 Chron. ii. 5. [compared with vi. 14—16.]

Stand before him, and in place near him; near his sanctuary, the place of his presence; placed there, so it seems. Placed on high, and near him; as near as the title of gods can make them,—made judges of the earth; so *stare in conspectu* is sometimes intrepreted. This is a second proportion answering to their obedience to commands: they shall be commanders. Under command they kept, now they are above it; above the people, equal with the princes of the earth. A famous, a pious, an honourable posterity, the second reward of obedience.

(iii.) All this is much, exceeding much. Yet honour and virtue are created things, and therefore mutable, may fail at last. Theirs shall not. *Stans in conspectu.* In honour they shall be, and in honour they shall stand. In virtue they shall be, and in virtue they shall stand. Standing is a posture of continuance.

Stand; and stand in his sight, dear as the apple of his eye. That must not be touched; no more must they; and then nothing can change them to be sure.

Cunctis diebus, puts all out of question. They shall stand so all their days, says the text. What speak I of days? Stand so for ever; continue ever; Christians succeed into their order and obedience; they survive into Christians; live in them for ever.

When succession shall have done, successive motions have their periods, and all days shall have an end, yet then Jonadab shall not want a man to stand then before him, and see his face for ever. This is indeed the last reward, a firm, a perpetual, an eternal succession.

And now we are come up to the tops of the mountains, the everlasting hills. Eternity is a circle, and there we wind about in everlasting rounds. There we turn about to the beginning of the verse, the Lord speaking and confirming all; that so the certainty may embrace with the eternity. That you may see I tell you no more than God himself will make good, "Thus saith the Lord of hosts, the God of Israel."

He hath promised it, and shall he not bring it to pass? He hath said it, and shall it not be done? Said it by his prophet; and prophecy, though it sometime wants light, yet never certainty. He engageth his honour, "Thus saith the Lord." Kings will not fail upon the word of their honour.

Sermon LII.

He engageth his power: "Thus saith the Lord of hosts;" he that doth what he will in heaven and earth.

He engageth his goodness, his tried, experienced goodness: "Thus saith the God of Israel;" their God, who can witness he never broke his promise, nor failed his word.

But doth God take care only for the Rechabites? or says he it for your sake too? For yours also, doubtless; it is the reward of obedience, wherever it is found, as it is in the text. Will you give me leave to inquire?

Has the king at any time commanded some of your superfluities, and has he obtained them? Have you been content to part with any of your delights, in diet, apparel, in your houses, to endure some abridgements to obey him, to supply him?

Have the inferior magistrates demanded the execution of the laws, and have you assisted them?

Has the Church required your presence, your order and assistance—for I speak not now of your private fathers—and can you say with these Rechabites, "We have obeyed and kept all their precepts, and done according to all that hath been commanded us?" Then, and not till then, dare I warrant you, "You and your seed shall stand before him for ever."

For it is not a reward only to private and personal obedience, but the obedience of cities, of nations, too. Obedient cities and kingdoms, as well as families, shall not want men to stand before him for ever; but disobedient and rebellious shall.

For kingdoms, cities, and countries have their fates; and, when they have rent this bond of union that kept them to their head, they must expect their funerals. You then to look to it. Remember that of the Prophet, "How is the faithful city become a harlot!" *Et quam facta est desolata!* "How is she become desolate!" Remember that; what becomes of her for it?

Isa. i. 21.

I have done with the Rechabites' obedience, and God's *dicit* to it. I come nearer home; and I cannot tell you but

I must change my phrase into *dicit homo*. Men talk abroad there is no such matter here.

If it be otherwise, you have the better of it. And I shall say no more than what Jotham to the men of Shechem, when they had made Abimelech king: "If you have then dealt truly and sincerely with Jerubbaal, and with his house this day, then rejoice you in Abimelech, and let him rejoice in you: but if not, let fire come out from Abimelech, and devour the men of Shechem, and the house of Millo; and let fire come out from the men of Shechem, and the house of Millo, and devour Abimelech." I will not say so much with an imprecation; but thus: If you have now dealt truly and sincerely with King and Church, in setting up your own profits, privileges, and humours to reign over you, by preferring them before their precepts, then rejoice you in them, and may they prosper with you. But, if not, fire will come out of them—those very privileges and profits—and devour you; and fire will come out from you to devour and ruin them, as sure as you thought once to be happy by them.

It is true, and I think I may justly quit some of you before God and man—say for you, You have obeyed; but as it is enough for the whole man to be thought guilty, when only one part sins, so it is enough for a punishment upon a kingdom that there be among us those, though hands and feet, that disobey.

Though make no doubt of it, you who have obeyed, but, however the world look on you—as certainly it looks but scurvily upon such—God from above will one day see it and reward it, give you the blessing of the text. His word is passed; go on and believe "there shall not want a man of your seed to stand before him for ever."

You are not all, then, of the same practices. I shall but mind you therefore of my text in a double sense: as it implies the punishment of disobedience; as it expresses the reward of obedience; and I have done.

The Rechabites that obeyed shall want no length of days, no posterity, nor they no heavenly grace or honour: you will thence infer, they that do not shall want all.

And have they not so in all generations? What got Jannes and Jambres by withstanding Moses but *non procedent ultra*, they should proceed no further, neither in their projects nor in their posterity? What got Korah and his company by rising up against Moses and Aaron, but a death that amazes us to read of? "They, and their wives, and their children, went down quick into hell." The grave was not low enough, nor could they die soon enough to receive their punishment. What got Absalom by his rebellion but an ignominious cruel death in the heat and fervour of his sin, and no posterity to survive him? What got the ten tribes by their discession in matter of taxes, but the loss of their religion and their God, a perpetual successive idolatry, and a thousand calamities? No *in conspectu meo* left them, that, God's presence, taken from them for ever. Lastly, what got Judas, that rose in the days of the tribute—all upon fair pretences, you see, with the people—but *Ipse periit, et omnes dispersi?* He perished, the rest made rogues and runagates upon the face of the earth.

And can we, after all this, look for better success either in Church or State, when we rise up against them both?—anything but an utter desolation? Lay it home: *non deficiet* in the text will prove *deficiet* here; nor posterity, nor honour, nor government, nor religion continue with you.

The very setting light by our superiors has brought a doom somewhat like it. Michal, scoffing at King David, had no child for ever, lost *vir de stirpe*. The little children, that did but taunt the prophet as he passed by, were at *deficiet* straight in their childhood; could go no farther. The very savage bears out of the wilderness rebuked the incivility of the children. If children found so sharp a punishment, what may men expect? In a word, God, the God of mercies, who holds out beyond our hopes or thoughts, could hold out no longer, when they came once to "despise his ministers."

And let me tell you too, you shall find it home in your own bosoms; be paid in kind, in your children and servants. For with what face can you expect obedience from your children who disobey by your example? How can you but expect rebellion from them, who see you in all your actions

Sermon LII.

2 Tim. iii. 8.

2 Chron. xxxvi. 16.

SERMON LII.

resolute to disobey? Where should they learn it? From your example? Alas! they cannot: you obey nor spiritual nor temporal fathers. From your words? They will not, because your actions contradict them. From God's commandments? Why do not you? Thus, while you study by disobedient practices to stand, you and yours fall down for ever.

But I dwell too long upon so harsh a theme. I shall lead you to obedience by sweeter thoughts—by example, by reward.

By example: shall these Rechabites, their wives and children give aside at no inconvenience, and must we, Christians, startle at everything that is not just as we would have it? Shall they hear, and hearken, and submit, and rest upon their father's will, and must we alway prefer our own; scarce read or mind a command which we first prescribe not? Shall they fail in nothing, not a circumstance; do according unto all? And are not we ashamed to question all so long till we do nothing? I appeal to yourselves. Would you be so used in your own houses?—have your commands disputed, questioned, denied, done by parts and pieces, by your children and servants? With what conscience, then, can you deal so with your superiors? Do as you would be done by, is the law of nature. Out of this only principle it is probable the Rechabites at first obeyed, in one man, the carnal, spiritual, temporal authority: and does our Christianity serve us to no better use than to contemn them?

If example will not, will reward prevail? It is a reward to be approved by God. But he rewards us not with words. What would you have?

Your city, your companies, your own families cannot subsist without obedience; and can you desire it of others, when you will not pay it yourselves? This the way to keep your city from destruction. You labour for succession; this is God's way to obtain it. You travel for lands and riches; this is his means to gain and keep them. You desire honours; these you may have for you and your posterities. You strive for privileges; they are surest obtained and held by obedience. You endeavour all for perpetuities; here you may find all for ever. You study to make all as sure as you can; God's promise is the best assurance; and here it is : do what he here commands, and you shall not fear what man can do unto you. The Lord of hosts is on your side.

Else I cannot but tell you, all may fail you. The wine and delicates you eat and drink; the houses and stately palaces you lord it in; the lands and possessions, the riches, state, and pomp you have to this day triumphed in; your wives and children; all you think so everlastingly to enjoy by rising up so much to defend them, may in a moment vanish, and your high-flown thoughts die before you. You have no assurance from heaven so to settle your estates and fortunes; no *dicit Dominus* for that. This is only God's way for thriving, by obedience.

Nay, and the religion you so much seem to contend for, against innovations, by the greatest innovations in Church and State—tumults, riots, and profanest usages,—that also will for ever fail you. You want men to stand before God for ever; and instead of them find men to stand before you— Micah's Levites; do what seems good in your sight, not in God's; so stand before you, as to hinder you from standing before God; stand in your sight, and blind you from seeing the right way to heaven. Thus you will want your old honours, profits, liberties, religion, all.

But, if you will return, and hear, and hearken, and submit to your ancient fathers, your King and Church, your magistrates and clergy,—observe, and keep, and do your ancient laws and customs, I dare warrant you, what God promises to the Rechabites, he shall perform to you.

Your city shall flourish, your places be renowned, your liberties increase, your persons rise up in honour, your estates prosper, your affairs succeed, your children be famous, your posterity happy, your religion display the glories of her first primitive purity, and all go on successfully for ever.

And when this "ever" shall have swallowed up the days of time, you shall stand still, immovable, immortal, glorious before him, in whose sight is the fulness of joy, where you shall one day meet your children, and stand all together: kings and subjects, priests and people, fathers and children,

SERMON LII. before your heavenly Father; see him face to face in the beatifical vision for ever and ever.

To which He bring us through his eternal Son, who was obedient unto death to teach us obedience of life unto life, Jesus Christ; to which Two Persons, with the Holy Ghost, be all praise, and glory, obedience, and worship, for evermore. *Amen.*

THE END.

R. CLAY, PRINTER, BREAD STREET HILL.

www.ingramcontent.com/pod-product-compliance
Lightning Source LLC
Chambersburg PA
CBHW022138300426
44115CB00006B/248